Threats to international financial stability

International Center for Monetary and Banking Studies

The International Center for Monetary and Banking Studies is an independent, non-profit foundation, placed under the supervision of the Swiss Federal Department of the Interior. Established in 1973, and located in Geneva, the Center is devoted to the scientific study of international monetary, financial and banking problems. In pursuing this aim, the Center relies on the collaboration of specialists from central banks, international organizations, the private sector and the academic community to bridge the gap between theory and practice in the field of international finance. It is financed by contributions from Swiss and international public and private financial institutions

In addition to organizing management training programs for finance professionals, the Center regularly sponsors international scientific conferences, public lecture series, and original research and publications.

The Center is associated with the Graduate Institute of International Studies in Geneva, and is administered by a Foundation Board with the assistance of a Scientific Committee.

The views expressed in this volume are those of the authors and not those of the International Center for Monetary and Banking Studies.

1 February 1987

Centre for Economic Policy Research

The Centre for Economic Policy Research is a registered charity with educational purposes. It was established in 1983 to promote independent analysis and public discussion of open economies and the relations between them. Institutional (core) finance for the Centre has been provided through major grants from the Economic and Social Research Council, the Leverhulme Trust, the Esmée Fairbairn Trust and the Bank of England. None of these organizations gives prior review to the Centre's publications nor do they necessarily endorse the views expressed therein.

The Centre is pluralist and non-partisan, bringing economic research to bear on the analysis of medium- and long-run policy questions. The research work which it disseminates may include views on policy, but the Board of Governors of the Centre does not give prior review to such publications, and the Centre itself takes no institutional policy positions. The opinions expressed in this volume are those of the authors and not those of the Centre for Economic Policy Research.

Board of Governors

Chairman
Mr Jeremy Hardie

Vice-Chairman
Sir Adam Ridley

Governors

Dr Christopher Bliss	Mr Michael Posner
Mr Gavyn Davies	Lord Richardson
Admiral Sir James Eberle	Professor Amartya Sen
Professor Frank Hahn	Professor David Stout
Ms Sarah Hogg	Mr Angus Walker
Ms Kate Mortimer	Sir Douglas Wass
Sir Kit McMahon	

Officers

Director
Professor Richard Portes

Administrative Directors
Mrs Wendy Thompson   *Programme and Finance*
Mr Stephen Yeo   *Research and Publications*

1 February 1987

Threats to international financial stability

Edited by

RICHARD PORTES

and

ALEXANDER K. SWOBODA

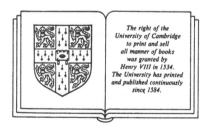

The right of the
University of Cambridge
to print and sell
all manner of books
was granted by
Henry VIII in 1534.
The University has printed
and published continuously
since 1584.

CAMBRIDGE UNIVERSITY PRESS
CAMBRIDGE
New York   New Rochelle   Melbourne   Sydney

CAMBRIDGE UNIVERSITY PRESS
Cambridge, New York, Melbourne, Madrid, Cape Town, Singapore, São Paulo, Delhi

Cambridge University Press
The Edinburgh Building, Cambridge CB2 8RU, UK

Published in the United States of America by Cambridge University Press, New York

www.cambridge.org
Information on this title: www.cambridge.org/9780521347891

First published 1987
Re-issued in this digitally printed version 2009

A catalogue record for this publication is available from the British Library

ISBN 978-0-521-34556-9 hardback
ISBN 978-0-521-34789-1 paperback

Contents

List of figures

List of tables

Preface

On 11–13 September 1986, fifty academics, bankers and officials met in Geneva for an international conference on 'Risk, International Financial Markets and Public Policy' organized by the International Center for Monetary and Banking Studies. This volume contains the proceedings of that conference under the title *Threats to International Financial Stability*.

Although the conference was organized by the International Center for Monetary and Banking Studies, this publication is the product of a cooperative effort with the Centre for Economic Policy Research. This cooperation grew naturally out of early contacts between the two Centres' directors, and we hope that this will be but the first instance of an ongoing collaboration. The views expressed by participants are their own and not necessarily those of the institutions with which they are affiliated nor of either Centre.

We have incurred many debts of gratitude in the organization of the conference and in the preparation of this volume. Our greatest debt is to the participants in the conference: to the authors, who provided provocative papers and revised them promptly; to the discussants, who let themselves be provoked and brought their experience to bear on sometimes difficult intellectual issues; to the other participants, who made for a most stimulating and lively general discussion; to session chairmen (P. H. Cassou, R. Dale, B. Dennis, J. l'Huillier, L.-E. Thunholm, S. Ogata and R. Zecher), who managed to keep that discussion civilized but never dull; to our panelists for their insights; to Joan Pearce for taking on the heroic task of summarizing the panel and general discussion; and to Markus Lusser for his keynote address which provides this volume's conclusion.

We also would like to thank the Ford Foundation for providing the essentials, financial support for the conference, and Thomas Bayard of the Foundation's staff, whose early interest in the project constituted a much appreciated encouragement. We should also like to record our appreciation to the International Center for Monetary and Banking Studies which supplied the remaining financial support.

Organizing the conference would have been impossible without the untiring help of Martine Nguyen-Phuoc, the administrator of the International Center for Monetary and Banking Studies. Rapid changes in financial markets and their global economic and political implications made timely publication of these conference proceedings especially important. The speed achieved is due largely to the efforts of Stephen Yeo, Administrative Director for Research and Publications of the Centre for Economic Policy Research, and of the production editor, John Black of the University of Exeter.

To all, our thanks. We hope that they, and our readers, will like the final product.

RICHARD PORTES
ALEXANDER K. SWOBODA

Conference participants

Ubaldo Aguirre   *Financial Representative Office, Republic of Argentina, Geneva*
Johnny Akerholm   *Bank of Finland*
Ernst Baltensperger   *University of Bern*
Thomas O. Bayard   *The Ford Foundation, New York*
Michael Beenstock   *The City University Business School, London*
Robert R. Bench   *Office of the Comptroller of the Currency, Washington*
Arturo Brillembourg   *The World Bank*
Simon H. Broadbent   *Foreign and Commonwealth Office, London*
Pierre Henri Cassou   *Banking Regulatory Committee, Bank of France*
Pierre Cosandier   *Banque Paribas (Suisse) S.A., Geneva*
Sam Y. Cross   *Federal Reserve Bank of New York*
Richard S. Dale   *Heriot-Watt University, Edinburgh*
Christian de Boissieu   *University of Paris I*
Michael Dealtry   *Bank for International Settlements*
Bengt Dennis   *Sveriges Riksbank, Stockholm*
Jean Dermine   *INSEAD, Fontainebleau*
Christine V. Downton   *County Investment Management Ltd, London*
Barry Eichengreen   *Harvard University and CEPR*
Ernesto Feldman   *Central Bank of the Republic of Argentina*
Jean-Pierre Fevre   *Commission Bancaire, Paris*
Charles Freedman   *Bank of Canada*
Robert Gemmill   *Federal Reserve Board, Washington*
Hans Genberg   *Graduate Institute of International Studies, Geneva*
Richard Herring   *Wharton School, University of Pennsylvania*
Daniel Kaeser   *Federal Department of Finance, Bern*
Edward J. Kane   *Ohio State University*
Nicholas Krul   *Financial Adviser, Geneva*

Jacques l'Huillier   *Graduate Institute of International Studies and University of Geneva*
Markus Lusser   *Swiss National Bank, Bern*
Donald Mathieson   *International Monetary Fund*
Shijuro Ogata   *Bank of Japan*
Joan Pearce   *N. M. Rothschild & Sons Ltd, London*
Rinaldo Pecchioli   *OECD*
Richard Portes   *CEPR and Birkbeck College, London*
Lionel D. D. Price   *Bank of England*
David H. Pyle   *University of California at Berkeley*
Werner Rein   *Union Bank of Switzerland, Zurich*
Georg Rich   *Swiss National Bank, Zurich*
Harold B. Rose   *Barclays Bank Plc., London*
T. M. Rybczynski   *Lazard Brothers & Co. Ltd., London*
Anthony Saunders   *Graduate School of Business, New York University*
Stephen Schaefer   *London Business School and CEPR*
Peter Schmid   *Deutsche Bundesbank*
Aloys Schwietert   *Swiss Bank Corporation, Basle*
Claudio Segre   *Company Director, Geneva*
Alexander Swoboda   *International Center for Monetary and Banking Studies and Graduate Institute of International Studies, Geneva*
Lars-Erik Thunholm   *formerly Skandinaviska Enskilda Banken, Stockholm*
Niels Thygesen   *University of Copenhagen*
J. Richard Zecher   *The Chase Manhattan Bank, New York*
Daniel Zuberbuehler   *Swiss Federal Banking Commission, Bern*

Introduction

RICHARD PORTES and
ALEXANDER K. SWOBODA

The debt crisis, the extraordinary pace of financial innovation, policy
conflicts among major industrialized countries, the enormous variability
of exchange rates and interest rates, and the growing interdependence of
national banking systems all represent threats to international financial
stability. Such threats are of course not new. Before Mexico in 1982,
there were Franklin National and Herstatt in 1974–5, and the Credit
Anstalt in 1931. The more recent episodes, which also include Ambrosiano, Continental Illinois and Johnson Matthey, have not resulted in
either national or international financial crises, and shades of the 1930s
have remained shades.

To understand why and to assess the likelihood of a recurrence of a
deep international financial crisis, we must consider three questions. The
first concerns the extent and nature of the shocks that buffet the system.
Do they originate in asset markets, more specifically foreign exchange
markets, goods markets, or both? Are they the result of outside shocks,
particularly from policy, or do they arise as bubbles endogenous to asset
markets? Second, are international financial markets resilient in the
sense that they tend to dampen shocks or, on the contrary, fragile in the
sense that they tend to amplify and propagate disturbances?

Answering this question requires an understanding of the nature and
role of the institutions that characterize any international financial
regime in its historical manifestation. This immediately raises the third
set of issues, namely questions concerning appropriate policy responses
and the design and regulation of institutions, both private and public.
Should there, for instance, be an international lender of last resort?
Under what circumstances, if any, are controls over capital movements
appropriate?

There are three reasons why it seemed appropriate for the International Center for Monetary and Banking Studies to organize the
conference that took place on 11–13 September 1986 in Geneva and for

the Centre for Economic Policy Research (CEPR) to become associated with it. Topicality is the first: the questions are familiar from history, but current events heighten their importance. Second, recent developments in the theory of finance as well as in the economics of uncertainty provide promising tools to analyse the functioning and institutions of international financial markets and the roles of regulation and supervision. Third, the Center in Geneva has some comparative advantage in bringing to bear on these issues the triple expertise of academics, bankers and officials. Academics seek to understand the risks generated in and impinging on financial markets; so do the bankers who have to face and manage such risks; and supervisors have a direct stake in the risks the bankers take. Assessing and coping with threats to international financial stability is one issue which requires a joint intellectual endeavour by all these groups. CEPR was motivated by these same considerations; in particular, it is keen to make academic research comprehensible and relevant to policy-makers in the public and private sectors. Moreover, financial innovation and the international financial system are central to its programmes of research on macroeconomic interdependence and financial markets.

At the conference, the division of labour was to let the academics survey the issues in the papers that constitute the first six chapters of this book and ask private sector economists and officials to act as discussants and panellists. Their input is in the comments, the summary of the discussion and Panel, the country studies and the concluding chapter. It is, however, also to be found in the papers by the academics, since these ultimately deal with issues defined by the everyday actions of practitioners, private and official.

Other considerations motivate the order of the chapters in this book. Chapter 1 provides a general framework for understanding the anatomy of financial crises, their origins and international propagation. Chapters 2 and 3 deal respectively with the practice and theory of financial regulation and supervision designed to ensure financial stability. The perspective here is comparative and national rather than specifically international. The next three chapters, in contrast, focus on three of the main issues that arise in an international context. They deal, respectively, with the dynamics of the international (and subsidiary national) cycle of regulation/deregulation/reregulation; how to provide emergency liquidity assistance in the absence of an international lender of last resort; and the role of the interbank market in the international propagation of financial crises. In Chapter 7, the rapporteur pulls together the various strands of the discussion and of individual chapters, while Chapter 8 peers into the future and deals briefly with a topic that is only touched upon in other papers, the implications of financial innovation for monetary rather than supervisory policy.

Understanding the anatomy of international financial crises requires a definition of the phenomenon; the definition, to be useful, should suggest a framework that helps organize thought about the origins and nature of crises. The paper by Eichengreen and Portes provides such a framework and puts it to use in comparing the experience of the 1930s and 1980s. It is necessary to distinguish between the shocks to the international financial system and the structure of the system itself; the latter determines whether the shocks will be amplified into crisis or not. Eichengreen and Portes identify three main types of disturbances (debt defaults, bank failures and exchange-market disturbances) and characterize the linkages by which one type of disturbance can spread to other markets and thus create other disturbances. A financial crisis, characterized by plummeting asset prices and a disruption of the system's ability to allocate capital, tends to occur when there are no mechanisms to break or attenuate these links, and the financial system is too fragile to withstand the shocks.

International financial crisis in the 1930s but not, so far, in the 1980s is attributable, according to Eichengreen and Portes, to differences in the nature and extent of the shocks, of the linkages, and of both regulatory and macroeconomic policies. In particular, shocks to debtor economies were largely external in the 1930s and more mixed in the 1980s. Macroeconomic and trade policies were disastrous in the earlier period. Both macroeconomic and regulatory policies recently appear to have been informed by the lessons of the past. And sovereign debt may be more manageable today, when that debt mainly takes the form of bank loans, than when it consisted mainly of bonds. Eichengreen and Portes conclude on a fairly sanguine note, though they do emphasize the overriding importance of coordinated and appropriate macroeconomic policies in avoiding and containing international financial crises. Their discussants, however, add cautionary remarks, Gemmill by stressing the potentially destabilizing role of the interbank market (see also Chapter 6) which was only of minor importance in the earlier period, and Rybczynski by considering the role of the international monetary (in contrast to financial) regime, whose current form he finds wanting.

Different countries adopt different methods to cope with potential financial instability. These measures can, as Baltensperger and Dermine remind us, be divided into prudential/preventive measures on one hand, and protective measures, on the other hand. The former include capital adequacy and liquidity requirements, diversification rules, and so forth; the latter include mainly various deposit insurance schemes and lender of last resort facilities. Two fundamental problems arise in bank and financial institution regulation. Regulatory measures (mainly of the first type) that seem to limit the risk taken by financial institutions may decrease the efficiency of the resource allocation process. Moreover, protective measures introduce well-known problems of moral hazard, since they are likely to lead financial institutions to pursue higher-risk policies than would be warranted in their absence. These dilemmas are hard to solve. Intellectually, much is to be said for a clear choice between a minimalist system where risk falls squarely on private institutions, leaving the monitoring to depositors and stockholders, with the regulators confined to ensuring transparency and honesty; and a tightly regulated system where the *quid pro quo* of the provision of deposit insurance and LLR facilities is adherence to strict prudential regulation.

In practice, however, the choice is never clear-cut, as the country studies in this volume show. Calls for protective measures, however self-interested, are difficult to resist when the solvency of the banking system is at stake. Implicit guarantees are as fraught with moral hazard as explicit ones; the problem of the authorities is credibly to deny such guarantees rather than credibly to grant them. On the other hand, competitive forces and innovations make it very hard to enforce strict regulatory standards without seriously damaging the efficiency and international competitiveness of national banking systems.

The compromises that are typically adopted are surveyed in a general manner in the paper by Baltensperger and Dermine and exemplified more specifically in the country studies that were presented at the conference in the discussion of that paper. These studies are appended in this volume. They present concisely the regulatory and supervisory measures, institutions, and philosophies of six countries chosen for their importance or for the contrasts they provide. Whereas the systems prevailing in the United States, the United Kingdom and the Federal Republic of Germany are relatively well known, the remaining three are not. The case of Finland illustrates an important point that is often valid elsewhere but also often forgotten, namely that regulatory control is often a by-product of monetary control. That of Argentina starkly illustrates another point: when the government's budget runs out of control, monetary policy loses all independence. Supervision and regulation then serve to enforce deficit financing through the inflation tax at the cost of mounting inefficiency in financial markets.

The general motivation for bank regulation, if we follow Baltensperger and Dermine, arises from the asymmetry of information between banks and their customers and the exposure of a major portion of bank liabilities to the possibility of withdrawal on demand at par. The interaction between these two characteristics of deposit banking raises the spectre of contagion effects and bank runs that threaten the integrity of the payments system or, in the perspective of Eichengreen and Portes, the ability of the financial system to allocate capital. The policy implications may appear simple: improve information through disclosure requirements; and design protective measures, deposit insurance and LLR facilities that minimize moral hazard problems. To do the latter, relate insurance premia to risk in much the same way as capital adequacy is (or should be) based on the asset structure of banks and the riskiness the latter entails.

There remains the question of how these very general principles should be implemented in practice. We would suggest that useful hints are provided by recent developments in the theory of finance, industrial organization, and the economics of information. This volume offers a number of examples. Chapter 3 by Stephen Schaefer draws some lessons from the theory of finance for the design of bank regulation. Schaefer makes three main points. First, relating capital adequacy to the riskiness of a financial institution's assets requires that riskiness be estimated properly. The methods currently used by regulators are by and large inappropriate partly because they do not take into account the all-important covariance between asset returns, partly because they assume that the risk that various asset classes contribute to the portfolio remains fixed over time. Schaefer suggests that often a fairly simple procedure would permit a much more accurate assessment of the riskiness of banks' asset portfolios. Improving existing measures is quite important, since Schaefer's rough and illustrative calculations show that currently used measures appear well wide of the mark. Second, regulators should take into account the liability structure as well as the asset structure of an intermediary, both on and off balance sheet, when assessing the risk to which its capital is subjected. The point is particularly relevant for banks, given their rather special liability structure and the recent proliferation of off-balance-sheet transactions. Third, Schaefer finds a puzzle in the contrasting views of regulators and banks as to capital structure. Bankers seem to prefer a small capital base even though the theory of corporate finance (the Modigliani–Miller theorem) does not justify any such preference. This suggests that the theory may be inadequate to deal with the capital structure of financial intermediaries that would presumably not exist if markets were complete.

This challenge that practice raises for theory is taken up briefly by Harold Rose, who supplies a number of insights into the determinants of banks' capital structure that should be pursued further. Recent developments in agency theory may well provide one key to the puzzle. As for policy implications, one conclusion can already be stated: improved information and greater transparency are essential. Robert Bench, in his comment, also underlines the importance of accurate and timely information in the supervisory process. Whether he would agree with Rose that supervisory authorities should not have a monopoly on such information is not for us to say. His comments do show that supervisors are well aware of the problems identified by Schaefer and others too – even if there is no general agreement on how to solve them. As we write this Introduction, however, there has just been a *limited* agreement that makes Schaefer's paper and the discussion of it especially topical. On 8 January 1987, the Bank of England and the US Federal Banking Regulatory Authorities announced their accord on a common system for measuring capital adequacy.[1] The risk asset ratio to be used is very similar to that already calculated by the Bank of England for several years and discussed by Schaefer.

The process of financial innovation, both national and international, and the rapid growth of international markets such as the Eurodollar markets, have often been ascribed to the dynamic interaction of technological and regulatory changes. Edward Kane borrows from the economics of industrial organization, particularly the theory of contestable markets, to illuminate the dynamic interaction between regulatees and regulators. This leads him to propose a Hegelian dialectic of the regulatory process. Starting (arbitrarily) in the dialectic chain with an act of regulation as the initial synthesis one would observe avoidance as the antithesis and reregulation as the new synthesis. And the process repeats.

The usefulness of this scheme comes with identifying the determinants of the speed of the diffusion process and with applying it to specific instances. Kane shows how the dialectic describes not only competition among regulators within the United States but also at the international level. Indeed, as he and his discussants stress, today the main arena for competition among regulators and for avoidance by regulatees is international. Conflicts between efficiency and stability arise once again. While international regulatory competition prevents arbitrary concentration of power and yields efficiency gains, it also hinders monitoring of regulatory agencies by the public and may bring destabilizing overcompetition. This is especially dangerous insofar as it results in underpricing conjectural government guarantees, which constitutes a subsidy to risk-taking. Kane makes a case for greater international regulatory cooperation, at least as an interim step in dealing with the problem. As both David Pyle and Aloys Schwietert note, it is difficult to ensure the degree of competition (or 'structural arbitrage') required to break down inefficient regulation while providing incentives to adopt the efficient regulation that is in the common interest. Schwietert's comment also makes it clear that Kane's regulatory dialectic is close to a banker's view of the actual dynamics of the international regulatory process.

The pricing of governmental guarantees is a main issue in any discussion of the role of, and need for, lenders of last resort (LLR). Guttentag and Herring discuss the origins of the concept, its rationale, and its meaning in an international context. To justify LLR activities requires that there be a market failure that can transform a liquidity problem into a solvency problem, and that failure of a bank might have social costs greater than those of providing LLR facilities. Once this is established (and Guttentag and Herring make a strong case), it is necessary to determine the appropriate modalities of last-resort lending. The main problem is again one of moral hazard and, subsidiarily, whether it is possible and desirable to distinguish between solvent and insolvent banks. In the end, Guttentag and Herring argue, LLR facilities will be made available at least to large banks, whether one likes it intellectually and morally or not. They therefore propose that banks that are eligible for such facilities be clearly identified in advance, at an international as well as a national level. They also argue, convincingly to us, that vagueness about the availability of LLR facilities may increase rather than reduce the moral hazard problem.

That LLR facilities are controversial will be clear from the comments of the discussants. Michael Beenstock traces the need for LLR facilities back to asymmetries of information between the banks and the non-bank public (as depositors, shareholders and taxpayers). Though some of these asymmetries are 'natural', in his view most are not but arise from regulators' attempts to keep a monopoly of information. He would confine the role of regulators and supervisors mainly to disseminating this information as widely as possible, while abstaining from the provision of LLR facilities. Freedman, in contrast, sees a need for lenders of last resort but insists on the necessity of trying to distinguish between solvent and insolvent institutions. Helping the latter is the role of the investor of last resort, not that of the lender of last resort. Richard Zecher recognizes the necessity of protecting the payments system. He finds, however, that the *quid pro quo* of LLR facilities has been additional regulation of bank activities that may have nothing to do with the banks' payments function, at the cost of inefficiencies and loss of competitiveness of some groups of banks (such as the New York money center banks). The result is an intriguing suggestion that the money-issuing, payments-system function of banks be separated from their other functions, at least when it comes to regulation and supervision.[2]

One rationale for LLR facilities is to avoid or contain bank runs or, more generally, contagion effects that spread an individual institution's problem to the rest of the financial system. Anthony Saunders's paper examines both the mechanisms by which the interbank market may spread shocks and existing evidence on instances of such contagion in the postwar world. Contagion effects are modelled as affecting interest rate spreads in international deposit and loan markets; the quantities of such deposits and loans supplied; and bank equity returns. Perhaps surprisingly, such contagion effects do not appear to have been very strong except immediately around a crisis: the Mexican debt crisis of 1982 and Continental Illinois for the first of these effects; and for bank equity prices in 1973–74, after the Franklin National and Herstatt failures. That contagion effects have been weak, especially after 1982, may be due either to the unaided resiliency of the system or to the existence of explicit or implicit guarantees. If the latter, however, the stabilization may have been achieved at the cost of creating serious moral hazard problems for the future.

Whether contagion effects would have been as limited under a serious shock to the settlement system (mainly CHIPS) is an issue raised by Arturo Brillembourg who, like Zecher, would focus the regulators' attention on the integrity of the payments and settlement system, leaving it to better information and the market to assess and deal with other types of risk. Lionel Price in his comment emphasizes the role of preventive (e.g., capital-adequacy) measures as well as protective ones in explaining the market's stability. He also argues that moral hazard is reduced because shareholders and management are not protected from the consequences of a bank failure, even if depositors are.

Financial crises are always unexpected. Each new crisis appears in a different guise from the last. Preventing the next crisis thus requires identifying its likely source, a task rendered particularly difficult by the rapid pace of financial innovation and changes emerging from the regulatory dialectic. This is perhaps the main message of the Panel discussion. Points of stress include not only new instruments which regulators find difficult to assess (Sam Cross), but also the settlement system and the integration of very different managerial cultures in the personnel of financial institutions (Christine Downton). The Panel discussion also explored the interaction between macroeconomic policy and regulatory efficiency, or rather between macroeconomic and regulatory mismanagement (Ernesto Feldman). A further perspective was added by considering how successful crisis management in the short run may sow the seeds of financial fragility, inefficiency and future crises in the long run (Alexander Swoboda).

So where do we end up if we peer into the future? In his evaluation, Markus Lusser is fairly optimistic on where we could and should go. Financial innovation has many positive aspects and does not pose insurmountable problems for monetary policy. Deregulation is a step in the right direction. Less optimistically, however, Lusser concludes that there is no guarantee that the macroeconomic mistakes that led to the inefficiencies undone by innovation and deregulation will not be repeated in the future.

Taken together, the papers in this volume provide, we believe, not only a rich survey of the threats to international financial stability, but also several insights into the role of both policy and markets in containing them. We hope that these insights will stimulate further work and eventually lead to the design of a more resilient international financial system.

NOTES

1 *Bank of England* (1987).
2 For a similar suggestion, see Fama (1980).

REFERENCES

Bank of England Quarterly Bulletin (1987), **27** No. 1 (February).
Fama, Eugene F. (1980). 'Banking in the Theory of Finance', *Journal of Monetary Economics*, **6** No. 1 (January), pp. 39–57.

1   The anatomy of financial crises

BARRY EICHENGREEN and
RICHARD PORTES*

Much as the study of disease is one of the most effective ways to learn about human biology, the study of financial crises provides one of the most revealing perspectives on the functioning of monetary economies. Indeed, epidemiological metaphors like fever and contagion feature prominently in the literature on financial crises. Financial crises, like contagious disease, threaten not only the host organism, namely the financial market, but the entire economic environment in which that host resides.

There exists a voluminous historical literature concerned with episodes labelled financial crises.[1] Yet the usefulness of much of this literature is limited by the absence of any definition of the phenomenon under consideration and hence of a minimal structure around which historical observation can be organized.[2] This criticism is not limited to the historical literature, since recent theoretical analyses of financial crises are uniformly deficient in this same regard. While no single definition may be appropriate to all purposes, any work on financial crises should proceed on the basis of an explicit statement of meaning. Since our purpose in this chapter is to provide a perspective on the present and prospective danger of a serious disruption to the global financial system, which we propose to explore by comparing the last full-fledged financial crisis – that of the 1930s – with conditions prevailing today, we adopt the following definition. A financial crisis is a disturbance to financial markets, associated typically with falling asset prices and insolvency among debtors and intermediaries, which ramifies through the financial system, disrupting the market's capacity to allocate capital within the economy. In an international financial crisis, disturbances spill over national borders, disrupting the market's capacity to allocate capital internationally.

This definition suggests an agenda for research, of which the following

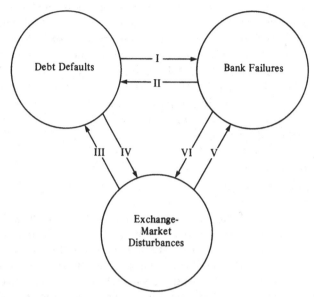

Figure 1.1 Asset-market linkages

questions form only a part. What are the distinguishing features of disturbances which give rise to financial crises? Rather than the nature of the disturbances, is it the financial system's response that differentiates crises from perturbations to financial markets? What is the mechanism through which a disturbance specific to a single market is generalized to the entire system? In particular, what are the roles of asset prices and solvency problems in the process of generalization and propagation? How are the market's allocative capacities disrupted, and what are the implications of this disruption for the course of the crisis itself?

Our definition implies a distinction between generalized financial crisis on the one hand and bank failures, debt defaults and foreign-exchange market disturbances on the other. This distinction is the presence of linkages, which are represented schematically in Figure 1.1. These linkages within the body economic give the essential anatomy of financial crisis.

Consider two examples which play a leading role in our historical analysis. Defaults on sovereign bonds, if sufficiently widespread and disruptive, impede the ability of the bond market to allocate capital across countries. But if these defaults are not accompanied by bank failures (if in Figure 1.1 the linkage labelled 'I' is interrupted), there may exist alternative channels, notably bank loans, through which the capital market's allocative functions may be carried out. Debt default need not give rise to financial crisis. But if, on the contrary, debt default heightens the commercial banks' susceptibility to failure, the danger of a generalized crisis is intensified. To take another example, an anticipated devaluation may threaten the banking system if depositors liquidate their accounts in an effort to avoid capital losses on their overseas assets (an example of the linkage labelled 'V'); but if they hold government securities instead, this linkage is broken and exchange-market difficulties need not be associated with financial collapse. Clearly, the extent and speed of transmission along these linkages depend on institutional arrangements in financial markets, including any institutionalized responses of policy-makers.

In this paper, we focus on the generalization and propagation of financial crises in an international setting. Ideally, these issues of generalization and propagation are studied historically: while all serious disturbances threaten the stability of financial institutions, it is only from the comparison of historical episodes during which different institutional arrangements prevailed that generalizations about the fragility or resilience of monetary economies can be derived. By analyzing the contrasting institutional arrangements of the 1930s and 1980s, we hope to identify configurations which render the international financial system particularly susceptible to collapse.

Our analysis of the generalization of financial disturbances underscores the critical role played by institutional arrangements in financial markets as a determinant of the system's vulnerability to destabilizing shocks. In both the 1930s and 1980s, the institutional environment was drastically altered by rapid change in foreign exchange markets, in international capital markets, and in the structure of domestic banking systems. But the implications of institutional changes have not all been similar. In the earlier period, they generally worked in the direction of heightening the system's vulnerability to shocks; recently, however, some have tended to work in the opposite direction. Our review of the course of crises suggests that the banking system and the linkages by which it is connected to the rest of the financial sector play a pivotal role in the propagation of crises. Our analyses highlight the importance of two sets of factors in the process of propagation: asset-market linkages running from debt defaults and exchange-market disturbances to the stability of the banking system (linkages I and V in Figure 1.1), and the role of economic policy in blocking these linkages and thereby insulating the banking system and the macroeconomy from threats to their stability.

I   The international financial crisis of the 1930s

A.   The environment

The 1920s were marked by three sets of developments which increased the international financial system's susceptibility to destabilizing shocks: flux in the foreign exchange market, rapid institutional change in the banking system, and dramatic shifts in the volume and direction of international lending. Each set of developments had its immediate origins in the dislocations associated with World War I.

Foreign exchange markets   The war and its aftermath marked the end of the classical gold standard. Most countries initially succeeded in maintaining their gold reserves and customary exchange rates by withdrawing gold coin from circulation and embargoing bullion shipments. But as hostilities dragged on and were financed through the issue of money and bonds, pressure mounted in foreign exchange markets. The German and Austrian exchanges collapsed by 1918. The British and French rates were propped up by American intervention but depreciated with the termination of support in 1919.[3] The postwar inflationary boom, the reparations tangle and deficit finance of reconstruction all wreaked havoc with national efforts to peg the domestic-currency price of gold.

Policymakers then confronted the question of the appropriate level at which to stabilize exchange rates. The history of subsequent efforts to reconstruct the system of fixed parities is familiar: Britain restored sterling's prewar parity in 1925 following a period of deflation; France opted against reversing half a decade of inflation, pegging the franc price of gold at five times the prewar level; Germany and other countries experiencing hyperinflation established new currency units; and Latin American countries reestablished gold standard parities in conjunction with budgetary reforms and newly independent central banks.[4]

The characteristics of the reconstructed gold standard added to the strains on the financial system. Paramount was the problem of misalignment, starting with the pound sterling, the traditional linchpin of the monetary mechanism. Due to high wages and to changes in the direction of trade, Britain's restoration of the prewar parity rendered the pound overvalued and difficult to defend with the Bank of England's slender reserves. Keynes (1925) estimated sterling's overvaluation at 10–15 per cent. In conventional accounts, an undervalued French franc figures also among the misaligned currencies.[5] Misalignment was related to the problem of maldistributed gold reserves, which came to be concentrated in the United States and France. This maldistribution gave rise elsewhere to complaints of a 'gold shortage', which induced countries to expand on prewar practice and supplement gold reserves with foreign deposits. The growth of foreign deposits rendered the reserve currencies increasingly vulnerable to destabilizing shocks.[6] Each of these difficulties reflected the failure of governments to coordinate their choice of exchange rates and to harmonize their monetary policies. Ultimately, the consequences of this failure would be far-reaching.[7]

International lending The impact of the war on patterns of international lending and borrowing was equally profound.[8] The 1920s marked the rise of the United States and decline of Britain as external creditors. The transfer of business from London to New York, initiated by wartime closure of the London market to foreign borrowers and by the Liberty Loan campaign in the United States, was reinforced following the conclusion of hostilities by informal capital controls in the UK and abundant savings in the US. Before the war, Britain's foreign assets roughly matched the combined total of the remaining creditor countries, while the US was a creditor of negligible importance. In the 1920s (with the exception of 1923, when transfers to Europe were depressed by the Ruhr invasion), lending by the US, especially to countries outside the British Empire, consistently exceeded that by Britain.

The other side of this coin was rapidly mounting indebtedness in Central Europe and Latin America. Loans to Europe were used to finance the reconstruction of industry and infrastructure, the purchase of imported inputs and the provision of working capital. At the same time, the growth of lending can be understood as a response to the need to recycle German reparations in much the same way that OPEC investment in the US, in conjunction with US lending to LDCs, recycled oil revenues in the 1970s.[9] Loans to Latin America, in contrast, reflected favourable publicity and growing awareness of economic prospects in developing regions.[10] Table 1.1 summarizes the direction of US and British lending. American lending was widely distributed, going most heavily to Europe (where Germany was the leading debtor in absolute terms) and then to Latin America and Canada; British lending was directed predominantly towards the Empire, especially at the end of the decade.

Then, as recently, there was much discussion of the soundness of foreign loans, embellished by tales of loan pushing, excessive commissions, corrupt administration, and squandering of funds. Indeed, placing much of the business in relatively inexperienced American hands may have increased the market's tendency to fund risky projects.[11] It is important to note, therefore, that the macroeconomic performance of

Table 1.1. **US and British lending in the 1920s**

| | US lending abroad by region (millions of dollars) | | | |
	Europe	Canada	Latin America	Far East
1924	526.6	151.6	187.0	96.1
1925	629.5	137.1	158.8	141.7
1926	484.0	226.3	368.2	31.7
1927	557.3	236.4	339.7	151.2
1928	597.9	184.9	330.1	130.8
1929	142.0	289.7	175.0	51.5

| | British investment in government and municipal securities (millions of pounds) | |
	Foreign	Dominion and Colonial
1926	392.0	676.5
1927	406.7	703.3
1928	364.5	1036.0
1929	351.0	1061.6

Sources: For the US, Department of Commerce (1930); for Britain, Royal Institute of International Affairs (1937).

the debtors, and the consequent growth in their ability to service external debt, was more than respectable, and in the Latin American case rather impressive, during this period of large-scale foreign lending (1925–9). With the exception of Costa Rica and El Salvador, real GDP in those Latin American countries considered in Table 1.2 increased at then historically unprecedented rates in excess of five per cent per annum. Except for Brazil, Guatemala and (to a lesser extent) Costa Rica, the same is true of exports, despite a persistent decline in the prices of primary products. Initially, the ratio of debt service to exports (excluding reparations) remained manageable.[12]

Thus, in the 1920s as in the 1970s, foreign lending was associated with expanding trade and rosy prospects, at least in the short run, for economic growth in the borrowing regions. Whether the loans were sound in the sense that export receipts would prove adequate to service them is essentially the question whether it was realistic to assume that the growth rates and financial stability (e.g., absence of real interest rate

Table 1.2. **Annual growth rates of real GDP, industrial production and exports 1925–9, and debt/export ratio, 1929**

(in percentage points)

	GDP	Industrial production	Exports in US dollars	1929 Central govt foreign debt as percent of exports
Germany	1.7	5.0	9.9	6.6
Austria	2.7	6.3	4.0	77.5
Hungary	7.1	−0.4^a	5.9	123.2
Australia	−0.4	4.1	−3.8	112.5
Canada	6.3^a	8.8	−1.1	46.2
Argentina	5.7	5.2	4.8	41.8
Brazil	7.2	4.6	−1.6	66.3
Costa Rica	0.2	1.6	3.1	95.4
Chile	10.8	0.0	5.8	101.7
Colombia	7.5	4.5	11.6	55.7
Honduras	5.6	6.8	20.2	43.3
El Salvador	1.7	5.9	12.4	105.4
Guatemala	5.5	3.0	−3.4	54.0

Note: European figures exclude reparations. ^{a} indicates 1926–9. For Australia, industrial production is proxied by manufacturing production at constant prices. *Sources:* Latin American figures computed from Thorp (1984), Appendix Table 4. European figures computed from Mitchell (1976). Canadian figures computed from Urquhart and Buckley (1965). Australian figures computed from Butlin (1984).

shocks) of the 1920s would persist. The answer is surely more obvious with hindsight than it was at the time.

Banking structure and regulation   These changes in the direction of foreign lending were accompanied by equally profound developments in the structure and regulation of commercial banking. Following the lead of the United States, which had created the Federal Reserve System in 1914, in the 1920s many countries either established central banks or gave them added independence, in Latin America in conjunction with visits by US economic experts, in Central Europe as a condition of League of Nations stabilization loans.[13] One function of these central banks was to act as lender of last resort, although as we shall see there was considerable variation in the effectiveness with which they carried out this role. In a number of countries monetary reform was accompanied by new banking regulations patterned on the US model. In Chile, for example, a law of September 1925 established a 'Superintendencia de Bancos' charged with inspecting the books of banks and publishing a statement of their position annually. Banks were prohibited from extending individual loans in excess of ten per cent of the sum of paid-up capital and reserves and were required to observe minimum capital requirements which differed by city size and liability composition. Since there was considerable variation in the appropriateness of the US model, these reforms varied in their efficacy and implications for the stability of national banking systems.

A number of countries including Germany and Poland established publicly owned or controlled agricultural credit and mortgage banks which engaged in all forms of deposit and industrial banking and expanded rapidly.[14] Their implications for the stability of the financial system are not clear: on the one hand, public banks for political reasons sometimes extended loans to risky undertakings which did not attract private banks; on the other, the central authorities were particularly disinclined to let public enterprises fail.

A further feature of the development of banking structure in the 1920s was a pervasive amalgamation movement. While the immediate incentive for amalgamation was often savings on administrative costs, another advantage was the greater facility with which risk could be diversified and stability ensured through the dispersion of loans over different regions and sectors of the economy. Although present earlier, the amalgamation movement in commercial banking accelerated after World War I, spreading from England and Wales to Latin America, Hungary, Poland and Greece. In Germany and Czechoslovakia, large banks increasingly acquired control of their smaller counterparts, while in the US, restrictions on branch banking were circumvented through such mechanisms as the securities affiliate.

Along with the spread of the securities affiliate, financial innovation in the 1920s took the form of the adoption of 'investment' or 'industrial' banking on a national scale in the Succession States of what had been the Austro-Hungarian Empire. In English-speaking, Scandinavian and Latin American countries, intermediaries specialized in deposit banking, soliciting money on deposit and extending short-term advances to commerce and industry. The alternative of investment banking, which entailed long-term loans to industry, had traditionally prevailed in Central Europe. When the Succession States created new banking systems in the wake of World War I, they naturally emulated Austrian and German practice. Given the specialization of industry and agriculture in the newly partitioned Central European states, the fate of the

Table 1.3. **Business cycle indicators for advanced countries, 1929–38 and 1973–83**

	GDP	Import volume	Terms of trade	Net capital outflow at 1929 prices $ million	World price level (US export unit values)
1929	100.0	100.0	100.0	355	100.0
1930	94.6	94.8	106.1	−145	89.6
1931	89.3	89.5	111.8	−1,422	69.4
1932	83.0	76.5	113.7	−1,661	59.0
1933	84.0	78.4	114.8	1,006	61.9
1934	89.2	79.6	111.1	−1,254	72.4
1935	94.3	81.8	108.0	−406	74.6
1936	101.6	85.7	100.6	−176	76.1
1937	107.0	97.4	103.9	−1,677	80.6
1938	109.3	87.0	108.3	−1,413	74.6
1973	100.0	100.0	100.0	8,919	100.0
1974	100.4	101.1	88.4	7,020	127.6
1975	99.8	92.7	90.3	12,507	142.6
1976	105.1	105.5	89.8	12,416	147.5
1977	109.1	109.5	88.7	13,429	152.7
1978	113.5	115.4	91.1	17,241	163.3
1979	117.3	124.0	87.3	16,265	185.9
1980	118.8	121.8	81.3	14,215	211.0
1981	120.4	118.4	80.2	15,792	230.4
1982	119.9	117.6	81.9	14,340	232.9
1983	122.8	122.0	83.4	11,702	236.5

Notes: GDP, import volume and terms of trade are weighted averages for 16 countries. The capital flows are deflated by the US export unit value index. The US export unit value in 1973 was 251 per cent of its 1929 level.
Source: Maddison (1985, p. 13).

banks' loan portfolios was tied to the fortunes of narrow industrial or agricultural markets. When a particular crop or industry was hit by the Depression, the shock to the banking system would prove severe.

B. The crisis and its management

Our analysis of the financial crisis of the 1930s highlights two factors: first, the singular importance of linkages running from debt defaults and exchange market disturbances to the instability of banking systems; second, the critical role of policy in interrupting these linkages, thereby insulating the banking system and the macroeconomy from threats to their stability.

Table 1.4. **Business cycle indicators for 11 developing countries, 1929–38 and 1973–83**

	Latin America				Asia			
	GDP	Export volume	Terms of trade	Import volume	GDP	Export volume	Terms to trade	Import volume
1929	100.0	100.0	100.0	100.0	100.0	100.0	100.0	100.0
1930	96.1	81.2	81.5	77.4	101.1	91.3	90.4	89.5
1931	90.0	90.0	67.9	51.9	101.4	86.6	83.5	82.3
1932	86.7	73.0	71.4	39.5	103.8	77.7	84.2	78.5
1933	93.2	75.7	68.8	45.5	104.5	80.0	82.1	71.2
1934	101.0	85.4	76.5	52.5	99.4	82.6	86.6	76.7
1935	106.3	91.9	75.2	56.4	104.2	84.7	92.3	82.6
1936	113.4	93.3	80.6	61.7	109.9	94.1	94.9	81.0
1937	120.8	101.8	89.1	76.8	110.0	n.a.	n.a.	n.a.
1938	121.4	(81.4)	(84.9)	(70.9)	106.9	n.a.	n.a.	n.a.
1973	100.0	100.0	100.0	100.0	100.0	100.0	100.0	100.0
1974	106.7	100.4	95.8	126.4	101.6	101.7	97.5	109.1
1975	109.7	100.1	88.5	119.5	110.0	107.8	91.9	110.9
1976	116.0	112.1	94.1	112.0	110.2	132.0	97.0	121.9
1977	122.3	123.2	94.7	110.9	119.3	142.9	102.0	132.9
1978	127.3	141.2	87.9	121.2	131.7	163.6	97.7	157.5
1979	136.1	152.6	87.5	141.8	136.8	171.8	94.5	165.3
1980	143.9	167.7	92.1	169.7	145.2	189.6	91.2	176.3
1981	143.9	190.3	85.6	175.1	153.0	209.6	86.4	183.0
1982	142.3	194.0	83.1	132.3	161.6	220.4	81.2	176.5
1983	139.3	214.7	80.2	103.7	174.1	245.7	75.9	193.3

Notes: The above indices are all weighted averages. Latin America includes Argentina, Brazil, Chile, Colombia, Cuba and Mexico. Asia includes China, India, Indonesia, Korea and Taiwan.
Source: Maddison (1985, p. 14).

Exchange market disturbances   The first indication of serious financial distress was exchange-rate depreciation by primary producers starting in 1929. While misalignments within the North Atlantic community may have played some role in early exchange-market difficulties, the most disruptive pressures originated on the real side, notably in markets for agricultural commodities and primary products. So long as US import demands and foreign lending were maintained, these pressures remained tolerable. But in 1928–9 the indebted countries of Central Europe, Latin America and Oceania were subjected to dual shocks. First, the Wall Street boom both reflected and induced portfolio shifts by US investors, choking off American capital exports: after peaking in the summer of 1928, they fell by 46 per cent within a year (see Table 1.1). Next, commodity exports declined precipitously following the US cyclical downturn commencing in the summer of 1929 (see Table 1.3). Primary-producing countries were seriously affected (as shown in Table 1.4), since the US accounted for more than 40 per cent of the primary-product consumption of the 15 leading industrial countries.

The exchange rate and the external debt were directly linked through the government's reserve constraint. Gold and foreign-exchange reserves could be allocated either to debt service or to merchants and currency dealers who, under gold standard statutes, could demand gold for export. In principle, borrowing countries could have chosen to default on their external debts while defending the gold standard, to let their exchange rates go while maintaining debt service, or to default and depreciate simultaneously. Initially, they chose to sacrifice the exchange rate and honour the debt. One might speculate that policymakers viewed debt as even more sacrosanct than the gold standard, although that is doubtful in view of the frequency of default in the nineteenth century (matched only by the frequency of suspensions of convertibility). In fact, their motives were pragmatic: while default automatically precluded additional foreign borrowing, depreciation had less impact on credit-worthiness. It was even suggested that, insofar as depreciation stimulated exports, it might facilitate foreign bond flotations. Nevertheless, policymakers themselves saw depreciation as a threat to the national credit, albeit one less serious than default.

The pre-sterling depreciations were a Latin American and Antipodean phenomenon, starting with Uruguay in April 1929 and followed in rapid succession by Argentina, Paraguay, Brazil, Australia, New Zealand, Venezuela, Bolivia and Mexico. Australia's experience is especially revealing, since both default and devaluation were resisted so strongly.[15] The Australian economy was adversely affected by both declining wool and wheat prices and increasingly stringent London credit conditions. As early as the first semester of 1929, the Commonwealth Bank had been alarmed by the decline in its sterling balances and by its inability to float new loans in London. But despite the rising opportunity cost of debt service, little consideration was given to the option of default, in the hope that faithful maintenance of service might permit floating new loans in London. Instead, to curb imports the banks rationed foreign exchange and increased their rates against sterling while attempting to stay within the gold points. These expedients were viewed as temporary, and their reversal was anticipated as soon as new loans could be floated. The authorities obtained additional breathing space through the passage of legislation (patterned after the British Gold Standard and Currency and Bank Notes Acts of 1925 and 1928) which concentrated Australian gold holdings in the authorities' hands. Citizens were required to exchange gold for notes, and specie exports were discouraged by specifying a minimum quantity of gold (400 ounces fine) which could be obtained on demand. Hence there was additional scope for depreciation without destroying the gold standard facade.

To strengthen the trade balance and stave off depreciation, Australia adopted no fewer than seven new tariff schedules between April and December 1930. Exports were promoted by a 'Grow More Wheat Campaign' and by bounties or bonuses for wine-making and gold mining. Ultimately, these efforts proved inadequate due to deteriorating world market conditions and to resistance within Labour circles to further deflationary policies. When in December 1930 a political impasse over the budget deficit threatened to unleash a wave of capital flight, those in banking circles who viewed devaluation as damaging to Australian credit acceded to the others who insisted that devaluation would be acknowledged instead as a beneficial step 'towards recognition of the true state of affairs'.[16] In January the currency was depreciated substantially, at which point it held until sterling's devaluation the following September. The authorities continued to hope that additional borrowing on the London market might prove possible; hence little serious consideration was given to the alternative of default except by Labour heretics such as Jack Lang in New South Wales.

Debt default Even after suspending convertibility, many countries found it difficult or impossible to maintain service on their external debt.[17] The debt crisis that followed fell into three phases.[18] The first, spanning calendar year 1931, is dominated by Latin American defaults. During the second, from January 1932 through June 1933, default spread to Southern and Eastern Europe. The third, whose opening coincided with the Monetary and Economic Conference of 1933, was dominated by Germany's reduction of service on its foreign debt.

Macroeconomic events, rather than disturbances limited to financial markets, played a leading role in the onset of the debt crisis. The Great Depression affected the ability of governments to generate both the tax revenues needed to service debt and the foreign exchange required to transfer revenues abroad. Plummeting economic activity and rising unemployment increased budgetary expenditures at the same time as revenues fell. The decline in export values and volumes led to a rapid contraction of foreign exchange earnings (see Table 1.4). In much the same manner that an isolated bank failure can be infectious given depositors' incomplete information about the solvency of other banks, defaults by a few countries caused investors to revise their expectations for continued debt service by others. International lending all but evaporated following Bolivia's January 1931 default, and with the collapse of lending, the incentive to keep debt service current was further reduced.[19]

The Latin American defaults that dominated the first phase of the crisis exhibited common features. Typically they resulted from the interaction of declining primary-commodity prices with government budget deficits (due both to expenditures on nonproductive projects and to the macroeconomic slump).[20] Debt crisis and domestic political instability interacted in a vicious circle: political instability hindered attempts to achieve fiscal reform, while the crisis environment and the draconian policies adopted to redress the debt and budget problems threatened to undermine the most stable of governments. Although Bolivia's default was in large part a function of a 40 per cent fall in the dollar price of tin, a long history of budgetary mismanagement culminating in the government's overthrow also played a role, as the British consul had recognised fully three months before default:

> The unlimited depredations on the State coffers by the late head of the country and his minions have left the country bled white, and there are no resources left on which to fall back. In fact there is every prospect that Bolivia will be obliged to default on her obligations in connection with foreign loans falling due in December.[21]

In Peru, as in Bolivia, the onset of the Depression exacerbated political unrest which culminated in revolution. While Peru's new government put a stop to what the British consul described as the previous administration's 'reckless squandering' of funds, it was still forced to halt debt service in March 1931 on the grounds that the Treasury was bare of funds.[22] Chile, which also experienced revolution and suffered greatly from the decline in nitrate and copper prices, defaulted four months later. Brazil, hit by a disastrous fall in coffee prices and similarly undergoing revolution, defaulted in October.

Default spread to Europe one year to the day after its appearance in Latin America. Compared with the Latin American republics, most Central and East European countries had suffered less from the collapse of primary-commodity prices (due to greater export diversification) and had pursued more austere budgetary policies. They were hesitant to interrupt service on the grounds that much of their debt had been arranged under League of Nations auspices. Nonetheless, Hungary's default in January 1932 was followed in rapid succession by those of Greece, Bulgaria and Yugoslavia.

The final phase of the crisis was ushered in by Germany's default. The German authorities had previously limited the transfer of funds to extinguish maturing loans but refrained from interfering with interest transfers. As in Latin America, default was associated with political upheaval. One of the first steps of the National Socialist Party upon taking power in 1933 was to convene a conference of bondholders' representatives with the intention of rescheduling the debt. Arrangements were made to transfer a share of accrued debt service into foreign currency, to issue scrip in place of the rest, and to convert maturing coupons into funding bonds. With few exceptions, the dollar obligations of German states, municipalities and corporations were brought under the control of the Reichsbank's Conversion Office.

Strikingly, debt default had limited repercussions in the foreign exchange market. The currencies of most defaulting Latin American countries had already depreciated, while the currencies of the major European debtors were under exchange control. Moreover, in contrast to the 1980s, the deterioration of long-term foreign assets posed no direct threat to the banking systems of the creditor countries. Links from debt default to bank failures were broken because foreign lending took place not through bank loans but through the issue of bonds, few of which were held by banks in the creditor countries. Banks might participate in the syndicate which organized the loan and serve as purchasers of last resort if the market failed to take up the entire issue. But even in such instances, banks could resell their share of the issue once bond-market conditions improved.

Commercial banks also purchased foreign bonds as investments, although information on the extent of this practice is sketchy and incomplete. For the United States, the Comptroller of the Currency provided only aggregated information on the foreign bond holdings of National Banks. According to these data, foreign bonds accounted for but a small share, on the order of 7.5 per cent, of the bond holdings of National Banks, and bonds for less than a third of total assets. The Comptroller provided no information which might be used to estimate what share of these foreign bonds were subject to default risk. But unlike the Comptroller, who listed foreign bonds only as a group, the Vermont Bank Commissioner in 1930 reported the book value of the individual foreign bonds held by each state-chartered bank and trust company.[23] Table 1.5 lists foreign government bonds held by mutual savings banks, trust companies and savings and loan associations in Vermont on 30 June 1930. *Ex post*, and perhaps also *ex ante* given the relatively small discounts from par, most of these bonds appear to have been subject to relatively little default risk. Of the 58 banks under the Commissioner's supervision, one closed its doors in 1930, but due to a bad domestic loan rather than foreign bonds, of which the bank in question in fact held

Table 1.5. **Foreign government bonds held by Vermont mutual savings banks and trust companies, 30 June 1930**

	Book value $000
National Debt	
Dominion of Canada	453
Government of Argentina	277
Government of Newfoundland	296
Kingdom of Belgium	1,083
Kingdom of Denmark	1,209
Kingdom of Norway	896
Kingdom of Sweden	4
Republic of Chile	751
Republic of France	54
Republic of Uruguay	437
United Kingdom of Great Britain and Ireland	159
United Kingdom of Great Britain and Northern Ireland	23
Provincial Debt	
Province of Alberta	317
Province of British Columbia	195
Province of Manitoba	69
Province of New Brunswick	20
Province of Nova Scotia	14
Province of Ontario	913
Province of Quebec	48
Province of Saskatchewan	245
Miscellaneous Canadian bonds	927

Source: State of Vermont (1930).

none. While foreign bonds accounted for a larger share of the portfolios of the banks of certain other states, it is hard to see how foreign defaults alone could have posed a serious threat to the US banking system. It is likely that the same conclusion holds for the UK and other creditor countries.

A more serious threat was posed by the liquidation of foreign bank deposits. The exception to the debtor-country rule of giving priority to debt over convertibility concerned the treatment of short-term credits. These credits typically originated in connection with commercial trans-actions. As the Depression deepened, not only did credits to finance international transactions become redundant, but financial uncertainty induced foreigners to convert them into domestic currency. Commercial banks in the indebted regions consequently experienced sudden with-drawals of foreign balances. Their governments responded with exchange control and prohibitions on the repatriation of short-term capital. For example, when in October 1931 Argentina experienced accelerating depreciation, it imposed exchange control and froze short-term liabilities, which were owed predominantly to British creditors. After nineteen months an agreement was reached with Britain, under the provisions of which a long-term loan was floated to provide funds to transfer the frozen accounts. What is noteworthy is that Argentina, at the same time as it faithfully maintained service on its long-term debt, did not hesitate to restrict foreign access to short-term liabilities. The difference is attributable to the higher costs of leaving short-term debt unfettered, given its volatility in response to changes in anticipated returns, and the greater benefits of leaving service on long-term debt uninterrupted in the hope that additional long-term borrowing might again prove possible for the creditworthy.[24]

Short-term credits, bank failures and intervention

The preceding discussion has focused on links between exchange-rate convertibility and debt. A noteworthy aspect of Argentine experience is the absence of the next link in the chain, from debt and exchange rates to bank failures. While, as noted above, sovereign default was not a major source of instability of creditor-country banking systems, the same was not always true of debtor-country banks. Short-term debt was an important item on the liability side of many debtor-country-bank balance sheets, even if, due to their greater size, it represented a small item on the asset side of creditor-country-bank balance sheets.

In particular, foreign attempts to repatriate short-term credits in the summer of 1931 posed major threats to the solvency of the Austrian and German banking systems. Serious difficulties surfaced in Europe with the run on the Austrian Credit-Anstalt in May 1931. The problems of the Credit-Anstalt, while largely of domestic origin, were greatly complicated by its dependence on foreign credits. Austria had been the second European state (after Sweden) to stabilize its currency, and the early date of its stabilization in conjunction with League of Nations sponsorship promoted a sizeable inflow of foreign funds to the banking system. The Credit-Anstalt had participated fully in the amalgamation movement of the 1920s, absorbing the Bodenkreditanstalt and its portfolio of dubious industrial loans, and in 1929, when the market value of these loans declined precipitously, this amalgamation returned to haunt it.[25] Regulations forced the Credit-Anstalt to publish its 1930 balance sheet on 11 May 1931, revealing that it had lost more than half its capital, the criterion according to which it was officially declared insolvent. This announcement provoked large-scale withdrawals by domestic and

Table 1.6. **Short-term indebtedness of selected European countries, 1930–3**

(millions of US dollars)

Country	Date	Central Government	Local authorities	Central bank	Other banks	Other debtors	Total	Gross Foreign Debt
Austria	IX 1932	14.1	0.3	121.9		19.4	156	583[a]
Hungary	XI 1931	42.8	21.8	25.3	106.7	124.0	320	695[a]
Bulgaria	XII 1931	4.2	3.4	1.1	10.3	23.4	42	n.a.
Poland	XII 1931	0.4	—		5.1	27.9	33	1,130[a]
Romania	1932			13.5	23.7	41.9	79	965
Denmark	XII 1932		—	25.0		36.2	61	361
Finland	XII 1932	7.5	1.4	4.7	24.4	17.5	55	296
Norway	I 1933		2.2		19.7	106.9	129	373
Germany	IX 1932		148.0		193.6	918.4 963.3	2,223	4,670

Note: [a] denotes 1930 value; n.a. denotes not available. Gross foreign indebtedness for Poland includes direct foreign investment.
Sources: League of Nations (1933, 1937, 1938) and Royal Institute of International Affairs (1937).

foreign creditors.[26] A $14 million credit obtained through the Bank for International Settlements was exhausted within five days, and a subsequent loan from the Bank of England lasted little longer. The government's next step was to freeze foreign balances, and on 16 June 1931 foreign creditors agreed to a two-year suspension of transfers provided that the Austrian Government guaranteed the debts. A second standstill between other Austrian banks and their creditors followed. Although this freeze of foreign transfers did not put a halt to domestic withdrawals, which continued through 1931, the Credit-Anstalt's doors remained open by virtue of large rediscounts with the National Bank. This aspect of Austrian experience suggests a lesson common to Europe and Latin America: shocks with the potential to destabilize the banking system did not lead to generalized collapse because central banks acted in lender-of-last-resort capacity and simply did not permit this to occur.[27]

The Austrian run alerted creditors to the precarious position of other countries dependent upon short-term credits from abroad, notably Germany and the Successor States of Eastern Europe. Table 1.6 indicates the extent of short-term foreign indebtedness of the German banking system. Even had German banks not shared many of the weaknesses of their Austrian counterparts, they would have suffered withdrawals given depositors' incomplete information about their position and the signal provided by the Credit-Anstalt crisis.[28] The Darmstadter Bank, which failed on 13 July 1931, had invested heavily in textiles in general and in the bankrupt Nordwolle firm in particular, as well as in the nearly insolvent municipalities of the Rhine–Ruhr region. Foreign deposits figured prominently on the liabilities side of its balance sheet. Between mid-1930 and July 1931, German statistics show withdrawals of 2.5 to 3 RM billion in short-term foreign credits, or roughly half of the gross short-term liabilities of the 28 most important German banks. In the six weeks ending 13 July 1931, the Darmstadter lost 30 per cent of its deposits, culminating in a run that forced the closure of all German financial institutions. As the price of state support, the Reich fused the Darmstadter with another bank and replaced its board of directors. To prevent capital flight, the Reichsbank was given a monopoly of trans-actions in foreign exchange. Under the provisions of an agreement coming into force in September, transfers of short-term debt were suspended for six months and then for a year starting February 1932. Nonperforming assets were written down and new capital was secured with the aid of the Treasury and, indirectly, the Reichsbank.

Next to Austria and Germany, Hungary was most seriously affected by the liquidation of short-term credits. In the Hungarian case, first the Credit-Anstalt disclosures led to a withdrawal of foreign credits, and then the German banking crisis precipitated a domestic run. The government declared a three-day bank holiday, limited withdrawals and instituted exchange control. Together with heavy rediscounts by the Central Bank, these measures prevented widespread failures. The experience of Romania, the next largest short-term external debtor, differed in that official exchange control was only introduced in May 1932, and in its absence rediscounts with the National Bank were provided even more liberally.

The role of the lender of last resort in containing bank failures is evident in Latin America as well. As noted above, Argentina escaped bank failures because of the substantial rediscount and other credits extended to commercial banks by the Banco de la Nacion: rediscounts rose from 80 million pesos at the end of 1928 to 160 million pesos in April 1931, while advances to banks against government bills rose from 190 to 250 million pesos. Where rediscounts were less liberally provided, instability was greater: in Peru, for example, the Banco del Peru y Londres suspended payments in October 1930, occasioning a banking moratorium lasting through the end of the year. The authorities

Table 1.7. **Indices of prices of bank shares and industrial shares, 1930–3 (1929 = 100)**

		VI 1930	XII 1930	VI 1931	XII 1931	VI 1932	XII 1932	VI 1933	XII 1933
Belgium	Banks	66	55	47	36	30	35	35	35
	Industrial	72	55	52	35	29	36	35	29
Canada	Banks	85	80	72	69	45	50	54	47
	Industrial	62	45	34	28	18	22	39	40
Denmark	Banks	93	96	92	75	70	78	91	101
	Industrial	92	90	88	81	71	74	85	90
France	Banks	89	76	73	46	47	54	52	50
	Industrial	85	66	62	41	44	47	48	43
Germany	Banks	88	74	66	n.a.[a]	35	35	37	...
	Industrial	86	62	53	n.a.[a]	36	47	56	52
Netherlands	Banks	94	83	82	56	47	57	66	58
	Industrial	73	51	43	30	21	30	33	32
UK[b]	Banks[c]	92	97	89	68	82	96	96	104
	Industrial	75	64	56	49	45	57	63	70
USA	Banks[d]	67	43	38	21	14	23	21	15
	Industrial	77	55	47	29	18	24	42	43
Sweden	Banks	104	101	93	70	50	53	53	58
	Industrial	90	80	73	48	31	35	39	39
Switzerland	Banks	98	96	97	61	49	61	60	60
	Industrial	89	75	77	50	45	54	68	66

Notes: [a] No quotation.
[b] 31.XII.1928 = 100.
[c] Banks and discount companies.
[d] New York bank shares.
Source: League of Nations (1934).

responded by encouraging amalgamations and, after 1931, by increasing rediscounts.

The United Kingdom and the United States are the two prominent exceptions to this pattern, the UK because the banking system was not threatened, the US because of the extent to which it was. The relationship between the prices of industrial and bank stocks shown in Table 1.7 can be taken to indicate the condition of national banking systems relative to the condition of national economies. The table confirms that the British banking system weathered the crisis exceptionally well while the American banking system suffered profoundly.

In the British case, external credits again play a role, but in a rather different fashion.[29] The extent of Britain's short-term liabilities, while known to experts, was heralded by the publication of the Macmillan Committee Report in the summer of 1931. Combined with uncertainty about the defensibility of the sterling parity due to a budgetary impasse and British creditors' inability to withdraw funds from Austria and Germany, it led to a run on the pound which forced Britain from the gold standard in September. But since the discount market and the Government, not only the banks, relied on foreign funds, and since the run took the form mainly of sales of foreign-owned Treasury bills and withdrawals of credits previously granted to the discount market, it posed little threat to the banking system. In the three months ending September 1931, total deposits of the ten London clearing banks fell by £70 million, not an insignificant amount but small in comparison with experiences on the Continent.

Even in the United States, where agricultural foreclosure and industrial insolvency are typically emphasized as explanations for bank failure, foreign credits played a role. Signs of widespread financial distress surfaced in June 1931, when foreigners reduced their holdings of dollar acceptances and transferred their deposits from commercial to reserve banks. With Britain's abandonment of the gold standard these movements accelerated. In part these withdrawals of foreign deposits reflected the imposition of exchange control abroad, which rendered the United States one of the few remaining sources of liquidity for foreigners scrambling for funds.

Foreign withdrawals were particularly damaging to the banking system because they reinforced domestic sources of weakness. In the course of the 1920s, US commercial banks had greatly augmented the security and real estate components of their portfolios.[30] Collapse of the security and mortgage markets therefore rendered their asset position especially vulnerable. Real estate loans, which tended to be geographically undiversified due to restrictions on branch banking, increased the vulnerability of thousands of small unit banks to sector-specific shocks. Their desperate attempts to restore liquidity induced them to call in open-market loans and sell securities. Similar responses occurred in other countries although, as Table 1.8 makes clear, the liquidity position of US banks had eroded particularly dramatically over preceding years.[31] In response, US banks restricted loans, giving rise to widespread complaints among manufacturing firms about a shortage of credit. The scramble for liquidity reinforced the collapse of the bond market. The prices of domestic bonds fell so dramatically that by June 1932, when the rate on 3-month acceptances had fallen below one per cent, domestic industrial bonds were quoted on an 11 per cent yield basis and second

Table 1.8. **Bank cash resources as percentage of total deposits, 1929–32 (end of June)**

	1929	1930	1931	1932
France	7.4	9.7	13.9	33.6
Switzerland	n.a.	n.a.	11.3	22.9
United Kingdom	11.3	11.5	11.7	11.5
United States	7.3	7.4	7.6	8.2
Italy	6.9	6.6	6.2	5.9
Germany	3.1	2.7	3.6	3.4
Poland	8.5	8.8	10.7	9.0
Sweden	2.1	2.3	2.1	3.8
Czechoslovakia	6.7	7.3	7.2	7.4
South Africa	10.3	10.0	9.1	10.1
Argentina	17.9	14.2	13.4	17.5
Australia	15.6	13.4	19.2	17.8
Canada	13.3	12.1	10.9	12.2
Chile	14.4	12.6	9.5	26.4
Japan	9.1	9.0	10.1	9.8
New Zealand	12.3	13.0	13.7	11.5

Note: n.a. signifies not available.
Source: League of Nations (1934).

grade rails yielded 19 per cent. While some component of these yields indicates the magnitude of the risk premium, their high level may also reflect distress sales and therefore the generalized effects of the financial crisis, which severely disrupted the domestic bond market's ability efficiently to allocate funds among competing uses in much the same manner that the collapse of the market in foreign bonds reduced international investment to a trickle.[32]

Although the literature on the American Depression emphasizes the two waves of bank failures in the late autumn of 1930 and early spring of 1933, in fact failures continued throughout. In October 1931, for example, 522 banks with deposits amounting to $470 million were forced to suspend payments, and in the 12 months ending in June 1932, 2,429 US banks failed. Again, the pattern of failure mirrors the actions of the authorities. In the spring of 1932 the incidence of bank failures declined as the Federal Reserve expanded credit through rediscounts and open market operations, but this expansionary initiative was reversed soon thereafter, permitting a resurgence of commercial bank insolvencies.[33]

The US case provides a graphic illustration of linkages running from bank failures to other markets and to the macroeconomy. Although it is still disputed whether monetary stringency, much of which resulted from bank failures, was a factor in the onset of the Great Depression, it is widely agreed that these monetary factors were central to its singular depth and long duration. The inability of the Federal Reserve to prevent widespread bank failures, along with its inability to interrupt the linkages running back from bank failures to financial markets and to the macro-economy, is a central explanation for the severity of the crisis in the United States. Thus, one reason for the exceptional depth of the Great Depression in the US was that policy was used less effectively than in other countries to prevent the transformation of financial market disturbances into a generalized financial crisis.

II   Fifty years later

A.   The periods compared

A summary of the apparent similarities and differences between our two periods will be useful background for our analysis. In the 1930s as in the 1980s, illiquidity was not confined to any one country or region. In neither instance can the problems of debtor countries be attributed exclusively to domestic causes – external shocks from the world economy were transmitted through sharp rises in real interest rates and falls in commodity prices and the economic activity of industrial countries. The burden of reparations inhibited expansion just as the burden of debt service does in many countries today (McNeil, 1986).

There can be no exact dating of recent troubles in international financial markets, nor *a fortiori* a precise correspondence between 1929 and 1979. Nevertheless, to take 1979 as the beginning of the contemporary period of interest is not merely a convenient metaphor. Admittedly, one cannot identify at that point a classical panic, preceded by 'mania', then 'distress', and followed by sharp, generalized price falls (Kindleberger, 1978). But conditions in the world economy and financial system clearly did deteriorate from the second oil shock to the Mexican collapse of August 1982, which marks the onset of the 'debt crisis' in popular consciousness.

Any simple analogy with 1932, however, would be equally inappropriate. For just as the contemporary debt crisis began the American economy entered a period of strong expansion which compensated, until recently, for the drag on world economic activity caused by the overhang of LDC debt and restrictive macroeconomic adjustment policies adopted to deal with it.

We have seen many debt reschedulings but not widespread, extended interruptions of service and amortization on the scale of the 1930s; even the deterioration of relations between Peru and the IMF in August 1986 is not strictly comparable to the defaults which began in January 1931. There have been wide swings in nominal and real exchange rates but no significant currency collapses, nor any resort to inconvertibility or new exchange controls to protect any major currency. Real interest rates rose to historically exceptional heights, but there was no worldwide dramatic fall of investment. Large government budget deficits in industrialized countries have in most cases (with a major exception!) been brought under control, with many crisis budgets but no collapse of government finances. There have been large trade imbalances and repeated threats of a plunge into overt protectionism, but in practice we have seen only the gradual accretion of non-tariff barriers to trade. Failures of individual financial institutions have been isolated, without generalized runs or significant contractions in the credit base. One authority judges that the crisis was worst in 1982–4 and is now over (Kindleberger, 1986).

We are less sanguine, and we stress in particular the need for continued and improved international policy coordination in providing the regulatory and macroeconomic environments necessary to prevent financial crisis. But despite greater interdependence in the world economy – and partly in response to it – institutional change and economic policies have tended to break, block or attenuate the linkages of Figure 1.1. A further difference from the 1930s is more difficult to analyse: the growing assertiveness of the United States and the political consensus among the major industrialized countries in dealing with international debt problems (Diaz Alejandro, 1984; Portes, 1986). It has been more difficult for any single debtor country, particularly in Latin America, to break ranks, and the cohesion of the creditors' cartel contrasts sharply with feeble efforts at coordination among debtors.

As noted, in both the 1930s and 1980s, the preceding decade had been marked by major changes in the structure and management of the international political economy. Before World War I, the United Kingdom played the pivotal role in the world economy, using its investment income to run a trade deficit that allowed other countries to pursue export-led growth. When World War I and its aftermath cut that income, the United States assumed the financial role of the world's leading creditor without taking on the corresponding responsibility of running an import surplus with open markets, thus leaving a structural weakness in the system. Now the transition from the United States to Japan as dominant lender is similarly occurring without a shift by Japan into import surplus (though in this case, with little immediate weakening of American political dominance).

Yet differences between the periods preclude simple generalizations. In the 1970s, the banks did not act merely as intermediaries in placing LDC bond issues among many dispersed bondholders, but rather took on very large direct exposure, with corresponding risk to themselves and the financial system.[34] Although there was significant cross-border lending among banks in the earlier period, the density of international interbank relationships now is incomparably greater. For both reasons, creditors have been much better organized in the 1980s than in the 1930s, a change that has favoured rescheduling rather than default.[35] But banks appear to have paid no more attention to sovereign risk in the lending of the 1970s than in that of the 1920s. And they lent at considerably shorter maturities than those of the 1920s bond issues.

An institutional difference of considerable practical importance is the International Monetary Fund. To some extent, the IMF acts as international lender of last resort, while also serving the capital market in a signalling capacity, providing information on domestic adjustment programmes and helping to differentiate among borrowers. There are also stronger domestic lenders of last resort (new, in some countries), with more extensive supervisory and regulatory roles now than fifty years ago despite recent moves towards deregulation; and there is deposit insurance in many countries. The macroeconomic background differs as well, with much greater experience of stabilization policies, a system of floating exchange rates in existence for over a decade, and extended international discussion of domestic macroeconomic policies in economic summits, the OECD and the EEC. Finally, there is greater political stability in relations among the industrialized creditor countries, and perhaps greater internal political stability in the LDC debtors.

B. The environment

Our description of the international financial environment begins with the breakdown of the Bretton Woods payments settlement and exchange rate systems in the early 1970s. A detailed history is not needed here. But the major events have brought deep structural change closely analogous to that of the 1920s, in the exchange rate system, in international lending, and in financial institutions.

The changes in the exchange rate system during 1971–73, while in the opposite direction to those of the mid-1920s, were equally profound and far-reaching.[36] Official convertibility of dollars into gold was abandoned in August 1971, and the adjustable-peg exchange-rate mechanism gave way to unrestricted floating in March 1973. The 'reform' negotiations of the C20 and its successors could not reconstruct or replace the constraints

which Bretton Woods had imposed on the autonomy of national monetary authorities. The new freedoms and powers were *de jure* rather than
de facto, however, as policy-makers, academic analysts and the markets
soon discovered. The same capital mobility which made the old exchange
rate system untenable also made true autonomy infeasible.

Among the many complementary explanations for the breakdown of
the Bretton Woods exchange rate system, we stress capital mobility as
fundamental. So did the architects of the system and their predecessors.
Nurkse (1944) identified 'disequilibrating' capital flows as a major cause
of the disturbances of the interwar period. Keynes insisted that controls
over capital movements be an essential component of the postwar
monetary order, and the Bretton Woods Agreement made no provision
for convertibility for capital account transactions. But the progressive
relaxation in the early 1950s did extend to capital flows. Their volume
and speed grew dramatically as a function of technological innovation
and profit opportunities. Since the authorities were unwilling to make the
Bretton Woods exchange rate system their sole policy target, official
convertibility and the adjustable peg could not withstand the pressures
arising from the growing sophistication, scope and integration of international capital markets. This process has of course continued, and we
return to it below.

Currency convertibility and the international institutions established
at Bretton Woods survive. Moreover, the political relationship between
France and Germany in the context of the European Community gave
rise in 1979 to the European Monetary System, with its exchange rate
mechanism providing a 'zone of (relative) monetary stability' among
most of the EC currencies.[37] Even outside the exchange-market intervention in the EMS, the major currencies have not floated freely since
1973. Exchange rates have been regarded as important indicators or even
targets for monetary policy, leading to intervention, whether unsterilized
or sterilized.[38] This raises the question whether, by the end of the 1970s,
the resulting exchange rate system was well-suited to absorb major
macroeconomic and financial shocks, or whether the system propagated
or even magnified such disorders, which might then be transmitted to
capital markets and the financial system (linkages III and V in
Figure 1.1).

The explosive growth of international lending in the 1970s is also
familiar to contemporary observers.[39] Analysts still differ, however, in
the importance they assign to supply and demand factors affecting
international lending during the period. Econometric explanations of its
volume and price perform no better than econometric models of
exchange rate behaviour. It is clear that the 1970s saw a striking,

unexpected growth of liability financing of balance-of-payments deficits under little apparent constraint for most countries; and that aggregate liquidity in the world economy was correspondingly demand-determined.

The process of institutional change in the banking system during the 1970s was also driven by the powerful forces of internationalization and the technological change which stimulated and facilitated it. The pace of internationalization may have slowed somewhat in the past five years.[40] This has not eased the regulatory authorities' task in keeping abreast of these changes. The problems of the banking system in 1974–5, from spectacular bank failures like Franklin National and Herstatt to many lesser difficulties, were surmounted.[41] But the Basle concordat of 1975 was just the beginning of a much more active, continuous process of consultation among central banks, in good part through the continuing work of the Cooke Committee. This internationalized prudential supervision also forms an important part of the environment in which the events of the past several years have transpired.

C.   Disturbances and their management

The two major sources of recent instability are those of fifty years earlier: disturbances in the foreign exchange market and sovereign debt.

Major exchange rate swings and misalignments, as well as sharp deterioration in the debt-servicing capacity of individual countries, have undoubtedly threatened domestic financial institutions and the international financial system. There have been isolated, individual cases of bank failures, some quite spectacular, at least judging by the reaction of the media. Banco Ambrosiano, Johnson Matthey and Continental Illinois offered high-grade material to all from sensational journalists to sober academics. The scandals and political fallout were greater in Rome and London than in Chicago, but financially the most serious was Continental Illinois, then the twentieth largest US bank and a major participant in the international interbank market. Despite a classic run by foreign holders of its CDs, the bank was saved by the regulators (without bailing out its officers and shareholders), and there were no spread effects nor generalized financial crisis resembling the 1930s.

Stresses in foreign exchange markets, international lending and the banking system are striking, and they suggest analogies with the interwar period. These comparisons help to explain why there has so far been no collapse like that of the 1930s and shed light on the continuing vulnerability of the financial system. We shall therefore turn to data on the size of imbalances and shocks, on the capacity of the exchange-rate system to cope with misalignments and volatility, and on how the debt crisis has been managed. We then consider the linkages represented in Figure 1.1 and the roles of policy and institutional change in attenuating them.

Exchange rates   The exchange rate system operating since 1973 has survived both unexpectedly high volatility and substantial misalignments without exchange-market collapse or any overall drift towards controls.[42] Central bank intervention has doubtless helped; few would argue that it has been destabilizing, though many would judge its influence to be marginal. It has certainly not eliminated short-run volatility. Nor has market learning reduced volatility as the floating-rate period has gone on. Even the EMS has had only limited effects: among the major EMS currencies, only the Deutschmark and lira experienced clear declines in overall volatility (with respect to all currencies) from 1978 to 1984.[43] On most assessments, however, the EMS has succeeded in reducing volatility among the currencies participating in its exchange-rate mechanism, as one would expect.[44]

Yet more than a decade of learning among market participants and the authorities has apparently not delivered the supposedly stabilizing effects of speculative activity. The EMS may be interpreted as one response to this disappointment, while the rapidly developing forward and futures markets now provide ample opportunities to protect against exchange-rate instability. Recent evidence suggests, however, that these opportunities are not used fully to insulate trade, and that exchange-rate volatility does in fact have empirically significant effects on the volume of international trade.[45] And the new markets and instruments can be used not only to hedge but also to gamble. We must therefore regard short-run volatility still as evidence of instability which might itself spread through the financial and real economies.

Even more dangerous, however, are the large exchange-rate swings and misalignments of long duration which have characterized the period since 1973. Williamson (1985, p. 17) cites maximum swings in real effective exchange rates during 1973–82 of 22 per cent for the Deutschmark, 19 per cent for the French franc, 32 per cent for the US dollar, 35 per cent for the yen, and 60 per cent for the pound. His graph (reproduced as our Figure 1.2) is striking testimony to the magnitude of these gyrations and their extended duration. His calculations of misalignments give one measure, admittedly controversial, of the exchange-rate imbalances creating strains on other elements of the financial system. Table 1.9 gives these estimates of divergencies from 'fundamental equilibrium exchange rates' in 1984:Q4. One need not fully accept the methodology or conclusions to judge that the misalignments are likely to

Table 1.9. **Estimates of exchange-rate misalignments, 1984:Q4**

	Effective exchange rate relative to estimated fundamental equilibrium	Fundamental equilibrium rate US dollar	Nominal appreciation needed against US dollar (percentage)
US dollar	137	n.a.	n.a.
Japanese yen	89	¥ 198	24
Deutschmark	87	DM 2.04	50
French franc	92	FF 6.51	44
Pound sterling	107	$ 1.52	25

Note: n.a.: not applicable.
Source: Williamson (1985, p. 79).

1976-77 Fundamental equilibrium exchange rate = 100

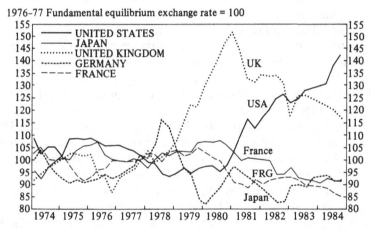

Figure 1.2 Composite measures of real effective exchange rates, five major countries, 1974–84.
Source: Williamson (1985, p. 103)

have been two to three times the magnitude of those estimated by Keynes for the 1920s.

Even in the absence of an agreed model of exchange-rate determination, there is consensus that changes in such fundamentals as the current account and purchasing power parities (or even 'safe haven' effects) cannot fully explain these shifts. Nor are they solely due to inappropriate monetary policies and exchange-rate targets (as represented by the pegs of the 1920s). An unbalanced *mix* of monetary and fiscal policies within the United States and among the major industrial countries is a more comprehensive explanation, especially insofar as it underlies the wide swings in nominal and real interest rates and international interest rate differentials. Yet it is increasingly agreed that speculative 'bubbles', with or without rational expectations, also played a role in accentuating recent exchange-rate swings.[46] If so, then the exchange rates are still highly uncertain for participants in trade and financial markets, however much they hedge.

This longer-run uncertainty may reduce trade volumes just as volatility appears to do, and direct investment may suffer as well. Large and sustained misalignments impede trade by encouraging protectionist policy responses. Since debt servicing capacity derives from trade flows, there is an indirect link from the exchange-market disturbances of the past decade to debt defaults (linkage III in Figure 1.1). Yet this differs from the link we identified for the earlier period, in which convertibility crises and the threat of exchange control induced withdrawals of short-term funds, which in turn could provoke default. Nor do exchange-rate misalignments appear to have threatened the banking systems in either creditor or debtor countries (linkage V). But exchange-rate uncertainty and volatility may have increased the importance of this link by offering banks new opportunities for speculation. Some have participated aggressively in these markets (often seeking to build up earnings depleted by bad loans), and some of these have not succeeded (Franklin National and Herstatt were early victims).

A more important example of linkage III can be found in the LDC debtor countries themselves. In several cases, exchange-rate over-valuation has led to massive capital flight by domestic residents, seriously exacerbating debt-servicing difficulties.[47] Insofar as overvaluation is a direct result of government policy, exchange-market intervention rather than post-1973 exchange-rate flexibility is the cause of the problem.

On balance, we are inclined to accept the judgment of Cooper (1983) that flexible exchange rates have served more as a shock absorber than as a source of destabilizing influences in the financial system or as a link in their transmission. The misalignments which this flexibility has permitted, by removing a constraint on monetary and fiscal policies, have not themselves provoked financial crisis or exacerbated financial instability, whatever their negative effects on trade and investment. Indeed, it is the process of correcting the misalignments without the appropriate coordination of macro policy mixes which might be highly destabilizing.[48]

Debt   As in the 1920s, the growth and export performance of major borrowing countries in the latter half of the 1970s gave some cause for optimism regarding the recycling process and the prospects for debt

Table 1.10. **Annual growth rates of real GDP and exports, 1975–9**

	GDP	Exports in US dollars
Argentina	1.1	27.2
Brazil	6.6	15.9
Chile	7.4	25.7[a]
Mexico	6.2	32.7[a]
Venezuela	4.7	13.1[a]
Peru	0.9	28.0[a]
Nigeria	1.2	22.5[a]
India	2.6	15.7
Indonesia	7.4	21.6
Korea	10.6	30.9
Malaysia	8.8	30.3
Philippines	6.6	18.6
Egypt	n.a.	6.9
Turkey	3.7	12.5
Yugoslavia	6.4	12.4

Note: [a] more than 50% increase in 1979 over previous year.
Source: International Financial Statistics 1983 Yearbook.

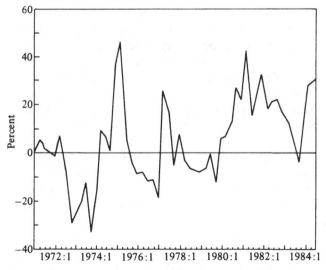

Figure 1.3   The real interest rate of nonoil LDCs, 1971:1–1984:3.
Note: The real rate is measured as the six-month lagged LIBOR adjusted with the three-month forward rate of inflation of export unit values of nonoil LDCs.
Source: Dornbusch (1985, p. 341)

service.[49] Table 1.10 gives data comparable with Table 1.2 for the earlier period. In both cases, however, the assumption that expansion would continue without major shocks proved to be false.

The problems which ensued were indeed similar. The major external shocks which hit the debtor countries were global, not country-specific. The second oil shock, the OECD recession and the industrialized countries' restrictive monetary policies created serious fiscal problems in the debtor countries (aggravated by domestic mismanagement) and cut the prices and volumes of commodity exports. Nominal interest rates finally rose to meet and exceed inflation, bringing a sharp switch from negative to positive real rates. Higher nominal rates also reduced debtor liquidity by shifting the burden of debt repayment towards the present (the tilt effect). Then as inflation subsided, nominal interest rates fell less quickly, and real rates rose further (see Figure 1.3).

Voluntary lending to LDCs by the commercial banks evaporated after the Mexican crisis of August 1982; the Polish debacle of early 1981 had already hit lending to Eastern Europe and put Hungary and Romania in deep trouble.[50] A wave of debt reschedulings followed: there were a total of 36 'multilateral debt renegotiations' in 1975–81 covering $19.6 billion of debt; then 10 in 1982 ($2.4 billion), 32 in 1983 alone ($51.7 billion), with some slackening in 1984, but a record number of 41 reschedulings signed in 1985 dealing with $92.8 billion of debt.[51] Lenders reacted to new information about global economic conditions and individual debtors with a generalized, discrete change of regime in credit markets. Rather than a continuous tightening of terms and constraints for borrowers, there was a shift to credit rationing.

This change of credit-market regime was a response to macroeconomic shocks exogenous to the credit markets whose effects conveyed new information to lenders.[52] Imperfect information about one or at most a few borrowers was generalized to others, and lenders' overall perceptions changed. The 'disaster myopia' emphasized by Guttentag and Herring (1984, 1985) was dispelled by such information; and when the disaster scenario suddenly took on a non-negligible subjective probability, lenders whose sole protection was to try to maintain short loan maturities could react only by pulling out of the market wherever possible.

The magnitude of the shocks which so dramatically affected lenders' behaviour can be seen in Tables 1.11–1.18 and Figures 1.3 and 1.4. The rise of 20 percentage points in real interest rates on floating-rate debt from 1980 to 1981 is extraordinary. The fall in the real commodity price (excluding oil) of 26 per cent from 1980:Q1 to 1983:Q1 is of a similar magnitude to fifty years previously. Although the terms of trade of

Table 1.11. **Average real percentage interest rate on LDC floating-rate debt, 1977–83**

1977	1978	1979	1980	1981	1982	1983
−11.8	−7.4	−9.7	−6.0	14.6	16.7	15.9

Source: Maddison (1985, p. 47).

Table 1.12. **Commodity price indices, 1979–85 (1980 = 100)**

	1979	1980	1981	1982	1983	1984	1985
Coffee (NY)	112.5	100.0	76.8	83.4	84.9	93.7	88.6
Copper (London)	90.3	100.0	79.8	67.8	72.9	63.0	64.9
Petroleum (Venezuela)	60.8	100.0	116.1	116.1	101.6	97.9	97.9^a
Rubber (Singapore)	88.6	100.0	78.8	60.2	74.7	67.2	53.3
Sugar (EEC Import price)	87.4	100.0	83.7	82.0	79.5	72.6	72.4
Tin (London)	92.1	100.0	84.5	76.5	77.4	72.9	68.7

Note: ^{a} Quarter II.
Source: International Financial Statistics 1985 Yearbook.

Table 1.13. **External shocks, 1979–83**

	Percentage change in terms of trade from 1975–78	Real income effect as percentage of GDP	Sum of real interest rate and terms of trade effects on GDP (percentage)
Argentina	3	0.2	1.6
Brazil	−29	−2.3	−5.0
Chile	−27	−4.9	−6.2
Mexico	26	1.8	1.2
Peru	−22	−3.7	−4.2
Venezuela	64	15.9	16.2
Colombia	−18	−2.0	−2.8
Indonesia	36	6.1	6.2
Korea	−3	−0.9	−3.8
Malaysia	14	4.9	4.8
Thailand	−14	−2.9	−3.3
Philippines	−16	−3.2	−3.9

Source: Sachs (1985, pp. 527–28).

Table 1.14. **Gross external liabilities and short-term component, 1978–83**

(billion US dollars, end-year)

		1978	1980	1981	1982	1983
Argentina	Total	13.3	27.3	33.7	43.6	46.0
	S	3.4	10.5	11.0	16.5	9.4
Brazil	Total	53.4	70.0	79.9	91.0	95.5
	S	7.1	13.5	15.3	17.4	14.2
Mexico	Total	35.7	57.1	77.9	85.5	93.7
	S	4.9	16.2	25.0	26.1	10.1
Peru	Total	9.7	10.0	10.3	12.2	12.4
	S	2.1	2.1	2.5	3.1	1.4
Venezuela	Total	16.8	29.6	31.9	31.8	32.2
	S	8.0	15.5	17.0	14.7	14.5
Nigeria	Total	5.5	9.0	11.9	14.2	19.7
	S	2.4	3.5	4.4	4.3	6.7
Korea	Total	17.3	29.3	34.2	38.3	40.4
	S	4.5	10.1	11.6	13.6	12.1
Indonesia	Total	18.0	29.9	22.7	26.5	30.2
	S	1.8	2.8	3.3	4.8	4.6
Philippines	Total	10.8	17.4	20.8	24.2	23.9
	S	3.9	7.6	9.4	11.3	9.4
Yugoslavia	Total	12.5	18.5	20.7	20.0	20.3
	S	1.2	2.1	2.5	1.8	1.9

Note: Short-term liabilities S are those of *original* maturity less than one year.
Source: World Bank, *World Debt Tables, 1985–86.*

Table 1.15. **Ratio of gross external liabilities to exports of goods and services, 1978–84 (percentage)**

	1978	1980	1981	1982	1983	1984
Argentina	169	244	285	449	471	464
Brazil	369	301	296	388	392	345
Mexico	313	232	256	310	327	301
Peru	401	206	243	292	323	331
Venezuela	154	133	130	158	186	182
Nigeria	45	33	61	110	179	160
Korea	101	130	125	135	133	128
Indonesia	159	94	91	125	151	147
Philippines	220	214	242	302	294	304
Yugoslavia	147	134	131	131	154	144

Source: World Bank, *World Debt Tables, 1985–86.*

Table 1.16. **Exposure of US banks to LDC debtors, 1982 and 1986**

| | Percentage of capital | | | | Billion $US March 1986 |
| | June 1982 | | March 1986 | | |
	9 money center banks	All US banks	9 money center banks	All US banks	All US banks
Mexico	50	38	38	22	24.2
Brazil	46	31	37	22	23.7
Korea	19	14	11	9	9.4
Venezuela	26	16	16	9	9.7
Argentina	21	13	14	8	8.5
Chile	12	9	9	6	6.3
Philippines	14	8	8	5	5.0
Colombia	8	5	4	2	2.3
Non-OPEC LDCs	227	154	141	88	96.4
OPEC	35	60	33	18	19.4

Note: Banks' capital defined as equity, subordinated debt and loan-loss reserves. 'All US Banks' are those completing Country Exposure Report. Their total capital base rose from $66.2 b in June 1982 to $109.7 b in March 1986.
Source: Federal Reserve Board.

Table 1.17. **Exposure of US and UK banks in Mexico, Brazil, Argentina and Venezuela as percentage of capital, 1982 and 1984**

	End 1982	End 1984
Bank of America	128	122
Chase Manhattan	139	142
Manufacturers Hanover	234	173
Chemical	155	134
Bankers Trust	131	114
First Chicago	123	103
Citicorp	n.a.	140
National Westminster	n.a.	73
Barclays	n.a.	62
Lloyds	n.a.	165
Midland	n.a.	205

Sources: Cline (1983, p. 34) for 1982 and Lever and Huhne (1985) for 1984.

Table 1.18. **Bank share price/earnings ratio as percentage of overall market P/E for UK and US, 1970–86**

	NYSE	London
1970	n.a.	66.9
1975	n.a.	118.4
1980	62.0	52.5
1981	69.8	49.7
1982	48.8	39.7
1983	49.5	51.4
1984	45.5	47.5
1985	49.6	56.7
1986 (Jan–July)	56.8	46.1

At 15 August each year except 1986.

Source: Financial Times, Datastream.

non-oil LDCs (NLDCs) had peaked in 1977:Q1, the decline of 18 per cent from 1979:Q1 to 1983:Q1 was still substantial. The total effect in terms of real income is shown in Table 1.13; for the non-oil debtors (excluding Argentina), there were losses in GDP from three to six per cent. As a real income loss, this might be tolerable; as a required increase in transfer abroad, it was indeed onerous.[53]

Consequences for the debt burden are shown in Tables 1.14 and 1.15. Beginning in 1980, total indebtedness rose rapidly for the NLDCs, and by 1982 their debt-export ratios far exceeded the levels recorded in Table 1.2 for 1929 (which refer, however, only to central government debt, whereas the recent data cover all foreign liabilities). Most may still have been 'solvent' on a suitable long-run calculation,[54] but with uncertain expectations, the distinction between insolvency and illiquidity for a sovereign debtor is both theoretically imprecise and politically untenable. Certainly liquidity was impaired by the withdrawals of short-term funds in 1982–3 evident in Table 1.14; together with capital flight, they significantly increased the disaster probability. That reaction could have activated the linkages I, V and VI which proved so devastating in the 1930s. The 'debt strategy' was designed entirely to contain it.

The dangers are evident from the data on bank exposure in Tables 1.16 and 1.17 and on bank share prices in Table 1.18. The US banks did not begin to recover from the 1982 plunge in their relative price/earnings ratios until 1986, partly because of their subsequent problems with energy and real estate loans. The UK banks have fared somewhat better but show no sign of regaining the standing they enjoyed in the 1970s.

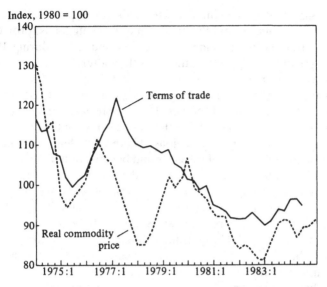

Figure 1.4   The nonoil LDCs' terms of trade and the real commodity price, 1974:1–1985:1.

Note: The real commodity price is the *Economist* index of commodities deflated by industrial countries' unit export values. Terms of trade are exports unit value index divided by imports unit value index. Terms-of-trade data extend through 1984:3.

Source: Dornbusch (1985, p. 324)

Many useful case studies treat the impact of the debt crisis on individual countries and regions and their responses.[55] Nevertheless, we require much more empirical evidence on the role of information about debt-servicing difficulties and their causes. How do the markets perceive such information, process it, and then react to individual borrowers and classes of borrowers? For example, we have two contradictory assessments of market evaluations of Mexican securities in the period leading up to August 1982, one finding a continuous deterioration from the previous winter, the other observing a discontinuous plunge shortly before the crisis became manifest.[56] How the market performs before a crisis is important in assessing whether shifting more sovereign debt into the market through securitization is likely to make the system more or less stable.

The response of policy-makers to the debt crisis assumed that it was essentially and almost everywhere a problem of liquidity rather than solvency, ignoring questions about the legitimacy of that distinction. This approach may have been adequate in the short run, when the key to avoiding financial crisis was maintaining confidence. On plausible assumptions about growth, interest rates, adjustment policies, industrial-country macro policies, and the provision of bridging loans, projections showed substantial improvement in the debt indicators during 1984–6 and a progressive dissipation of the crisis thereafter.[57]

The US government's optimism did not last; hence the Baker Plan in autumn 1985. For the objective of avoiding a financial crisis, however, the strategy has been almost completely successful so far in keeping both creditors and debtors on board. Neither the reasons nor the prospects for continued success are entirely obvious. There exist clear, level-headed, well-informed evaluations of the costs and benefits of default to debtors which imply that there are cases in which the benefits exceed the costs.[58] As long as rescheduling continues to eschew debt relief, this will remain the case; yet historical comparisons suggest the likelihood of some element of write-off, some ultimate sharing of the burden between creditors and debtors.[59] The question is whether there are circumstances in which debt relief or write-offs are possible without financial crisis.

The answer requires a judgment of the overall health of the international banking system and a scenario for how the authorities would react. Recently the banks have been building up their capital base while writing off some sovereign debt (see Table 1.16). There remain problems on the asset side. Keeping maturities short has little systemic advantage, since that just increases the competition, when trouble threatens, to exit first and leave the problem to other banks. It can be argued that some of the banks' off-balance-sheet activities that have grown so fast recently are relatively risky. On the other hand, securitization on the liability side of banks' balance sheets reduces their dependence on the highly volatile international interbank market.

Linkages   The discussion of recent disturbances and their management now permits a comparison between the two periods of the operation of the linkages we have stressed.

(I)   Whereas the events threatening debt default endangered the banks of some debtor countries in the 1930s, the creditor-country banks did not then hold enough sovereign debt to make it a problem for them. In the current period, there have been a few instances of the former linkage (Argentina had domestic financial difficulties at a critical juncture in its debt-servicing problems). The major effort today, with banks having assumed the credit risks formerly borne by purchasers of sovereign bonds, is to contain any menace this poses for the financial system. So far, direct policy intervention by national authorities and international institutions has succeeded almost entirely in protecting the banking system from major harm.

(ii) There have been no bank failures so spectacular as themselves to provoke debt default.

(iii) In the 1930s, withdrawals of short-term funds sometimes brought the authorities to restrict convertibility in order to avoid debt default. Recently, exchange-rate overvaluation without exchange controls has brought capital flight, which has played a greater role in the buildup to debt crisis than in the earlier period (although capital movements were important in the *propagation* of crises in both periods). Failure to block this linkage has been a key weakness in present-day arrangements relative to those of the 1930s. There is a further, indirect linkage from exchange-market disturbances to debt-servicing difficulties which is a major threat today: exchange-rate misalignments have caused pressures for protectionist trade policies, which impede the ability of debtor countries to earn the export surpluses they require.

(iv) Whereas debt default did not generally force down the debtor's exchange rate in the 1930s, the burden of debt service has clearly had that effect even for non-defaulting debtors today. Pressures from the government budget and the need to run current account surpluses both work in this direction, insofar as depreciation relieves the financial burden of supporting an overvalued rate while raising net exports.

(v) Instability in the foreign exchange markets was a major cause of generalized financial instability in the 1930s. In the recent period, it has endangered banks only insofar as some of them have sought too aggressively to profit from speculation in these markets.

(vi) In the earlier period, bank failures caused pressures on the home country's currency by provoking capital flight, and occasionally on the currency of a major foreign creditor (recall how the pound weakened due to the problems of Austrian and German banks). Recently, tremors in the US banking system appear to have made the foreign exchange markets nervous, but this has not been a significant consideration.

Institutional change and public policy

Partly in reaction to the problems faced by the banks, international credit flows have in the past few years shifted from bank lending towards direct credit markets. Simultaneously, there has been an explosion of new financial markets and financial instruments, primarily because technological innovation has substantially reduced transactions costs.[60]

In principle, reduction in interbank linkages should reduce systemic vulnerability. The 'Cross Report' (Bank for International Settlements, 1986), however, points out some countervailing aspects of recent trends: the quality of banks' loan assets may decline; the narrower base of the system may make it less responsive to sudden liquidity needs; non-bank capital markets may have less information on borrowers, less opportunity to screen and to monitor performance, and less capacity to arrange refinancing packages for those in debt-servicing difficulties; and many of the new services banks are providing appear to be underpriced, so that they are not providing earnings commensurate with their risks.

These trade-offs are complicated, and the pace of change has been so rapid that there is little contemporary experience from which to generalize. On the basis of interwar experience, these developments appear to be mainly positive from the viewpoint of financial stability. Our study of linkages suggests that incomplete and imperfect information favours the generalization of adverse shocks into full-fledged crises; that macroeconomic instability is the prime source of those shocks; and that appropriate action by the regulatory and monetary authorities can block the most dangerous linkages. Such action in the 'debt strategy' has avoided defaults and widespread bank failures to date. But it was the system of bank lending to sovereign borrowers that permitted the accumulation of excessive debt burdens, and the rescheduling process which has so far prevented defaults is maintaining almost the full weight of those burdens on the debtors.

In the 1930s, as during the century of international lending before World War I, creditors too assumed a share of the losses created by adverse shocks. The problem then was that when the shocks were global, the contagious, infectious nature of default contributed to financial crisis, disrupting the allocative mechanisms of the international capital market. We now have much more sophisticated public health measures, both macroeconomic and regulatory. They can cope with the dangers of securitization while the financial system switches from relationship-towards transaction-based banking.

Securitization will get more information into the market place. This should reduce adverse selection; substitute more frequent, smaller, visible shocks for the major upheavals which arise when relationships go wrong; and remove from the banking system the heavy burden of having to act as a buffer when shocks do occur. It is not evident that underpricing of new financial services exceeds the inadequacy of spreads in allowing for the default risk on bank lending to sovereign borrowers in the 1970s ('disaster myopia'); while the *ex-post* rates of return on international lending of the 1920s appear to have been relatively favourable for the lenders.[61]

Calls for more formal international-lender-of-last-resort (ILLR) arrangements[62] should not obscure the substantial development of both domestic and international LLR facilities over the past fifty years, as well as a much more sophisticated regulatory system. In the 1930s, financial weakness affected mainly the large banks in Europe, while in the United States it characterized the entire spectrum of the banking system. Now small banks are protected on the liability side by deposit insurance which limits runs,[63] and large ones in difficulty are handled directly by domestic LLRs. Internationally, the 'Paris Club' arrangements have for over two decades effectively handled rescheduling of official or government-guaranteed lending to sovereign debtors. The International Monetary Fund acts in a signalling capacity, providing the capital market with information on debtors and so reducing the risk that the difficulties of one will be transmitted infectiously to others who are creditworthy. IMF conditionality helps to maintain the standing of the debtor and its obligations, thereby limiting the risk of contagious transmission of financial illness to its creditors. And in contrast with the 1930s, the IMF can act to promote a rescheduling before default, whereas then default was needed to provoke direct negotiations between a sovereign debtor and representatives of its creditors.[64] This *ex ante* bargaining should in principle benefit both creditors and debtors; in practice, who gains how much from rescheduling is highly controversial.

Coordination of prudential supervision has taken place primarily under the auspices of the Bank for International Settlements. The Basle concordat of 1975, as revised in 1983, explicitly disclaims any ILLR responsibilities. The authorities' key principle is to exercise supervision on a consolidated basis. They do have a clear understanding of how responsibilities are shared between home and host central banks, and the individual regulatory authorities are much more experienced than they were fifty years ago. It has been difficult for them, however, to keep abreast of internationalization and financial innovation.

The key problem facing any LLR is moral hazard.[65] The classic answer is that the LLR is responsible for the money supply – avoiding financial crisis by containing any threat to the credit base – rather than for the survival of any particular financial institution. The internationalization of the interbank market has made this distinction harder to maintain, however, and no authority or institution currently has responsibility for the world money supply. There is no true ILLR, although the functions which one might fulfil are much better understood now than they would have been in the 1930s (as can equally be said of domestic LLRs).

Nevertheless, success in blocking the transmission of destabilizing shocks in the 1980s owes much to the ILLR-style activities of certain participants. The US Federal Reserve Board and Treasury sometimes seem to forget that the United States is supposed to have lost its hegemonic role. Whether by itself, as when domestic monetary policy was eased in autumn 1982 in response to signs of financial distress,[66] or in collaboration with the IMF, notably in dealing with Mexico in both 1982 and 1986, or coordinating its major Western partners, as at the Plaza Hotel in 1985, the United States has shown itself capable of leadership. Neither the commitment to 'hands-off' economic policies nor the decline of internationalism in the United States has inhibited decisive action when American vital interests are at stake.

Sometimes others play this role, as did the Governor of the Bank of England in arranging a bridging loan for Hungary through the BIS in spring 1982. Yet unless and until more formal institutional arrangements are established, the United States will continue to be the key player – if it wishes – in forcing action on debt strategy, exchange rates and macro-economic policy coordination, and hence in preventing financial crisis.

III   The future

There are still plausible disaster scenarios. Marris (1985) on macro policy imbalances and their consequences (the 'hard landing') and Lever and Huhne (1985) on debt both permit the imagination to run to deep financial crisis. We believe, however, that greater understanding today of the linkages in financial crisis may have helped to reduce the danger of a serious crisis. Market participants and policy-makers may have learned from the experience of several smaller disturbances since the early 1970s that disaster probabilities are not negligible and appropriate precautions should be taken.

The main dangers lie not in disturbances originating in financial markets but in malfunctions of the real economy. Even though we have not experienced a crisis that seriously disrupted its allocative role, the international capital market still does not appear to be working properly, with the bulk of net flows now going from areas of high real marginal productivity to areas of lower productivity. Sustained high unemployment still fosters protectionism and threatens trade policy conflicts, with the 'inward-looking' consequences characteristic of the 1930s.[67] Although there has been more international macroeconomic policy cooperation recently, it is not fully institutionalized and may prove transient[68] – there is no international monetary constitution providing rules on exchange-market intervention and choice of reserve asset, constraints on fiscal and monetary policies, or responsibility for the ILLR function. Policy-makers still try to maintain their autonomy in an increasingly interdependent world. Paradoxically, even that objective, in the sense of expanding their opportunity set, might best be achieved through international economic policy coordination. Markets could not do the job, even if individual domestic policies were independently 'optimal'.

IV Conclusions

In this paper, we have contrasted the international financial crisis of the 1930s with the recent performance of the global financial system. We have sought to provide a perspective on the prospects for continued stability in international capital markets. While exhibiting fundamental differences in the operation of these markets currently and during the 1930s, our analysis nonetheless yields conclusions regarding conditions conducive to both the maintenance of stability and the onset of crisis.

The most important of these conclusions concern the roles of regulatory and stabilization policies. Financial crises spread most quickly when information is least complete, and they result in major externalities for particular sectors and the macroeconomy. On both imperfect information and externality grounds, there is a rationale for government intervention. Financial crises pose a greater threat under some institutional configurations than others. Even when the benefits of financial deregulation are apparent, there is a role for regulatory policy in channeling financial innovation in directions that leave the world economy less vulnerable to financial collapse. Finally, we have seen that financial crises are as much the result of macroeconomic shocks as they are of perturbations originating in financial markets. Perhaps the most important policy to prevent financial crises is therefore to provide a stable – and, in an increasingly interdependent world, internationally coordinated – macroeconomic environment within which financial markets may function.

The main difference between now and fifty years ago is that we have been there before and do not want to return. Informed policies can help us to avoid epidemic and keep our anatomy lesson to the conference room rather than the mortuary.

NOTES

* We thank H.M. Stationery Office for permission to cite documents from the Public Record Office, Anita Santorum for research assistance, and Jane Maurice for cheerful secretarial help beyond the call of duty. Anthony Harris, Joan Pearce and our discussants offered very useful comments, as did the seminar group at the Institute for International Economic Studies (Stockholm), where an early version of the work was presented in April 1986.
1 The most comprehensive recent survey is by Kindleberger (1978).

2 This same point is made by Goldsmith (1982), p. 42.
3 Other exchanges, including those of Italy, the Netherlands, Spain, Sweden, Japan, Argentina and Brazil, remained stable even at the end of the war.
4 See the introduction to Eichengreen (1985a) for details.
5 Documenting the franc's undervaluation is problematic, however; see Eichengreen and Wyplosz (1986). Conventional accounts typically suggest that the franc was some 10 to 15 per cent undervalued relative to the dollar.
6 The transition from the gold to gold-exchange standard is analysed in Eichengreen (1985b). We return below to the role of foreign deposits.
7 Two views of the policy coordination problem are Clarke (1967) and Eichengreen (1985b).
8 The information summarized here is taken from Eichengreen and Portes (1986).
9 The parallels between the two experiences are explored by Balogh and Graham (1979).
10 Many articles in the financial press could be cited. An example is the *Financial Times* (18 December 1929), which even at this late date calls Peru 'apparently a country with a bright future.'
11 See for example Winkler (1933) or Securities and Exchange Commission (1937). Mintz (1950, ch. 4) presents evidence that a few aggressive issue houses were responsible for a disproportionate share of the loans which ultimately went into default.
12 The Table 1.2 data on ratios of public debt to GNP must be interpreted with care, since the importance of state and municipal borrowing varied enormously across countries. The low ratio for Germany, for example, reflects the tendency for borrowing to originate with municipalities and not the Reich.
13 Latin American experience is described in Eichengreen (1986) and Central European reforms in Nurkse (1946).
14 League of Nations (1931), p. 14.
15 Details are to be found in Schedvin (1970).
16 Schedvin (1970), pp. 166–7.
17 Insofar as exchange-rate fluctuations due to devaluation disrupted trade, a linkage to which contemporaries attached much importance, export receipts and debt capacity were reduced still further. For example, Condliffe (1933, p. 221) writes that 'exchange instability resulting from the breakdown of the international gold standard was one of the principal causes of further economic deterioration in 1932 and figured prominently among the factors which limited and checked the revival of prices and productive capacity in the third quarter of that year'. For similar comments, see Nurkse (1944). We return below to evidence on the impact of exchange-rate volatility on trade.
18 This periodization follows Condliffe (1933), chapter ix.
19 The situation in 1931 differs from Sachs's (1982) description of pre-World-War-I lending and default. Before World War I, Sachs argues, default by one country did little to interrupt the flow of capital to other borrowers. The difference between the periods may be that default in 1931 was seen as a response to global rather than country-specific shocks.
20 Eichengreen and Portes (1986) report regressions in which both the extent of terms-of-trade deterioration and the growth of the central government budget deficit are significantly correlated with the incidence and extent of default.

21 British Public Record Office (PRO) FO371/14198, Dispatch to Foreign Office by R. C. Mitchell, 'Political Situation in Bolivia', 22 September 1930.

22 PRO FO 371/14253, Dispatch from Mr Gurney (Lima), 'Annual Report of the Peruvian President to Congress', 18 September 1930; Madden *et al.* (1937), p. 111.

23 Bank Commissioner of the State of Vermont (1930). Vermont appears to be the only state for which this information is available. See White (1984) for further discussion of these data.

24 See Leguizamon (1933) for additional analysis.

25 Kindleberger (1984), p. 372. It is popularly thought that origins of the run were both economic, caused by the bank's uncertain liquidity, and political, caused by French alarm over the recently proposed Austro-German customs union.

26 A recent account of this episode is James (1984).

27 It could be argued that the provision of deposit insurance and improvements in bank regulation have reduced the extent of these externalities. We return to this point below.

28 See League of Nations (1934) for another statement of this view.

29 Details are to be found in Cairncross and Eichengreen (1983) and the references cited there.

30 Between June 1922 and June 1929, the real estate loans of commercial banks had risen by 128 per cent and their security loans by 77 per cent, in comparison with all other loans and investments, which rose by only 30 per cent.

31 The ratio of cash reserves to total deposits was consistently lower only in countries which ultimately turned to exchange control (Germany, Austria, Czechoslovakia) and in the exceptional Swedish case.

32 This is similar to the argument advanced by Bernanke (1983).

33 This episode is the subject of Epstein and Ferguson (1984).

34 Beenstock (1984) argues that this difference has no significant systemic consequences; and the 1970s may turn out to have been a quite exceptional period in this regard, with the growth of securitization and off-balance-sheet operations in the past few years.

35 There were negotiations between debtor countries and the bondholders' organizations after the defaults of the 1930s, but they were difficult to organize. See Eichengreen and Portes (1986).

36 See Williamson (1977) for an account of this period.

37 See Padoa Schioppa (1985) for background on the operation of the EMS and the detailed discussions and assessments in the report (and background documents) of the Treasury and Civil Service Committee of the UK House of Commons (1985).

38 The studies which supposedly showed the inefficacy of sterilized intervention were ignored when the United States changed its policy stance in September 1985.

39 Recent accounts, from somewhat different viewpoints, include Cline (1984) and Lever and Huhne (1985).

40 OECD (1983) describes the picture at the beginning of the 1980s, and Bryant (1987) offers a more recent and more analytical assessment.

41 See Kindleberger (1978, 1986) and Spero (1980).

42 Generally, capital controls have been progressively liberalized or removed, notably in the UK. It can be argued that they have played an important role in

keeping the EMS together – or that the demands of keeping the system together have required capital controls (Giavazzi and Giovannini, 1986). This view is likely to be tested soon, as France and Italy proceed to relax exchange controls.

43 See Kenen and Rodrik (1986).

44 See Rogoff (1985), Padoa Schioppa (1985), and House of Commons (1985).

45 See de Grauwe and de Bellefroid (1986) and Kenen and Rodrik (1986).

46 See Frankel and Froot (1986) and references cited there.

47 The estimates in *World Financial Markets* (March 1986) are particularly striking, though controversial (according to the *Financial Times*, 21 August 1986, the Bank of Mexico estimates capital flight under the current government at $2 billion, in contrast to the Morgan Guaranty estimate of $17 billion). A more academic but still debatable analysis stressing the role of capital flight in Latin American debt problems, and the root cause of exchange rate overvaluation, is given by Sachs (1985).

48 The views of Marris (1985) are discussed below.

49 Diaz Alejandro (1984) argues that an observer in 1980–81 could not reasonably have foreseen a crisis of the magnitude experienced in 1982–4. On the other hand, Portes (1977) predicted a debt-servicing crisis for several East European countries in the early 1980s, beginning with a rescheduling for Poland in 1980–1.

50 See Portes (1982).

51 World Bank (1986).

52 As suggested by theory; see, for example, Guttentag and Herring (1984). Their argument that an extended period without adverse shocks creates conditions in which a shock will then provoke discontinuous market behaviour is more specific and rigorous than the 'financial instability hypothesis' of Minsky (1982), who argues that the danger of financial crisis builds up over an extended period of prosperous times.

53 Cf. note 20 above.

54 See Cohen (1985).

55 Notable among these are Kraft (1984), who gives an 'inside', circumstantial narrative of the negotiations which dealt with the initial Mexican crisis, and Fraga (1986), who makes an interesting comparison of Brazil's recent experience with Germany and reparations fifty years before.

56 Compare Guttentag and Herring (1985) with Edwards (1986).

57 'With reasonable recovery in the global economy, the problem of international debt should prove manageable and the degree of its current risk to the international system should decline' (Cline, 1983, p. 121).

58 See Kaletsky (1985) and Lever and Huhne (1985).

59 See Eichengreen and Portes (1986) for calculations of the *ex-post* rates of return earned by creditors in such cases.

60 Cooper (1986) describes these changes and argues convincingly that they are explained better by technical change than as innovative risk-sharing arrangements or as responses to cross-border differences in taxation and regulation.

61 Eichengreen and Portes (1986).

62 For example, see Guttentag and Herring (1983).

63 The models of the US Federal Deposit Insurance Corporation and Federal Savings and Loan Insurance Corporation have been increasingly followed in Europe and elsewhere.

64 Eichengreen and Portes (1986).
65 Solow (1982) provides a recent discussion of the theory relevant to LLR functions, which are treated further in Kindleberger (1978) and Kindleberger and Laffargue (1982). It can be argued that financial deregulation has led to more risk-taking by financial intermediaries, hence to more LLR intervention, exacerbating moral hazard (and weakening monetary control). This goes beyond our scope here.
66 See Carron (1982).
67 See Cooper (1983).
68 See Portes (1986).

REFERENCES

Balogh, Thomas and Andrew Graham (1979). 'The Transfer Problem Revisited: Analogies Between the Reparations Payments of the 1920s and the Problem of the OPEC Surpluses', *Oxford Bulletin of Economics and Statistics* **41**, pp. 183–92.
Bank for International Settlements (1986). *Recent Innovations in International Banking*, Basle.
Beenstock, Michael (1984). *The World Economy in Transition*, London: Macmillan.
Bernanke, Ben S. (1983). 'Nonmonetary Effects of the Financial Crisis in the Propagation of the Great Depression', *American Economic Review* **73**, pp. 257–76.
Bryant, Ralph (1987). *International Financial Intermediation: Issues for Analysis and Public Policy*, Washington: Brookings Institution.
Buiter, Willem and Richard Marston (eds) (1985). *International Economic Policy Coordination*, Cambridge: Cambridge University Press.
Butlin, N. G. (1984). 'Select Comparative Economic Statistics, 1900–1940', Source Paper No. 4, Department of Economic History, Australian National University.
Cairncross, Alec and Barry Eichengreen (1983). *Sterling in Decline*, Oxford: Blackwell.
Carron, Andrew (1982). 'Financial Crisis: Recent Experience in US and International Markets', *Brookings Papers on Economic Activity*, No. 2, pp. 395–422.
Clarke, S. V. O. (1967). *Central Bank Coordination, 1924–31*, New York: Federal Reserve Bank of New York.
Cline, William (1983). *International Debt and the Stability of the World Economy*, Washington, DC: Institute for International Economics.
  (1984). *International Debt: Systemic Risk and Policy Response*, Washington, DC: Institute for International Economics.
Cohen, Daniel (1985). 'How to Evaluate the Solvency of an Indebted Nation', *Economic Policy* **1**, pp. 139–67.
Condliffe, J. B. (1933). *World Economic Survey, 1932–33*, Geneva: League of Nations.
Cooper, Ian (1986). 'Financial Markets: New Financial Instruments', paper presented to CEPR Workshop, London.

Cooper, Richard (1983). 'Managing Risks to the International Economic System', in Herring, Richard, ed., *Managing International Risk*, Cambridge: Cambridge University Press.

Diaz Alejandro, Carlos (1984). 'Latin American Debt: I Don't Think We Are in Kansas Anymore', *Brookings Papers on Economic Activity*, No. 2, pp. 335–89.

Dornbusch, Rudiger (1985). 'Policy and Performance Links between LDC Debtors and Industrial Nations', *Brookings Papers on Economic Activity*, No. 2, pp. 303–56.

Edwards, Sebastian (1986). 'The Pricing of Bonds and Bank Loans in International Markets', *European Economic Review*, **30**, pp. 565–90.

Eichengreen, Barry (1985a), ed, *The Gold Standard in Theory and History*, London: Methuen.

(1985b). 'International Policy Coordination in Historical Perspective: A View from the Interwar Years', in Buiter and Marston (1985), pp. 139–78.

(1986). 'House Calls of the Money Doctor: The Kemmerer Missions to Latin America, 1923–1931', in Ronald Findlay *et al.* (eds), *Debt, Stabilization and Development: Essays in Honor of Carlos F. Diaz Alejandro*, Oxford University Press, forthcoming.

Eichengreen, Barry and Richard Portes (1986). 'Debt and Default in the 1930s: Causes and Consequences,' *European Economic Review* **30**, pp. 559–640.

Eichengreen, Barry and Charles Wyplosz (1986). 'The Economic Consequences of the Franc Poincare', unpublished manuscript.

Epstein, Gerald and Thomas Ferguson (1984). 'Monetary Policy, Loan Liquidation, and Industrial Conflict: The Federal Reserve and the Open Market Operations of 1932', *Journal of Economic History* **44**, pp. 957–86.

Frankel, Jeffrey and Kenneth Froot (1986). 'The Dollar as an Irrational Speculative Bubble', Marcus Wallenberg Papers on International Finance, **1**, No. 1.

Fraga, Arminio (1986). *German Reparations and Brazilian Debt*, Princeton Essays in International Finance No. 163, Princeton, NJ: International Financial Section, Princeton University.

Goldsmith, Raymond (1982). 'Comment on Minsky', in Kindleberger and Laffargue (1982), pp. 41–43.

Giavazzi, Francesco and Alberto Giovannini (1986). 'The EMS and the Dollar', *Economic Policy* 2, pp. 455–85.

de Grauwe, Paul and Bernard de Bellefroid (1986). 'Long-Run Exchange Rate Variability and International Trade', mimeo.

Guttentag, Jack and Richard Herring (1983). *The Lender-of-Last-Resort Function in an International Context*, Princeton Essays in International Finance No.151, Princeton, NJ: International Financial Section, Princeton University.

(1984). 'Credit Rationing and Financial Disorder', *Journal of Finance* **39**, pp. 1359–82.

(1985). *The Current Crisis in International Lending*, Washington, DC: Brookings Institution.

House of Commons, Treasury and Civil Service Select Committee (1985). *The Financial and Economic Consequences of UK Membership of the European Communities: The European Monetary System*, Vols. i, ii, and Memoranda, London: HMSO.

James, Harold (1984). 'The Causes of the German Banking Crisis of 1931', *Economic History Review* **38**, pp. 68–87.

Kaletsky, Anatole (1985). *The Costs of Default*, New York: Twentieth Century Fund.

Kenen, Peter and Dani Rodrik (1986). 'Measuring and Analyzing the Effects of Short-Term Volatility in Real Exchange Rates', *Review of Economics and Statistics*, pp. 311–15.

Keynes, John Maynard (1925). 'Is Sterling Overvalued?' *The Nation and Athenaeum*, 4 April.

Kindleberger, Charles (1978). *Manias, Panics and Crashes*, New York: Basic Books.

(1984). *A Financial History of Western Europe*, London: Allen & Unwin.

(1986). 'Bank Failures: the 1930s and the 1980s', in *The Search for Financial Stability: The Past Fifty Years*, San Francisco, California: Federal Reserve Bank of San Francisco.

Kindleberger, Charles and Jean-Pierre Laffargue (eds) (1982). *Financial Crises: Theory, History and Policy*, London: Cambridge University Press.

Kraft, Joseph (1984). *The Mexican Rescue*, New York: Group of Thirty.

League of Nations (1931), *Commercial Banks, 1913–1929*, Geneva: League of Nations.

(1934). *Commercial Banks, 1925–1933*, Geneva: League of Nations.

(1937). *Balance of Payments 1936*, Geneva: League of Nations.

(1938). *Balance of Payments 1937*, Geneva: League of Nations.

Leguizamon, Guillermo A. (1933). 'An Argentine View of the Problem of Exchange Restrictions', *International Affairs*, pp. 504–17.

Lever, Harold and Christopher Huhne (1985). *Debt and Danger: The World Financial Crisis*, London: Penguin.

Maddison, Angus (1985), *Two Crises: Latin America and Asia 1929–38 and 1973–83*, Paris: OECD.

McNeil, William C. (1986). *American Money and the Weimar Republic*, New York: Columbia University Press.

Marris, Stephen (1985). *Deficits and the Dollar: The World Economy at Risk*, Washington, DC: Institute of International Economics.

Minsky, Hyman (1982). 'The Financial Instability Hypothesis: Capitalist Processes and the Behaviour of the Economy', in Kindleberger and Laffargue (1982), pp. 13–38.

Mintz, Ilse (1950). *Deterioration in the Quality of Foreign Bonds Issued in the United States, 1920–1930*, New York: National Bureau of Economic Research.

Mitchell, B. R. (1976). *European Historical Statistics*, London: Macmillan.

Morgan Guaranty Trust Company of New York, *World Financial Markets*.

Nurkse, Ragnar (1944). *International Currency Experience*, Geneva: League of Nations.

(1946). *The Course and Control of Inflation*, Geneva: League of Nations.

OECD (1983). *The Internationalization of Banking*, Paris.

Padoa Schioppa, Tommaso (1985). 'Policy Cooperation and the EMS Experience', in Buiter and Marston (1985), pp. 331–55.

Portes, Richard (1977). 'East Europe's Debt to the West', *Foreign Affairs* **55**, pp. 751–82.

(1982). 'La crise polonaise et les relations économiques est-ouest', *Politique étrangère*, no. 1, pp. 75–90.

(1986). 'Finance, Trade and Development: Issues in Transatlantic Cooper-ation', CEPR Discussion Paper No. 100.

Rogoff, Kenneth (1985). 'Can Exchange Rate Predictability be Achieved without Monetary Convergence? Evidence from the EMS', *European Economic Review* **28**, pp. 93–116.

Royal Institute of International Affairs (1937). *The Problem of Foreign Invest-ment*, London: Oxford University Press.

Sachs, Jeffrey (1982). 'LDC Debt in the 1980s: Risk and Reforms', in *Crises in the Economic and Financial Structure*, ed. Paul Wachtel, Lexington, Mass.: D.C. Heath.

(1985). 'External Debt and Macroeconomic Performance in Latin America and East Asia', *Brookings Papers on Economic Activity* No. 2, pp. 523–64.

Schedvin, C. Boris (1970). *Australia and the Great Depression*. Sydney, Sydney University Press.

Securities and Exchange Commission (1937). *Report on the Study and Investi-gation of the Work, Activities, Personnel and Functions of the Protective and Reorganization Committees*, Washington, DC, GPO.

Solow, Robert (1982). 'On the Lender of Last Resort', in Kindleberger and Laffargue (1982), pp. 237–47.

Spero, Joan (1980). *The Failure of the Franklin National Bank*, New York: Columbia University Press.

State of Vermont (1930). *Annual Report of the Bank Commissioner of the State of Vermont for the Year Ending June 30, 1930*, Rutland, Vermont: The Tuttle Company.

Thorp, Rosemary (1984), ed., *Latin America in the 1930s*, London: Macmillan.

Urquhart, M. C. and K. A. H. Buckley (1965). *Historical Statistics of Canada*, Cambridge: Cambridge University Press.

U.S. Department of Commerce (1930). *American Underwriting of Foreign Securities*, Washington, DC: GPO.

White, Eugene (1984). 'A Reinterpretation of the Banking Crisis of 1930', *Journal of Economic History* **44**, pp. 119–38.

Williamson, John (1977). *The Failure of World Monetary Reform*, London: Nelson.

(1985). *The Exchange Rate System*, Washington, DC: Institute for Inter-national Economics.

Winkler, Max (1933). *Foreign Bonds: An Autopsy*, Philadelphia: Roland Swain.

World Bank (1986). *World Debt Tables*, Washington, DC: IBRD.

Discussion

ROBERT F. GEMMILL

We should be grateful to the authors for probing history to identify the parallels and differences; we do have a habit of meeting the same problem in different guises, sometimes more frequently than a half century apart.

I endorse a good many of the broad conclusions, and in particular I would underline their judgement on the importance of the macro-economic environment – both as an element in producing the problems and as an essential setting for working out of the problems. The diagram of asset market linkages should rest firmly on this point, somewhat like the ancient view of the turtle that supports the world.

The paper draws a number of parallels between the present and the 1930s.

(a)   In both periods there have been structural imbalances. Fifty years ago they arose out of the exchange rate policies of the 1920s and culminated in the depression; recently we had the oil price gyrations and the relatively short recession, together with worldwide structural problems we still wrestle with (notably in agriculture but also, for example, in steel), making it difficult to work out of the present situation.

(b)   Another parallel is the rapid increase in lending that led to the problem. In both periods, market observers apparently believed that the economic climate was good, at least superficially. There may be a lesson for us here: *any* rapid sustained burst of lending is likely to be storing up trouble for the future. (In terms of the current debt situation, it was probably not feasible for the borrowers to invest such large amounts of funds productively in ways that would contribute to the ability of their economies to service debts.) Lenders of the future, whether banks or bondholders, should take note of the dangers of eating too fast.

There are also differences cited between the present and the earlier period.

(a)   The form of credit was different: differences in maturities (more a formal distinction than a real one, it turns out); differences in yield premiums; and different procedures for working out delays in payment and adjustment of terms. The formalities are more striking, and perhaps less reversible, when nonpayment of interest occurs on securities. One of the strengths of the present situation is that, while we have seen numerous cases of arrears in interest, we have not had a default. Banks have much experience with workout situations, whereas security holders as a group do not.

(b)   While in the 1930s factors outside the debtor countries were primarily responsible for their troubles (notably depressions in creditor countries), in the recent period the policies in the debtor countries that led to substantial capital flight appear to have played a *greater* role than in the 1930s. I am a bit unnerved by the comment in the paper (page 47) that failure to block the linkage between overvalued exchange rates and capital flight has been a main shortcoming of the present institutional arrangements, compared to the 1930s.

(c)　A third difference is the new international institutions. The paper points to the IMF, but treats it too narrowly in focusing on the Fund's role in assistance packages and as providing a signal to financial markets. The essential element of Bretton Woods (which is still with us) is the long history (with a few notable exceptions) of international consultation on economic and financial policy and conditions in a number of forums – including the IMF, but also the BIS and OECD.

The consultation that occurs is not the same as policy coordination, which the paper mentions longingly at the end. But just as we can live with rough agreements and understandings on supervisory matters and in matters dealing with support and rescue operations (p. 50), so can and (doubtless for the foreseeable future) *must* we live with cooperation on policy matters that is less than what one could call full coordination.

(d)　One element in the present institutional arrangements that was not present in the 1930s – and which is not mentioned in the paper – is the interbank payments system, and the role of banks in making payments for their customers as well as for themselves. This was not a crucial factor in the current debt situation, but it is central to thinking about the anatomy of possible financial troubles and of the critical linkages, domestic or international. (The celebrated discount window borrowing of more than $20 billion by the Bank of New York and the daily transactions of roughly $250–$300 billion are sufficient to establish the standing of this issue.) And potential payments system problems point up the difficulty of framing the analysis in terms of simple schematic diagrams.

Where do we stand now in September 1986?

There is a much publicized trend toward securitization of international credit flows. To date, this involves primarily borrowing by OECD countries. Developing countries have accounted for only 3 to 5% of total gross issues (from 1983 through the first half of 1986, $17 billion out of $460 billion), and these developing countries are not the ones that banks are worrying about at the moment. In fact, most developing countries have perforce relied on bank credits and credits from international institutions in the postwar period.

Should we expect securitization of credits to developing countries to expand further? Probably not a lot, although in principle it may be preferable to the borrower to have debt in a number of different forms, rather than relying exclusively on one group of lenders. If banks were willing to re-emphasize customer relationships in their planning (and to lessen their interest in moving into the securities industry) it would seem in the interest of the developing countries to seek to establish their traditional banking relationships, rather than to try to go it alone in the international bond market.

Will the banks be interested again? I would guess yes. Banks must decide what is unique to banking. Their role in the payments system is one unique feature; another is probably the re-establishment of long-standing customer relationships, although that is not in vogue now.

For US banks, exposure to developing countries (in relation to capital) is down to the levels of 1977. Thus some time in the future I would expect to see bank lending growing in importance in international credit flows.

That brings us back to bank supervisory issues for the future. I have just a couple of brief points.

(a)   Over the past decade cooperation and consultation in supervision (not coordination, cf. p. 49) have developed progressively. The Cooke Committee has served a valuable function – not so much for the Concordat as for contacts between supervisors.

(b)   In this era of rapid innovation, supervisors will be put to hard tests. They will likely have to put emphasis on the need for banks to have sound management control systems, since supervisors will always be catching up with specific innovations. Supervision will not be able to substitute for use of sound credit judgment by banks and other financial institutions, and supervisory systems must try to ensure that banks assess credit (and other) risks realistically, and price services appropriately.

If banks read history, it will help.

Discussion

T. RYBCZYNSKI

There are two approaches to historical exercises. They are exemplified in two sayings; 'history is bunk', as Henry Ford put it, and 'historia docet', as the Latin phrase has it.

The case for the institutional approach

The authors of the paper appear to take the second view, though in a cautious, guarded and circumspect manner. They seem to hold the view that the historical approach at best can provide no more than helpful and useful insights. This is a pity because their efforts show very clearly that the institutional approach, so long out of fashion, has a legitimate place in the body of economics. The basic claim of institutionalists that the nature and character of institutions do affect the workings of economic forces – as shown by this paper – could not be justified better than by reference to the operations of the financial sector.

Basic questions, analytical approach and the crucial position of the banking system

The basic questions the authors endeavour to answer are, firstly, what are the sources of financial crises; secondly, what role does the financial system play either in generating them and containing, attenuating or enlarging them; and, thirdly, to what extent does the response of macroeconomic policy and the structure of the financial system and the supervisory framework affect the generation and transmission of the primary disturbances?

Their starting point is the definition of a financial crisis: a disturbance to financial markets associated with falling asset prices and insolvency among debtors and intermediaries, which breaks forth through the financial system, disrupting the market's ability to allocate capital domestically and, in the case of international crisis, internationally.

At the heart of the authors' approach is what they call a 'minimum structure' around which they place their historical observations. This consists of linkages between the three main elements; debt defaults, bank failures, and exchange rate disturbances. The extent to which the original disturbance is propagated and can change into a crisis will depend, first, on how changes in the assets and liabilities situation of all wealth holders, working through debt defaults and exchange rate market disorders, affect the banking system; and, second, on the degree to which economic policy can insulate the banking system and macroeconomy from the pressures so arising. The first factor (the propagation of the disturbance and the probability of its changing into a crisis) is in turn influenced by the character of the financial system; the second factor (insulation of the banking system and macroeconomy from a shock) is conditioned by the approaches to and the constraints on economic policy and the relationship among economic policies pursued by various countries.

The crucial position in this structure, however, is occupied by the banking system. If the banking system can be insulated from shocks and their impact attenuated or contained, the real economy can be insulated from any adverse consequences. If the banking system cannot be insulated the original disturbance becomes a crisis, bringing down the real economy with it and resulting in a depression.

Changes in four major areas in the inter-war period and the last 15 years and their repercussions

Within this framework the authors trace and compare the repercussions of changes both in the inter-war period and in the recent past, in four major areas. These are a major shift in international lending, and major changes in the financial system, in the exchange rate system and in the structure of world economic and political power.

Although in some ways the nature (though not the size and direction) of changes in these two periods was similar the results they produced were markedly different. In the 'twenties and 'thirties the result was to accentuate the shock. The three basic linkages enhanced the impact of the original disturbance, leading to a collapse of the financial system through the banking sector and eventually to the great depression. In contrast, in the recent past the three linkages have been attenuated, blocked or broken. They in fact insulated the banking system and so far have led to the continuing functioning of the world financial system as well as to reasonably satisfactory behaviour of world production and trade.

These contrasting results are attributed by the authors, first, to institutional changes bearing on the linkages in the banking system and above all to a better and more efficient supervisory structure nationally and internationally; and, second, to markedly different posture of and changes in economic policy and its success in insulating the banking system from outside shocks and perturbations.

The main conclusions

There are three main conclusions which the authors draw from their comparison of the inter-war and post-1970 experience. They are, firstly, that disturbances which become crises arise either from the malfunctioning of the real economy *or* the workings of the financial markets; secondly, that governments should be actively involved in creating a regulatory framework that prevents the occurrence of disturbances in the financial area and weakens and isolates their impact if they originate in the real economy; and thirdly, that to prevent and contain the occurrence and propagation of disturbances in the real economy and financial system there should be international coordination of economic policies.

All these three conclusions flow naturally from the analytical structure employed and can be said to conform to and indeed form a part of the new conventional wisdom. But are their analytical underpinnings adequate to answer meaningfully and in an operationally helpful manner the questions the authors consider so important?

The need to link the international monetary system and the financial system

There are three basic comments I wish to make. The first is that from a wider perspective it would appear, firstly, that the authors' concentration on the financial system with only occasional and scanty references to the international monetary arrangements has restricted unnecessarily and severely the scope of their exercise and has limited the value and usefulness of their study and the conclusions they arrive at. The second is that the proposals to disconnect the linkages have been more apparent than real and can be regarded as tantamount to dealing with symptoms rather than causes. The third is that the success so far achieved in holding the world financial system in a fairly good shape may represent merely temporary containment of the pressures which will burst out once again in the future.

I shall concentrate merely on the first point and refer only in a summary way to the second and third points.

The important point to start with is that the functioning of the financial system cannot be divorced from the structure and functioning of the monetary system. A well-structured and properly functioning monetary system is a necessary, although not sufficient, condition for a healthy and well-functioning financial system. However well-structured and supervised is the financial system it will not function properly and indeed will probably collapse if the monetary system fails.

The financial system (domestic and international) is a man-made institutional arrangement for transmission of savings from those who generate them to those who use them. In performing this basic function the financial system determines the total amount and the distribution of risk that an economy undertakes. These in turn are influenced by the character and the stage of evolution of the financial system and the nature of the supervisory framework.

I have outlined the stylised evolution of the financial system in various papers I have produced. The evolution – associated with economic growth – involves the transition of the financial system from a bank-orientated system to a market-orientated and securitized system. During each of these stages the total volume of risk, its distribution and linkages differ. This must be taken account of when looking at the supervisory and other arrangements.

During each of the phases of the evolution of the financial system the purpose of supervisory rules and the regulatory framework is to ensure that if excessive risk is taken by those who channel their savings to ultimate users the consequences of risk, if materialising, are contained or so attenuated that they have no important repercussions (i.e. that linkages emanating from debt default and other defaults by users of savings are blocked). Excessive risk here means the risk which cannot be met out of the resources of those who originally assumed it.

However, the volume and distribution of risk (real and financial) which an economy and financial intermediaries (i.e. depository and other savings-collecting institutions) carry are also influenced by the character of the international monetary system (i.e. exchange rate arrangements which solve the problem of adjustment, liquidity and expectations). Evidence available (quoted in the study) indicates that fluctuating rates of exchange, accompanied by a lack of an anchor and absence of 'rules of the game', cause the various economies and financial intermediaries and savers channelling their savings directly to users to assume excessive risk. This is so, firstly, because such arrangements result in a very high and basically unpredictable volatility of exchange and interest rates; secondly, because they weaken and defer the process of adjustment (i.e. shift of resources); thirdly, because they introduce a new dimension of uncertainty attaching to the course and mix of economic policy pursued by various countries.

Under an unmanaged exchange rate regime the world financial system not only functions (i.e. channels the flow of savings) less efficiently but also becomes more vulnerable and fragile. In addition the volume of savings coming forward declines (at least in relative terms) because such arrangements permit governments to pursue inconsistent and conflicting policies which lead to a significant misallocation of real resources and, consequently, a misalignment of exchange rates.

A managed exchange rate system with clear and unambiguous 'rules of the game' reduces the vulnerability of the domestic and world financial system, reduces its willingness to assume excessive risks and, together with a proper supervisory framework, contains the volume of risk to that broadly commensurate with the ability of savings-providers and distributors to bear that risk. It also blocks the linkages that facilitate the propagation of a disturbance originating in the real economy or the financial system.

A managed exchange rate system, by removing uncertainty, facilitating the process of adjustment and spreading its cost among all economic units (through changes in government policy) and easing the phasing out of debt (i.e. accepting in a non-propagating manner the cost of misalignment of real resources in the past) reinforces the robustness, resilience and efficiency of the financial system.

Let me now move to my second point, that the disconnection of linkages has been more apparent than real and has been tantamount to dealing with symptoms rather than causes. The very breakup of the monetary arrangements in fact means that the impact of the shocks experienced has been contained by introducing new and different distortions into the system. These distortions have temporarily redirected the impact of the original disturbance. However, they have not dispersed them. Moreover some of the changes in the financial system have probably enhanced the consequences of the disturbances, resulting in the assumption of a higher level of risk than can be carried and its worse distribution and greater interlinking.

This brings me to my third point, that the risks now carried are probably excessive and that what has happened is probably a temporary deferment of the consequences of the disturbance which is likely to materialise in the future.

There is no doubt that the approach adopted in the study provides useful insight into the position and the role of the financial system in the two major crises of the last 60 years. However, it would appear to me that the value of the study would be significantly enhanced if the analysis had been extended to and linked with that of international monetary arrangements and if the extent to which the post-1973 changes have temporarily blocked the linkages had been examined. This task, as well as the wider question of the role of the state in a market economy, are still to be taken up.

2 The role of public policy in ensuring financial stability: a cross-country, comparative perspective

ERNST BALTENSPERGER and
JEAN DERMINE

I   Introduction

It is a common feature of countries around the world that the financial sector of the economy, and the banking system in particular, is highly regulated and supervised. The effects of regulation on the economy and the comparison of alternative regulatory systems are of great interest, both from a practical and from an academic point of view. Any reform of banking legislation, and of financial regulation in general, requires that these issues are studied. In recent years, there has been a revival of interest in questions of this type, as illustrated by the discussion of deregulation and reregulation in the United States and in numerous other countries. A major reason for this renewed occupation with bank regulation has undoubtedly been the large amount of financial change (development of new financial instruments and institutions, domestic integration of financial markets and internationalization) which has occurred in recent years, partly due to developments on the technological side (electronic data processing, telecommunications), but partly also as an innovative response to existing regulations and constraints. A further ingredient in this discussion has been the international debt crisis of recent years.

The regulation issue raises a number of basic questions. To what extent is regulation of banking and financial markets justified, and why? What are the reasons for an unregulated financial system leading to suboptimal and 'undesirable' results? What forms of regulation can improve on these results and thus be economically justified? What kinds of regulation, on the other hand, prove detrimental to market efficiency and performance? In this context it is important to keep in mind that regulations normally have their costs. Thus, even if a regulation is judged to have beneficial effects, it is important also to investigate its costs and weigh them against the associated benefits.

While banking is regulated in every country around the world, the specific forms of regulation employed vary to a considerable degree. This paper offers a discussion of alternative approaches to ensuring the stability of the financial system of an economy. It should be made clear at the outset, however, that it is not the purpose of the paper to give a country-by-country description and comparison of regulations. This would be a task requiring far more space than is allowed here, and more detailed knowledge than the authors have. Rather, we try to identify and discuss different approaches to the issue of financial stability, using the regulatory systems and resulting banking structures of individual countries as examples. Very useful descriptions of the regulatory systems of major countries around the world are to be found in Welch (1981) or Dale (1982 or 1984). Specific details on some individual national systems are also found in the country papers prepared for this conference.

II   Motives for banking regulation

It is sensible to begin a discussion of bank regulation with a brief review of the basic motives and justifications for it. Traditionally, most regulations in the banking area have been justified in terms of one of the following three considerations:

Concern for bank safety and overall financial stability. Bank safety can be seen as important from two points of view: the protection and safety of bank customers (especially depositors) on the one hand, and the avoidance of banking panics and crises on the other hand. The former of these refers to the safety of individual banks and their customers and is comparable to concerns for consumer protection in other areas. The latter, on the other hand, refers to the safety of the banking and financial system as a whole.

Concern for monetary control (especially money supply and price level control and stability). Without regulation, such control is sometimes said to be impossible, leading to indeterminateness of the money supply and price level. More frequently, and less extremely, the money stock and the price level are said to be subject to an excessive amount of variability without such controls, with consequent costs to the economy as a whole. The former possibility is feared by authors who believe that, without regulation of banking, there would be no effective constraint on banks and other financial enterprises creating money in the form of bank deposits and other, similar liabilities (near-monies). The latter view stems from the related (but less extreme) concern that the banking system, via its participation in the money creation process, injects an undesirable instability into the monetary and financial system (through unpredictable variations in reserve behaviour, etc.), and that in this sense it is 'inherently unstable' and thus needs to be regulated. In contrast to the 'global' stability of the financial system referred to in the first point above, we are talking about its 'local' stability here. The most important regulatory device usually proposed in this context is the institution of a reserve requirement (Baltensperger, 1982).

Concern for monopoly, concentration and inadequate competition in banking. This concern is usually based on the presumed existence of economies of scale or scope in banking. In this instance, regulation is seen as a measure protecting the banking sector from inadequate competition – somewhat in contrast to the other two types of considerations mentioned above, which often result in a tendency to ask whether, and to what extent, competition is appropriate in banking. While this third type of approach to bank regulation has played a certain role in the United States, especially with regard to branch banking restrictions, it has been considerably less important, generally speaking. Although some economies of scale probably exist in banking for small bank sizes (see Baltensperger, 1972; Benston, Hanweck and Humphrey, 1982, and Gilligan, Smirlock and Marshall, 1984), it is less clear that these are important enough to justify branching restrictions of the sort employed in the United States or that these restrictions actually reduce the likelihood of the emergence and maintenance of monopoly positions in banking.

Of course, these motivations for bank regulation cannot always be fully separated. To some extent, they are related to each other. Nevertheless, it is useful to separate them analytically, since the arguments and types of regulation usually proposed and recommended under them differ to a considerable degree (and in some cases, as just noted, can become contradictory). In this paper we are concerned with the first of these three issues alone, and we deal with the other two only to the extent that they are related to the first.

III   The need for public policy in ensuring financial stability

Concerns for bank safety are often based, in essence, on the idea that, without regulation, there would be too much competition and that banks would take excessive risks. Competition in this view is seen as less appropriate for banking than for other industries. Banks which assume excessive risks and overextend themselves ('overbanking') reduce bank safety to unsound levels and increase the probability of bank failures and of a collapse of the financial system. These worries, which have been behind most existing bank regulations (especially those introduced in response to the financial crises of the 1930s) have been reinforced again by foreign exchange losses in the mid-70s and by maturity mismatching and the international debt crisis in the 80s. This, together with the large amount of financial change occurring in the world economy, has led to a substantial reconsideration of regulatory issues during recent years. It should be noted, however, that it is important to distinguish between overextensions caused by public interventions themselves (regulations or, especially, compulsory deposit insurance, or implicit guarantees of a similar sort by governments) and inefficiencies caused by free markets in the absence of regulation. Thus, simply pointing to recent developments (international debt crisis) is not enough to prove market failure and to justify regulation.

Thus, before discussing specific regulations, in order to give a clear focus to the subsequent discussion, we must briefly ask why regulation is necessary at all for ensuring financial stability. What is the nature and the source of the failure of the unregulated market which regulations are supposed to correct? Once such a failure has been identified, we can ask what type of regulation would help to improve the situation. What are the consequences, including the costs, of possible regulations? In all this, it is important to remember that it is not enough to establish a 'failure' of the market vis-à-vis some idealized state of the world, for example the state which could be reached if everybody had perfect information. A case must be made that specific regulations will improve on the unregulated market's solution, given the actual environment characterizing the economy. Often such a case is much more difficult to make than is thought at first sight.

The following argument, which has been much emphasized in recent years, is based on the presumption of imperfect information, especially information asymmetries between the bank and the bank customer (borrower and lender) and the resulting problems of moral hazard and adverse selection. Depositors are said to be unable to judge adequately the quality of bank assets and thus the default probability of individual banks. That is, depositors know that there are high quality and low quality banks, but they are unable to tell which is which, while the banks themselves know their own status. This is often reinforced by the low level of disclosure in many countries. Research in information economics during recent years has shown that such an asymmetry, if it exists in a field, may lead to a breakdown of markets or to unusual types of market equilibria. Whether this, as such, justifies speaking of 'inefficiencies' is a difficult and subtle question. (Inefficient with respect to what?) However, in banking it is pointed out that such an asymmetry creates a special problem because a large part of the banks' liabilities are withdrawable on demand or short notice at par (Diamond-Dybvig, 1983). Depositors face the question whether an observed bank failure is due to bank-specific causes (a bad draw from a given distribution of returns) or whether it represents a shift in the risk of the banking system as a whole (an overall change in the state of the economy). As technological progress reduces substantially the cost of deposit transfers, the fear of a bank run becomes more relevant. In this way, a form of externality arises: 'good' banks may be hurt by the existence of 'bad' banks. This can lead (a) to a misallocation of resources (a suboptimal level of risk taking) generally, and (b) to the danger of bank runs: the failure of a 'bad' bank may cause a run on 'good' banks, and thus create a risk of the collapse and destruction of the banking system and the money supply, with high social costs, due to the vital importance of the banking and monetary system for the smooth operation of an economy (Bernanke, 1983).

It should be stressed that what is special to banking, according to this kind of argument, is the liquid nature of the liabilities of banks and the 'contagion effect' of bank failures; that is, the effects which an individual failure may have on the banking system as a whole. This thought has always been, in one way or another, at the heart of the justification of bank regulation. Information problems and uncertainty as such create the possibility of bank failures and depositor losses. In principle, this fact alone does not much differentiate banking from other fields. A creditor or shareholder of any firm may suffer losses of this kind (and may be subject to the sort of information asymmetry referred to above), but this is not normally taken to be cause for a call for regulations – at least not of the kinds which are customary in banking. Thus, as far as individual banks and their risk of failure are concerned, special bank regulations would seem to be comparatively hard to justify. It is the potential effect of individual failures on the safety of the banking and credit system as a whole which forms the basis for regulatory concern.

Although some authors (e.g. Kareken and Wallace, 1978) claim that an unregulated banking system would imply a zero probability of default, and hence also of banking crises, it cannot be denied that in terms of historical experience fears of the sort just mentioned do not entirely seem to lack justification. This suggests that the models on which this alternative view is based (perfect information) do not adequately reflect the complexity of the bank-customer relationship and the role of confidence and trust for this relation and the financial system overall. In any case, this kind of fear has probably been the overriding concern behind bank safety regulations, and the main reason for the call for institutions and regulations preventing, or at least containing, the risk of such an event. From this perspective, deposit insurance is generally perceived as an efficient way to reduce the risk of a bank run while allowing for short-term deposit funding and maturity transformation. This point has occasionally been formulated in the following way (e.g. Meltzer, 1967): individual bank failures are comparatively easy to insure and can, in principle, be covered by private insurers, like any other risk. The possibility of multiple failures (chain reactions), on the other hand, makes private insurance very costly and, possibly, unavailable.

The crucial question, of course, is what is the best solution to this problem. As just mentioned, an obvious solution to propose is some sort of insurance scheme, maybe run by the government. Such an insurance can be supplemented, or possibly even substituted by a lender of last resort authority. Both of these types of institutions can assume a variety of forms in practice. Furthermore, they may or may not be supplemented by various additional controls (capital adequacy requirements, disclosure laws, entry restrictions, to name but a few); or, finally, they may be largely substituted by these. Different countries use different combinations of these regulatory devices. We turn to the most important of these next.

IV   Characteristics of regulatory systems

There are a number of characteristics of regulatory systems which can be employed to distinguish between different approaches to regulation. We will first describe these briefly. Afterwards, we will discuss them in more detail, with references to countries relying on these different approaches.

A first distinction is between *prudential*, or *preventive*, regulations on the one hand and *protective* measures on the other hand (Dale, 1984). Prudential, or preventive, measures are those aimed at controlling the levels of risk assumed by banks and thus affecting the probability of bank failures. Protective measures, on the other hand, offer protection to bank customers or to the banks themselves in the case of actual or impending bank failures. Indirectly, thus, they concern the capacity of the system to handle bank failures and runs. Prudential measures can include capital adequacy requirements, liquidity requirements, interest (especially deposit rate) regulations, asset diversification rules (including foreign exchange exposure), restrictions on permissible business activities, restrictions on market entry, and general banking supervision and inspection. Protective measures include various forms of deposit insurance and lender of last resort facilities.

However, it should be seen clearly that this separation is not a clearcut one. The two types of measures interrelate in several ways. First, a basic idea of protective regulations (deposit insurance and lender of last resort facilities) is the creation of confidence in the banking system, with subsequent beneficial effects on the probability of bank runs and system crises. At the same time, however, protective measures involve the danger of moral hazard and adverse effects on the riskiness of banks. Therefore, the two types of measures are interrelated. In particular, protective measures often call for supplementary preventive regulations. That is, there are particular bundles, or packages, of regulations which go together. Of particular importance in this regard is the form in which protective measures are designed.

This brings up another important distinction which can be made, namely that between a *discretionary* approach to protecting the safety of the banking system and an *institutionalized* contractual approach. Discretionary interventions are all those that are at the discretion of government: lender of last resort (possibly at a subsidized rate), public guarantees and subsidies of all sorts, or nationalization. The main characteristic of a discretionary intervention is that it is not granted 'for sure', so that some amount of private risk remains. This uncertainty creates obvious incentives for lenders to monitor the riskiness of the financial institutions they are lending to. Until recently, this was the only form of public intervention in many countries, especially in Europe. Nevertheless, there was often a common understanding that a public intervention was almost certain, especially for large banks. In a discretionary intervention system, the costs of bailing out are shared by the central bank (the taxpayers) and by the private banks. Contractual interventions, on the other hand, include the institutionalized deposit insurance systems familiar from the United States and recently introduced in numerous other countries. Since in this case help is granted for sure, these institutions, while creating confidence in the banking system, are also prone to create problems of moral hazard, as is well known from the US experience.

In the case of institutionalized deposit insurance, the specific form of the insurance schemes employed can vary in a number of ways. Important dimensions which have to be kept in mind in this context are the following:

- *the fee structure* (flat fee versus variable, risk-related fees)
- *degree of coverage* (full versus particular coverage, maximum limits)
- *funding provisions* (funded versus unfunded systems)
- *public* versus *private* solutions
- *compulsory* versus *voluntary* participation.

In the case of discretionary interventions, an important issue evidently concerns the determination of the circumstances under which help is granted. As mentioned above, it is characteristic of a discretionary approach that these conditions are not known with exact certainty. Nevertheless, over time certain traditions and practices can evolve, and authorities can be more or less generous in determining the thresholds beyond which help is supplied. Important aspects here are the relation of these discretionary measures to formalized deposit insurance on the one hand, and to routine discount window operations of the central bank on the other hand. Another difficult question concerns coordination between different national authorities. (Who is responsible for foreign subsidiaries of domestic firms? Should home or host country principles apply?)

In all cases of regulation and intervention, an important question refers to the *definition of the institutions* which are covered (only banks in a narrow sense, or financial firms in a broad definition) and of the items which are covered (e.g. balance-sheet versus off-balance-sheet items).

In the following sections, we will discuss the major dimensions of bank regulation in more detail, and we will indicate how different countries have relied on different combinations of regulations and institutional structures in order to ensure the stability of their financial systems. We will organize the discussion in the following way: we will begin with the main form of institutionalized protective regulation, deposit insurance. We will then continue with a discussion of discretionary protective interventions, in particular lender of last resort facilities. Finally, we will review the role of prudential measures. Here, one can distinguish between two groups of regulations: those which, in one form or another, exist in virtually every country (e.g. capital requirements, diversification rules) and those which are used in some countries only, but not in others (e.g. entry restrictions based on demonstration of 'need', restrictions on lines of business).

V   Deposit insurance

From the point of view of the depositor, deposit insurance makes all deposits equally attractive, independent of the bank's insolvency risk. It removes the necessity for the depositor to distinguish between different quality types of banks and – in case such differences are perceived by the depositor – for the bank to include a bank-specific risk premium in the rate of interest paid to the depositor. In the case of a bank failure, the insurer pays off the insured depositors, thereby preventing direct effects of the failure on the deposit and money holdings of the economy. Most important, however, the need for depositors at other banks to be concerned about the safety of their deposits is removed, and thus the danger of chain reactions and of collapse of the banking system disappears. This is so, in particular, if delays in reimbursing depositors are avoided. This argument, if valid, applies to all liabilities which can be withdrawn on short notice – under whatever name they may appear in the balance sheets of financial firms.

Today, a large number of countries have institutionalized schemes of deposit insurance or protection funds. While in some cases these were created some time ago (e.g. United States: 1933, Canada: 1967, Japan: 1971, revised in 1986), in many countries, especially European ones, they have been introduced only recently (e.g. United Kingdom: 1982, Germany: 1977, France: 1979, Belgium: 1985, Netherlands: 1979). The stated motivations are usually the traditional ones of protection of small deposits and of stability of the banking system. Nevertheless, there are still important countries without formal deposit insurance (e.g. Italy, Switzerland, Luxembourg, Hongkong, Singapore). However, in countries without formal deposit insurance, a more or less implicit guarantee by the government or the central bank usually takes its place. Furthermore, the introduction of institutionalized deposit insurance is under discussion in some of these countries (e.g. Italy, Switzerland).

Deposit insurance has been discussed by a variety of authors; see, for example, Friedman (1959), Black, Miller and Posner (1978), Kareken and Wallace (1978), Baltensperger (1980), Cooper and Fraser (1984), Kane (1985), or Dermine (1986).

Deposit insurance can take a variety of forms. A first basic question is whether or not it should be compulsory. Voluntary insurance may be enough if the only objective is to offer bank customers the opportunity of holding a risk-free deposit. However, since the avoidance of bank runs and system crises is usually seen as one of the main goals, the normal call is for enforced insurance. Therefore, many countries have deposit insurance on a mandatory basis and, even when it is voluntary (Belgium, Netherlands, Germany or United States; Johnson and Abrams, 1983), in fact it covers almost the entire banking system.

Deposit insurance systems can be either public (e.g. United Kingdom, United States, Canada, Belgium) or private (usually created on a collective basis by the banks themselves, via some sort of insurance pool, e.g. Germany, Netherlands, France). These private solutions are normally run under the control and supervision of the government, however, so that the difference from public insurance may not be as fundamental as it appears at first. Another case of a mixture between public and private systems is the Japanese one, a kind of joint effort by the government, the central bank, and the banking industry. There are, in principle, good reasons for introducing some competition and, consequently, adaptive efficiency into the business of supplying deposit insurance, e.g. by allowing private insurers to participate in this business by offering supplementary deposit insurance (Kane 1986, Benston 1983).

A basic question of any insurance system, especially with mandatory insurance, concerns the way in which insurance fees payable by the insured banks are set: flat fees or variable, risk-related premia? The answer to this question has great significance with regard to what further types of complementary regulations may be necessary. Economists almost invariably have, in principle, expressed a preference for risk-related premia. An efficiently organized insurer would graduate insurance premia according to the bank's risk of insolvency, and consequently according to the risk of the bank's asset portfolio and the adequacy of its capital holdings. Such a system would minimize the danger of adverse incentive effects which may otherwise result from deposit insurance. Under such a system, the individual bank bears the consequences of a higher risk portfolio or a lower capital-deposit ratio in the form of a higher insurance fee. If this is not the case, banks have an incentive to hold higher risk portfolios and lower capital-deposit ratios than they otherwise would. In reality (as in all insurance markets) it is probably impossible to avoid these problems totally. But this is no reason not to try to approximate such a solution as far as possible.

Arguments against this form of deposit insurance (often brought forward by administrators of government agencies) usually emphasize the administrative difficulty in calculating the appropriate fee structure. However, this argument does not seem to be a very convincing defence of a flat fee structure. A differentiation among just a few risk classes would probably go a long way towards a reasonable first approximation and be much superior to a flat fee which is not related to insolvency risk. It is not clear why the problem of setting adequate insurance premia should be intrinsically more difficult in this area than for other types of insurance. Another argument points to the 'private nature' of bank portfolios, which makes it impossible to ask banks to reveal the relevant information without giving away private information vital for their survival in the marketplace (Batchelor and Fitzgerald, 1982). However, there is no need for information about a bank's individual portfolio items to become public information. It is true, of course, that adequate information disclosure to the insurer is a prerequisite of such a system (as with any other insurance contract – or loan contract, for that matter). However, the overall risk of a bank (which may become publicly known under such a system) does not allow inferences about individual portfolio items. Maybe a more serious difficulty is the opportunity of banks to change their risk exposure within short spans of time. However, this does not mean that high-risk banks can hide their status forever. Furthermore, as Kane points out, risk-related premia need not consist entirely of *ex-ante* payments, but may include provisions for an *ex-post* settling up of gains and losses between a bank, its stockholders, and the insurer (Kane, 1986). Recent developments in the American financial markets, where private insurance contracts exist on bonds, money market funds and swap transactions, give support to the feasibility of private insurance.

Thus, theoretical support for such a system is strong. Usually, its proponents see no need for further, complementary public controls (like capital requirements, etc.), beyond adequate asset inspection and information disclosure to the insurer. As will be pointed out below, this is in marked contrast to the case of a flat fee insurance system. According to Meltzer (1967), an insurance system of the type discussed here could be voluntary, with variable coverage to be chosen by the depositor. This is, in principle, tempting to a market oriented economist. It must be noted, nevertheless, that a large participation would be essential, since otherwise the safeguard against chain reactions (seen above as the main underlying problem) would be weakened.

However, actually existing deposit insurance systems almost invariably use a flat fee per unit of deposits, regardless of a bank's insolvency risk. Such a system is well-known, in particular, from the FDIC in the United States. But this feature is common to insurance schemes around the world. As already pointed out above, this has important effects on debtor behaviour and will, in general, create an adverse incentive (moral hazard) problem. Since under this system the bank does not bear the consequences on its cost of funds of increasing the risk of its portfolio or of lowering its capital ratio, it has an incentive to pursue such policies beyond the point it otherwise would. Thus, deposit insurance of this sort, as such, has the effect of actually making banks less safe than they would otherwise be. In recent years, under the developments of deposit insurance, especially in the United States, this aspect of flat-fee deposit insurance has been much discussed in the literature (see, for example, Kane 1985). It is quite clear that this logically calls for certain controls to be imposed on the debtor (the bank) by the insurer – the same types of controls and constraints as the depositor/lender would like to have imposed in the absence of insurance. This is a basic reason for the concern of bank regulators and deposit insurers with the adequacy of bank capital (and reserves) and the riskiness of bank assets, and it tends to lead such a system to the introduction of a host of additional controls, such as required capital and liquidity ratios, prohibition of certain (risky) assets from bank portfolios, and diversification rules – all imposed on the bank in order to minimize the risk of bank failures.

It is important to emphasize the difference between a flat fee and a variable fee insurance system which manifests itself in this. While the variable fee system discussed above does not care about the risk of individual bank failures as such and constrains it via its influence on insurance premia, the flat fee system is forced to care directly about this risk and to limit it through certain nonprice measures. That is, it must attempt to force banks to be safe, in order to protect the insurance fund. But note again that, in principle, there is no reason why we should be more concerned about an individual bank failure than about the failure of any other firm. It is only the possibility of chain reactions which should be our concern, that is, the possibility of the failure of sound banks and the banking system as a whole through bank runs. The failure of an individual bank, as such, probably implies no social costs beyond the direct costs to the depositors, shareholders and employees. A collapse of the whole banking system, however, represents a heavy social cost, given the importance of the banking and money system for the efficient operation of an economy. But this does not require minimization of the probability that even one bank will fail; it only requires the elimination of the risk of adverse chain reactions.

While non-reliance on risk-related fees is virtually universal, there exist nevertheless some differences between different countries with regard to other aspects of funding practices. Most national insurance systems proceed on a funded basis, but the size of the insurance fund, relative to the insured volume of deposits, varies quite considerably (e.g. about 1 percent in the United States, 0.067 percent in Japan; see Dale 1984). However, this is a rather meaningless number, of course, as the insurance fund must be seen in relation to potential payouts and the possibility of raising additional funds. Nevertheless, the capacity to make large payouts is quite limited in the case of many national systems, meaning that there must be some implicit backup support of a discretionary nature for the case of severe problems (including, as an ultimate solution, nationalization). Some national systems (e.g. France, Netherlands) even operate without any explicit funding, relying instead on *ad hoc* contributions by the insured banks when payouts have to be made.

Maybe the most important differences between different national systems of deposit insurance can be found with regard to the extent of coverage they offer. In all systems, there exists a maximum amount per depositor and institution beyond which there is no insurance. In most cases, this maximum is stated as a fixed amount, which varies considerably between countries, however (United States: $100,000; Canada: $60,000; France: FF 250,000; Belgium: BF 500,000; Japan: 10 million Yen). The German system provides full coverage up to 30 percent of the failed bank's equity capital. The British system is exceptional in that it covers only 75 percent of the loss, up to a maximum of £10,000, while the remaining 25 percent has to be borne by the depositor. Most systems usually attempt to merge troubled banks, so that actual payouts can be avoided as far as possible. The 'small deposit' criterion can be questioned if the objective is to protect the less-wealthy depositors. Income or wealth criteria would appear more appropriate and would eliminate the recent problem of brokered-deposits, i.e. large sums of money which are divided by brokers into small insured deposits.

The degree of coverage can be quite important for the working and consequences of a deposit insurance system. On the one hand, partial and incomplete coverage weakens the potentially beneficial effect of insurance on the stability of the financial system (creation of confidence, avoidance of bank runs). On the other hand, especially with flat-rate insurance, a limitation of coverage may be necessary in order to induce a certain minimum amount of monitoring of banks by bank customers. It should be clear that the very limited coverage by current deposit insurance systems is unlikely to completely eliminate the risk of a run (especially in view of the large amount of uninsured deposits raised on the interbank markets), but that it helps to achieve a politically acceptable solution to banks' default as small deposits are insured. This is especially true for the United Kingdom where the 75% provision only partially reduces the incentive to run even for insured deposits. Moreover, the existence of deposit insurance systems is largely unknown to the public in Europe as they are not advertised by banks. There is no such thing as the American 'FDIC-insured' sticker on the front door of a European bank. This raises again the question of supplementary interventions by other parts of the government, e.g. the central bank in its role as a lender of last resort.

VI   Lender of last resort facilities (and related emergency measures)

Typically, monetary authorities (usually the central bank) stand ready to provide help when banks, or the banking system as a whole, are experiencing temporary liquidity problems. However, we should distinguish between routine operation of the discount window for normal monetary policy purposes, with often formalized access (e.g. Canada, France, Japan), for example for short-term interest rate stabilization or to meet seasonal variations in liquidity demand, and emergency type measures for troubled banks made on a more discretionary basis. It is especially the latter which we are addressing here.

Usually, the view taken is that such help should only be given to banks which are temporarily illiquid but solvent (and therefore fit for long-run survival). This immediately raises the question why basically sound banks should need help to begin with. With perfect or nearly perfect credit markets, a solvent bank should always find it possible to obtain credit from the private markets. Therefore, one philosophy of the lender of last resort function is that the central bank, as lender of last resort, should never be concerned about the fate of individual banks, but only about the banking system as a whole. That is, it should see it as its duty to maintain an adequate volume of liquidity for the system as a whole, but should leave the distribution and redistribution of funds to the private markets (Humphrey, 1975).

However, another position – which is in fact usually taken by central banks – is that, due to imperfections in credit markets, basically sound banks may find it difficult or impossible to obtain sufficient credit from the market when experiencing a temporary liquidity shortage. Therefore, in this view, lender of last resort assistance should take the form of help to individual banks experiencing temporary liquidity problems when these problems endanger their survival (and possibly that of other banks and the banking system, too). In this view, the lender of last resort facility is a response of the authorities to the imperfections of the credit markets. Of course, this view is based on the implicit assumption that the authorities have a better judgment of the soundness and long-term survival potential of individual banks than the market. Another case for concern would be a breakdown in large wire transfer systems which would create a liquidity problem.

Although, on a conceptual basis, liquidity and solvency can be distinguished, it is difficult for them to be completely separated in practice. In practice, the public perception of a 'liquidity problem' usually means that some doubts about the bank's solvency exist, too. In fact, some relations between the two states cannot be denied. Unwise liquidity management implies the risk of corresponding adjustment costs; in the case of a 'bad draw', these may assume an extent which can threaten the solvency of an institution. Publicly observed liquidity difficulties can to some extent be self-enforcing, by leading to further withdrawals, thereby aggravating the problem. Conversely, solvency problems, by inducing precautionary withdrawals, may quickly generate a liquidity problem, at least in the case of noninsured deposits. If this spreads to other banks, threatening the stability of the banking system as a whole, this is a matter of obvious concern to the lender of last resort, even under the most conservative view of its role. Generally speaking, if a problem (liquidity or solvency) of some bank(s) creates the danger of an imminent liquidity crisis for the system as a whole (conditions for a bank run), then it is a classical duty of the central bank to step in as a lender of last resort and to protect the liquidity level and the money supply of the economy. A key issue is whether central banks should take a macroeconomic view in protecting the liquidity through, for instance, open market operations or whether they should lend directly to the banks facing a deposit outflow.

As mentioned above, the non-existence of, or the very limited coverage offered by, deposit insurance systems and fears of a contagious run help to explain why the lender of last resort (the central bank) also steps in in the case of insolvent banks and provides not just liquidity help but, effectively, public guarantees or even subsidization. Recent cases are the Bank of England with the mid-70s secondary banking crisis and the recent Johnson Matthey Bankers affair or the Federal Reserve with Continental Illinois. These are clearly not 'pure classical' lender of last resort interventions, as liquidity and solvency problems were clearly mixed. The '*de facto*' insurance function of central banks helps to explain why regulation and supervision are often achieved (partially or totally) by central banks. As Volcker expresses it: 'To be effective in carrying out its interrelated responsibilities for monetary policy and the stability of the banking and financial system, the Federal Reserve needs to maintain a strong position as a "hands-on" regulator and supervisor, not just as an advisor or a bystander' (Volcker, 1985, p. 316). Primary central bank responsibility is the case in the United Kingdom, Italy, Netherlands and France. Joint responsibility between the supervisory institution and the central bank applies in Belgium, Germany, Japan, Switzerland and the United States.

As with deposit insurance, lender of last resort assistance, in principle, creates a problem of moral hazard. However, the discretionary nature of lender of last resort support helps somewhat to constrain this adverse effect, compared to institutionalized protective schemes like (flat fee) deposit insurance. For this reason, the precise conditions under which lender of last resort assistance is given are always and consciously left somewhat open and vague. Of course, the danger of moral hazard can also be lowered by making it known that the banks using this form of help will have to pay a penalty rate of interest.

In accordance with the philosophy mentioned above, in numerous countries lender of last resort support can only be granted, in principle, to solvent banks and on a secured basis. Examples for countries where such a policy is stated are the United States, Canada, Germany, Netherlands, or Switzerland. In some countries, help can be granted even when insolvency is at stake (United Kingdom, Belgium, Italy and France). To some extent, of course, these differences may simply reflect the presence or absence of an institutionalized deposit insurance with an established tradition. Where such a tradition exists (United States, Canada) the division of labour is usually such that the insurance body is responsible for problems of insolvency, and the central bank (lender of last resort) for problems of liquidity. However, even where lender of last resort support is allowed only for solvent banks, the crux of the matter is, of course, the precise operational definition of insolvency. Therefore, these distinctions are less clearcut in practice than they are on paper. Also, the above division of labour is hard to enforce when the funding of the insurance scheme is insufficient to cover large losses.

In most countries, the lender of last resort function is performed by the central bank. In some cases, however, another form of government agency can take its place (Hongkong: Exchange Fund), or a mixed institution operated jointly by the authorities and the banks may be created for this purpose (Germany, Belgium). Sometimes the function can even be assumed, to some extent, by a dominant private bank (e.g. Hongkong Bank in Hongkong). Even where the official responsibility rests entirely with the central bank, large private banks frequently become involved in actual rescue operations. Examples: UK clearing houses in the secondary banking crisis of 1973/5, the Banco Ambrosiano case in Italy in 1982, the Herstatt case in Germany in 1974, Continental Illinois in 1984 and Johnson Matthey Bankers in 1985 (these cases resulting from solvency problems originally).

Additional issues arise in the context of international banking. What are the responsibilities of the domestic lender of last resort and deposit insurance system? Do they include the deposits of branches and subsidiaries of domestic banks operating abroad? Do they include the deposits of branches and subsidiaries of foreign banks operating domestically? As far as deposit insurance is concerned, the 'host country' principle applies as only the deposits of domestic and foreign banks operating domestically are insured. The deposits of domestic banks operating abroad are excluded. This is the case in the United States, Netherlands, Belgium, United Kingdom and Germany (Welch, 1981). Furthermore, a distinction has to be made between local currency deposits which are insured and foreign currency deposits which are only insured in the Netherlands and United States. The discretionary nature of lender of last resort facilities prevents a precise definition of responsibility, but the role of central banks in protecting the soundness of national financial markets implies that lender of last resort facilities, when they exist, will be extended to all banks operating domestically. Also, liquidity assistance between the central banks of the Group of Ten is likely to occur in the case of foreign currency withdrawals.

The 'host country' nature of deposit insurance and lender of last resort facilities raises regulatory issues that will be addressed in the next section.

VII Prudential regulation

Deposit insurance, be it explicit or implicit, and similar measures of support involve the danger of moral hazard. As discussed, this is so particularly in the case of flat rate deposit insurance. For this reason, but partly also because of a general distrust of unconstrained competition in banking, governments around the world have subjected banks to a variety of prudential regulations aimed at limiting their risk exposure and their probability of failure. While some types of regulation exist, in one form or another, in practically every country, others are used in some places only, but not in others.

An important kind of control which can be employed in banking as well as in other areas of business is the *control of market entry* through some sort of authorization procedure and licensing practice. In a formal way this kind of control exists in the banking area in every country. As a formal check of adherence to the law and of the professional reputation of prospective management (absence of a record of fradulent behaviour, etc.), this may be seen, along with general banking inspection and supervision, as an obvious and unobjectionable part of any prudential, safety-oriented policy.

However, this form of admission procedure must be clearly distinguished from 'real' entry controls based on the requirement of demonstration of economic 'need' for additional banking facilities (new firms or new branches of existing firms), i.e. a 'public interest' criterion. The objective of this kind of regulation, which usually results from fears of 'overbanking' under unconstrained competition, is to restrain competition and affect market structure by protecting existing banks and their profits. Bhatacharya (1982) discusses how appropriate combinations of entry controls and interest rate ceilings can limit the probability of bank failure. Entry controls, however, have further effects which economists typically are inclined to judge as highly detrimental. For one, they confer monopoly rents on those banks fortunate enough to be admitted, and lead to corresponding inefficiencies, well-known from general economic analysis. In particular, they result in a tendency to prevent bank failures by shielding existing banks, regardless of how inefficient they may be, from competition by new, and potentially more efficient, banks. For this reason, from a long-run perspective, it is not even clear whether the objective of establishing a safe and resilient banking system is actually reached.

Entry controls based on a 'need' criterion are well known, e.g. in the United States. Other countries with similar provisions include Japan, Italy and France (although the actual use of these provisions by admission authorities can differ considerably). In the last two countries, the 'need criterion' should be phased out by 1989, as is provided by the 1977 European Commission directive on 'the coordination of laws, regulations and administrative provisions relating to the taking up and pursuit of the business of credit institutions' (Dassesse and Isaacs, 1985).

In recent years, the emphasis on this kind of 'anticompetition' measure has been somewhat downgraded, as the insight has gained acceptance that competition is basically as healthy and appropriate in banking as in other areas, leading to increased reliance on other methods of regulation.

Another form of regulation which is widely used and has, at least partly, a similar motivation as entry controls is the *control of deposit rates* (through the introduction of rate ceilings, or even the prohibition of payment of interest on certain types of accounts). This kind of regulation, which limits price competition among banks, usually leads to increased reliance on other, substitute forms of competition, for example the provision of free (or underpriced) services to deposit customers (bundling of services), branching, or advertising. But normally this allows only a partial evasion of price controls (costs of evasion, imperfect competition), so that deposit rate regulations retain a certain amount of effectiveness. This generates rents for the controlled institutions, and can create serious distortions in controlled markets when the government-determined rates are much out of line with market-clearing rates. A basically similar situation can result from the setting of cartel rates ('concerted pricing'), although the flexibility of such rates with respect to changes in underlying market conditions is probably greater than in the case of legally fixed rates. Deposit rate controls are sometimes also defended from a monetary policy point of view, rather than a prudential one.

In the case of deposit rate controls, the general tendency again is towards reduced reliance on this sort of regulation, although they have been reinforced in Belgium and France in the last few years. But restrictions still exist in many countries, especially with respect to demand deposits. In Europe, market rates are paid today on demand deposits in Italy (but with concerted pricing) and the United Kingdom; in a limited sense also in Switzerland ('salary accounts', concerted pricing). In a number of other countries, there is an increasing reliance on other types of interest-bearing accounts which can be used for transactions purposes, although normally not with market rates (e.g. Sweden,

Finland, Netherlands, Norway; see Bingham 1985). Deposit rate controls on savings and term deposits were also known in the United States (Regulation Q) but they have been completely phased out since April 1986 (Calem, 1985). With respect to demand deposits, they formally still exist (for business deposits), but have become less and less important during the last decade with the growth of automatic transfer services and other accounts designed to circumvent the legal restrictions. In the case of savings deposits, the trend towards allowing payment of market rates is even clearer.

The easing of controls on entry and deregulation of deposit rates are quite beneficial from an economic efficiency point of view, especially as the risk of failure may be limited by other widely used constraints such as *capital adequacy requirements*. As emphasized before, capital adequacy requirements are necessary with flat rate deposit insurance, because of that system's moral hazard feature which induces banks to lower their capital ratio below what it would be otherwise. Beyond that, it again results from a general distrust of unconstrained competition in banking, even where no deposit insurance of explicit form exists. Capital requirements are necessary not only because they reduce the risk of failure but also because they limit the incentives to take risk. Indeed, the more equity there is, the larger are the shareholders' losses in case of bankruptcy.

Capital adequacy requirements can take a variety of forms. Most countries impose a minimum level of required capital (an absolute amount). Beyond that, many countries require the maintenance of some capital- or solvency-ratio; that is, a minimum ratio between capital and an overall balance sheet magnitude, such as total assets or liabilities, or some weighted measure of risk assets. However, not all countries have such a requirement. No formal and generally applicable capital ratio is established, for example, in Italy, Japan, the United Kingdom, or Canada. Nevertheless, even in these cases, capital adequacy is carefully monitored by the authorities, if in a less formal way. The formal regulations range from relatively simple gearing ratios (e.g. Luxembourg, Germany) to complex risk-weighted arrangements (e.g. Netherlands, Switzerland, France, Belgium).

Important problems in the implementation of such capital adequacy controls are the definition of capital on the one hand (treatment of subordinated debt; hidden reserves, including franchise value of established firms under restricted competition and appropriate valuation of assets; Dermine, 1985), and the determination of 'adequacy' of capital on the other hand (appropriate evaluation of the different risks assumed by banks and their potential consequences). In relation to capital adequacy and solvency controls, a distinction must be made between countries (e.g. the United States) that disclose information (such as non-performing loans, off-balance-sheet business and country exposure) and countries (e.g. Belgium, Germany and Switzerland) which rely heavily on hidden reserves to smooth reported profit and equity.

In analogy to capital adequacy requirements, many countries employ prudentially motivated *liquidity requirements* (as distinguished from monetary policy oriented reserve requirements, which exist in most countries). This is not the case everywhere, however. No formal (prudential) liquidity requirements exist, for example, in the United States, Canada, Japan or Belgium (although the authorities normally monitor liquidity and have the power to regulate it). Countries with formal and in some cases quite complex rules designed to restrict the extent of maturity transformation by intermediaries include the Netherlands, Germany, Switzerland and France. Sometimes, separate restrictions for foreign and domestic currency liquidity are used (France).

Important differences between different countries exist with regard to the regulation of *admissible lines of business*. Some countries have a history of attempting to separate banking from other (nonbank) areas of business by prohibiting or restricting equity investments by banks. Regulations of this sort may partly be based on other (non-prudential) considerations, such as the prevention of concentration of economic power. To some extent, however, they usually reflect prudential concerns, the idea being to exclude common stock investments from bank portfolios because of their high risk – although, from a prudential perspective, it is not quite clear that this kind of constraint is really justified, since from a risk-return efficiency point of view the availability of an additional asset should prove beneficial for bank portfolio performance, rather than detrimental. A less restrictive form of regulation is 'corporate separateness' whereby a risky activity is legally separated from the banking entity.

Two polar types of banking systems resulting from adherence or nonadherence to this kind of control are the universal banking system in, for example, Germany, the United Kingdom, or Switzerland on the one hand (with virtually no restrictions on admissible activities) and the specialized banking system traditionally known in, for example, the United States, Canada, Italy, or Japan on the other hand, with its separation of commercial banking from investment banking. A variety of intermediate positions exist, too, allowing engagement in nonbank activities only indirectly, through the formation of holding companies or subsidiaries, or allowing such an engagement on a limited scope only. For a survey of European practices on equity investments, see Langohr and Santomero (1985).

Finally, almost all countries have *diversification rules* of one sort or another aimed at restricting a bank's loan concentration to individual customers or groups of customers constituting a single economic risk. While the precise form and content of these regulations varies considerably, they normally restrict loans to an individual customer to a certain percentage of the lender bank's capital (15% in the Netherlands, 50% in Belgium, 75% in Germany and 100% in Italy). Sometimes, loans to an individual customer beyond a stated limit are possible, but only under special conditions (e.g. with a higher solvency requirement in the Netherlands and Belgium).

More recent, but similarly oriented areas of concern relate to a bank's loan concentration in individual currencies (foreign currency exposure) or in individual countries (country risk). Foreign currency exposure is monitored by the authorities in most countries today, but formally regulated in some countries only. In Germany, for instance, open positions on foreign currency and precious metal may not exceed 30 percent of own funds. In some cases (e.g. Netherlands, Switzerland) a special capital requirement applies to open positions in foreign currencies. Country risk is monitored increasingly by central banks, but usually no explicit rules have been specified until now.

The regulation and supervision of international banks raise the issue of division of responsibility between the home and host authorities. Since the coverage of deposit insurance and lender of last resort is mostly domestic, it seems logical for supervisors to control the risks taken by banks (domestic and foreign) operating domestically. However, since in many cases there is likely to be pressure on the parent bank to intervene (legal commitment in the case of branches and moral or commercial pressures), one can expect that the parent bank will often be involved in the crisis of its foreign extension and that the supervisors of the parent bank will rightly want to control the bank on a consolidated basis. A case is therefore made for a joint supervision by the host and home authorities. This is the view taken by the Basle Concordat. In June 1983, the European Commission adopted a directive on the supervision of credit institutions on a consolidated basis and, similarly, the United States, Japan and Switzerland control their banks on a consolidated basis (Pecchioli, 1983).

A final question in regulation concerns the type of institutions to include in the prudential net. This is becoming an increasingly important issue as there is a clear tendency for various types of financial (and non-financial) institutions to offer a full range of financial services. Some countries have already merged several regulatory agencies. For instance, in Belgium and France commercial banks and savings banks are regulated by the same supervisor. An opposite case is the United Kingdom where commercial banks are regulated by the Bank of England while the building societies fall under the supervision of the Chief Registrar of Friendly Societies. Also, to provide a 'fair level playing field', there is the issue in the United Kingdom of organizing supervision along functional lines (rather than institutional), so that the same prudential rules would be applied to banks and non-banks.

VIII Conclusions

The cross-country, comparative survey on institutional structures reveals both common trends and differences. Most countries are heading towards formal deposit insurance systems with flat premium and limited coverage. This creates a need for lender of last resort facilities and recent interventions show that the liquidity and solvency motives are often blurred. Major differences appear in prudential rules such as loan limits, capital and liquidity ratios, 'economic need' criteria or foreign exchange positions. The progressive abandonment of control on entry, the deregulation of deposit and loan pricing and the recent emphasis on capital adequacy have improved the efficiency of the banking systems. Substantial progress remains to be made with respect to the disclosure of information and the pricing of deposit insurance. Imperfect information being the principal source of market failure, it seems to us that increasing disclosure will improve market discipline, and reduce moral hazard incentives and the danger of contagious runs. As to insurance premiums, they should be related to the risks taken by the individual banks in much the same way as capital requirements are related to their asset structure. The integration of financial markets both at the domestic and international levels and the arrival of non-financial firms on the markets will no doubt create a need for a major rethinking of regulation, deposit insurance and lender of last resort mechanisms.

REFERENCES

Baltensperger, E. (1972). 'Economies of Scale, Firm Size, and Concentration in Banking', *Journal of Money, Credit, and Banking* **4**.
  (1980). 'Alternative Approaches to the Theory of the Banking Firm', *Journal of Monetary Economics* **6**.
  (1982). 'Reserve Requirement and Economic Stability', *Journal of Money, Credit, and Banking* **14**.

Batchelor, R. A. and M. D. Fitzgerald (1982). 'The Regulation of Financial Markets and Financial Institutions', in *Geld, Banken und Versicherungen*, Vol. II (Göpp, H. and Henn, R., eds) Karlsruhe.

Benston, G. J. (1983). 'Deposit Insurance and Bank Failures', *Economic Review*, Federal Reserve Bank of Atlanta.

Benston, G. J., G. A. Hanweck, and D. B. Humphrey (1982). 'Scale Economies in Banking', *Journal of Money, Credit, and Banking* **14**.

Bernanke, B. S. (1983). 'Nonmonetary Effects of the Financial Crisis in the Propagation of the Great Depression', *American Economic Review* **73**.

Bhatacharya, S. (1982). 'Aspects of Monetary and Banking Theory and Moral Hazard', *Journal of Finance* **37**.

Bingham, T. R. G. (1985). *Banking and Monetary Policy*, OECD, Paris.

Black, F., M. H. Miller, and R. A. Posner (1978). 'An Approach to the Regulation of Bank Holding Companies', *Journal of Business* **51**.

Calem, P. (1985). *The New Bank Deposit Market, Good Bye to Regulation Q*, Federal Reserve Bank of Philadelphia.

Cooper, K. and D. R. Fraser (1984). *Banking Deregulation and the New Competition in Financial Services*, Cambridge, Mass.

Dale, R. (1982). *Bank Supervision Around the World*, Group of Thirty, New York.

(1984). *The Regulation of International Banking*, Cambridge.

Dassesse, M. and S. Isaacs (1985). *EC Banking Law*, Lloyds of London Press, London.

Dermine, J. (1985). *Accounting Framework for Banks, a Market Value Approach*, SUERF Series.

(1986). 'Deposit Rate, Credit Rate and Bank Capital: the Klein-Monti Model Revisited', *Journal of Banking and Finance* **10**.

Diamond, D. and P. Dybvig (1983). 'Bank Runs, Deposit Insurance and Liquidity', *Journal of Political Economy* **91**.

Friedman, M. (1959). *A Program for Monetary Stability*, New York.

Gilligan, T., M. Smirlock, and W. Marshall (1984). 'Scale and Scope Economies in the Multiproduct Banking Firm', *Journal of Monetary Economics* **13**.

Humphrey, T. M. (1975). 'The Classical Concept of the Lender of Last Resort', *Economic Review*, Federal Reserve Bank of Richmond.

Johnson, G. and R. Abrams (1983). 'Aspects of the International Safety Net', *Occasional Paper 17, International Monetary Fund*.

Kane, E. J. (1985). 'The Gathering Crisis in Federal Deposit Insurance', Cambridge, Mass.

(1986). 'Appearance and Reality in Deposit Insurance; The Case for Reform', *Journal of Banking and Finance* **10**.

Kareken, J. H. and N. Wallace (1978). 'Deposit Insurance and Bank Regulation: A Partial-Equilibrium Exposition', *Journal of Business* **51**.

Langohr, H. and A. M. Santomero (1985). 'The Extent of Equity Investment by European Banks', *Journal of Money, Credit, and Banking* **17**.

Meltzer, A. H. (1967). 'Major Issues in the Regulation of Financial Institutions', *Journal of Political Economy* **75**.

Pecchioli, R. (1983). *The Internationalization of Banking*, OECD, Paris.

Volcker, P. A. (1985). 'Statement Before the Subcommittee on Commerce, Consumer and Monetary Affairs, of the Committee on Government

Operations, U.S. House of Representatives, March 27, 1985', *Federal Reserve Bulletin*, May.
Welch J. (1981). *The Regulation of Banks in the Member States of the EEC*, The Hague.

3 The design of bank regulation and supervision: some lessons from the theory of finance

STEPHEN M. SCHAEFER*

I Introduction

Bank regulators and supervisors have an important and increasingly difficult job. Their responsibilities include: ensuring the integrity of the payments mechanism, protecting the interests of depositors and promoting efficiency in the banking sector. At present they must carry out these tasks against a background of highly variable asset markets, an unprecedented increase in the number and variety of financial instruments which banks trade and in which they have positions and against the complexities created by the growing internationalization of banking and financial markets.

Despite all this, the task of banking supervision has attracted relatively little public debate.[1] Moreover, much of what little debate there has been has taken place in the wake of one or other of the more spectacular bank failures, and has given little consideration to the methods and approach used by regulators.

In this paper I want to consider some aspects of the regulator's task from a theory-of-finance perspective. It is certainly not my claim that financial theory provides a panacea for the many problems which banking supervision presents. But I hope to show that it is useful in some areas, e.g. risk assessment and the regulation of bank capital, and I shall focus on these. Most of the discussion in this paper refers to the system of supervision used in the UK though, for our purposes, the similarities between the UK and other countries, particularly the US, are more important than the differences.

II Do the sums matter?

The process of bank supervision is in large measure a private discussion between the supervisor and the supervised. Hints of the substance of the discussion sometimes emerge through, for example, the decision of a bank to raise capital or to divest itself of a particular asset. However, the details of the supervisory process are unobservable to the outsider and, whether or not such discretion is actually necessary, it undoubtedly makes public debate more difficult.

Part of the supervisory process involves the use of technical tools for tasks such as risk assessment. The details of these methods are usually in the public domain although often the data they require is not. There are many examples here, e.g., the Bank of England's Risk Asset Ratio and Gearing Ratio, and the Federal Reserve's 'ABC' form.[2] What is much less clear, however, is the way that these tools are actually used. Certainly supervisors do not rely on them exclusively: discretion and judgement play an important role. This means that technical measures are not viewed as *sufficient* to determine, say, capital adequacy. It may even be the case that the calculation of formal risk and gearing measures is no more than a way of organizing the data for informal discussions. In this case supervisors may not regard the development of more reliable technical measures (of risk, for example) as important. On the other hand, it may be that supervisors place little weight on these formal methods because they are seen as unreliable. If so, improvements may induce supervisors to shift the balance between the formal and informal parts of the process.

III   Measuring the risk of bank asset portfolios

Much of the technical apparatus of the regulation of financial institutions has to do with risk assessment. Examples include the two already mentioned, the Bank of England's Risk Asset Ratio, and the Fed's 'ABC' form, as well as the Bank of England's recently introduced system of supervision for gilt-edged market makers.[3]

What measure is appropriate for assessing the risk of bank assets? The correct approach will depend on the form of both the joint distribution of asset values and the associated loss function, but a simple metric, widely used in portfolio theory, is the standard deviation of asset value. The relationship between the standard deviation of the value of total bank assets and the standard deviation of individual assets is:

$$\sigma_v = (\sum_i \sum_j x_i\, x_j \sigma_{ij})^{1/2} \qquad (1)$$

where σ_v is the standard deviation of the change in value of total assets, x_i is the quantity held of asset i, $i = 1, \ldots, N$ and σ_{ij} is the covariance between the changes in value per unit of asset i and changes in value per unit of asset j. If we define K as the difference between the market value

Table 3.1. **Bank of England risk asset ratio**

	Weight	Example asset
(i)	0.0	Notes and Coin
		Deposits with Bank of England
(ii)	0.1	Foreign Currency; Notes and Coin; Treasury Bills
(iii)	0.2	Market Loans with Banks
		Gilts up to 18 months Maturity
(iv)	0.5	Gilts Over 18 Months
		Guarantees and Contingent Liabilities
(v)	1.0	Advances
(vi)	1.5	Connected Lending
(vii)	2.0	Property

Source: Bank of England Quarterly Bulletin (1980).

of assets and the default-free value of non-capital (assume riskless) liabilities, and if asset values are normally distributed, the probability that K becomes negative depends on the ratio

$$\frac{K}{(\sum_i \sum_j x_i x_j \sigma_{ij})^{1/2}} \qquad (2)$$

where K is the value of capital.[4]

It is interesting to compare expression (2) with the form of the risk asset ratio. This is defined as the adjusted capital base divided by the 'adjusted total of risk assets'. The latter is defined by:

$$\sum_i x_i w_i \qquad (3)$$

where x_i is the amount of asset category i and w_i is the corresponding 'risk weight'. The risk weights used by the Bank of England are shown in Table 3.1. The risk asset ratio is therefore given by:

$$\frac{K}{\sum x_i w_i} \qquad (4)$$

In very broad terms, then, there is a correspondence between the ratio (2) and the risk asset ratio (4). Ignoring questions to do with the definition of capital, the risk asset ratio will be a good proxy for expression (2) if the adjusted total of risk assets is a good proxy for the standard deviation of the changes in value of the risky asset portfolio (1). Some differences between (3) and (1) are obvious. Firstly, (3) is a linear function of the asset quantities x_i whereas (1) is non-linear. Secondly, and more fundamentally, (3) depends only on quantities connected with each individual asset whereas (1) depends on quantities which have to do with the interdependence between asset values, the covariances. This difference is by no means unimportant. For example, with a large number of assets and an equal investment in each, the variance of a portfolio depends *entirely* on the covariances. The only circumstances when (1) and (3) coincide exactly, irrespective of the quantities x_i, is when there is perfect positive correlation between all asset values. The evidence presented in Section V suggests that these conditions have little empirical relevance in the case of banking assets.

In the risk asset ratio the risk weights are fixed, as if they represented a set of accounting rules or statutory requirements. There is, on the other hand, ample evidence that relevant risk measures, such as the variability in, and the correlation between rates of return on different asset classes, change over time.[5] A system which implicitly assumes that risk measures are constant is unlikely to achieve any great degree of reliability.

The use of fixed versus changing risk measures raises another, rather different, problem. Other things being equal, the methods of assessment that bank supervisors use should be both simple and sufficiently stable over time that banks are able to take regulatory constraints into account in their own planning (on capital structure, for example). But there is no reason to suppose that the requirements of simplicity, stability *and* accuracy are mutually compatible. Measures such as the risk asset ratio place more weight on the first two of these criteria. As banks become more sophisticated in their own techniques for managing risk it may be appropriate to re-examine the emphasis in supervision.

IV   Further aspects of risk in supervision

The risk asset ratio focuses on the risk of the asset portfolio and the quantity of capital. As shown earlier, this is appropriate if non-capital liabilities bear no risk. If this condition does not hold, then three further issues arise.

First, suppose that non-capital liabilities consist entirely of deposits which pay the default-free floating interest rate. If there were no default risk the value of these liabilities would always equal their face value. With default risk, the value of capital *and* deposits will depend on the value of assets. If depositors bear part of the risk of the bank's assets, then the risk asset ratio approach will tend to overstate the risk, and understate the value, of capital.

Secondly, suppose that the deposits in the previous example paid a fixed interest rate. Now, if some of the assets are also fixed rate, the presence of fixed-interest-rate liabilities will reduce the risk attached to capital. In this case issuing fixed-rate liabilities hedges fixed-rate assets and some 'netting-off' of fixed-rate assets against fixed-rate liabilities is appropriate.[6]

Thirdly, many banks nowadays engage in a wide variety of contracts which do not fit easily into the categories included in the risk asset ratio. Examples here include futures contracts, options of various types, loan commitments, underwriting agreements and so forth. The risk and value of these contracts, particularly in the case of options, can change substantially with changes in the price of underlying assets. The use of fixed risk weights is therefore even less appropriate in these cases than in the case of more conventional assets. Assessing the value and risk of such contracts is often technically more involved than in the case of more conventional securities. There is, however, a substantial body of theory – option pricing theory and contingent claims analysis – which can be applied to these problems.[7] It is also worth mentioning that increasingly this theory forms the basis of valuation, hedging and risk assessment procedures used by banks themselves. The theory is also applicable to the first problem described in this section, that of risky deposits.

V   An alternative linear risk measure

The linear risk measure implicit in the risk asset ratio – the 'adjusted total of risk assets' – has the great virtue of simplicity. How can this important feature be preserved if the risk measure is also to capture correctly the covariance between different asset classes?

A solution to this problem is possible if the asset portfolios of individual banks are sufficiently similar. Define the 'risk weight' z_i as the covariance between the change in value of an individual asset i and the change in value of the portfolio:

$$z_i = \text{cov} \left(\Delta v_i, \sum_j x_j \, \Delta v_j \right) \tag{5}$$

where Δv_i is the change in value of one unit of asset i and x_i is the number of units of asset i which are held. The relationship between the risk weights z_i and the variance of the asset portfolio, σ_v^2 is simply,

$$\sigma_v^2 = \sum_i x_i \, z_i \tag{6}$$

The viability of this approach depends on bank asset portfolios being sufficiently similar that common covariance measures can be employed. If this condition is not met then the full form of (1) must be used. It is also worth noting that (6) gives the variance rather than the standard deviation and so, to compute the denominator of (2) – the analogue

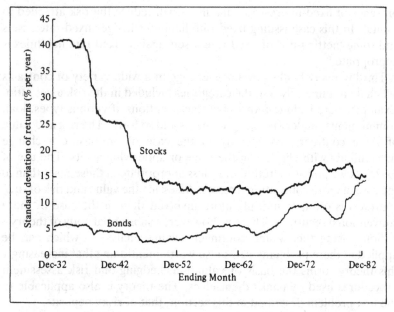

Figure 3.1   Standard deviations of bond and stock indices 1927–82.
Source: Sharpe (1985).
Note: Standard deviations taken over five-year periods.

of the adjusted total of risk assets – we must first take the square root of
(6).

One of the features of the approach suggested here is that it is quite
explicit about the nature of the risk weights. In the Bank of England's
risk asset ratio the interpretation of the weights is left (perhaps deliberately) vague:

> ... the standard risk asset calculation will take into account three types
> of risk inherent in the assets themselves but that weightings should be
> applied to different assets reflecting the extent to which they are
> susceptible to these risks. The three types of risk are: (i) credit risk ...,
> (ii) investment risk ... (iii) forced sale risk. (*Bank of England Quarterly
> Bulletin*, September 1980)

The z_i's in the alternative approach depend on the proportions of each
asset class in bank portfolios and on the covariance matrix of changes in
asset value. The latter must be estimated, most probably from past data
and, in contrast to the weights in the risk asset ratio, it is extremely
unlikely that these will remain constant over time. Figure 3.1 shows the
standard deviations of representative equity and bond indices in the US
over the period 1932–84. Even over the past 20 years there have been
substantial changes in the estimates. For example, the standard deviation

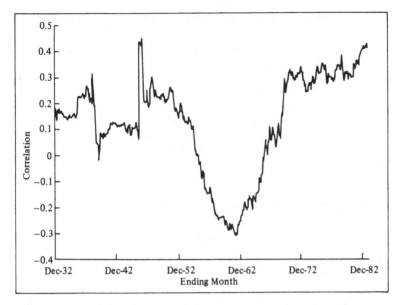

Figure 3.2   Correlation between bond and stock indices 1927–82.
Sources: Sharpe (1985).
Note: Correlation taken over five-year periods.

of bond returns has increased from around 5% to nearly 15% per annum and, even more strikingly, the correlation between bonds and equities (Figure 3.2) has reversed in sign: from around −0.3 to +0.3. Differences of this magnitude would clearly have a substantial effect on the z_is and, while it would be convenient if the situation were otherwise, to ignore such changes would be to throw away much of the benefit that a more soundly based system might bring.

Implementation of a system of risk assessment along these lines involves first allocating bank assets to a number of classes in much the same way as in the adjusted total of risk assets. To illustrate this approach, Table 3.2 shows assets divided into four categories: sterling market loans, UK gilts, UK advances and foreign currency assets. The proportions in Table 3.2 are aggregate data for UK banks averaged over the period November 1984–December 1985.[8] These data are book values; wherever possible, and particularly in the case of advances, it would be preferable to use market values.

The asset categories in Table 3.2 are not those that would be used in a practical application of this approach. The category of 'Foreign currency assets', in particular, is too broad to be useful and the distribution of assets by currency and by type would be important. The same applies to advances in general, whether in domestic or foreign currency, as default

Table 3.2. **Average asset category proportions for UK clearing banks, 1984–5**

Asset category	Average % in balance sheet	Proxy
Sterling market loans	14	Salomons UK Treasury bill index
Gilts	3	FT gilt index (5–15 year)
Sterling advances	42	Salomons Eurosterling bond index
Foreign currency assets	41	Salomons Eurodollar FRN index

Source: Committee of London and Scottish Bankers, Statistical Unit (1986).

risk may vary substantially across different loans in the portfolio. At the portfolio level, risk will depend significantly on the extent to which the portfolio is diversified. A well diversified portfolio of loans, each of which has a high probability of default but where the risks are independent across loans, will have less risk than a portfolio where the loans have lower default risk but where the risks are highly correlated. Thus 'average loan quality', i.e. the average probability of default, is a good guide to the expected cash flow on a loan portfolio but a poor guide to its risk. Some measure of diversification *within* the loan portfolio would therefore be important in practice.

Implementation of the proposed linear risk measure requires estimates of the covariances between different asset categories, and to estimate these we require proxies for the rates of return. There are many possibilities here and the proxies used in the calculations which follow are put forward in order to illustrate the approach rather than as those which regulators, with better information on the characteristics of individual assets, would use.

Finding suitable proxies for rates of return on sterling Treasury bills and gilts is relatively straightforward. For bills we use an index computed by Salomon Brothers and for gilts we use the FTA 5–15 year gilt price index.[9] On the other hand the task of finding appropriate proxies for advances, both domestic and foreign, is much more difficult. The ideal proxy would be a traded instrument which mirrors the changes in market value of the net asset in question. For sterling advances we face two problems. First, the market for corporate debt in the UK is neither extensive nor particularly active. The second problem is that most traded corporate debt in the UK is fixed rate whereas most bank debt is floating rate. Both fixed- and floating-rate debt will be influenced by changes in

Table 3.3. **Summary statistics and relative risk weights for bank asset categories**

	T-bills	Gilts	Sterling advances	Foreign currency assets	Portfolio
(a) Portfolio weights and monthly standard deviation of rates of return					
Weight in portfolio	0.14	0.03	0.42	0.41	1.00
Annualised S.D. of returns (% p.a.)	0.80	10.53	7.97	12.47	5.54
(b) Correlation coefficients					
T-bills	1.00	0.36	0.25	−0.23	
Gilts		1.00	0.70	−0.21	
Sterling advances			1.00	−0.22	
Foreign currency assets				1.00	
Portfolio	−0.02	0.30	0.45	0.77	
(c) Relative risk weights					
$\hat{z}_i$ (see text)	−0.001	0.063	1.000	2.644	
Risk Asset Ratio	0.100	0.500	1.000	1.000	

default risk, but fixed-rate debt has greater sensitivity to interest rate changes. Traded floating-rate debt would be quite appropriate but no publicly available index exists for sterling instruments of this type.

In the absence of a sterling floating-rate index we have used a fixed-rate index. One possibility we investigated was the FT – Debenture Index but its behaviour appeared anomalous at various times and we have instead used the Salomon Brothers Eurosterling bond index.[10] This is not an ideal choice both because it is based on fixed-rate instruments and because it reflects the idiosyncracies of the Euromarket. It is, however, adequate for purposes of illustration.

The problems in the case of foreign loans are compounded by the need to reflect the distribution of loans by currency. In our example we assume that all foreign loans are denominated in US dollars and we use the Salomon Brothers Eurodollar floating-rate-note index as a proxy.[11] Rates of return are computed from the sterling price of the index.

Panel (a) of Table 3.3 gives the annualised standard deviation of monthly returns on the four asset category proxies described above together with the asset proportions given earlier. The individual standard deviations range from 0.80% p.a. for Treasury bills to 12.47% for Foreign Currency assets. It is also interesting to note that the weighted average standard deviation of 8.9% is over 60% higher than the true standard deviation (one interpretation of the adjusted total of risk assets) on the portfolio of 5.54%.

Surprisingly, the standard deviation of returns on (risky) Sterling Advances (7.9%) in Table 3.3 is significantly lower than the standard deviation of (default-free) gilts (10.53%). There are several possible reasons for this including the different maturity characteristics of the two indices used. If this is the reason it serves to emphasise the importance of interest rate risk.

Similarly, currency risk represents a large fraction of the risk associated with foreign currency assets. As described earlier the index for foreign currency assets is computed as the sterling price of a Eurodollar floating-rate-note index. Denominated in dollars, the annualised standard deviation of return is only 1.4% p.a. The difference between this figure and the standard deviation of the same index denominated in sterling (12.5% p.a.) is accounted for entirely by fluctuations in the exchange rate.

Panel (b) in Table 3.3 gives the correlation coefficients between the rates of return on the asset categories and between each asset category and the portfolio. Finally, the risk weights in Panel (c) are derived using expression (5) and the estimates in Panels (a) and (b). Expression (5) defines the risk weight z_i as the covariance between the value change for asset category i and the value change for the portfolio. In the Bank of England's Risk Asset Ratio the weights are defined relative to the weight for Sterling Advances. Therefore, if we define:

$$\hat{z}_i = z_i / z_A, \tag{7}$$

where z_A is the risk weight for Sterling advances, the revised risk weights can be compared directly with the Bank of England weights. The relative risk weight $\hat{z}_i$ may be written as:

$$\hat{z}_i = \frac{\alpha_i \, \sigma_i \, \varrho_{iP}}{\alpha_A \, \sigma_A \, \varrho_{Ap}} \tag{8}$$

where α_i is the fraction of the portfolio invested in asset i, σ_i is the standard deviation of the rate of return on asset i and ϱ_{ip} is the correlation between the rate of return on asset i and the rate of return on the portfolio. The subscript 'A' denotes Sterling advances, the numeraire asset. Using (8) the risk weights $\hat{z}_i$ may be computed from the data in Panels (a) and (b) of Table 3.3; these are given in Panel (c) together with the corresponding Risk Asset Ratio weights. The nature of the proxies used for the asset categories means that the results should be treated with some caution. Nonetheless the substantial differences between the two sets of weights are interesting. In particular, the results certainly do not suggest that the risk asset ratio weights will approximate the $\hat{z}_i$ weights for any plausible proxies for rates of return on the assets.

VI   The bank capital structure puzzle

An important part of the reason that bank supervisors monitor the risk of bank assets is to decide on the minimum quantity of capital which a bank ought to have. There are two reasons why this monitoring on the part of supervisors might be necessary. First, banks might wish to adopt the same approach as supervisors but make mistakes. Bank supervisors in this case merely check the bank's calculations. The second reason is that banks might want to have less capital than supervisors think is necessary. For monitoring to be required in these cases the cost of bank capital must exceed the (risk adjusted) cost of other liabilities. If this were not the case supervisors could set a minimum capital requirement which was sufficiently high to eliminate the risk of failure and, if capital were no more costly than other forms of funding, banks would find it costless to comply with this requirement.

Among practical bankers there appears to be an oral tradition that capital is indeed more expensive than non-capital liabilities. For example, in an article in the financial press on the recent moves towards harmonisation in UK and US banking supervision, the author referred to the desire on the part of UK and US supervisors to extend their system to other countries:

> They will now be leaning on their counterparts in other countries to get things moving. Their main target will be Japan which has frequently been accused of *allowing its banks to operate with low capital levels, which gives them a useful cost advantage.* (*Financial Times*, 9th January 1987, emphasis added)

Despite (in the author's experience at least) the prevalence of this view it is difficult to find written accounts of the basis of the hypothesis, perhaps because it is regarded as self-evident. In contrast, most financial economists would not accept as in any way self-evident the proposition that one form of funding is, on a risk adjusted basis, cheaper than another. The dominant paradigm in this context is the Modigliani–Miller (M&M 1958) theorem and, while refinements to the original argument have been suggested (most notably by M&M themselves in 1963 and by Miller in 1977) the main thrust of their argument would still find much support.[12] Perhaps the first question a financial economist would ask is: What is special about banking that makes capital (and in particular equity capital) costly whereas we see no evidence of a similar preoccupation in other industries? Successful non-bank companies, e.g., IBM and Shell, do not seem to think that, in order to compete, they must operate on the smallest possible equity base.

There are several ways in which economists might rationalize the incentive to minimise capital, but few of these would find much support among bankers. For example, if deposit insurance, whether explicit or implicit, is under-priced it is in the interests of banks to increase the risk of assets and to minimise the amount of capital.

It must be admitted that the M&M theory is not an ideal framework within which to analyse the problem of bank capital. The original theory depends on the existence of complete markets and this seems a poor standpoint from which to analyse financial intermediaries. Presumably, if markets were actually complete, there would be no role for inter-mediaries. It may very well be that the practical bankers are right and there is a well founded incentive on the part of banks to minimize capital. Simply knowing this, however, does not enable the supervisor to carry out his task fully; he also needs to know why.

VII   Conclusions

Over the past 25 years financial economics has advanced considerably in areas such as portfolio theory, the pricing of risky assets and corporate finance. Many of the problems faced by bank supervisors are, in principle, amenable to the methods of financial economics but, at least as regards the public aspects of supervision, they do not appear to be much used. This paper has attempted to show how the basic tools of portfolio theory can be used to highlight some shortcomings of the methods of risk assessment currently used in banking supervision and how alternative measures can be formulated.

It goes without saying that the approach proposed in this paper has its own drawbacks. But at least the new theory is explicit about what it is the method is intended to measure. It would therefore be possible, in principle, to establish the degree of precision that the method had under different conditions. In contrast, some of the measures currently used by supervisors appear to involve rather too much in the way of definition and too little in the way of measurement. As markets become more complex and participants more sophisticated, perhaps it is time to re-examine the balance.

NOTES

* I should like to acknowledge the many helpful discussions I have had with Harold Rose on this topic and also the very capable research assistance provided by Ian Rowley. Responsibility for the remaining shortcomings of the paper rest firmly with the author.
1 Deposit insurance is an exception here. See e.g., Merton (1977) and papers in a Symposium on Bank Regulation published in the *Journal of Business* (January, 1986).
2 *Bank of England Quarterly Bulletin* (1980), and Board of Governors of the Federal Reserve System (1956).
3 Bank of England (1985).
4 If non-capital liabilities are fixed then the standard deviation of K is equal to the standard deviation of the value of assets.
5 See Section V.
6 Duration provides a simple measure of the degree of interest rate sensitivity of an asset. See e.g. Schaefer (1984).
7 See e.g., Black and Scholes (1973), and Brealey and Myers (1984), chapter 20.
8 The data in Table 3.2 are asset proportions for London clearing banks averaged over the values for November 1984 and September 1985. Source: Committee of London and Scottish Bankers (1986).
9 The Treasury Bill index is taken from Weher and Badyna (1986). The FTA Gilt indices are published daily in the *Financial Times*.
10 Weher and Badyna (1986).
11 Weher and Badyna (1986).
12 Modigliani and Miller (1958, 1963) and Miller (1977).

REFERENCES

Bank of England Quarterly Bulletin (1985). 'The Future Structure of the Gilt Edged Market' (April).
(1980). 'The Measurement of Capital', **20**, No. 3 (September), pp. 324–30.
Black, F. and M. Scholes (1973). 'The Pricing of Options and Corporate Liabilities', *Journal of Political Economy* **81**, pp. 637–54 (May–June).
Board of Governors of the Federal Reserve System (1956). Form for Analyzing Bank Capital (April).
Brealey, R. A. and S. C. Myers (1984). *Principles of Corporate Finance*, McGraw-Hill (2nd edition).
Committee of London and Scottish Bankers, Statistical Unit (1986). *Abstract of Banking Statistics* **3** (May).
Merton, R. C. (1977). 'An Analytic Derivation of the Cost of Deposit Insurance and Loan Guarantees; an Application of Modern Option Pricing Theory'. *Journal of Banking and Finance* **1**, pp. 3–11 (March).
Miller, M. H. (1977). 'Debt and Taxes', *Journal of Finance* **32**, pp. 261–76 (May).
Modigliani, F. and M. H. Miller (1958). 'The Cost of Capital, Corporation Finance and The Theory of Investment', *American Economic Review* **48**, pp. 261–97 (June).

(1963). 'Corporate Income Taxes and the Cost of Capital: A Correction', *American Economic Review* **53**, pp. 433–43 (June).

Schaefer, S. M. (1984). 'Duration and Immunisation: A Review of Theory, Performance and Applications', *Midland Corporate Finance Journal* **2**, pp. 41·58.

Sharpe, W. F. (1985). *Investments*, 3rd edition, Prentice Hall.

Weher, K. P. and S. Badyna (1986). 'International Bond and Money Market Performance, 1978–1985', Salomon Brothers.

Discussion

ROBERT R. BENCH

The purpose of this short note is to discuss briefly and generally the design of bank regulation and supervision, in response to the Chairman's request.

Just about every country in the world has established public policies for the regulation and supervision of banks, since banks are the depositories of the public's savings, allocators of capital in the economy and managers of nations' payments systems. The policies vary depending on the history of each country's governance. For instance, authorities for bank regulation and supervision may be delegated to a concentrated point, such as the central bank, or the delegation may be dispersed among a number of parties, as in the US, where the Federal Reserve, OCC, FDIC, SEC, Congressional Committees, and the public at large all participate in policy development as well as the direction of regulatory and supervisory activities. The history of governance also will determine the degree of regulation and supervision in particular areas such as market entry, degrees of competition, and the variety of product and asset powers banks may have. US governance traditionally promotes a banking system comprising thousands of banks with limited geographical and product powers. Governance in other countries permits banking systems comprising a relatively small number of very large banks which can operate on a nation-wide basis and in all areas of finance.

One aspect of governance common to all countries is that the regulatory and supervisory schemes support the lender of last resort, deposit insurance, and/or investor of last resort functions that governments may have to perform to maintain confidence in the financial system. During any government assistance effort, the central decision makers need current and accurate information to determine the level of assistance required. Without such information, the government may under-react or over-react to a problem, thus exacerbating it. While crisis assistance is never an exact science, the more decision makers know about a problem, the better the assistance they can provide to restore confidence.

The regulatory and supervisory process in all countries usually covers three areas: corporate authorizations, risk assessment, and sanctions. The corporate process authorizes new charters, geographical and product expansion, mergers and acquisition, and bank failure. The risk assessment function determines the risks in individual bank operations, the condition of each bank in the system and the condition of the banking system. Risk assessment traditionally has been a static, point-in-time analysis. Increasingly, supervisors are making this assessment process more dynamic, assessing risks prospectively by learning more about banks' future operations and strategies. Sanctions comprise the enforcement and compliance process which can include formal agreements, cease and desist orders, removal of bank management, civil penalties and criminal penalties.

This conference is focusing on risks. Supervisors' methodologies for assessing risks vary from country to country. A methodology common to all countries is assessment of banks' risk through the analysis of data which banks submit in prudential returns. This off-site assessment may be supplemented in some countries with on-site visitations by supervisors and/or bank audits by firms selected by the supervisors. In the US, regular on-site examinations by supervisory staff, supplemented by visitations and off-site computerized performance analysis, provide US supervisors with continual flows of current and accurate information on banks' condition. A corps of trained professional examiners, knowledgeable about bank operations, can provide governments with immediate and valuable assistance in sorting out a bank problem.

The assessment of capital adequacy is a fundamental aspect of bank supervision. Capital is required to start a banking business as well as to make investments in fixed assets and subsidiaries. It also provides a disciplined measure of bank management's performance. Capital can be used to absorb unexpected losses, match certain risks and maintain market confidence, although market expectations for capital vary with changing perceptions of risks in the banking system. The determination of capital adequacy is difficult, however. There is first the problem of how to define capital, and second, there is the problem of how to measure capital adequacy. The definition of capital may vary depending on what are considered as the components of bank capital, such as hidden reserves, inner reserves, or loan loss reserves.

Common measures of capital adequacy are gearing ratios, such as the ratio of capital to assets or capital to liabilities. However, these measures do not include off-balance-sheet activities. The other common measure is the risk-weighted approach, which tries to relate risks borne by banks to their capital. However, financial liberalization is changing this traditional risk measurement, which generally concentrated on the riskiness of the various kinds of assets banks held. While some of these risks remain, they may be reduced or eliminated through newly developed hedging techniques. In addition, open dealing positions, interest-rate sensitivity, concentrations of credit, sovereign risks, as well as off-balance-sheet risks are expanding and traditionally have not been included in risk-weighted assessments of capital adequacy.

Bank supervisors in many countries, including the US, are revising their capital adequacy measurements to incorporate these changes arising from the new activities of banks. Active work is going on nationally as well in the Basle Supervisors Committee. The main job here for all supervisors seems to be to forge ahead and provide leadership on the subject, achieve compatibility on definitional and measurement questions, establish a simple framework and methodology which addresses the obvious questions, and implement the scheme with enough bite that bankers take it seriously.

Financial liberalization and innovation also oblige supervisors to review their traditional attitudes to and measurement of liquidity, especially in a cross-currency environment. While supervisors should continue to insist on some survival stock of liquid assets, the marketization of finance also requires supervisors to view liquidity as a dynamic phenomenon in banks rather than as a static, point-in-time measurement. Supervision of bank liquidity needs to go beyond stock and flow concepts to dynamic considerations, such as: overall balance sheet symmetry, variety and sensitivity of funding sources available, asset credit concentrations, assets that can be securitized and the market's perception of a bank's current and future asset quality, as well as present and future earning capacity. Overall, the supervision of banks' liquidity has become very complex and supervisors are revising their expectations about the adequacy of banks' internal controls, management reports, and contingency plans for managing liquidity.

The design of bank regulation and supervision is also concentrating more on the quality of management and earnings capacity during this period of financial change. As the business of banking changes, new skills and knowledge are required of bank management. The changing business also leads to new sources of income. The quality of those earnings and the abilities of bank managements to plan, control, and respond to change are becoming more important considerations in the assessment of banks' conditions.

In this regard, there *is* a private side to bank regulation and supervision in those countries where governance promotes private ownership of banks. It is first and foremost the responsibility of banks' management and directors to establish the policies, practices and procedures for the banks under their fiduciary stewardship. Second, communities of banks have responsibilities for establishing standards and controls for bank activities. Third, public disclosure and accuracy of financial statements are the responsibilities of public accountants. Fourth, financial innovation in banks' liability products, securitization of banks' assets, and expanded distribution of banks' capital instruments have led to the development of 'private supervisors' which increasingly rate or grade the financial assets distributed by banks. Greater disclosure by banks and the increase in rating services creates market discipline as a supplement to official regulation and supervision of banking.

Finally, the design of bank regulation and supervision increasingly incorporates the needs to be more internationally compatible as well as more integrated with securities regulation and supervision. While financial liberalization is bringing mutual opportunities to the world, it may also raise mutual vulnerabilities. In response, bank regulators and supervisors are developing broader and more dynamic ways to ensure financial stability during this period of change.

Discussion

HAROLD B. ROSE

Like Professor Schaefer I want to take up the question of capital ratio control and the problems caused by the crude allocation of risk co-efficients to asset classes such as that adopted by the Bank of England. As Professor Schaefer says, it is not clear how seriously regulators treat such systems; but in Britain, at any rate, banks do use such prescribed risk weightings to determine the rate of return required from different assets.

A system that is intellectually flawed has practical consequences for bank pricing and resource allocation.

In addition to the distortions that arise from the prescription of risk coefficients that take little account of co-variances, an important set of problems results when the laudable desire to avoid overcomplication leads, as in the Bank of England's method, to the allocation of a single risk coefficient to bank advances as a whole. Banks are still free to allocate their own risk ratings to individual classes of loan, but the (minimum) risk rating for advances as a whole is prescribed by the regulators. This means that banks which depart from a 'representative' portfolio are obliged to assign risk coefficients for *individual* assets classes that are different from those in the 'representative' portfolio. For example, a bank which has an unusually high proportion of low-risk business, such as mortgage loans, will be penalized. The system could actually encourage banks to tilt their loan portfolios in the direction of risky advances, which is presumably not what the supervisors intend.

Do capital ratios matter in a free market? Financial theory has gone through several stages in trying to answer this question. The foundation of modern theory in this field is of course the work of Modigliani and Miller, who in 1958 showed that, in efficient markets without taxes, capital structure would have no effect on the value of the firm, if the operating assets of the firm were taken as given. Allowing for the effect of debt on financial risk, the costs of debt and of equity would be the same.

More recently, it has been argued (by Miller) that the tax-deductibility of corporate interest payments should have no effect once borrowers have exhausted the lending resources of relatively low-tax-rate lenders and the marginal tax rate of lenders equals that of borrowers. This would leave only possible insolvency costs as the main determinant of an optimal capital structure. Today, however, economists are not so sure; and there are signs that they are prepared to allow choice of capital structure to re-enter the scene for other reasons, if only through the back door of agency theory.

In the case of the banks it is not hard to understand why they should want to have at least a *minimum* equity capital ratio. In a world of uncertainty and possible credit rationing, the ability of banks to attract deposits will be reduced if capital ratios fall short of some level. This amounts to saying that the assumption that operating assets can be taken as given, short of insolvency, is invalid. What is less easy to explain, at least in terms of what has become standard theory, is why banks dislike a *high* capital ratio; for this should be reflected in a correspondingly lower cost or greater supply of deposits.

Two possible answers might be given. One is that banks may still regard the moneyness of deposit liabilities as providing an economic rent, so that deposit ratios are kept as high as possible, subject to a minimum capital constraint. This view, however, has less justification in a world of extensive competition between deposits and non-bank liabilities as liquid assets.

The other possible answer is a paradox; namely that with imperfect information the adoption of a very high capital ratio might even be regarded by depositors as a sign that the bank concerned saw its assets – current or prospective – as being of relatively high risk. The effect on deposit supply might even be perverse. (There is an analogy here with dividend changes as possible signals.) If so, the knowledge that the regulators have asked a bank to increase its capital ratio, or even asked this of banks as a whole, might actually be adverse as far as the market's view of bank risk is concerned. This is not so fanciful as it may sound, as usually banks which have failed have previously reported relatively high capital ratios.

I have two suggestions to make to reduce the costs which result from the imposition of more or less arbitrary capital requirements by regulators. The first is that, if regulators insist on prescribing minimum capital ratios, they should take a leaf out of nineteenth century practice and allow banks to meet these requirements by having some of this capital in uncalled form. This would give banks more flexibility and avoid some of today's distortions.

To those who say that shareholders might refuse to pay up when capital was called, I would answer that the cost of refusal could be made very high by designing new capital in such a way that dividends would not be paid unless the call were met. If calls were unpopular, so that the share price fell as the expectation of a call increased, banks would be deterred from allowing their portfolios to become unduly risky. The case for uncalled capital is also that variance of returns may not be the best measure of risk in bank portfolios. As Professor Schaefer says, the shape of the distribution of returns may be important. In particular it may be the possibility of infrequent but extreme losses that have to be guarded against most of all.

My second suggestion is simpler but more fundamental. Much of the justification for regulation is based on the idea of asymmetric information, namely that depositors do not have sufficient information about the solvency of individual banks, a state which most of the papers prepared for this conference seem to take as given. If information about the riskiness of bank portfolios is scarce, the obvious solution is to require banks to supply it, in the form, for example, of statistics of the industrial and geographical composition of loan portfolios, and with the frequency already required by supervisors.

At present there is hardly any incentive for banks to do this voluntarily, because they gain very little if their capital and liquidity ratios are already prescribed by regulators. The provision of more published information would be tantamount to loosening what is a monopoly of information held by regulators and one which sustains the trend towards increasing prudential regulation itself.

4 Competitive financial reregulation: an international perspective*

EDWARD J. KANE

Even though the precise purposes and techniques of financial-services regulation vary from place to place and time to time, financial-services regulation is a veritable fixture of economic life. On average, across the world, the financial sector (and particularly the banking industry) is probably more closely regulated than any other segment of the private economy.

Instruments of regulation focus primarily on arrangements for monitoring solvency and conflicts of interest, supervising institutions' prices and risk-taking, and limiting the range of institutional activity. These instruments include: site examinations (i.e., direct inspections of institutions' account books), reporting requirements, capital requirements, liquidity ratios including reserve requirements, deposit-rate controls, loan quotas, asset-growth and usury ceilings, product-line restrictions, margin requirements, foreign-exchange restrictions, and capital export controls. In addition, many countries limit cross-border deposit-taking and lending by domestic banks and differentially restrict opportunities for market entry and expansion by foreign and foreign-controlled financial firms (OECD, 1984).

*Re*regulation occurs whenever an inherited system of regulatory instruments is adjusted in any way. This paper portrays reregulation as an economically endogenous process, in which politicians and regulators respond self-interestedly to political and economic pressure. During the 1980s, selective relaxations of longstanding government restrictions on the operations of foreign and home-country financial-services firms have been spreading in seemingly epidemic fashion across the face of the globe. Although many observers deem the resulting net lowering of the world-wide burden of financial regulation to be an exogenous process, deregulation is best viewed as a special case of reregulation. Deregulation is not something like an ideological infection that develops inexplicably among swing voters. It is spread by programmed responses to changes in the political and economic landscapes that regulators (including politicians) face.

While acknowledging the impact of changing technological and investment opportunities on regulators' opportunity sets, the paper attributes the rapid spread of regulatory relaxations (as does Giddy, 1984) to heightened competition in what is in fact an international market for financial-services regulation. Discretionary adjustments in regulatory restraints are rational and multidimensional acts of reregulation. These acts are rooted reactively in the prospective *economic* returns that individual regulators can self-interestedly reap from relieving or accentuating inefficiencies and inequities. Opportunities to earn additional regulatory profits develop as inherited strategies and frameworks of financial-services regulation come into increasingly fuller contact with changing investment opportunities and new technologies of information processing and telecommunications.

The paper shows that competitive reregulation is potentially beneficial and that the paradigm of competitive reregulation can make sense of many current events. It concludes by noting that many of the potential benefits of competitive reregulation can be dissipated by explicit and implicit government subsidies to regulatory risk-bearing. Because subsidies inherent in conjectural government guarantees of the debts of multinational financial corporations are implicit rather than explicit, they are hard to measure, monitor, and control. This makes a case for requiring that market-value measures of institutional performance and capital be employed internationally and may even support cooperative regulatory efforts to control the risk exposure of multinational financial institutions.

I   A contestable-markets view of regulation

Treating suppliers of regulatory services (national, supranational and sub-national politicians, regulatory agencies, and self-regulatory industry cooperatives) as multiproduct firms, the argument makes considerable use of the economists' paradigm of imperfectly contestable markets. A market may be defined as a body of persons carrying on extensive and at least partly voluntary transactions in a specific good or service. Individual markets are perfectly contestable when entry and exit costs are zero, so that the possibility of hit-and-run entry by outsiders serves to constrain the profit margin sought by incumbent firms (Baumol, Panzar, and Willig, 1986). The analysis posits the existence of a 'market for regulation'. Exploring this market, its participants, and their motivation is a principal task of this paper.

Purchases and sales of regulatory services typically occur in the context of an ongoing client relationship rather than on an item-by-item basis. Much as medical patients do, regulatees contract for a range of contingent services without haggling over individual prices.

In attempting to explain what and whom various regulators control, the analysis focuses on the response of different regulatees and regulators to exogenous and endogenous decreases in the costs of entry into and exit from different financial product markets. The argument portrays evolving differences in the structure of the market for financial regulatory services as driven by rivalry between suppliers of financial regulatory services within and across countries. It takes as the motive force these parties' efforts, subject to a long-run profitability constraint, to extend or to defend their share of the market for regulatory services in the face of exogenous and endogenous disturbances in the economic environment (cf. Niskanen, 1971).

Voters (consumers *and* producers) demand solutions to recognized economic problems and this demand creates rewards for parties who can supply potential solutions that service this demand. The demand is driven by perceived opportunities to reduce or share particular risks, correct economic inefficiencies, and redistribute resources (for example) between rich and poor, big business and small, housing and luxury goods. Economic-efficiency objectives are promoted primarily by coordinating, standard-setting, and certification services. Redistributional objectives are pursued by intervening in the financial system to create tax or regulatory preferences for selected customers, instruments, or investment opportunities. Introducing such preferences regulatorily seems a deceptively painless and quick way to correct social ills and to improve the pattern of economic results. The use of financial regulation for redistributional purposes seems less hypocritical in European countries than in the US, where an ideological schizophrenia exists between citizens' theoretical preference for a minimal state and their *de facto* support of politicians who view the government as the chief solver of their constituents' economic problems.

Our contestable-markets conception makes the demand for a particular regulator's services into a form of derived demand. A regulator's market share may be defined as the aggregate market share in financial-services markets enjoyed by firms that fall within its jurisdiction, adjusted for the extent to which jurisdiction in these markets is effectively shared with other regulators. Any regulator's share rises and falls with surplus and deficit spending units' worldwide demand for the financial services provided by its particular regulatory clientele (i.e., its regulatees). This perspective makes it useful to distinguish between *active* and *passive* movements in a regulator's market share. Passive movements occur when regulatees gain or lose market share on their own, unrelated to prior or concurrent adjustments that may be carried out by their traditional regulators. Active movements are those brought about by regulators' efforts to realign the operative regulatory structure. In turn, active adjustments may be either aggressive or defensive in intent.

In line with these distinctions, sequences of interregulator market-share adjustment differ according to the nature of the initiating disturbance. In a defensive sequence, the process begins when passive gains or losses in a regulator's market share alert its managers to opportunities for using reregulation as a way to defend their traditional turf. Aggressive sequences begin with a regulator's pursuit of opportunities for market-share gains that are generated by exogenous changes in the economic environment. Passive sequences are marked by a regulator's (possibly temporary) acquiescence in an observed gain or loss of its regulatees' market shares.

II   The regulatory dialectic

In turn, these sequences represent special cases of a dynamic model of regulator-regulatee action and reaction known as the 'regulatory dialectic' (Kane, 1981 and 1984a). In this model, every adjustment in applicable regulations engenders at least partially offsetting reactions on the part of regulatees and their differentially regulated competitors. In turn, regulatory adjustments are conditioned on past regulatee reaction patterns. Individual acts of reregulation are directed at resolving prior conflicts between attempts by regulators to control the behaviour of regulatees and regulatees' efforts to avoid (i.e., to minimize) the net burdens that regulation ultimately places upon them. Equilibrium regulatory structures (if they exist at all) unfold adaptively over a long time span.

The regulatory dialectic views regulation and regulatee avoidance behaviour as forces linked like the pedals on a bicycle. The alternating rise and fall of associated stresses drive a single process. Whether a particular observer sees one pedal or the other as more important generally depends upon where he or she is located along the chain of wealth redistribution that a specific regulation is intended to create. Whereas the intended beneficiaries of a given pattern of regulation tend to praise the ostensible benefits attributed to their favourite regulatory walls and to denounce loopholes in these walls that regulatee avoidance activities exploit, regulatees tend to malign the walls and to extol the noble ends that loopholes permit them to pursue. Irrespective of whether individual acts of avoidance promote the goals of horizontal and vertical equity, to the extent that they relieve net economic inefficiencies that perfectly effective regulation would cause, they advance social welfare. Even in trying to undo politically approved patterns of wealth redistribution, avoidance behaviour may actually promote the common good. This depends on whether or not the planned redistribution that they at least partially undo would merit the approval of what welfare economists would term a 'properly instructed' ethical observer.

Dialectical processes are driven in Hegelian fashion by forces of conflict (a thesis and antithesis) and conflict resolution (a synthesis). Each new synthesis becomes a fresh thesis in a succeeding three-part dialectic. Dialectical evolution takes the form of an unending and not necessarily convergent sequence of action and reaction: Thesis–Antithesis–Synthesis (Thesis)–Antithesis–Synthesis (Thesis)...

When dialectical thinking is used to interpret observed patterns of regulatory and financial innovation, the thesis and antithesis become acts of *regulation* and *avoidance*. When an act of regulation serves as the thesis, the third-stage synthesis becomes an act of *reregulation*: a deliberate rewriting of inherited rules to facilitate the achievement of various ostensible goals such as economic stability, economic efficiency, system integrity, social equity, and hidden goals such as wealth redistribution. When an act of avoidance kicks off the dialectic, reregulation becomes the antithesis and further patterns of avoidance constitute the synthesis.

The regulatory dialectic depicts financial regulation as an endless game of strategy in which two teams of players (regulators and regulatees) make alternating moves. Changes in the economic environment, in technology, and in competitive systems of regulation alter the potential moves available to both teams at each turn. The freedom and speed with which different players formulate and execute their moves constitute their adaptive efficiency. Players' average adaptive efficiencies may be ordered as follows:

(1) Less-regulated players move faster and more freely than more tightly regulated ones;
(2) Private players move faster and more freely than governmental ones;
(3) Regulated players move faster and more freely than their regulators;
(4) International regulatory bodies move more slowly and less freely than all other players.

This ordering implies that the lag of avoidance behind regulation is on average shorter than the lag between avoidance and reregulation. Although not denying that government regulators may deal quickly with situations (such as cases of spectacular fraud or scandal) in which voters show an intense interest, it implies further that reregulation lags are shorter for industry-based self-regulatory cooperatives than for government regulatory agencies. Self-regulatory bodies are also apt to follow strategies that are more proactive than those that typically appeal to government agencies. Finally, lags in regulatory response are particularly severe for activities that take place in the international sphere.

In the pages that follow, a justification for regulatory services is developed and the structure of regulatory competition is described. Finally, recent trends in worldwide financial reregulation are linked to temporally prior developments in four areas: information and communications technology; government intervention strategies in markets for foreign exchange; markets for differentially regulated financial products; and competitive adjustments made by alternative suppliers of financial regulatory services.

III   Two layers of financial-services competition

Traditional models of financial-services firms emphasize two dimensions of competition: explicit price and user convenience (Klein, 1971; Sealey, 1980; Baltensperger, 1980; Santomero, 1984). Historical analysis (Mullineaux and Gorton, 1985) and contemporary concern over the need to establish credible guarantees of institutional performance (Kane, 1984b) make clear the value of adding a third dimension: that of public confidence. Convenience, confidence, and (when interest-rate ceilings obtain) even explicit prices can be regarded as intermediate goods produced jointly with providers of regulatory services. These three characteristics govern the demand for an intermediary's loan-commitment and deposit services alike.

Because explicit pricing has been thoroughly analysed elsewhere, we focus here on the other two characteristics. Recognizing that the etymologically key syllable in both convenience and confidence is the middle one, we symbolize each of them by the first letter of its second syllable. 'Con-' is merely one of several variants of 'com-.' When linked to the 'veni' (a form of the Latin verb 'to come') in convenience, con- means 'with' or 'together'. When linked to the 'fide' (Latin for faith or trust) in confidence, con- means 'full' or 'total'.

Domestically, confidence in any institution, F, relates to the perceived probability that this institution's financial commitments will be met. F is primarily a function of: (1) the institution's explicit plus implicit net worth, NW; (2) the variability of its earnings, σ; (3) the cost and possible unreliability, c_F, of the accounting data available on NW and σ; and the market value of its external guarantees, G:

$$F = F(\overset{(+)}{NW}, \overset{(-)}{\sigma}, \overset{(-)}{c_F}, \overset{(+)}{G}) \tag{1}$$

The market value of external guarantees depends (among other things) on the pattern of cash flows covered and on the capacity and willingness of the guarantor to make good on its explicit and implicit promises. In the US, the most relevant formal guarantees consist of federal deposit insurance and federal insurance of the repayment capacity of various farmers and mortgagors. Viewed from an international perspective, NW and σ may be affected unfavourably by fluctuations in exchange rates and G includes a number of informal conjectural guarantees as well. Hence, these variables link up inextricably with foreign confidence in an institution's home currency (i.e., its macroeconomic policies) and in the perceived soundness of the home-country and world financial system.

User convenience is a matter of the geographic reach of the firm and the speed and reliability with which it can service customer needs. Speed means minimizing delays in executing transactions, answering balance and credit inquiries, and rectifying errors. Reliability means having low error rates in all service functions. Technological advances in information and communications technology are transforming financial institutions' geographic reach in two ways. First, convenience is no longer dependent mainly on the geographic spread and density of a firm's own network of branch offices. Real-time connections with subsidiaries, affiliates, and *ad hoc* partner firms through electronic and other servicing networks make it possible for financial institutions to execute distant or nontraditional transactions for their customers (including respondent banks) indirectly with relative ease and efficiency. Second, improvements in technologies for handling and communicating information make it easier for customers in distant locations to order and take delivery directly of various of the services a financial institution offers. Remote access is provided by customers' telephones, computer modems, or satellite dishes and by partial-service automated teller machines owned by either the institution or a transactions network to which it belongs. User convenience, V, may be represented as a function of: (1) the radius of the aggregate market area, M, its shared and owned facilities span; (2) average cost to individuals located within this market area of accessing these facilities, c_v;[1] (3) the diversity of the transactional products the firm offers its customers, D; and (4) the speed and reliability of the services the institution performs, S:

$$V = V(\overset{(+)}{M}, \ \overset{(-)}{c_v}, \ \overset{(+)}{D}, \ \overset{(+)}{S}) \tag{2}$$

In exchange for what we may term explicit and implicit regulatory revenue, producers of regulatory services can help an institution to effect favourable movements in every argument of V and in the last two arguments of F. Explicit regulatory revenue, R_R, consists of fees and other cash receipts (including seigniorage) that accrue from a regulator's operation. Implicit revenue, R'_R, consists of noncash benefits such as improvements in an agency's prestige, size, effective autonomy, or market share. A regulator's profit or net budget deficit, Π_R, may be defined as its implicit and explicit regulatory revenue, $R'_R + R_R$, minus the total cost, C_R, of producing the services it supplies:

$$\Pi_R = R'_R + R_R - C_R \tag{3}$$

Politicians typically wish to transfer regulatory profits either explicitly to the national Treasury or implicitly to designated constituents. Earning either a target level of net explicit regulatory profits, a target profit margin, or delivering a target pattern of subsidies may be an important national goal.

Financial regulatory services consist of efforts to monitor, discipline, or coordinate the behaviour of individual financial-services firms for the benefit either of these firms, their customers, or society as a whole. Financial regulatory services are produced and marketed by a combination of private and governmental entities. In most Western countries, the fairness and legitimacy of regulators' actions are subject to judicial review.

Private regulators range from independent financial analysts, auditors, and credit-rating agencies to self-regulatory organizations such as clearinghouses, securities or commodities exchanges, accounting-standards boards, and trade associations. On the governmental level, private regulators are supplemented, overseen, and sometimes superseded by specialized national, subnational (state, canton, province, prefecture, etc.), foreign, and even international governmental agencies. Although the regulatory dominions of a country's alternative financial regulators often overlap formlessly, the central bank is often paramount. As a nation's most far-reaching financial regulator and stabilizer of last resort, the central bank's ability to enter any regulatory submarket in emergencies and to evoke top-level government support for its actions permits it to impose a degree of cartel-like discipline on other members of its country's domestic financial regulatory industry. However, a central bank's role in regulating domestic institutions and financial markets is importantly constrained by its need to compete for regulatory business with central banks of other countries.

Financial analysis has focused traditionally on competition for customers by those who produce and distribute financial services. But running parallel to this competition between private financial institutions is a less-visible layer of competition for rights to produce and deliver regulatory services to financial institutions. Examining this level of competition is the focus of this paper. In the deposit-institution sector, this competition is mainly among alternative national and subnational politicians and regulatory agencies. As lobbyists and as purveyors and enforcers of codes of professional ethics, trade associations join in this rivalry. Moreover, particularly in the nondepository sector, industry self-regulatory cooperatives such as securities and future exchanges, clearinghouses, and registration societies play a particularly important role.

In principle, the invisible hand works at both levels of competition. Rivalry among alternative regulators for clients and budgets should not be viewed merely as wasteful duplication. In many cases, duplication of regulatory missions across different agencies promotes long-run efficiency in the production and delivery of regulatory services much as duplication of service functions across private institutions promotes efficiency in the provision of financial services. This competition promotes inefficiency when, by exploiting and perpetuating impediments in taxpayers' access to information relevant to judging their performance, regulators can extract unintended and economically inappropriate subsidies. As long as taxpayers do not permit inefficiency to be subsidized, interregulator rivalry protects borrowers, depositors, and investors from the overregulation to which a monopoly supplier or regulatory cartel would tend in the long run.

In the financial-services industry today, regulatory conflict is in as furious a state of turmoil as the conflict between alternative financial-services providers. In the main, this conflict is driven *not* by acts of bureaucratic imperialism but by structural changes undertaken by each side's various regulatees. In turn, these structural changes represent profit-seeking efforts by individual financial institutions either to invade nontraditional markets or to fashion an improved regulatory climate for themselves. Individual financial institutions are revising their organizational structures and extending their product lines and geographic reach to serve new markets and in the process selecting a cost-minimizing set of regulatory micro climates for themselves. Because these structural changes disrupt the inherited regulatory equilibrium, they force individual regulators to struggle to defend or redefine the borders of their domains.

Incentives to monitor and minimize the costs of producing regulatory services are weaker for government agencies than they are for private producers. When the effects of financial innovations are aggregated across society, much of the cost advantages that multinational and multipurpose financial firms are currently achieving is more apparent than real (Clarke, 1983; Kane, 1984a). Unintended subsidies flowing from the improper pricing of explicit and implicit government and international guarantees lower the costs of product-line and geographic-market extension for individual firms. But they do this only by imposing unaccounted expense and unrecognized liabilities onto governmental guarantors and through them onto unwary taxpayers and conservatively run competitors who knowingly or unknowingly backstop these contingent governmental commitments.[2]

Underpriced opportunities for shifting risk onto governmental guarantors are especially great for innovative activities. Governmental information, monitoring, and regulatory-response systems inevitably lag behind market perceptions of relevant risks, and estimates of changes in the market value of these guarantees are not published in timely fashion for taxpayers to monitor. Mispricing governmental guarantees creates incentives for financial institutions to search out new forms of risk and for nonfinancial institutions to look for inventive ways of folding guaranteed financial subsidiaries into their operations. These defective incentives are undermining the stability of the world's financial system (Kane, 1985).

IV   Net regulatory burdens as incentives for structural arbitrage

Regulators restrain the activity of individual financial-services firms to develop both societal and industry-wide benefits. These benefits take the form of: (1) minimizing the cost of certifying the integrity and competence of individual institutions and other contracting parties; (2) improving productive efficiency by providing coordinating services that lower transactions costs; (3) assuring the stability and orderliness of the system over time; and (4) monitoring industry pricing arrangements for anti-competitive behaviour.

From the point of view of the regulatees, revenue losses imposed on them by effective regulatory constraints and regulators' explicit charges need to be set against the value of regulatory services. We define the balance between the costs and benefits that a given regulator imposes on its regulatees to be its 'net regulatory burden'. Because some of the costs imposed on regulatees may not produce regulatory revenues and because the value of regulatee benefits may exceed or fall short of regulator costs, this burden need not be merely the mirror image of the regulatory net profits specified in equation (3).

From the point of view of society as a whole, whether a governmental agency or a self-regulatory body produces a given set of regulatory services, the regulator confronts a fundamental incentive conflict. Self-regulators face socially beneficial incentives to minimize certification costs and to promote efficient arrangements for their members on the one hand. However, they face socially harmful incentives to foster cartel pricing on the other. Moreover, over time, cartel pricing encourages the expansion of uncertified firms that operate outside of the aegis of the self-regulatory organization. Hence, under a purely self-regulatory system, market-structure adaptation to undo the effectiveness of cartel pricing tends to expand the market share of unregulated firms. In cases where the oversight being avoided promotes safe-and-sound operation, this process can undermine the soundness and integrity of the financial system as a whole. When regulation is supplied by a governmental organization, the nature of incentive compatibility and conflict is reversed. Socially beneficial incentives exist to promote at least the appearance of stability and to restrain cartel pricing (although, as Stigler (1971) emphasizes and recent US experience with deposit-rate ceilings demonstrates, regulatee political activity can subvert this incentive), but incentives to minimize certification costs and to produce coordinating, guarantee, and other regulatory services efficiently have little force at all. Hence, when regulation is purely governmental, regulatory services tend to be produced at unnecessarily high resource costs and to be employed as an engine of redistribution.

The amorphous market structure of world-wide (and, to the extent that a country's subnational political structure permits, domestic) financial regulation serves as an entry-facilitating system of competition among alternative regulators. Viewing this competition merely as a 'competition in laxity' is a grave conceptual error. Much as in other kinds of competition, regulatory competition is guided by Adam Smith's invisible hand to resolve apparent incentive conflicts, producing subtle and long-run benefits that are imperceptible to uncritical observers (Bloch, 1984; Giddy, 1984; Kane, 1984b). Even though regulatory overlaps impose avoidable short-run costs, on average and on balance, they diversify against narrow or inflexible approaches to problem-solving at individual agencies and facilitate dynamic adaptations in market structure necessary to achieve evolutionary optimality.

Overlapping jurisdictions lead competing regulators to develop a series of alternative patterns of coping with common problems that are routinely tested against each other in the crucible of experience. This allows regulatory problems to be resolved without betting all of society's chips on the problem-solving ability of any particular set of regulators.

Duplicate regulatory functions and overlapping administrative boundaries that may seem inefficient from a purely static point of view provide dynamic opportunities for structural arbitrage that entails the adaptive affiliation and disaffiliation of individual regulatees. Such behaviour is labelled as arbitrage to emphasize that differences in net regulatory burdens are akin to differences in quoted prices on any set of substitute services. Structural adaptation by regulated firms (especially by new entrants into markets for products and services that substitute for regulated ones) punishes poor regulators.

Regulation may be inefficient in either of two ways. First, the services a particular regulator offers may be produced at more than minimum cost. Second, the services offered may be maladapted to the evolving needs of producers and consumers of financial services. Patterns of regulation which are inefficient in either sense impose excessively burdensome taxes either on regulatees or on the general taxpayer. Assuming that at least in the long run taxpayers extract the information necessary to guard their economic interests, as clients shift their business from the regulatees of inefficient regulators to the regulatees of efficient ones, jurisdictional domains and budgetary resources must eventually shrink for regulators whose production costs prove inefficiently high or whose response to the evolving needs of the marketplace consistently proves short-sighted or inflexible.

Opportunities for regulatees to relabel products, relocate production, or adjust their legal form to switch regulators and for regulators to enroll additional classes of regulatees constitute a type of social insurance. These opportunities protect financial firms and their customers from having to bear the excessive burdens which a cartel or monopoly supplier might be expected to impose. Especially when ongoing technological and regulation-induced change impels regulators and market participants endlessly to learn new ways of competing, regulatory competition induces more timely and economically better-adapted adjustments in regulatory structures than a set of monopoly regulators would choose to make. The combined threat of judicial review and competition from other regulators encourages an agency's regulatory brainstrust to produce its regulatory services more efficiently: to adopt regulatory strategies that serve the needs of new forms of business organization and would-be producers of new or improved products. In particular, interregulator rivalry tends to smooth out 'bubbles' of overly severe regulation that would develop in response to intermittent financial-market crises and scandals if financial-regulation 'barriers to entry' were more significant. High exit costs, statutory constraints on regulatees' and regulators' entry into new realms, and regulatory lags slow the adaptation of the market structure for financial-services providers. For example, in the case of US antitrust regulation, the Supreme Court is the dominant regulator. The Court's adherence to outmoded concepts of banking as a single line of commerce, of banking market areas as narrow economic regions, and of seller concentration ratios (i.e., market structure) as a reliable guide to seller performance have deflected other federal regulators' attention away from regulatee entry and exit costs. Although the pre-1978 absence of explicit deposit-insurance premiums on the foreign deposits of US banks and restrictions on these banks' domestic insurance and investment-banking activities have been more important forces, the inappropriate emphasis on measures of industry concentration in US antitrust supervision has encouraged large US banks to plant important parts of their capacity for servicing the needs of large corporations in foreign locations.

Although the nature of bureaucratic competition for regulatory jurisdiction differs from country to country, it is imbedded in the multinational character of the world economy and in any federal system of government. In the United States, this competition reflects its founders' deep respect for individual freedom. Because it makes for messy organization charts and an overabundance of government agencies, this competition could not have survived and expanded unless it also improved the long-run adaptive efficiency of government regulation. It is part of a system of constitutional checks and balances that restrains the arbitrary exercise of political power in the United States. By rearranging its activities and organizational form in prescribed ways, a regulated entity may change the regulatory climate within which it functions. The term 'regulatory climate' serves as a shorthand expression for the set of laws and the particular regulatory bodies by which an institution is governed.

Structural arbitrage consists of substituting differentially regulated (often *new*) products, processes, and organizational forms for traditional ones. Secular expansion in bank use of off-balance-sheet activities constitutes a vivid example of structural arbitrage. Such arbitrage is constrained by various legal obstacles. But opportunities for regulators to extend their dominion to new types of institutions and the existence of even greatly constrained options for regulatees to switch regulators create incentives for efficient regulator adaptation. Without tough sunset laws, it is almost prohibitively costly to effect the complete exit of a government regulatory agency (particularly a national one). Nevertheless, declines in either market share or regulatory profits are bureaucratically embarrassing. Potential losses in regulatory domain undermine agency goals and bring economic pressure on a bureau's top management to lighten many of the burdens that in a changing marketplace the inherited system of regulation would otherwise impose on regulated firms and their customers.

In a complex and dynamic world economy, it is unlikely that an unchanging pattern of either financial contracting or national regulation could remain optimal over time. Rather, tension between alternative regulators and between regulated and less-regulated purveyors of substitute financial instruments is needed to hold the burdens of regulation and industry profit margins in the vicinity of their long-run optimal levels. Concern for dynamic efficiency creates a presumption against imposing substantial barriers to entry into the financial-services game either for new financial instruments or especially for additional self-regulators. Currently, the high costs of effecting the exit of an inefficient government competitor, the dominant market position of the world's leading central banks, and underpriced governmental or quasigovernmental guarantees of financial-institution liabilities constitute important barriers to entry for self-regulatory bodies.

V   Technological change and international competition for regulatees

Restrictions on the entry and expansion of foreign banks and on domestic-bank capital exports exist in most developing countries and in a majority of developed countries, too. To document the latter claim, Tables 4.1 and 4.2 describe restrictions that applied in early 1984 to foreign-bank entry into each of the 24 member countries of the Organization for Economic Cooperation and Development (OECD). One way to measure the pace of competitive reregulation is to note how many of these countries have revised their policies during the intervening 2.5 years and eased foreign entry into domestic securities markets, too. (On this issue, Germany and Morton 1985, pp. 750–2, provide useful information.)

To establish a hypothetical point of reference from which to assess the effects of reductions in barriers to international competition in financial services, let us imagine a world in which the following costs or risks are zero: (1) costs for foreign and domestic banks to enter or leave any foreign or domestic banking market; (2) costs of converting between home-country and foreign currencies (in a risk-adjusted sense, these

Table 4.1. **Status in early 1984 of policies of OECD member countries regarding the establishment of foreign-bank agencies or branches and subsidiaries**

	Branches or agencies	Subsidiaries
Australia	X	X
Austria		
Belgium		
Canada	X	R
Denmark	C	C
Finland	X	R
France	C	C
Germany		
Greece		
Iceland	X	X
Ireland	C	C
Italy	C	C
Japan	R	R
Luxembourg		
Netherlands	C	C
New Zealand	X	X
Norway	X	
Portugal		
Spain	R	R
Sweden	X	X
Switzerland	R	R
Turkey	R	R
United Kingdom		
United States	Q	Q

Note:
X – Foreign entry prohibited
R – Some reciprocity provisions
C – Some reciprocity tests for Banks headquartered outside the European Economic Community
Q – Some states prohibit foreign bank establishment or impose reciprocity requirements
Source: OECD (1984)

costs are probably higher with fluctuating exchange rates than under a fixed-rate system); (3) costs of delivering banking services to and from any office location in the world; and (4) sovereign risk. In such a world, national markets would be completely integrated. Production of banking activities would migrate to office locations in the single country whose regulators placed the lightest consolidated net regulatory and tax burden on these activities.

Table 4.2. **Status in early 1984 of policies of OECD member countries governing acquisition by foreign banking organizations of participations in indigenous banks**

Australia	– Forbidden under current policy
Austria	– License required
Belgium	– Mergers are subject to prior authorization. The banking control authorities must be notified of any significant change in equity ownership
Canada	– For Schedule A banks, permitted up to 10 percent of capital for each shareholder (maximum 25 percent held by non-residents). Free for Schedule B banks
Denmark	– Permitted up to 30 percent of share capital (but possibility of authorization for higher percentages)
Finland	– Nonresident ownership limited to 20 percent of share capital (but possibility of authorization for higher percentages)
France	– Authorization required by Conseil National du Credit
Germany	– Free, subject to antitrust law
Greece	– Permitted up to 40 percent of share capital (but possibility of authorization of up to 51 percent)
Ireland	– Subject to the same requirements as for establishment of foreign-bank subsidiaries
Italy	– Free
Japan	– Free up to 5 percent of equity capital; authorization by the Fair Trade Commission required for higher percentages
Luxembourg	– Free
Netherlands	– Free up to 5 percent of voting shares; higher participations subject to a declaration of non-objections
New Zealand	– Authorization required for foreign acquisition of 25 percent or more of equity of New Zealand incorporated banks
Norway	– Free up to 10 percent of share capital (but possibility of authorization up to 25 percent)
Portugal	– Forbidden 1977–83. Liberalized by law of November 1983. New regulations to be published shortly
Spain	– Subject to individual authorization
Sweden	– Forbidden
Switzerland	– Authorization required for majority participations
Turkey	– Authorization may be granted for participations between 10 and 49 percent of share capital
United Kingdom	– Free up to 15 percent of share capital; higher participations are subject to supervisory approval by the Bank of England and controlling majority participations may be subject to investigation
United States	– Free up to 5 percent of voting shares; for higher participations, federal regulatory approval is required

Source: OECD (1984)

Regulatory burdens that fail to generate sufficient regulatory revenue or enough supplementary budgetary support from informed taxpayers to cover the minimum costs of producing a given set of regulatory services may be termed unsustainable. When a regulator sets its burdens at unsustainably low levels, the induced inflow of world activity into its domain produces substantial budget losses that, by definition, taxpayers sooner or later prove unwilling to finance. Reregulation ultimately forces – albeit not without the possibility of considerable interim disruption – unsustainable burdens back into line.

On the other hand, sustainable forms of reregulation force regulators in other domains to reregulate. Faced with sustainable cuts in one country's regulatory burden, regulators in other countries who wanted to attract production back to their shores confront two choices. They have either to lower their respective burdens until they equal that of the minimum sustainable-burden country for each activity or to introduce taxes and other restraints designed to control movements of currency, financial instruments, and financial offices across their borders.

This analysis tells us that these three categories of costs (entry and exit costs; currency-conversion costs; and distance-related delivery costs), the risk of changes in these costs, and the threat of adverse trade, exchange, or capital controls constitute barriers to tax and regulatory equalization. Much as transportation and transactions costs establish gold points that in the gold-standard era defined a range of permissible differences across countries in the market price of gold, these costs set limits on observable differences in the net regulatory and tax burdens that may be imposed by different countries. The analysis also suggests that, other things equal, anything which tends to lower one or more of the three types of barriers to international tax and regulatory competition tightens links between national markets. Such a tightening tends to pull at least some of the heaviest tax and regulatory burdens toward their minimum sustainable levels.

To highlight the extent to which regulatory policy is an endogenous variable, it is convenient to conceive of a nation's authorities as setting a consolidated net burden. To keep this burden intelligible, in what follows we reduce individual burdens to a single conceptual dimension by assuming that differential burdens in explicit taxation are negligible. Alternatively, by viewing regulation as an implicit form of taxation that takes profitable business opportunities away from regulatees by force of law (Posner, 1974), the analysis could be unified along the tax dimension.

Markets for financial regulatory services are less directly contestable than markets for financial services themselves. The ideal of perfect contestability consists of zero entry costs and zero exit costs, which

assures opportunities for hit-and-run entry. Technological improvements in information handling have increased the contestability of
national markets for financial services by reducing distance-related and
currency-related entry and operating costs. Exit costs for high-tech plant
and equipment are also lower than for traditional capital and equipment.
The fixed costs of operating high-tech facilities are not sunk costs.
Capital invested in computer and telecommunication facilities may be
easily switched to nonfinancial uses and depreciates rapidly because of
obsolescence in any case. The sharply higher turnover rates currently
observed for financial firms in the US support this view.

In parallel fashion, technological change has increased the international contestability of national markets for financial regulatory services. As it has become harder and harder for individual countries to
keep out foreign financial-services firms and to keep domestic firms from
expanding their off-shore activities, competition in domestic markets
from foreign regulators has intensified. The domestic market structure
for financial regulatory services reflects: (1) delegations of market power
from elected politicians; (2) entry and exit costs faced by subnational,
foreign, and private regulators; and (3) regulatees' and their customers'
reactions to the net burdens the alternative regulators place on different
types of financial activities. Within each nation, central banks and
banking bureaus often play the role of dominant firm. However, except
for the need for *reputational capital*, entry costs and even exit costs are
relatively low even for subnational governments and self-regulators.

As regulatee market structures change, efficient parallel adaptation of
the market structure for financial services is hampered by legislatively
and judicially imposed entry barriers and by inflexible concepts of
appropriate regulatory strategy and tactics. In particular, the difficulty of
arranging durable patterns of international regulatory cooperation
reflects the difficulty of forming and maintaining a world-wide cartel in
any product or service. Although (for example) the US Comptroller has
been permitted to operate a London office, it is hard for national
regulators to negotiate even bilateral rights to open offices in each other's
regulatory territory. Significant progress has occurred primarily in
arrangements to improve the flow of information across the regulatory
community.

What further inhibits hit-and-run entry in the market for financial
regulatory services is the level of exit costs. For national government
regulators, these are so high that it is unusual ever to see any exit by these
entities. Because regulatory lags are longer than avoidance lags, the
ability of regulatees to shift specific operations to other nations or to
other domestic regulators permits competition for turf. Although the
effect of this competition is blunted by government regulators' need to

Table 4.3. **Number of US banks with indicated types of foreign or semi-foreign offices, 1950–85**

Date	Number of member banks with foreign branches	Number of foreign branch offices	Domestically owned Edge and agreement corporations and branches	Number of international banking facilities
1950	7	95		. . .
1960	8	131		. . .
1965	13	211		. . .
1970	79	532		. . .
1975	126	762	58	. . .
1980	159	787	91	. . .
1981	159	841	134	270
1982	162	900	164	430
1983	166	892	167	496
1984	163	905	162	524
1985	163	916	155	540

Notes: All data are yearend figures. Domestic nonmember banks have engaged in almost no foreign branching. Most of the 20 to 30 nonmember banks with foreign branches are foreign-owned. International Banking Facilities were first authorized on December 3, 1981. The figures given include foreign-owned as well as domestic IBFs. On June 30, 1986, about 60 percent of the IBFs were foreign-owned.

In examining data from different sources for this table and the next, some minor but hard-to-reconcile differences emerged.

Sources: First two columns: 1950 from Sinkey (1986), p. 653; 1960–85 from Telephone conversation with James Houpt, a staffmember at the Board of Governors of the Federal Reserve System. Data on Edges comes from computer runs supplied by Elizabeth Thorley of the Board of Governors staff. Figures on IBFs come from the Board of Governors' *Annual Reports.*

operate largely from within a set of national or administrative boundaries and the absence of national-regulator exits, it is encouraged by possibilities for regulating a multinational firm as a single entity. In the face of regulatee avoidance, this competition promotes long-run adaptation in regulatory structures by rewarding reregulation that validates and spreads efficient regulatory schemes.

VI Reciprocal expansion of foreign operations by US and foreign banking organizations

In a world of absolutely stationary exchange rates, the need for international portfolio diversification would be relatively small. As shown in

Table 4.4. **Presence of foreign banks in domestic United States banking markets, 1972–85**

Yearend	Number of banking families operating US branches and agencies	Number of uninsured branches and agencies	Number of insured branches and agencies	Number of foreign-owned Edge and agreement corporations (offices)	Number of foreign-owned majority positions in US banks	Percentage US banking assets controlled on June 30
1972	53	82	...	0	25	4
1975	79	147	...	0	33	n.a.
1979	154	295	n.a.	2	42	n.a.
1980	153	322	n.a.	11	40	12
1981	193	410	24	16 (21)	55	14
1982	205	389	33	28 (36)	69	14
1983	225	416	34	31 (43)	67	14
1984	248	442	38	25 (41)	69	15
1985	255	451	51	22 (37)	71	17

Notes: n.a. means 'not available'. When known, the number of offices operated by foreign-owned Edge and agreement corporations is given in parentheses.

We neglect a relatively few foreign-owned New York Investment companies. These were permitted in all years covered by the table. The International Banking Act of 1978 authorized foreign banks to own Edge corporations ('Edges') and permitted all Edges to branch domestically (Houpt, 1981; Key, 1985).

Sources: 1981–5, *Annual Reports of the Board of Governors of the Federal Reserve System*; 1972, 1975, 1979, and 1980: Telephone conversation with James Houpt of the Board of Governors, doublechecked against computer runs on Edge corporations supplied by Elizabeth Thorley of the Board's Staff.

Tables 4.3 and 4.4, since fluctuating exchange rates emerged in the early 1970s, individual US and foreign banks greatly expanded their presence in each other's domestic markets. A rapid reciprocal expansion of this type is consistent with the notion that a greater need to spread international assets was induced by increased volatility in exchange rates. Additional motives can be found in market and regulatory incentives to locate in foreign markets.

Abstracting (temporarily) from international differences in tax and regulatory burdens, since 1971, fluctuations in exchange rates and in the flow of petrodollars to OPEC countries created new opportunities for international deposit-taking and lending. The locations from which best to exploit such opportunities vary with the level and volatility of exchange rates. A strengthening dollar encourages foreign exports. The need to finance any accompanying deterioration in the US current account tends to make the US an attractive place in which to lend. This tends to increase the profitability of foreign-bank entry and expansion in US markets. On the other hand, a weakening dollar encourages US exports and bids up interest rates in foreign countries. This would increase the incentive of US banks to expand abroad. With increasingly volatile exchange rates, even slow growth in foreign trade and direct investment would create rewards for domestic banks that develop sufficient flexibility to be able to service the expanding foreign activities of their traditional business clients in the most favourable locations.

Moreover, throughout the period, banks' capacity to deliver out-of-country services increased secularly as technological changes lowered distance-related and currency-related operating costs and made these costs more predictable. Benefits to 'financial engineers' of introducing improvements in telecommunications and transactions efficiency increase with the financial sophistication of the transactors and/or the physical distance between these transactions. Electronic funds transfer (EFT) provides faster and more reliable transportation services for payments (e.g., same-day settlement), with important informational by-products. In ordinary transactions, faster execution tends to benefit the payee more than the payor. The symmetry of net benefits is apt to be greater for strictly financial transactions (such as interest-rate swaps) and to increase as well with the distance between transactors and with the opportunity costs of delays and uncertainties associated with alternative methods of effecting the transaction in question. Little market resistance has developed in applying EFT to international and particularly inter-continental transactions, especially where large amounts of money are involved. International EFT clearings networks are expanding in both retail (as exemplified by the 17-country American Express network of 8,200 automated teller machines) and wholesale (as exemplified by same-day international settlement under SWIFT) applications.

An additional incentive relates to the growth of financing opportunities in world trade as a whole. To reduce its exposure to regulatory risk, a world-class bank needs to establish a secure funding base in each of the world's principal vehicle currencies. Hence, irrespective of whether its home currency is weak or strong, any foreign bank striving to become an important player in international banking markets has good reason to establish a branch, subsidiary, agency, or representative office in the US, UK or Japan.

Of course, precisely because tax and regulatory burdens do vary substantially across countries, tax and regulatory incentives and the risk of future changes in these parameters must not be ignored. Shifting markets, flexible exchange rates, and higher and more-volatile world interest rates increased the burden of traditional regulatory structures based on liquidity requirements, capital standards, interest-rate ceilings, and activity limitations. By seeking out less-burdensome tax and regulatory climates, an institution could noticeably increase its after-tax profit margin on old business at the same time that it could harvest profitable forms of new business. A decision to conduct a particular financial activity in a foreign country rather than at home can easily be an act of pure structural arbitrage. To whatever degree the two countries' legal systems permit, it substitutes the tax and regulatory framework imposed on the activity in the host country for the framework obtaining in the home country. At the same time, it promotes the export of financial services supported by the continuation of what (because of the loss of associated regulatory revenues) tend during the period of associated regulatory lags to become subsidized home-country regulatory services. Such subsidies tend to expand foreign deposits at the expense of domestic ones and to lessen the home country's cost of financing current-account deficits in its balance of payments. If GATT is to be expanded to cover trade in financial services, such subsidies deserve to receive considerable attention.

Implicit financial-services subsidies have important effects on the distribution of wealth and financial opportunities. First, they redistribute the burden of financing home-country regulatory services that build confidence and facilitate transactions toward the general taxpayer and the stockholders, managers, and customers of smaller institutions that do not participate in international banking. Second, market adjustments tend to shift at least part of the subsidies from multinational home-country banks to host-country depositors and borrowers. In this way, the subsidies squeeze the lending margins of host-country intermediaries in their domestic markets. These events feed political demands on home-country regulators to impose regulatory assessments against domestic banks' foreign deposits or loans and lead host-country institutions to urge their regulators to impose countervailing restrictions on foreign firms and to negotiate offsetting concessions from foreign regulators for those domestic institutions able to expand reciprocally into their competitors' home countries. Third, questions arise about the credit-worthiness of the now typically more-leveraged regulatory arbitrageurs and about the reliability of conjectural home-country guarantees of their growing debts to foreigners.

In large part, the extent to which home-country or host-country regulators gain or lose market share and regulatory profits during the period of regulatory lag depends on the extent to which the services exported consist truly of new business for the relocating firm. New business creates home-country regulatory services by expanding to some

Table 4.5. **The ten largest investment-banking networks operated abroad by US commercial banks, 1986**

Bank	Number of offices	Number of foreign countries in which these offices lie
Citibank	45	40
Morgan Guaranty Trust Co.	28	26
Chase Manhattan Bank	18	18
Bank of America	7	6
Chemical Bank	7	7
First National Bank of Chicago	7	7
Manufacturers Hanover Trust Co.	5	5
Security Pacific National Bank	5	5
Bankers Trust Co.	4	4
Continental Illinois National Bank and Trust Co.	4	4

Source: The American Banker, July 23, 1986.

degree the home regulator's dominion over this class of activity in foreign markets. On the other hand, displacing business previously conducted domestically in the home country may be described as regulatory-service diversion. Whenever traditionally domestic business is simply displaced to foreign locations, home-country regulators are disadvantaged. They lose market share and regulatory revenue, while retaining at least some of the costs of producing confidence-building and coordinating services for this activity.

A particularly interesting case occurs when the home-country regulator losing volume in domestic markets differs from the home-country regulator of the class of institution that is expanding abroad. For example, to circumvent US regulations excluding US commercial banks from investment banking, the nation's major banks have established overseas investment-banking networks. Table 4.5 shows the number of foreign offices and countries served by the ten largest US bank purveyors of investment-banking services. Because the Securities and Exchange Commission and individual-state securities departments oversee corporate underwriting and deal-making in the US, ancillary foreign service volume that federal banking regulators pick up unambiguously improves their market share. While in the long run banking regulators may be expected to reregulate to recover the costs that this activity imposes on them, they are not apt to support efforts to close the associated loophole in domestic regulatory walls.

It is important to see that the foreign clients that a host-country regulator gains do not always improve its overall market position either. These clients must be *shared* in variable proportions with regulators in their home country. Although this sharing tends by itself to expand the host regulator's market share, foreign-bank entry tends simultaneously to lessen its autonomy, by putting downward pressure on the host country's domestic profit margin and increasing domestic demand for greater freedom for host-country institutions to expand abroad reciprocally. Foreign institutions must be expected to arbitrage differences in home and host regulatory structures and their entry into the domestic market creates incentives for their domestic competitors to consider expanding abroad. Unless host-country regulations comprehensively limit the rights and privileges of foreign banks (something which expansion-minded subnational regulators exemplified by the US state of Delaware may effectively thwart), foreign institutions are apt to enjoy regulatory freedoms that were not previously available to strictly domestic institutions. For example, although the International Banking Act of 1978 narrowed some of the differences, foreign bank operations in the US enjoy: lower capital requirements, fewer activity restrictions, more freedom to operate inter-state, and advantages in surmounting the concentration-ratio tests the courts use to regulate takeovers of large domestic institutions. Foreign-bank exercise of their differential freedoms tends to benefit consumers and to create and feed a demand for compensatingly lighter burdens for domestic regulatees. In Japan, for example, large domestic banks welcomed the exercise of investment-banking powers by foreign banks as a lever with which to pressure Japanese authorities for similar powers.

As we have emphasized, any loss of market share and the inevitable loss of regulatory profits tends to dispose home-country regulators to engage in defensive reregulation. Table 4.6 presents a time series of the geographic distribution of US banks' foreign branch assets. For US banking regulators, the observed secular expansion of these assets represents a mixture of gains and losses. The table indicates that, throughout the last 12 years, banking regulators in the UK lost market share they used to enjoy in regulating the foreign activity of American banks. Although regulatory havens in the Caribbean Basin gained considerable ground in 1973–6, their market share stabilized thereafter. The relative fixity of the Caribbean share after 1976 suggests that reregulation by the UK, the US, or competing regulatory havens (in Asia, for example) counteracted their differential burdens. However, because regulators in other locations on average gained market share and volume throughout the period examined, US and UK regulators may be said to have suffered a continuing decline.

Table 4.6. **The geographic distribution of US foreign branch assets, 1973–84**

	United Kingdom		Caribbean Basin		Other locations		Total US foreign branches	
Year	US $ billions	Percent	US $ billions	Percent	US $ billions	Percent	US $ billions	Percent
1973	62	50	25	21	39	29	122	100
1974	70	46	34	23	48	31	152	100
1975	75	42	49	28	53	30	176	100
1976	81	37	71	32	67	31	219	100
1977	91	35	84	32	84	33	259	100
1978	107	35	99	32	101	33	307	100
1979	131	35	121	33	112	32	364	100
1980	145	36	124	31	133	33	401	100
1981	157	34	149	32	157	34	463	100
1982	161	34	145	31	163	35	469	100
1983	159	33	152	32	166	35	477	100
1984	144	32	147	32	161	36	452	100
1985	149	32	142	31	167	37	458	100

Note: In May 1978, the exemption level for branches required to report their assets was increased, which lessened the comprehensiveness of the survey sample from which these data are constructed.
Source: 1973–84: Sinkey (1986), p. 659; 1985: *Federal Reserve Bulletin* (June 1986).

Direct US responses to its secularly declining regulatory market share, regulatory profits, and current-account position has lurched through several stages of reregulation. Some of the more notable developments include: (1) applications of loose capital controls, including the Voluntary Foreign Credit Restraint Program in the early 1970s; (2) sporadic experimentation with special reserve requirements on offshore deposits and borrowings; (3) redefinition by the International Banking Act of 1978 of the powers that foreign banks may exercise; (4) higher capital requirements for and closer supervision of US multinational banks authorized by the International Lending Supervision Act of 1983; and (5) expansion of opportunities for US banks to set up subsidiary corporations whose onshore facilities are granted 'offshore' privileges in transacting business with nonresidents.

Of these acts of reregulation, the last is theoretically the most interesting. For US banks, two main classes of onshore 'offshore offices' exist: Edge Act corporations (first authorized in the 1920s and given expanded powers by the 1978 Act) and IBFs (which have been allowed only since December, 1981). Growth in the number of these institutions, which is shown in Tables 4.3 and 4.4, surged dramatically in the 1980s.

Edge Act and agreement corporations are bank subsidiaries chartered by the Federal Reserve Board to conduct *international banking business* in US and foreign locations. They are permitted to have interstate branches (since 1978) and to make investments freely in foreign financial organizations that would be impermissible for US banks. An agreement corporation is a now-inconsequential form of state-chartered national-bank subsidiary that enters into an agreement with the Board not to exercise any power that is impermissible for an Edge corporation. A large percentage of Edge assets are located in New York and Miami.

An IBF is essentially a set of accounts or ledger books segregated from the other accounts of its parent. Its parent can be a US deposit institution, an Edge or agreement corporation, or a branch or agency of a foreign banks. Accounts are booked at these institutions *as if* they were located offshore. This means that IBFs are not subject to domestic reserve requirements, deposit-rate ceilings, or deposit-insurance premiums. However, as long as capital standards are applied on a consolidated basis to US banking corporations, US-owned IBFs are subject to capital requirements. IBFs are designed to reduce the flight of banks competing for US-connected international business to regulatory havens such as the Cayman Islands. Other countries are considering introducing an IBF option into their regulatory structures. For example, early in 1986, the Japanese Diet enacted legislation to set up similar corporations in Tokyo.

Data in Tables 4.3–4.6 cover only US-related components of the international market for banking regulation. Table 4.7, which compares the nationality of the leading banks in the world in 1964 and 1985, shows that the US is far from the only focus of pressures for competitive reregulation. Japanese banks and their regulators have made serious inroads into markets long dominated by North American, British, and Continental regulators. In 1964, measured by the dollar value of their deposits, the four biggest banks in the world and 6 of the top 10 were American. The other members of the top 10 were either British or Canadian. These three countries dominated the scene, with only one Italian bank (11th) and one French bank (14th) squeezing into the top 19 positions. The largest Japanese banks held positions 20 through 23. These four banks' aggregate deposits barely exceeded that of the then-largest US bank, the Bank of America.

In late 1985, a very different picture emerges. Assisted by a sharp appreciation of the yen, the four largest banks in the world are now Japanese, as are 7 of the top 10 and 7 of the next 15. Other members of

Table 4.7. The world's twenty-five largest commercial banks in 1964 and 1985, ranked by dollar value of deposits

1964 ranking	Bank name	1985 ranking	Bank name
1	Bank of America N.T. and S.A., San Francisco	1	Dai-Ichi Kangyo Bank Ltd., Tokyo
2	The Chase Manhattan Bank, New York	2	Fuji Bank, Ltd., Tokyo
3	First National City Bank, New York	3	Sumitomo Bank Ltd., Osaka
4	Manufacturers Hanover Trust Co., New York	4	Mitsubishi Bank Ltd., Tokyo
5	Barclays Bank Ltd., London	5	Banque Nationale de Paris
6	Midland Bank Ltd., London	6	Sanwa Bank Ltd., Osaka
7	Chemical Bank New York Trust Co.	7	Credit Lyonnais, Paris
8	The Royal Bank of Canada, Montreal	8	Citibank NA, New York
9	Morgan Guaranty Trust Co., New York	9	Norinchukin Bank, Tokyo
10	Canadian Imperial Bank of Commerce, Toronto	10	Industrial Bank of Japan, Ltd., Tokyo
11	Banca Nazionale del Lavoro, Rome	11	National Westminster Bank Plc, London
12	Lloyds Bank Ltd.	12	Bank of America NT & SA, San Francisco
13	Continental Illinois National Bank and Trust Co. of Chicago	13	Deutsche Bank, Frankfurt
14	Credit Lyonnais, Paris	14	Credit Agricole Mutuel, Paris
15	Security-First National Bank, Los Angeles	15	Societe Generale, Paris
16	Bank of Montreal	16	Barclays Plc, London
17	National Provincial Bank Ltd., London	17	Midland Bank Plc, London
18	Westminster Bank Ltd., London	18	Tokai Bank Ltd., Nagoya, Japan
19	Bankers Trust Co., New York	19	Dresdner Bank, Frankfurt
20	Fuji Bank, Ltd., Tokyo	20	Mitsui Bank Ltd., Tokyo
21	Mitsubishi Bank Ltd., Tokyo	21	Mitsubishi Trust & Banking Corp., Tokyo
22	Sanwa Bank Ltd., Osaka	22	Sumitomo Trust & Banking Co. Ltd., Osaka
23	Sumitomo Bank Ltd., Osaka	23	Long-Term Credit Bank of Japan, Ltd., Tokyo
24	First National Bank of Chicago	24	Bank of Tokyo, Ltd., Tokyo
25	Societe Generale, Paris	25	Mitsui Trust & Banking Co. Ltd., Tokyo

Sources: 1964: Orsingher (1967); 1985: *The American Banker*, July 29, 1986.

the top ten consist of two French and one American bank. In the next tier of 15 banks, one finds three British, two French, two German and one American bank. Now the largest Canadian bank (still the Royal Bank of Canada) ranks 26th.

According to the regulatory dialectic, a sustained redistribution of market share toward Japanese banks should create pressure for defensive and aggressive reregulation around the world. Moreover, the near-impossibility of exit for national regulators should serve to intensify the pressure these regulators feel to respond. Home-country governments and trade associations of 'guest' firms such as The Institute of Foreign Bankers in Japan have placed considerable international political pressure on Japanese authorities to improve foreign access to their domestic financial markets. The strong secular outlook for the yen has made it easier for Japanese regulators both to relax restrictions on foreign entry into Japanese financial markets and to acquiesce in permitting increased foreign demand for Euroyen instruments to be serviced.

VII   The larger picture: financial fusion

Although I lack the space to analyse them in detail, dialectical developments in international insurance, securities, and currency markets have been equally hectic. In effect, structural arbitrage has melted down longstanding geographic and functional barriers between financial activities so that institutional product lines are flowing together across the globe. It is convenient to call this globalized merger a long-term and short-term financial and currency markets 'financial fusion'. Financial fusion implies that the concerns of different government regulators and self-regulatory organizations for efficiently producing the 'right' amount of financial-system confidence and convenience and for redistributing resources through implicit taxes and subsidies are merging within and across countries.

To re-establish what coaches in sports like soccer and basketball call the principle of defensive symmetry, the market structure for financial regulatory services must be expected to become desegmented and global, too. To understand why nations all over the world are realigning their financial regulations in the 1980s, we have only to recognize that avoidance has broken down traditional patterns and strategies of regulatee competition and reregulation and that political power is shifting, too. Old regulatory strategies are proving as unreliable as a worn-out car. Authorities can't count on these strategies anymore to take them where they want to go when they want to go there. In particular, market adaptation has made a mockery of the strategies that place restrictions on:

(1) traditional patterns of raising funds and delivering services: e.g., of deposit-gathering and lending;
(2) limitations on the scope of firm activities and on the particular partners with whom a firm may merge or affiliate;
(3) explicit prices a firm may charge; and
(4) geographic office locations.

Whatever new strategies are finally adopted, to be fully effective, they must assign an expanding role to supranational quasi-governmental agencies and agreements, such as the European Economic Community, Bank for International Settlements, International Monetary Fund, Concordat, and International Conference of Bank Supervisors.

Structural arbitrage occurs by developing hybrid instruments, organizational forms, and financial positions that serve as perfect substitutes for adversely regulated instruments or arrangements. Regulatees arbitrage differences in foreign and home-country tax and regulatory frameworks. The effect is to alter importantly the effectiveness and the structure of the global market for financial regulatory services. Thanks to technological change, regulatory competition is intensifying within the US and across countries. Taken together, structural arbitrage and regulatory competition are diminishing regulators' capacity to control events and to prevent financial panics. The counterforce of international regulatory cooperation is lagging, i.e. developing at a slower pace.

Although the previous pages have emphasized competition involving government banking regulators, competition among alternative self-regulators and with other types of governmental financial regulators is visible world-wide. For perspective, let me briefly cite four examples of competition among private regulatory organizations:

(1) Private electronic transactions networks such as SWIFT and CHIPS are vying for the right to clear bank transactions among nations;
(2) What began as cooperatively shared ATM networks within the US or a single European country are increasingly competing with each other across countries;
(3) What began as strictly national securities or commodities exchanges are now competing hard for out-of-country business. Recent developments include the electronic linkage of securities and futures exchanges in different time zones to provide round-the-clock trading; opening of membership in the Tokyo and

London stock exchanges to foreign firms; the London Stock
Exchange's allowing banks and insurers into the securities business and New York subsidiaries of British brokers to trade in
American Depository Receipts; and the development of an automated exchange in Bermuda;

(4) Efforts to increase standardization and organize self-regulation in
Eurobond markets, as exemplified by the Association of International Bond Dealers' proposal to evolve itself into an international exchange.

Cases of additional competition among governmental regulators may
be found in government ownership of postal savings systems and various
Euro-banks and in relaxation of rules on the issue and redemption of
domestic-currency loans and notes. To keep financial-services production at home, successive relaxations of restrictions in individual
countries have curtailed the dominant share of offshore-banking, Euro-
dollar, and Eurobond markets that London enjoyed in the 1970s.
Recently, British regulators have found themselves in the position of
reregulating in response to the ways in which authorities elsewhere have
extended to their own countries the freedom of action long characteristic
of the British regulatory climate (i.e., minimal guidelines and flexible
supervision). In particular, authorities in tax-haven and regulatory-
haven countries such as the Bahamas, the Caymans, Luxembourg,
Singapore, and Hong Kong had taken this approach about as far as it can
go.

VIII Final comment on the need for regulatory cooperation

In 1986, key trends in the production and distribution of financial
services include robotization, electronification, remote delivery, networ-
king, and securitization. Key trends in the adapting organizational
structure of financial-services firms include simultaneous expansions in
geographic reach, in product lines, in organizational complexity, and in
the use of off-balance-sheet instruments such as swaps and guarantees.
Key trends in financial-services regulation include a heightening of
intergovernmental competition for the right to perform various financial
regulatory services, a growing harmonization of regulatory structures
across countries and industry segments, and a continuing explicit and
implicit shift of the deepest layers of financial-institution risk-bearing
onto governmental entities. On the self-regulatory front, private entities
have so far found it easier to cartelize their activities than governmental
entities have. The proposed merger between the London Stock
Exchange and International Securities Organization represents a

harbinger of the type of cooperative reregulation that financial fusion is apt eventually to promote.

Reflecting on these developments, three thoughts emerge. First, most of the trends we espy in patterns of financial production, distribution, and organizational structure are conditioned in large part on the existing character of: (1) inter-governmental competition for regulatory services and (2) implicit or conjectural government guarantees. Second, over long periods of time and around the world, conservative and liberal strategies of financial-services regulation tend to alternate with each other much like the seasons of the year. Each generation looks for fresh policy answers to the political problems raised by the waste and inequities of regulated competition in financial services. Third, private adaptations to changes in fundamental regulatory strategies take several decades to play themselves out. Inherited paradigms for regulating financial market structures are poorly adapted to the ways in which competitive conditions are changing today. Given the universality of subsidized implicit government guarantees of the debts of multinational deposit institutions, regulators and regulatees in different countries need to recognize that they have a community of interest in monitoring and standard-setting and in lender-of-last-resort arrangements for avoiding financial panics. The 'Concordat' of 1975 officially recognized this need for multinational regulatory forms and took some tentative steps in this direction.

Adverse balance-of-payments and employment consequences of a domestic or international loss of confidence in any major government's willingness or ability to make good its implicit institutional guarantees would drastically alter the operating risks of financial firms everywhere. It could push national governments back toward financial autarky and jolt the world's leading financial firms from a bullish expansionary stance into a bearish survival mode of operation.

If the world should be lucky enough to avoid a world war or an international run on a major country's deposits, it is hard not to suppose that in some important country sometime in the next few decades the off-budget costs and distributional inequities of expanding and largely unintended governmental guarantees will become a political pivot point. For whichever of these reasons confidence is disturbed, a general destruction of confidence in multinational institutions would shrink foreign trade in financial services and dispose individual-country regulators to experiment energetically with new and decidedly autarkic policy medicines. This new generation of policies could reimpose many of the measures that, during an era when the production costs of confidence seemed misleadingly low, experience taught our generation to reject.

These measures include: nationalization of domestic or foreign financial institutions and extensive manipulation of capital and entry controls, interest-rate ceilings, price controls, discriminatory taxes, and restrictions on permissible activities.

To forestall an implosion of confidence, players must come to see regulation of multinational firms as a mixed competitive and cooperative game. Their partial community of interest in avoiding financial instability must be seen as clearly as their obvious conflicts in seeking to increase their individual market shares. The world economy needs a joint decision making process which can impose binding risk-management responsibility on parent-country and host-country regulators. The current system merely divides authority to manage institutional liquidity and solvency risk. It does not face up to the subsidy to institutional risk-taking inherent in firms that have become too large for either home-country or host-country politicians to allow them to fail.

This paper argues that, whenever it is monitored by well-informed taxpayers, competition among regulators is beneficial. This rivalry constrains the ability of manipulators of the political system to use the financial system as a means for transferring wealth in hidden fashion from general taxpayers to constituencies able to build up political clout. However, difficulties of measuring and monitoring the market value of regulatory guarantees of specific forms of institutional risk-taking currently make it hard for taxpayers in some countries to stop competing government regulators from using subsidies to client risk-taking as a way of maintaining or expanding their market shares. International integration of financial markets extends the impact of imperfectly controlled subsidies to all countries.

When taxpayers do not adequately monitor the costs and revenues that accrue to individual-government players, the competition tends to get out of hand. In recent years, increases in the volatility of asset prices and foreign-exchange rates have sharply increased the cost of individual-country confidence-producing services in popularly unperceived ways. Because these dimly perceived costs have not been fully passed along to regulated institutions, explicit and implicit government guarantees in financial markets have become severely underpriced.

Subsidies to risk-bearing could be brought under control either by improving the flow of relevant information to taxpayers or by coordinating regulatory activity across countries. Although the first solution is preferable in principle, the latter solution is apt to have great appeal to the regulators and politicians who are formally responsible for instituting reforms. A case can be made, as an interim and second-best step, for greater international regulatory cooperation, even though this would at least temporarily cartelize the market for financial regulatory services. The near-term gain in world financial stability promises to offset what should be only a temporary loss in economic efficiency.

To reduce efficiency losses from cooperative reregulation, effort should be made wherever possible to employ schemes in which co-operating self-regulators are directly responsible to the regulated parties. However, because regulation imposes an implicit excise tax on position-taking, cooperating self-regulators must also be monitored by outsiders to make sure that they keep the tax on what can be clearly identified as socially desirable positions at a minimum and the tax on clearly undesirable positions high. Competition between politically motivated decisionmakers cannot be counted on to establish efficiency. The subsidy to risk-taking associated with federal deposit insurance and mortgage insurance in the US and with parallel bailout arrangements in other countries is administratively out of control. Such subsidies are producing distortions that are slowly undermining the world's financial system.

Finally, it is critical that authorities recognize that it is the hidden subsidization of risk-taking inherent in government bailout propensities, *not* competitive relaxation of archaic rules that threatens financial stability. Naive efforts to turn the hands of the regulatory clock back to earlier settings would only make things worse.

Regulatory competition must not be permitted to deteriorate into mere 'competition in laxity'. Improving the flow of information on regulatory performance to taxpayers would increase the odds that regulatory rivalry will function as competition in least-cost production of customer confidence and convenience.

NOTES

* Sections II and IV of this paper make use of and extend to an international context material in Kane (1986). For helpful criticism of an earlier draft, the author is grateful to Richard C. Aspinwall, James Bodurtha, Stephen V. O. Clarke, Catherine England, Richard J. Herring, Charles P. Kindleberger, Robert L. Hetzel, Allan H. Meltzer, Richard Portes, David H. Pyle, and Joseph F. Sinkey, Jr. The views expressed in this paper are my own and should not be construed to represent those of the National Bureau of Economic Research.

1 Institutions' own costs of servicing customer transactions may be decomposed into: (1) account entry costs; (2) name entry costs; (3) category entry costs, and (4) in-transfer and out-transfer processing costs.

2 One subtle reason that Western European countries may have begun to introduce explicit deposit insurance in recent years is that the deposit-insurance

contract provides a formal mechanism for targeting and extracting compensation for what may well be unavoidable commitments in any case.

REFERENCES

Baltensperger, Ernst (1980). 'Alternative Approaches to the Theory of the Banking Firm', *Journal of Monetary Economics* **6** (January), pp. 1–37.

Baumol, William, John C. Panzar, and Robert Willig (1986). 'On the Theory of Contestable Markets' in *New Developments in the Theory of Industrial Structure*, edited by G. F. Matthewson and Joseph E. Stiglitz, Cambridge, Mass.: MIT Press.

Bloch, Ernest (1984). 'The Benefits of Multiple Regulators', New York University, Graduate School of Administration (unpublished).

Clarke, Stephen V. O. (1983). *American Banks in the International Interbank Market*, Monograph Series in Finance and Economics No. 1983–4, New York University.

Germany, J. David, and John E. Morton (1985). 'Financial Innovation and Deregulation in Foreign Industrial Countries', *Federal Reserve Bulletin* **71** (October), pp. 743–53.

Giddy, Ian H. (1984). 'Domestic Regulation versus International Competition in Banking', *Kredit und Kapital* **8**, pp. 195–209.

Houpt, James V. (1981). 'Performance and Characteristics of Edge Corporations', Staff Studies No. 110, Washington: Board of Governors of the Federal Reserve System.

Kane, Edward J. (1981). 'Accelerating Inflation, Technological Innovation, and the Decreasing Effectiveness of Banking Regulation', *Journal of Finance* **36** (May), pp. 355–67.

(1984a). 'Technological and Regulatory Forces in the Developing Fusion of Financial-Services Competition', *Journal of Finance* **39** (June), pp. 759–72.

(1984b). 'Regulatory Structure in Futures Markets: Jurisdictional Competition Between the SEC, the CFTC, and Other Agencies', *Journal of Futures Markets* **4** (September), pp. 369–84.

(1985). *The Gathering Crisis in Federal Deposit Insurance*. Cambridge, Mass.: MIT Press.

(1986). 'Adapting Financial-Services Regulation to a Changing Economic Environment', forthcoming in a University of Arizona conference volume, edited by Gary Libecap.

Key, Sydney (1985). 'The Internationalization of U.S. Banking', in *Handbook for Banking Strategy*, edited by Richard C. Aspinwall and Robert A. Eisenbeis, New York: Wiley-Interscience, pp. 267–92.

Klein, Michael A. (1971). 'A Theory of the Banking Firm', *Journal of Money, Credit and Banking* **3** (May), pp. 204–18.

Mullineaux, Donald J. A., and Gary Gorton (1985). 'The Joint Production of Confidence: Commercial Bank Clearinghouses and the Theory of Hierarchy', University of Pennsylvania, The Wharton School (unpublished).

Niskanen, William (1971). *Bureaucracy and Representative Government*. Chicago: Aldine.

Organization for Economic Cooperation and Development (OECD) (1984). 'Obstacles to International Trade in Banking Services', *Financial Market Trends* **27** (March), pp. 1–16.

Orsingher, Roger (1967). *Banks of the World: A History and Analysis*, London: Macmillan.

Posner, Richard (1974) 'Theories of Economic Regulation', *Bell Journal of Economics* **5** (Autumn), pp. 335–58.

Santomero, Anthony M. (1984). 'Modeling the Banking Firm', *Journal of Money, Credit and Banking* **16** (November, Part II), pp. 576–602.

Sealey, C. W., Jr (1980). 'Deposit Rate-Setting, Risk Aversion, and the Theory of Depository Financial Intermediaries', *Journal of Finance* **35** (December), pp. 1139–54.

Sinkey, Joseph F., Jr (1986). *Commercial Bank Financial Management in the Financial Services Industry* (second edition), New York: Macmillan.

Stigler, George (1971). 'The Theory of Economic Regulation', *Bell Journal of Economics* **2** (Spring), pp. 3–21.

Discussion

DAVID H. PYLE

In his paper, Ed Kane used the concept of a regulatory dialectic to frame his discussion of financial regulation. I decided it might be useful to apply his framework to a specific case, deposit interest rate ceilings in the US.

Kane's regulatory dialectic: US interest rate ceilings

Thesis:	Net worth problems at thrifts.	

Antithesis:	Regulatory adjustment – The Interest Rate Adjustment Act of 1966.

	large time deposits	*small time deposits*
Synthesis: (Thesis)	Regulatee avoidance – offshore CDs, bank holding company commercial paper	Regulatee avoidance – free toasters, bicycles and gold coins, more branches
Antithesis:	Regulatory adjustment – penalty reserve requirements	Regulatory adjustment – one toaster per customer, no gold coins, no bicycles

Synthesis:	Non-regulated avoidance – growth of commercial paper market, growth of foreign offices	Non-regulated avoidance – money market mutual funds Regulated avoidance – finders' fees: bicycles for grandchildren
Antithesis:	Regulatory adjustment – ceilings eliminated on large CDs (1970)	Regulatory adjustment – ceilings eliminated on all time deposits (1983–86)
Synthesis: (Thesis)	Excessive reliance on borrowed funds – silent runs	Net worth problems at thrifts, too many branches, an American wins the Tour de France!

Kane's dialectic fits this case very well and it was fun to apply it. I almost had the illusion that I too had benefited from a high-class education from Jesuits. The regulatory dialectic applied to this case is also instructive. But first, a semantical point: Kane's use of 'reregulation' as a generic term for regulatory responses is somewhat confusing. Most of us, I believe, think of reregulation in contra-distinction to deregulation. A regulator relaxes a constraint (deregulates), doesn't like the outcome and subsequently adds a constraint (reregulates). Kane makes the point that 'regulatory adjustments often tighten one sub-set of rules as they relax other sub-sets' (i.e., 'pure' deregulation may be hard to find). This suggests that it might be clearer to use the generic 'regulatory adjustment', reserving deregulation for those adjustments that on balance reduce the regulatory burden and reregulation for those that increase it.

More importantly the dialectic structure reveals that in the case of interest rate ceilings regulatee avoidance led to reregulation while non-regulated avoidance (i.e., the loss of regulated market share) led to deregulation. This provides strong support for Kane's suggestion that regulatory relaxation is driven by 'heightened competition in the market for financial services regulation'. The fact that the sequences of action and reaction for large time deposits were played out more than a decade before those associated with small time deposits is testimony to the greater strength of regulatory competition in the former case, greater in large measure because of the international dimension of that competition. It is important to note that the ultimate deregulation of rate ceilings was not, on the whole, driven by competition among US regulators of depository institutions but by interindustry and international regulatory competition.

The last line of my table supports one of Kane's concluding points.

Many of the concerns about the current condition of US financial institutions, e.g., excessive reliance on borrowed funds by money centre banks and net worth problems at banks and thrifts, are the result of 'the ... subsidization of risk-taking inherent in government bailout propensities, *not* competitive relaxation of archaic rules'.

However, it is important to recognize that the case I selected is not the most controversial one with which to judge the desirability of competitive regulation. The problem that set off the deposit interest ceiling regulatory dialectic was a misguided attempt to subsidize mortgage lending in the US. A much more controversial case arises if international regulatory competition leads to a lack of confidence in short-term financial markets and in the international transaction system. Professor Kane reminds us that reductions in entry and exit costs, in currency conversion costs and in distance-related delivery costs have made it increasingly difficult for domestic bank regulators to maintain regulatory structures that were established when these costs were more of a barrier to 'structural arbitrage'. He looks with favour on this to the extent that it breaks down inefficient regulation. A dilemma arises because it also can break down efficient regulation. As noted earlier in this conference, the provision of confidence building and coordinating services through domestic regulatory structures creates a public good and attracts domestic and international free riders. This tends to make confidence building and the provision of coordinating services a losing proposition for the domestic regulators. So, as Kane notes, we need to overcome '... the difficulty of arranging durable patterns of international regulatory cooperation.' However, if we are too good at it, we will lose the advantages of regulatory competition. Whether Kane's suggestion that cooperative self-regulation at an international level will solve this dilemma is an open question, but it seems worth a try.

Discussion

ALOYS SCHWIETERT

Using industrial organization concepts and applying the regulatory dialectic is a comprehensive and valid approach to the problem of market supervision. Although bank executives may have difficulties in understanding Kane's language, they would agree with the basic results of his analysis if translated into business terms. As active players in the ongoing process of integration and globalization of financial markets they are well aware of the increased international competition among national regulators. Bankers have already realized the diminishing importance of traditional offshore centres (Panama, Cayman Islands, etc.) and are themselves a driving force in getting governments to put more pressure on some countries, e.g. Japan, to offer the reciprocity bankers feel they can now now demand.

Most of our executives – at least in Europe – probably would also agree that the subsidy implicit in today's lender-of-last-resort arrangements is a costly matter in the long run as it lowers incentives for the banks to maintain prudent liquidity levels and favours the large banks. But they would also argue that it was not their fault that the system itself is now at stake.

But what are the reasons for the present structural vulnerability of the banking system and of the financial system in general? Did we have too much regulation or not enough? Did the regulation aim too much at limiting *risk* instead of widening *opportunities*? In a market economy the ultimate goal of regulation is to secure a proper functioning of the market, and that also means amending the institutional framework if necessary to keep it geared to competition. Regulatory authorities basically have a subsidiary function; their tax collection or revenue targets should not be pursued directly (which puts a burden on regulatees) but indirectly. This will lead to better results due to the proper functioning of the financial markets as a whole.

What I am aiming at is the following question related to the US financial system, where markets were segmented for too long. We had, and still have, too many regulatory agencies there, some of them competing with each other, all of them aiming at activity restrictions, interstate restrictions and special performance prescriptions, which, taken together, create a highly complex regulatory system. In short, the result is a kind of over-regulation leading to a misallocation of resources and widespread efficiency losses. My question is whether the combination of the compliance costs of regulation and the perception that large banks will not be allowed to fail has contributed to the fact that we now have only one US bank with a triple-A rating.

My second question refers to the last two paragraphs in Kane's paper: his crash scenario with its attendant danger of a relapse into autarchic policy remedies and the request for international regulatory cooperation. Kane argues, and I agree with him, that – after the 'financial fusion' – there is a need for desegmentation of regulatory services as well as for globalization. However he does not see the expanding role of supranational quasi-governmental agencies – the EEC, IMF, BIS, etc. – as being sufficient to avoid a crash.

A supranational authority appropriate and able to become a global regulator does not exist. But keeping in mind the lessons of regulatory dialectic theory, we should not even ask to be served by such an authority because it could become a so-called '*perfectly effective regulator*' who – as a monopolist – would cause economic inefficiencies.

Kane therefore suggests employing schemes in which *cooperative self-regulators* do the job. But did not the theory also suggest that self-regulating systems create a tendency toward cartel pricing and could undermine the soundness of the financial system as a whole?

If neither a supranational authority nor self-regulation is the answer, what is? Shouldn't we put even more trust in competition on the national regulators' level? Is their performance at the moment really so bad – when you realise not only the *competitive nature* of their regulatory actions but also the *common interest* (of the general public and the business community as well) they pursue in monitoring and standard-setting? And couldn't it improve the efficiency of the regulatory system to draft and enact tough sunset laws for most of the watchdog agencies?

5 Emergency liquidity assistance for international banks

JACK GUTTENTAG and
RICHARD HERRING*

Since the nineteenth century, the lender of last resort (LLR) has been viewed as an agency with responsibility for preventing financial crises by lending directly and freely to a broad range of borrowers during periods of financial strain.[1] The LLR responsibility is usually associated with central banks, although in the absence of a central bank other agencies can assume the responsibility. Most types of central bank lending, however, are not LLR lending.[2]

Some contemporary experts (Humphrey 1975) argue that if Bagehot had known about open market operations, he would have dispensed with the notion of direct lending to individual borrowers altogether. They maintain that the LLR can fulfill its responsibility adequately by using open market operations to sustain the level of bank reserves and markets can be counted upon to allocate funds to solvent borrowers as needed. We have no quarrel with the proposition that it is important to control the general level of bank reserves.[3] And so we move on to ask whether there is a case for providing emergency liquidity assistance to individual banks even when the general level of liquidity is sustained. We argue that there is, because of the large social costs which may result from abrupt failures.

This paper is the result of our increasing dissatisfaction with our earlier analysis of the problem (Guttentag and Herring 1983). In light of the widely noted blurring of the distinctions between the different types of financial institutions that has occurred in recent years, we wanted to place greater emphasis on the characteristics of banks which make them peculiarly vulnerable to liquidity shocks. We also wanted to investigate how the recent trend toward 'securitization' has affected the vulnerability of banks to liquidity shocks. In addition we have welcomed the opportunity to probe more deeply into a number of issues including the social benefits that provide the ultimate rationale for an LLR function, why private markets do not meet the need adequately, whether LLRs really can (or should) lend only to solvent banks, and whether excessive reliance on LLRs can be controlled by charging a 'penalty' rate. Finally, the major policy recommendation of our earlier paper – that central banks should be more explicit about their commitment to provide LLR assistance – elicited a challenge to stipulate exactly what the explicit commitment should be. We have attempted to respond to that challenge here.

Section I examines why commercial banks are peculiarly vulnerable to liquidity shocks. Section II develops the rationale for shielding banks from such shocks by providing them with LLR assistance. Section III extends the case for providing emergency liquidity assistance and examines the social costs of providing it. Section IV discusses the terms and conditions under which LLR assistance should be provided in order to maximize the net benefit. Section V evaluates the special problems that arise when bank operations extend across national boundaries and proposes an international allocation of LLR responsibilities.

I.   The vulnerability of banks to liquidity shocks

A.   Definitions

A bank's 'liquidity position' is its ability to meet cash needs without loss. Given the bank's projected cash needs, its liquidity position is determined by its holdings of short-term, marketable assets plus unused borrowing capacity.[4] A 'liquidity shock' is an unexpected increase in cash needs that exhausts a bank's liquidity position. An 'illiquidity loss' occurs when, in order to meet a liquidity shock, the bank pays 'up market' on its liabilities, or suffers a loss on the sale of an asset relative to the price it could have obtained if more time had been available to locate the highest potential bidder. The bank is likely to have limited scope for attracting more funds by raising the interest rate because potential lenders tend to ration a bank that signals a willingness to pay more than the customary rate for a bank in its risk category (Aliber 1985, Giddy 1981, Guttentag and Herring 1985, Moffett 1986, and Saunders 1986). Liquidity assistance from the LLR enables a bank to reduce (perhaps to zero) the illiquidity loss that it would otherwise incur as the result of a liquidity shock.

Why modern societies have produced institutions that are so vulnerable to an illiquidity loss is a profound and important question. It is easy to imagine alternative institutional arrangements that would provide individual banking services without exposing the providers of such services to illiquidity losses.[5] Yet the development of commercial banks must be more than an historical accident because such institutions have arisen in many different historical contexts. This creates a presumption that combining the various basic banking functions in one firm involves important efficiencies, although technological and regulatory changes may be reducing these advantages over time. Development of this topic,[6] however, would require a lengthy digression from our central concern – how best to cope with the vulnerability of existing institutions to a liquidity shock.

The peculiar vulnerability of banks to a liquidity shock arises from two basic characteristics: (1) banks hold assets that are imperfectly marketable; and (2) banks issue liabilities that are redeemable at par on demand or at short notice.

B.   The Imperfect Marketability of Bank Loans

A sudden increase in a bank's cash needs would not cause an illiquidity loss if the bank's assets were perfectly marketable. But imperfect marketability is a fundamental characteristic of most bank loans. Indeed borrowers are often willing to pay for the services of banks in intermediating with depositors because they are unable to issue marketable securities. To understand why, it is useful to draw a sharp distinction between a loan and a security, although in practice the boundary may be somewhat blurred.[7] A 'loan' is a credit contract between a borrower and a single lender. It is often custom-tailored to meet the borrower's financial requirements and the lender's need for assurances regarding the borrower's creditworthiness. A 'security', in contrast is a credit contract between the borrower and many investors who are unknown to the borrower and have no other relationship to the borrower.

1. Why Some Borrowers Prefer Bank Loans   Some borrowers may occasionally choose to obtain a bank loan because they wish to avoid public disclosure of proprietary information or because they prefer the greater flexibility of a loan even though they could issue securities as cheaply; but more often borrowers opt for loans because loans are less costly. In many cases, security issuance is not feasible because the costs would be so burdensome to the borrower (and therefore so prejudicial to the borrower's prospects for servicing the security adequately) that no investment banker would be willing to assume the responsibility for placing the issue.

The cost of a bank loan will be less than the cost of security issuance in four overlapping situations.

(1) A loan will be cheaper when the determination of creditworthiness depends on non-objective information such as the borrower's 'character'[8]

that must be evaluated through direct personal contact. Such information is difficult to transmit to third parties and decays in value rapidly as it moves away from the original source.

(2) A loan will be cheaper when it is necessary to custom-tailor the credit contract and monitor the borrower's compliance in order to assure that the borrower is making appropriate use of the funds. A single lender is likely to be able to monitor a credit contract more efficiently than a group of unrelated investors because monitoring requires the exercise of discretion and the ability to renegotiate the credit contract in the event that some contingency arises that was not foreseen in the original agreement.

(3) A loan will be cheaper when the borrower is seeking to finance a very specialized type of project or to make use of collateral that is imperfectly marketable. A bank that has invested in credit analysis that is relevant to the borrower's project or collateral will be able to assimilate and evaluate information regarding the borrower's creditworthiness much more efficiently than unspecialized investors.[9]

(4) A loan will be cheaper when information bearing on the riskiness of loans arises out of a relationship between the bank and the borrower. Once the bank has made an initial investment in information about a specific borrower and has developed the right contract and monitoring arrangements for that borrower, additional loans can be made to the borrower at lower marginal cost than would be possible for another creditor who has not made the initial investment. Moreover, as trust and confidence in the borrower grows with experience, the lender may be able to reduce its monitoring costs.[10]

These factors which lead a borrower to seek a bank loan rather than to issue securities, also make it difficult for the bank to sell the loan subsequently if the bank should experience a liquidity shock. Any potential buyer of the loan realizes that the original lender knows more about the value of the loan. In order to avoid paying more than the loan is worth, the potential buyer must make the same investment in information that the original lender made. Even if the expected return to the potential buyer is high enough to justify the investment in 'hard' data to evaluate the loan, the potential buyer will have difficulty evaluating information that arises from the original lender's relationship with the borrower. Moreover, if monitoring is necessary, a potential buyer who does not have prior experience with the borrower will be at a disadvantage.

As a practical matter, any potential buyers are likely to be other banks who already have some sort of relationship with the borrower, or who have expertise in evaluating similar borrowers, projects or collateral.

Loans to small borrowers that have no other banking relationships, or that involve idiosyncratic projects or unusual collateral, are likely to be particularly difficult to sell. (These borrowers are also likely to encounter the greatest difficulty in finding an alternative source of credit if the bank should be unable to continue lending.) The selling bank may overcome these obstacles by guaranteeing the loan, perhaps by accepting an obligation to buy it back if the loan becomes non-performing according to some mutually-agreed criteria. But at a time when there is some doubt about the bank's creditworthiness – a fundamental aspect of a run – the value of such a guarantee may be heavily discounted by potential buyers.

2. Implications of Securitization   To what extent has the recent trend toward securitization eased the structural vulnerability of banks to illiquidity losses? 'Securitization' is used in a narrow sense to refer to the conversion of bank loans into marketable securities by packaging the loans into pools, and issuing securities collateralized by the pools of loans. In a broader sense 'securitization' refers to the development of markets for a variety of instruments including bank loans, and claims issued by nonbanks that allow them to bypass banks (BIS 1986, pp. 266–7). Both the narrow and broad sense of the term are relevant.

Securitization narrowly defined began in the United States with home mortgage loans insured or guaranteed by a US Government agency, and while the process was later extended to include non-insured loans, most of the securities issued against these loans are guaranteed by a Federal agency. Recently the process has been applied to other types of loans: mortgage loans secured by income-generated properties, automobile and truck loans, credit card receivables, and computer leases (Pavel 1986 and Olson 1986). Business loans of commercial banks have not yet (as of August 1986) been securitized. Although efforts are underway, the problems involved are formidable.[11]

To what extent can securitization of this type reduce the illiquidity loss which must be sustained when assets are sold at short notice? Since time is of the essence in meeting a liquidity shock, securitization must be accomplished very quickly to materially reduce a bank's vulnerability to illiquidity losses. But issuing securities collateralized by loans takes a considerable amount of time and for that reason is no more useful for meeting a liquidity shock than issuing a debenture or common stock (except that in the former case, potential investors need not have confidence in the creditworthiness of the bank). Thus securitization is likely to enhance the bank's liquidity position only if, before a liquidity shock occurs, the bank has swapped its loans for securities issued against those loans.[12] Most securitization, however, has been used to shift assets off bank balance sheets in order to generate fee income, not to replace loans with lower yielding, more marketable assets.

The same technological, economic, regulatory and institutional developments[13] that have led to the conversion of loans into marketable securities have also facilitated securitization in the broader sense. Markets have developed, often with the active support and involvement of commercial banks, which enable the most creditworthy of traditional bank customers to issue negotiable securities directly to investors rather than borrow from banks. This trend may have reduced the average marketability of loans remaining on bank balance sheets.

Banks have also attempted to increase the direct marketability of loans, without going through the elaborate process of collateralization and security issuance. In many cases, loan documentation has been modified to facilitate marketability. Examples are the elimination of clauses that restrict the original lender's right to make assignments under the terms of large-scale syndicated loan agreements and the introduction of transferable loan certificates (Guttentag and Herring 1986). In addition, banks have offered recourse arrangements or other guarantees to buyers. Nevertheless, the secondary markets for bank loans remain thin. Such markets contribute little to a bank's ability to meet a liquidity shock, although they clearly facilitate other portfolio adjustments.

In order to recoup some of the revenues lost from customers who have shifted to the securities markets, banks have sold contingent guarantees to security holders and back-up lines of credit to issuers of securities. The growth of such contingent claims may reduce the bank's ability to cope with a liquidity shock because the beneficiary of the back-up line or guarantee may exercise its claim on the bank at a time when the bank itself is experiencing strains on its liquidity position.

In summary, securitization both narrowly and broadly defined has not reduced the vulnerability of banks to liquidity shocks. The decline in average quality of the loans remaining on bank balance sheets increases the probability of a shock that will undermine confidence in the bank and lead to a run.[14] And the possibility that large amounts of contingent claims may be exercised when beneficiaries of those claims detect a weakening in a bank's condition may further weaken the bank's ability to deal with a liquidity shock.

C. Unpredictable Increases in Cash Needs

The imperfect marketability of bank loans makes banks vulnerable to an illiquidity loss because they are subject to unpredictable increases in cash needs. Sudden increases in cash needs may occur for three reasons.

1. Bank runs   First, because a substantial portion of a bank's liabilities are very short-term, news that causes depositors to question the bank's net worth ('bad news') can cause a run. So long as depositors have confidence that the bank can redeem all of its liabilities at par they will ask it to do so only in accordance with their individual cash needs; the bank will be protected by the law of large numbers from having to redeem a large amount of deposits at one time. Yet if some event causes depositors to lose confidence, the bank will be subjected to massive withdrawals as depositors rush to redeem their claims. Depositors have an incentive to run even though they believe that if the bank had sufficient time to get the best possible price for its assets it would be able to redeem all liabilities at par.[15] If other depositors run, the hurried liquidation of imperfectly marketable assets could result in losses that exceed shareholders' equity, so that any depositors who delay redeeming their liabilities may incur a loss. In the terminology of Benston *et al.* (1986, p. 42), the bank may be fire-sale insolvent.

The incentive to run is strengthened by the knowledge that declines in asset value may accelerate as the market value of assets approaches the book value of liabilities. This tendency for losses to increase as the bank's capital position deteriorates is attributable in part to the fact that the bank is likely to take increasingly desperate gambles to stay in business (Herring and Vankudre 1986) and in part to the fact that if the most marketable assets are sold first, illiquidity losses will accelerate as withdrawals continue. Thus the perception of deteriorating asset quality can lead depositors to take actions which will cause the value of assets to decline in fact. The run becomes a self-fulfilling prophecy.

Even deposit customers who are current or prospective borrowers are likely to join the run. The banking relationship has a value to such customers that is contingent on the continuing ability of the bank to provide credit and other services when needed (Flannery 1982). The threat of a disruption of the relationship provides a motive for customers to shift deposits away from a bank whose solvency is in question to another bank where the option to borrow is expected to be more valuable.[16]

2. Commitments to Lend   A second reason that banks are subject to sudden increases in cash needs has already been noted: banks offer stand-by credit to their commercial customers (including other banks and non-bank financial institutions), and are therefore subject to unexpected surges in loan demands. In effect banks provide emergency liquidity assistance for the rest of the economy. While in many cases banks do not have a legal obligation to meet such demands, failure to honour them may seriously damage a bank's reputation and its long-run competitive position.

3. Adverse Clearings A third reason banks are vulnerable to unpredictable surges in cash needs pertains to large banks which are the custodians of the payments system. A settlement failure may cause an enormous increase in cash needs. (This point is discussed further in Section II.C below.)

Thus banks are vulnerable to illiquidity losses because they are subject to large, unanticipated increases in cash needs which may force them to liquidate imperfectly marketable assets. Of course, the fact that banks are vulnerable to illiquidity losses does not imply that they deserve special public support. The case for public intervention rests on the social costs associated with the vulnerability of banks to illiquidity losses which are discussed in the following section.

II. Social costs of bank failures

The function of emergency liquidity assistance is to mitigate the social costs associated with bank failures where 'failure' is defined as an inability to meet cash obligations when due. Failures do not necessarily generate social costs that justify an LLR function. Much depends on whether the failure is abrupt – catching creditors by surprise – and on whether the bank terminates operations or continues operations through a merger, recapitalization or other arrangement.

In most financial systems the LLR does not assume sole responsibility for mitigating the social costs of bank failures.[17] Prudential supervision and regulation of banks performs a failure-prevention function. And deposit insurance reduces the incidence of abrupt failures by dampening the tendency of depositors to run from banks of questionable soundness. Of course, so long as banks are permitted to take risky positions, failures will occur, and so long as insurance does not cover all bank liabilities, there is a danger that failures will be abrupt.

The responsibility of the LLR in this institutional context is to assure that solvent banks do not fail for want of liquidity and to help prevent the abrupt closure of an insolvent bank that might lead to a contagious loss of confidence in other banks. This latter responsibility may be shared in varying degree with the deposit insurance agency (if any) which is naturally interested in arranging a disposition that will minimize capital losses to itself (and other creditors of the bank); this is likely to be a secondary concern for the LLR.[18]

Potential social costs from the abrupt failure of a bank include the impacts on transactions balances, borrowers, the payments system and confidence in other banks.

A.   *Impact on Transactions Balances*

A bank failure that imposes losses on holders of transactions balances will reduce aggregate demand. In principle, this effect is no different from that associated with the failure of any firm upon which the public owns claims except that, because bank claims are highly liquid, the decline in aggregate demand may be larger for a loss of any given size. Depositors of the failed bank may be forced to borrow or sell assets in order to rebalance the liquidity structure of their portfolios. If these reactions result in a general contraction of bank reserves, which could be the case if the rebalancing of liquidity involved larger holdings of currency, the decline in aggregate demand could be substantially greater.

In a system where the monetary authorities sustain the general level of bank reserves, however, the reduction in aggregate demand will be only slightly greater than the reduction attributable to the initial loss of wealth.[19] While the failure may cause economic distress to the local economy, this may be true of any failure and the fact that the failed firm is a bank does not provide any special rationale for public intervention beyond that of monetary control.

This potential social cost of a bank failure has received the most attention in the literature; but we regard it as unimportant in a system where the monetary authorities sustain the general level of bank reserves.

B.   *Impact on Borrowers*

If the failure of a bank causes borrowers dependent on that bank to lose access to credit, real economic activity may decline as borrowers are forced to interrupt production and investment projects. Such borrowers may be impacted even though the general level of bank reserves is sustained. The extent of the impact depends on the availability of alternative sources of credit. In many cases bank borrowers have no other banking relationship and are unable to issue marketable securities. Hence, finding an alternative source of credit may require substantial time and search costs.[20]

Note that both illiquidity costs to deposit holders and loss of credit lines by borrowers are a result of failure as we have defined it (the inability of a bank to meet its cash obligations), which necessarily leaves depositors without access to their money and borrowers without access to credit. These costs need not follow from the closure of a bank because of financial difficulties – the FDIC definition of failure. If the closed bank is merged with another bank, for example, depositors are unlikely to be affected and there is a good possibility that borrowing relationships will be maintained.

C.   Impact on the Payments System

If the failure of a bank causes a loss (or threatens to cause a loss) to counterparties in the clearing process, it may disrupt the payments system. The aftermath of the collapse of Bankhaus Herstatt is a grim reminder that even the failure of a very small bank can have major repercussions on the volume of transactions. The failure of Herstatt on June 26, 1974 caused several counterparties in foreign exchange contracts to suffer loss on dollar balances that were to have been paid to them through the New York Clearing House Interbank Payments System (CHIPS) in exchange for Deutschmark balances that they had already paid to Herstatt earlier that day in Germany. For a few days trading was reported to have come to 'a virtual standstill' (*World Financial Markets* 1974, p. 1).[21] The repercussions would undoubtedly have been much more severe if a larger bank that was a settling participant had been involved.

More recently, Humphrey (1986) simulated the possible consequences of the sudden failure of a large CHIPS participant that would leave it unable to settle its net debit position at the end of a specified day. The results were dramatic. The unwinding of transactions to eliminate all transactions involving the failed bank resulted in some 50 banks having their net settlement obligation raised by an amount exceeding their capital. Furthermore, repeating the simulation on a different day gave similar results except that the list of affected banks was considerably different. Humphrey (1986, pp. 108, 110) noted that:

> These results suggest that the institutions most likely to be affected by a particular institution's failure cannot be readily identified beforehand. This day-to-day variation in systemic risk exposure means that an institution cannot limit its credit assessment to some small group of participants with which it most frequently deals. Rather, it must constantly monitor all participants in each network and its exposure across multiple networks. It also means that from a supervisory standpoint the consequences of an institution's default on its payments obligations cannot be easily predicted. ... (C)lose to half of the participants and one-third of the payment value could be subject to the CHIPS unwind provisions in the event of an unexpected settlement failure of a CHIPS participant.

The continuous and efficient functioning of the payments system requires that transactions balances be received and paid out rapidly and at very low cost. If perceptions of default risk associated with intra-day credit extensions to other participants in the system increase to the point that participants feel it necessary to verify that receipts due from specific banks will be met before they make payments to these banks, the payments system will be much more costly to operate. Mussa (1986, p. 104) notes that '. . . if transactors consistently feared a 1% chance of a 10% loss (due to bank failure) on every transaction through the banking system, it would be difficult to sustain the present payments mechanism. This small expected loss, compounded 500 times per year to take account of the turnover rate of transactions balances, amounts to more than a 50% annual rate of tax on each dollar of such balances.'

D.   Contagion

Most bank failures are isolated individual events that do not present a case for emergency liquidity assistance. If the bank is small the spillover costs would pass unnoticed, especially if deposits at the bank are insured and the failure was widely anticipated. Large bank failures, however, present a much greater risk of contagion.

Many observers associate contagion with cash drains stemming from the withdrawal of currency from a failing bank which attempts to replenish its cash by liquidating assets, thus pulling reserves away from other banks. In this view no problem will arise if the monetary authorities sustain the general level of bank reserves. However, contagion may occur even if the authorities sustain the general level of bank reserves.

Contagion may arise from an interbank settlements failure – interbank credit risk – even though the monetary authorities sustain the general level of bank reserves. When one bank fails, other banks may be in jeopardy if their claims on the failed bank are a significant proportion of their capital. Since the size of interbank lines is usually related to the size of the borrowing bank, the loss is likely to be a larger fraction of the capital of the counterparty in the event of the failure of a large bank.[22] As we have noted, this danger is particularly acute in the payments clearing system where intra-day extensions of interbank credits may be large relative to the settling banks' capital. But large positions also arise in other interbank markets.

The possibility of a contagious loss of confidence in the interbank market is heightened by the lack of timely data on interbank exposures. Market participants know that interbank credit positions may be very large, but the size of particular bilateral positions is not known. In the event of a failure, market participants do not know which banks have unsatisfied claims against the failed bank. Depositors may assume the worst and withdraw deposits from the bank that would least be able to sustain the loss if it were the counterparty.

A failure may also be contagious if other banks are believed to have asset portfolios that are similar to the failed bank and therefore to be vulnerable to the same economic disturbances. This too is a more serious problem for large banks than small banks. The larger the bank, the more likely is its failure to attract public attention and undermine confidence in the banking system generally, and in similar large banks particularly. The failure of a large bank, much more than that of a small one, is likely to be viewed as conveying information about the soundness of peer banks. In part this is because large bank failures are less often attributable to embezzlement or other idiosyncratic causes than to poor quality assets. And since large banks compete in the same national and international markets they face generally similar cost and demand conditions and tend to have similar portfolios (Mayer 1975).

The extent to which a contagious loss of confidence unrelated to currency drains has actually occurred is difficult to determine. The evidence of the 1930s when contagion was rampant is contaminated by currency drains which forced a contraction in the total stock of bank reserves. The evidence from the free banking era before 1860 is useless because bank liabilities took the form of circulating notes which, because of the high cost of redemption, traded at varying discounts from par depending on their presumed quality. This meant that a decline in the public's confidence in a bank resulted in a decline in the price of the bank's notes rather than in a run. A basic condition for a run is redeemability at par, at very low cost, and this condition was not met.[23]

The period between the Civil War and the 1930s may provide some relevant evidence. Benston and Kaufman (1986) investigate this period for evidence of contagion but they define contagion as simultaneous runs on large numbers of banks which they argue can only occur in the event of a currency drain. They conclude that since such drains 'current with a decline in aggregate deposits occurred in only three years – 1874, 1893 and 1908 . . . contagion could have occurred only in these three years and probably only in 1893' (Benston and Kaufman 1986, p. 18). Their approach, however, does not address the possibility of a contagious loss of confidence that may occur apart from a currency drain.

Saunders (1986) has reviewed several recent studies which indicate little evidence of contagion. But, as he notes, these studies must be interpreted in light of the fact that the Federal Reserve has clearly sought to prevent contagious bank runs. Thus the lack of clear evidence of contagion may simply indicate that the Fed has largely succeeded. The empirical evidence does not warrant dismissing a contagious loss of confidence as a potentially serious problem.

E.   Summary

Emergency liquidity assistance can mitigate the social costs which may result from the abrupt closure of a bank. If depositors have confidence that emergency liquidity assistance is available, they will be less likely to run when a bank's viability is in question. If a solvent bank experiences a liquidity shock nonetheless, emergency liquidity assistance will allow it to continue operations without interruption. If the bank is insolvent, emergency liquidity assistance provides the supervisory authorities with the time necessary to make an orderly and efficient disposition of the failed bank without interruption, avoiding the various social costs that might result from its abrupt closure – a disruption in the local economy due to illiquidity costs imposed on depositors, an interruption in the access to credit of bank borrowers, a breakdown in the payments system and a contagious loss of confidence in other banks.

III.   The provision of emergency liquidity assistance

A.   Emergency Liquidity Assistance and Market Failure

Why can't the private market provide emergency liquidity assistance to a bank in trouble? A partial answer is that markets for short-term claims do not work well when great uncertainty exists regarding the solvency of potential borrowers. Potential lenders faced with such uncertainty may ration the borrower instead of raising the rate to cover a greater potential for loss.

We have already noted the difficulty in evaluating imperfectly marketable bank assets and the lack of timely and relevant information. Thus, when a bank comes under suspicion, it may have great difficulty persuading the market that it is solvent. Bagehot (1873, p. 68) understood this problem well, noting 'Every banker knows that if he has to *prove* that he is worthy of credit, however good may be his arguments, in fact his credit is gone . . .'

Does Bagehot's point apply to deposit placements from other banks as well as from the public? Won't the self-interest of banks in preserving confidence in the banking system induce them to come to the assistance of a bank in trouble? Banks acting in their individual capacities have the same incentive to reduce their exposures to a bank of questionable solvency as the nonbank public. Indeed, bank creditors may sometimes be in the vanguard of a run, as some banks were in the case of First Pennsylvania and Continental Illinois. As one bank officer remarked to us after turning down an opportunity to lend to Continental, 'I'm not paid to take this type of risk.'

Banks will often overcome their self-interest narrowly conceived to act collectively in the broader interest of the banking system. For example, Morgan Guaranty organized a group of banks to provide liquidity assistance to Continental Illinois when it first fell under suspicion, although the amounts involved turned out to be wholly inadequate to meet Continental's mounting cash needs. Similar facilities were arranged for SeaFirst and First Pennsylvania. Such rescue efforts are usually organized by the central bank (Goodhart 1985, p. 34) and therefore provide only limited perspective on what banks might do in the absence of an official LLR. During periods of severe financial strain in the United States before the Federal Reserve Act, banks sometimes acted collectively through local clearinghouses, but sometimes they didn't.

The major difficulty with collective action is that it is uncertain. Success may depend on the leadership of one or two banks that may or may not be able to overcome the competitive impulses of the others. Moreover, collective action is most uncertain when a large bank encounters difficulties because usually the larger the bank the larger the amount of assistance required. Consequently more banks must agree to cooperate and negotiations become increasingly cumbersome. In contrast, a central bank acting as an LLR has the resources required to help a bank of any size (provided the bank needs domestic currency).

Thus, the market failure that underlies the need for a LLR is the problem of achieving collective action to mobilize the massive amounts of credit that might be needed by a large bank in sufficient time to meet the bank's needs. The Bank of New York case, where the bank found itself some $23.6 billion short near the close of business one day, is an extreme but instructive example. Although the need for emergency liquidity assistance was attributable to the breakdown of a computer system rather than a loss of confidence by depositors, the amount was so large and the need for assistance so urgent that it was impossible to confirm that the bank was solvent before granting assistance.[24]

B.   *The Solvency Condition for the Provision of Emergency Liquidity*
      Assistance

The traditional rule for the provision of emergency liquidity assistance is that LLRs lend only to solvent banks.[25] This principle is embodied in the statutes of many central banks, and has been repeated on numerous occasions by economists (Johnson and Abrams 1983, Guttentag and Herring 1983, Thornton 1802 and Bagehot 1873).[26] It is easy to understand why. If the bank isn't solvent, then liquidity assistance won't enable it to survive. Furthermore, the redistribution of wealth from taxpayers[27] to depositors, creditors and/or shareholders which occurs when an LLR offers assistance to an insolvent bank lacks political legitimacy and is difficult to justify on equity grounds.[28] Moreover market discipline may be seriously undermined if bank managers and creditors need not be concerned that the bank will lose access to emergency liquidity assistance when its net worth approaches zero. In addition, the effectiveness of emergency liquidity assistance will be enhanced if the market believes that the LLR lends only to solvent institutions, because the extension of assistance will constitute a signal to the market that the bank in question is sound. This will facilitate restoration of the bank's normal access to credit, and reduce the amount of credit the LLR must advance.

Practice, however, does not entirely square with principle. First, the practice of lending only on a collateralized basis undercuts the credibility of the signal regarding the bank's solvency.[29] If the LLR is confident the bank is solvent, why must it demand collateral? Is it reasonable to expect other creditors, who generally have less information and cannot monitor the bank or control its future behaviour as effectively as the LLR, to resume uncollateralized lending while the LLR lays claim to the bank's best assets?

Moreover, LLRs have lent to insolvent institutions on numerous occasions; for example: in the United States, Franklin National,[30] First Pennsylvania, SeaFirst, and Continental Illinois; in the United Kingdom, Johnson Matthey; in Canada, Canadian Commercial; and in Italy, Banco Ambrosiano. As a result, markets tend to associate unusually large credit extensions by the LLR as an indicator that the bank receiving assistance is likely to be insolvent rather than the reverse. A bank known to be borrowing more than routine amounts from the central bank thus runs the grave risk that it will quickly find that it can borrow *only* from the central bank.

Why, despite their stated intentions, do LLRs nonetheless lend to insolvent institutions? In part the reason is that solvency is often difficult to determine, especially on very short notice. Requests for emergency liquidity assistance do not come neatly labeled as 'liquidity problems' and 'solvency problems'. Serious liquidity problems usually develop because some event has raised questions about a bank's solvency and the LLR may be forced to act before it is possible to verify the soundness of the bank seeking assistance. When the LLR gives the troubled bank the benefit of the doubt it may sometimes turn out to be wrong. That the LLR is in effect making a bet on the solvency of the bank is part of the rationale for lending only on a collateralized basis.

Uncertainty regarding solvency may continue even after all the available data have been collected because the value of the imperfectly marketable assets which comprise the bulk of bank portfolios is difficult to establish. Moreover, the bank may be subjected to new shocks that push it into insolvency[31] even while it is receiving emergency liquidity assistance.

More fundamentally, the LLR may choose to grant emergency liquidity assistance even when it knows the bank is not solvent in order to prevent the potentially heavy social costs of an abrupt closure. The social costs from abrupt closure are likely to be just as high when the failed bank is insolvent as when it is illiquid. While the precedent created of assisting an insolvent bank may pose greater future hazards by dulling market discipline, when confronted with a clear and present danger of an impending crisis, concerns about the potential benefits of greater discipline seem invariably to give way.

C. Costs of Providing Emergency Liquidity Assistance

The provision of emergency liquidity assistance involves two related costs. Access to emergency liquidity assistance is a valuable contingent claim on the LLR,[32] which enables the bank to avoid illiquidity costs by exercising the option to discount assets with the LLR. Access to emergency liquidity assistance will be more valuable to shareholders the broader the range of contingencies under which it can be used, the greater the bank's vulnerability to an illiquidity loss, the more legally binding the bank's claim on the LLR, the greater the LLR's resources to meet the commitment, and the lower the price. The provision of emergency liquidity assistance may result in a subsidy to bank shareholders unless it is properly priced. We do not, however, view the wealth transfer to bank shareholders as a significant problem because it can be offset by other burdens imposed on banks including reserve requirements, direct taxes, reporting costs and portfolio restrictions.[33]

The second and more important cost is that access to emergency liquidity assistance allows a bank to operate with less liquidity than it would otherwise view as prudent.[34] It may choose to increase profits by holding smaller amounts of marketable assets, depending more heavily on its ability to place short-term liabilities to meet unusual cash requirements (Guttentag and Herring 1986b). Access to emergency liquidity assistance also may lead a bank to take on a greater risk of insolvency since it enables the bank to withstand a greater shock to its capital position without incurring illiquidity costs.[35]

This second cost of providing access to emergency liquidity assistance was emphasized in the earliest writing about LLR assistance. Thornton (1802, p. 188), for example, warned that it would not 'become the Bank of England to relieve every distress which the rashness of country banks may bring upon them; the bank, by doing this, might encourage their improvidence.'

LLRs are thus faced with a dilemma which Kindleberger (1978, p. 163) has aptly characterized: 'Central banks should act one way (lending freely) to halt the panic, but another (leave the market to its own devices) to improve the chances of preventing future panics.' This dilemma has its counterpart in the quandary of how to price emergency liquidity assistance. The problem is how to establish access terms that will assure the effectiveness of the LLR in dealing with liquidity shocks while minimizing the incentives for banks to increase their exposure to such shocks.

IV.   Terms of access to emergency liquidity assistance

Bagehot's solution to this problem was to exclude all banks which were not solvent from access to emergency liquidity assistance, to charge a penalty rate when assistance was required,[36] and to be very explicit about the availability of emergency liquidity assistance. Central banks have rejected all three aspects of his solution. As noted in Section III, central banks have accepted the solvency rule in principle while rejecting it in practice for compelling reasons. In this Section we will argue that the unwillingness of central banks to charge a penalty rate is probably well founded, but their rejection of Bagehot's explicitness rule is not.

A.   Price

We agree that the discount rate should be above the riskless rate, and the proposal by Kane and Kaufman (1986, p. 117) that it be set just above the equilibrium market value of the posted collateral is intuitively appealing. Yet it is clear that a rate set on this basis would not discourage banks from reducing their liquidity positions, since it amounts to a guarantee of the marketability of imperfectly marketable assets.

How does the LLR's discount rate affect the ways in which a bank manages its liquidity position and thus the extent to which it depends on the LLR? If the bank knew that the rate was so high that the cost of assistance would exceed the cost of liquidating illiquid assets, there would be no point in requesting emergency liquidity assistance and liquidity planning would be based on the assumption that no LLR assistance was available. Such a rate would obviously be self-defeating.

At less onerous discount rates, the bank will compare the cost of LLR loans with the opportunity costs of holding the additional volume of liquid assets needed to eliminate or reduce the need for emergency liquidity assistance. Since a bank is likely to anticipate that it will need LLR assistance infrequently and for very short periods, a high discount rate generates costs only for a very short period while the opportunity cost of holding low-yielding, liquid assets is a constant drain. Hence, any discount rate high enough to have an *ex ante* deterrent effect on the bank's liquidity management would have to be so high as to negate the purpose of the assistance. Indeed, it is the recognition of this fact by central bankers that underlies their penchant to be vague and non-committal about their willingness to provide emergency assistance.

To neutralize the tendency of banks to substitute LLR assistance for liquidity and capital would require an access charge (comparable to a fee for a line of credit) which would vary with the condition of the bank. In all respects, such a price would be the same as a variable deposit insurance premium, and the numerous problems involved in implementing such a scheme would be identical to those involved in implementing variable deposit insurance premiums (Horvitz 1983).

B.   Explicitness vs. Ambiguity

Bagehot favoured making the LLR's commitment explicit in order to sustain confidence in the system, and he strongly criticized the Bank of England for its unwillingness to do so (Bagehot 1873, pp. 208–9):

> The public is never sure what policy will be adopted at the most important moment: it is not sure what amount of advance will be made, or on what security it will be made. The best palliative to a panic is a confidence in the adequate amount of the Bank reserve, and in the efficient use of that reserve. And until we have on this point a clear understanding with the Bank of England, both our liability to crises and our terror at crises will always be greater than would otherwise be.

Central bankers have resisted Bagehot's position from his day to our own. Their major argument is that the more explicit they make their commitment the more they erode market discipline. Central bankers realize that they cannot dissuade banks from undue reliance on emergency liquidity assistance by threatening to charge a high discount rate. And they are undoubtedly aware that their own actions in providing emergency liquidity assistance give rise to strong expectations regarding their future behaviour. Nevertheless, they prefer not to encourage even greater erosion of market discipline by making an explicit declaration of a willingness to provide assistance in advance.

1. The case for market discipline   In principle, the case for encouraging depositors to discipline banks is quite compelling. In perfect markets, creditors have sufficient information to identify imprudent behaviour *ex ante*, before losses are incurred, and they would respond to the perception of imprudent behaviour by charging the bank a penalty premium which exceeds the expected return from the imprudent action. Hence, the rational bank would respond to the increase in the cost of funds by behaving more prudently. As soon as the bank revised its behaviour, creditors would reduce the penalty premium. Of course, if markets functioned this well, merely the anticipation that creditors will penalize imprudent behaviour would be a sufficient deterrent.

This type of market discipline would have clear advantages over traditional bank supervision. It is continuous, impersonal and non-bureaucratic. Penalties are automatically elicited by the perception of imprudent behaviour, the penalties are precisely calibrated to the degree of imprudent behaviour, and they continue until such behaviour is corrected. The direct costs of prudential supervision and regulation would be reduced since market participants would perform these functions. Indirect costs that arise when bank supervision and regulation impede the banking system's ability to adapt to changing market conditions would also decline. The market would arbitrate the issue of which activities a bank should undertake by making a case by case decision of whether a particular activity was being prudently managed by the bank and whether the activity would enhance or stabilize bank earnings. All users of banking services as well as shareholders would be better off. In principle the only losers would be bank regulators who would find their employment prospects greatly diminished.

2. How market discipline works in practice   In practice, however, market discipline often fails to deliver these advantages and under some circumstances may actually jeopardize the stability of the banking system. Part of the problem is that the market lacks sufficient information to evaluate the soundness of banks. It is intrinsically difficult for even supervisors and bank managers to value bank loans that are not actively traded on secondary markets. Depositors, with less access to information, face even greater obstacles in evaluating bank portfolios.

Published information is available only with a lag and is incomplete.[37] In almost every country regulators require that banks disclose a considerable amount of information that is not shared with the markets, but is presumably relevant to evaluating the soundness of the bank. The information gap has become increasingly large as the pace of financial innovation has accelerated. Several international banks now conduct a greater volume of activity off their balance sheets than on and there is as yet no clear agreement on what constitutes meaningful disclosure under such circumstances.

Largely because of the inadequacy of information, market discipline is often rather crude and unfocussed. Risk premiums on uninsured deposits seem to be determined largely by the size of the bank rather than by a careful assessment of its financial condition.[38] Tiering of deposit rates in the international interbank market is based less on careful assessments of the creditworthiness of individual banks than on perceptions of their access to governmental support and the ability of particular governments to provide it (BIS 1983, Clarke 1984, Guttentag and Herring 1985).

When markets react to questions concerning a particular bank's condition by rationing funds and raising rates, the bank may respond by prudently retrenching – allowing some liabilities to mature without being replaced and cutting dividends as earnings contract. Alternatively, the bank may attempt to maintain earnings by borrowing more from the sources still available while offering creditors greater comfort by shortening maturities. This seems to have been what Continental Illinois did after the failure of Penn Square. Such a reaction increases the bank's vulnerability to a future liquidity shock in the event that more bad news surfaces, which it did in the case of Continental two years later. Even when a bank responds constructively, relief from market discipline may be much delayed. Rationing and tiering often persist long after a problem has been corrected. The Japanese banks, for example, experienced tiering for several years after the Herstatt crisis despite their considerable financial strength.

Imperfect market discipline by depositors, however, may be preferable to no discipline. If depositors had not disciplined Continental Illinois in 1982 in the wake of the collapse of Penn Square, Continental might have grown more rapidly and caused an even more serious problem in 1984.[39] Thus, although we believe that the actual benefits of market discipline are much overdrawn, we would not dismiss them entirely. For this reason, we believe there may be some value associated with the traditional central bank policy of ambiguity toward the availability of emergency liquidity assistance.

3. Costs of the policy of ambiguity   The policy of ambiguity also imposes a very heavy cost; *ex ante* it provides a wholly unwarranted competitive advantage to the largest banks; yet *ex post* (after a liquidity shock) it does not protect these banks from a devastating run. These points will be considered in turn.

A policy of ambiguity does not affect all institutions equally. Depositors will formulate their own expectations regarding the banks that are most likely to receive emergency liquidity assistance.[40] These judgments will be based on simulations of the kind of *ad hoc* cost-benefit analyses the central bank has been observed to undertake in crisis situations. Depositors know that while the LLR will consider many factors including the condition of the bank, why the bank is in trouble, its prospects for recovery, and the state of the economy, the overriding consideration will be the potential spillover costs if support is not forthcoming. What would be the effect on public confidence in banks generally? Which banks might be threatened? And would an abrupt closure cause foreign depositors to suffer loss and jeopardize the country's external financial position?

The outcome of such analysis is very clear. Depositors are most likely to be protected at a large bank. The failure of a large bank that causes loss to depositors is likely to cause a greater drop in aggregate demand, interrupt more credit relationships, and pose greater threats to the payments system, than the failure of a small bank. But even more important, the failure of a large bank is more likely to undermine confidence in the banking system generally and to lead to runs on other banks. In addition, large banks are likely to have heavier foreign involvement, and an abrupt failure is therefore more likely to jeopardize external financial relationships.

Yet implicit guarantees do not prevent runs. In the event of trouble, the precise nature of the guarantees falls into question. Does the LLR merely guarantee that it will not close a major bank precipitately or does it offer complete assurance against loss? If the former, for how long is the guarantee good? If the latter, precisely which categories of creditors are covered? Ambiguity regarding answers to such questions is fatal to the maintenance of confidence. Uncertainty provides an incentive to run, and maturing liabilities provide the opportunity.

The consequences of not making guarantees explicit in advance of trouble are illustrated by the Continental Illinois case. Just nine days after the run on Continental began, the US authorities took the unprecedented step of explicitly guaranteeing 'all depositors and other general creditors of the bank.'[41] The guarantee was part of a comprehensive financial assistance programme that included a capital infusion of $2 billion ($1.5 billion from the FDIC and $0.5 billion from a group of commercial banks), an increase in unsecured credit lines from other banks to \$5.5 billion, and an assurance that the Federal Reserve was prepared to meet any extraordinary liquidity requirements of the bank during this period. Despite these actions, the run did not stop. Many banks were reluctant to resume lending to Continental Illinois because the FDIC guarantee was contained only in a press release and did not have sufficient legal safeguards. When Continental's solvency was in question, such a guarantee was not explicit enough.

Thus, a policy of ambiguity is tantamount to a policy of implicit guarantees for large banks that encourages depositors to place deposits with these banks on the basis of a cursory credit evaluation. However, it offers no real protection against a liquidity shock if some event raises questions about the bank's solvency.

4. The case for explicit commitments   As we have seen, central banks are strongly averse to making guarantees explicit *ex ante* because they wish to avoid weakening market discipline and they do not want to commit themselves to a course of action which they subsequently might prefer not to take. We believe this is a very weak case because the implicit guarantees offered large banks under the policy of ambiguity result in only minimal *ex ante* discipline, while experience suggests that the freedom of action that central bankers seem to prize so greatly is largely illusory. We know of no single case where an abrupt failure of a major bank threatened and an LLR with the power to prevent it failed to do so.

The Continental Illinois case is the most instructive in this regard because in early 1984 prior to the run the Federal Deposit Insurance Corporation (FDIC) had launched a new programme that was designed to increase market discipline by placing uninsured depositors at risk. (Under the usual merger or purchase and assumption procedure used with few exceptions by the FDIC all depositors were kept whole.) Between March 16 and May 4, 1984 seven small banks were closed using a new 'pay out-cash advance' procedure which did in fact impose losses on uninsured depositors in the cases where the failed bank's assets did not cover its liabilities. But when faced with the consequences of imposing losses on depositors of Continental Illinois, the resolve of the regulatory authorities crumpled.

If in fact an LLR would never allow a major bank to close precipitately, much would be gained if it committed itself in advance. Assuming the LLR has the means to make it credible, a policy of explicit commitments would prevent runs on major banks. Such a policy would not eliminate the unwarranted advantage possessed by these banks, but at least society would garner the benefit of greater financial stability to set off against this cost.

Such a commitment, we hasten to add, would not and should not represent a commitment to protect shareholders against loss, to continue the bank as a separate entity, to maintain the existing management if the bank is continued, or to protect creditors of a parent or affiliates of the bank. The only commitment would be to avoid termination of the bank's operations so that depositors and borrowers would be able to continue business as usual.

In addition to making explicit a policy that implicitly discriminates against banks that are *not* deemed too big to fail, this policy faces two objections. First, any market discipline now imposed on major banks by depositors would be diminished. We do not regard this objection to be of paramount importance, however, because we have doubts about how effectively depositors discipline large banks in practice and because we believe that holders of subordinated debt (who cannot run) are a preferable means of focusing market discipline on large banks.[42]

A more important objection, in our view, is that runs on major banks may sometimes serve a useful purpose. If regulatory controls are so weak that the authorities cannot prevent a major bank from operating imprudently, a run may provide the authorities with the leverage they need to exact changes in policies and/or management; LLR assistance can be made the *quid pro quo* for such changes. In some countries this may be the best means available to regulators for disciplining a bank. Even where regulators have the powers necessary to discipline a bank, furthermore, they may not do so for fear of political repercussions, because of bureaucratic inertia, or because they are simply unaware of how serious the problem is. In such cases, a run is an effective spur to action.

For this reason, we do not advocate that LLRs forswear the option of closing a major bank precipitately. Rather we argue for a more modest and logically prior step – that LLRs explicitly acknowledge *all* the specific banks for which they have responsibility, without committing themselves to any course of action in an emergency. This first step toward a more explicit policy is directed mainly toward international banking. It would allow markets to identify banks that have no LLR, while clarifying responsibilities toward some other banks for which existing lines of responsibility are uncertain. These points will be developed more fully in the following section.

V. Application to international banks

A. *Complications in Providing Emergency Liquidity Assistance*

We have argued (Guttentag and Herring 1983, pp. 10–15) that the internationalization of banking has complicated the problem of providing emergency liquidity assistance. An effective LLR should (1) be sensitive to the full range of social costs that may result from its failure to act so that it takes timely and appropriate action; (2) have resources that are large relative to potential demands for emergency liquidity assistance in order to sustain confidence that it will be able to act effectively when necessary; and (3) be able to limit the moral hazard which access to emergency liquidity assistance may create.

In an economy that is closed to international financial transactions the central bank usually meets these criteria. As a public (or in some countries, a quasi-public) institution it shares responsibility for providing the public good of a sound banking system. Since the central bank creates domestic bank reserves it has the resources to meet any potential demand for domestic liquidity. And the central bank usually has regulatory or supervisory powers (or has close relations with another public agency which has such powers) that enable it to control the extent to which banks rely on access to emergency liquidity assistance in managing their liquidity positions.

The internationalization of banking has extended deposit and loan relationships across national borders. Deposits at a bank located in one country may be denominated in the currency of another. Banks headquartered in the home country may have offices abroad. Banking offices in the home country may be controlled by foreign banks or by foreign residents who are nonbanks. A bank's residential jurisdiction may not correspond to the jurisdiction in which its owners reside or the jurisdiction of the currency in which most of its transactions are denominated.[43]

With the internationalization of banking, it is no longer obvious that the central bank where a bank resides will be or can be an effective LLR for that bank. If most of the bank's deposit and loan customers live outside the country, the central bank in the residential jurisdiction may not be sufficiently sensitive, or in some cases may be overly sensitive, to the social costs imposed on foreigners from an abrupt failure of the bank.[44] If most of the bank's liabilities are denominated in a foreign currency the central bank in the residential jurisdiction may lack adequate resources to provide emergency liquidity assistance without compromising its exchange rate objectives or undermining its own international liquidity position. And if the bank is controlled by foreign residents, the central bank in the residential jurisdiction may lack sufficient information to assess the condition of the bank seeking assistance and to exercise control over its use of emergency liquidity assistance.[45]

B.   The policy of ambiguity in an international context

The internationalization of banking has increased the uncertainty inherent in the traditional central bank policy of ambiguity regarding the availability of emergency liquidity assistance. Banks that are active in international markets are understandably anxious to know more about the availability of emergency liquidity assistance. Which (if any) central bank would offer emergency liquidity assistance to particular banks and/or banking offices? In what amounts? Under what conditions?[46]

Central banks, on the other hand, have been unwilling to provide clear answers. Just as the Bank of England in Bagehot's era was reluctant to announce the policies it would pursue in the event of a crisis, the central banks of the major industrial countries have been intentionally vague about arrangements to provide emergency liquidity assistance.

The official policy was set out in a communique issued by central bankers from the major industrial nations at the Bank for International Settlements in Basle in 1974 which states that: 'The Governors . . . had an exchange of views on the problem of the lender of last resort in the Euro-markets. They recognized that it would not be practical to lay down in advance detailed rules and procedures for the provision of temporary liquidity. But they were satisfied that means are available for that purpose and will be used if and when necessary' (Wallich, 1977, p. 95). This policy has been reaffirmed by central bankers in several leading countries (McMahon 1977, Wallich 1977 and Dini 1982).

The rationale is the traditional one for a policy of ambiguity: uncertainty regarding the availability of emergency liquidity assistance will strengthen market discipline. For example Henry Wallich (1977, p. 94) has argued that 'Giving too much advance assurance to management, stockholders and depositors risks losing some of the discipline of the market upon which regulators rely to some extent to keep banks "in line".'

We have already evaluated the weakness of this position. A policy of ambiguity is tantamount to a policy of implicit guarantees for the largest banks, which receive very little market discipline under normal conditions. Yet because such guarantees provide less than complete assurance against loss, they are not sufficient to protect a bank against a run if some event undermines confidence in the bank.

In an international context the policy of ambiguity has another possible purpose. It may be another example of what Fritz Machlup (1968, p. 2) has described as the achievement of international agreement through 'the avoidance of excessively clear language'. The danger of such a policy is that it may lead to unwarranted confidence in official arrangements. In the event of a crisis, if emergency liquidity assistance is not forthcoming as expected, the resulting disruption may be even greater than if no assurances had been offered regarding the availability of emergency liquidity assistance (Guttentag and Herring 1983, p. 20).

C. An Alternative Approach

Our proposal has two major objectives. The first is to increase market discipline over banks that do not have access to emergency liquidity assistance by identifying them. The importance of this can be illustrated by the collapse of Banco Ambrosiano Holdings (BAH) in Luxembourg. Bankers who were left with unsatisfied claims on BAH asked why the Bank of Italy was not responsible for the activities of its national banks abroad (*Wall Street Journal*, September 1, 1982). They were apparently unaware that the Bank of Italy did not consider BAH to be a bank. If market participants had been forewarned that the Bank of Italy would not offer emergency liquidity assistance to any entity it did not supervise (a defensible and entirely plausible position) it is likely that BAH would have undergone much closer market scrutiny. Because the policy of calculated ambiguity can undermine market discipline in instances where confidence in the availability of emergency assistance is completely misplaced, there is a compelling case for indicating which banks do not have access to an LLR.[47]

Our second objective is to clarify responsibility for those banks which *do* have access to emergency liquidity assistance. When responsibilities are not clearly allocated, there is a risk that a crisis will be exacerbated by delays in the provision of assistance. Delays may arise because of misunderstandings and disputes among LLRs regarding which LLR is responsible for a given bank, and because an LLR that had not assumed that it was responsible before the need for action arose may not have made prior arrangements for evaluating and perfecting claims to collateral and for obtaining information on a bank's condition.

Central banks may already have made an explicit allocation of responsibilities. (This is one possible interpretation of the 1974 communique.) If so, the apportionment of responsibilities should be disclosed to the market. An explicit apportionment of responsibilities need not undermine market discipline since each LLR will continue to make the availability of assistance depend on the costs and benefits under the conditions prevailing at the time. The objective of enhancing market discipline does not provide a rationale for a policy of ambiguity regarding the apportionment of responsibilities. If, on the other hand, there are disagreements among LLRs regarding the apportionment of responsibilities, it is misleading and potentially dangerous to encourage the market to believe that an allocation has been agreed upon.

In effect, our proposal is for each LLR to publish a list of banks for which it acknowledges sole or shared reponsibility. By implication, the market would be placed on warning that any bank which does not have an acknowledged LLR will not have access to emergency liquidity assistance.

The best approach to generating such lists would be through agreement among central banks. (We provide below an indication of how such an agreement might be structured.) We hasten to add, however, that such an agreement need not cover all central banks, nor must all those who participate in an agreement accept all of the provisions. Except where cross-border cooperation is called for, the principles developed below could be adopted by a single LLR. In fact, an LLR acting unilaterally may have a catalytic impact by publishing its own list. Multilateral agreement might, indeed, be the end of an incremental process rather than the beginning. Unlike the analogous problem of apportioning supervisory responsibility among the various national supervisory agencies, which had as a necessary goal making sure that every major bank was supervised by some agency, there is no analogous requirement that every major bank have an LLR. Hence, a piecemeal approach is quite feasible.

Since decisions regarding the provision of emergency liquidity assistance require information on a bank's condition, an LLR must cooperate closely with the relevant supervisory authority if that is another agency (which it often is). Such cooperation is likely to be much easier within a nation than between nations, and so it is useful to allocate responsibilities for providing emergency liquidity assistance in the same way that the Concordat allocates responsibilities for the supervision of solvency.[48] Such an allocation would assure that the LLR is in the same country as the supervisory authority with primary responsibility for monitoring the bank's solvency, which is also likely to be the country of the authority (usually the chartering authority and/or deposit insurance agency) responsible for making a disposition of the bank should it fail.

The Standing Committee on Banking Regulation and Supervisory Practices agreed in the Concordat (Blunden, 1977, p. 328) that the host supervisory authority has primary responsibility for supervising foreign subsidiaries and joint ventures, and the parent authority has primary responsibility for the solvency of foreign branches. We see an analogous division of responsibilities for providing emergency liquidity assistance as follows:

- The LLR in the parent country will give offshore branches of banks chartered in the parent country the same access to emergency liquidity assistance as the parent bank.
- The host country LLR will not provide emergency liquidity assistance to branches of foreign banks except as a conduit for the parent country LLR, at the latter's risk; however, it may cooperate with the parent country LLR in the provision of emergency liquidity assistance. Such cooperation may take the form of providing information to the parent country LLR or helping the parent country perfect a claim to the bank's assets in order to arrange a collateralized loan.[49]
- Foreign subsidiaries and affiliates of banks chartered in the parent country will not have direct access to emergency liquidity assistance from the LLR in the parent country. They may have indirect access to the extent that they are supported by the parent bank and the parent bank requires assistance; but the LLR in the parent country is free to deny assistance to the parent bank in such a case.
- Host LLRs may grant foreign-owned banks access to emergency liquidity assistance on equal terms with other locally chartered banks, or they may discriminate against them.

If all LLRs adopted these principles, banks without access to emergency liquidity assistance would include banks headquartered in countries that do not have an LLR and their foreign branches, and foreign-owned banks chartered in countries that have no LLR or do not offer emergency liquidity assistance to foreign-owned banks. These banks would be the focus of market discipline, along with banks located in countries that do not adopt the principles.[50] With an explicit apportionment of LLR responsibilities, furthermore, the market would tend to evaluate the capacity of an LLR to deliver. LLRs can usually provide completely credible commitments in their own currency but an LLR's credibility in making commitments in foreign currencies depends on the foreign exchange reserve position of its country.

With an explicit allocation of LLR responsibilities, entry might be difficult for banks not on the list. A policy of ambiguity, however, discriminates against banks that are presumed not to be guaranteed – a category which surely includes most potential new entrants. It is likely, moreover, that if LLRs choose to be explicit, they will experience political pressures to develop objective, equitable criteria that do not discriminate capriciously against new entrants. Thus the impact on competition relative to the current system of ambiguity is not clear.

A similar issue arises with regard to removing a bank from the list. Would not the announcement effect undermine confidence in the bank and destabilize the banking system? Again, this is plausible, but it is not obvious that an ambiguous policy is a preferable alternative. If the alternative to explicitly withdrawing access is to withdraw access secretly, without informing the market, it is not clear that the ultimate result will be more favourable. If the market falsely believes that an institution has access to emergency liquidity assistance, market discipline will be unduly slack and in the event access to emergency liquidity assistance becomes necessary, the blow to confidence in the system will be greater.

Being 'on the list' undoubtedly conveys a valuable benefit to a bank; but the list also gives the supervisory authorities powerful bargaining leverage which can be used to induce a bank to agree to higher quality prudential supervision. The list enhances the possibility of a bargain which could increase the stability of the banking system.

VI.   Concluding comments

This paper has developed principles for allocating responsibilities for the provision of emergency liquidity assistance among national LLRs. We believe that these principles make sense, but it is more important that responsibility for specific banks be explicitly acknowledged or denied, than that LLRs adopt these particular principles. If the allocation of responsibilities for LLR assistance is made more explicit, the market is likely to force banks that have no access to emergency liquidity assistance or whose acknowledged LLR has limited capacity to deliver, to offer higher deposit rates or hold more liquid assets. If a bank has no LLR (or an inadequate LLR) because it selected a chartering jurisdiction which is inadequately supervised, it may reconsider its location decision. Both responses would help improve the stability of the system.

NOTES

* The authors would like to thank (without implicating) Richard Emigh, Allen Frankel, Charles Freedman and Henry Terrell, for helpful advice regarding several aspects of this paper.
1 See Thornton (1802) and Bagehot (1873) for the classic description of the lender of last resort function. Kindleberger (1985, p. 15) asserts that the first use of the term 'lender of last resort' can be traced to Sir Francis Baring with regard to the crisis of 1797.

2 Broadly, other types of central bank lending fall into three categories. Adjustment credit loans are for very short periods, to meet unanticipated drains in reserves. Subsidy credit loans are generally for longer periods, and are designed to provide special benefits for designated beneficiaries and stimulate the flow of credit to particular sectors of the economy. Disaster credit loans are extended to banks or groups of firms that are subject to some common exigency, such as a natural disaster. If the solvency of banks receiving this type of credit falls into doubt, the loans may shift into the LLR category.

3 Although this proposition is by no means unanimously accepted. Hayek (1978) has argued that we would be better off without public control over the stock of money and several modern economic historians – for example White (1984) and Gorton (1985) – have concluded that the private market developed adequate mechanisms for preventing the cumulative collapse of credit without intervention by an official LLR.

4 'Unused borrowing capacity' is the additional amount of liabilities the bank could place without paying more than its customary rate.

5 For example, money market funds issue liabilities that can serve as a means of payments and hold only marketable securities. (See Goodhart 1985 for a provocative discussion of a hypothetical banking system that does not provide a means of payment.) And finance companies offer commercial loans financed by issues of liabilities of comparable maturity.

6 For further discussion of this topic see Bernanke and Gertler (1985), Diamond (1984), Goodhart (1985), and Gorton and Haubrich (1986).

7 The distinction correponds both to legal and to common usage with some major exceptions. Large-scale ('jumbo') syndicated bank loans come very close to being securities because they involve multiple lenders and usually are structured so that participations can be readily transferred among other banks which may have no other relationship with the borrower. On the other hand, private placements, which are generally classified as securities, are very much like loans in that a small number of lenders are involved who are known to the borrower and the credit instrument is not readily transferable to other lenders.

8 J. P. Morgan is reported to have used this criterion exclusively (Kindleberger 1978, p. 174).

9 Banks often find it advantageous to invest in the expertise needed to evaluate specialized loans when the amounts involved are not large enough to attract the interest of investors. When a bank invests to obtain expertise, it hopes to recover its investment in the rate charged. This is usually possible because the bank will have some degree of market power vis-a-vis the borrower who is unlikely to find many other banks with similar expertise.

10 See Flannery (1982) for a model in which the creditor's investment in information of continuing value engenders a customer relationship that is longer-lived than any particular loan transaction.

11 One commentator has noted that 'A selling bank's credit files are loaded with private information about corporate borrowers. ... When the commercial loan is securitized, there's an obligation to reveal all to the buyer. If the loan goes bad, I can face accusations that relevant information wasn't disclosed' (Brenner 1986, p. 2).

12 Such transactions have become a common feature in connection with special

programs established by the Federal National Mortgage Association and the Federal Home Loan Mortgage Corporation. Under these programmes, a firm may swap a package of mortgages for the same face value of marketable securities issued by these agencies against the same package of mortgages. It costs the institution giving up the mortgages around 25 basis points in foregone yield.

13 See BIS (1986, pp. 171–84) for a discussion of the factors influencing financial innovations.

14 The increase in bank capital that has occurred simultaneously may have offset this risk to some extent.

15 See Diamond and Dybvig (1983) for a model in which rational depositors may participate in a bank run caused by a shift in expectations, which could depend on almost anything; 'a bad earnings report, a commonly observed run at some other bank, a negative government forecast, or even sunspots.'

16 Advisory services take this factor explicitly into account in making recommendations to corporate treasurers about where to place deposits.

17 See Freedman (1986) for an illuminating discussion of how the various regulatory instruments interact to attain the intermediate and ultimate goals of regulation of depository institutions. See Guttentag and Herring (1982) for a discussion of the assessment and regulatory disposition of insolvent institutions.

18 For a discussion of this problem, see Guttentag and Herring (1983, p. 8).

19 See Kaufman (1986) for a strong defence of this proposition.

20 For an empirical analysis of the great depression that emphasizes this link to real economic activity, see Bernanke (1983). See also Blinder and Stiglitz (1983).

21 See Brimmer (1976) for an insightful analysis of the episode.

22 Just before the run on Continental Illinois National Bank, on April 30, 1984, 66 banks had exposures to Continental in excess of their capital and another 113 had exposures amounting to between 50% and 100% of their capital. See appendix to Committee on Banking, Finance and Urban Affairs (1984).

23 Because they ignore this point, Keeley and Furlong (1986) misinterpret a study of the free banking era before 1860 by Rolnick and Weber (1983) as indicating an absence of contagion during that period.

24 'The Federal Reserve Bank of New York required that the Bank of New York secure the advance with all of its domestic assets and all eligible customer securities. After the loan was made it was determined that the book value of all the assets and securities pledged to FRBNY was about $36 billion . . .' (Corrigan, 1985, p. 3).

25 Technically, this should be rephrased as: 'LLRs lend only to *viable* banks', since a bank which is solvent in the sense of having positive net worth may, nonetheless, fail to be viable if it does not have enough capital to justify the confidence of its customers.

26 For a contrary view, however, see Goodhart (1986). The Bank of Canada (1986, p. 3) has made a particularly clear statement: 'The Bank of Canada's decision to make extraordinary advances to a chartered bank depends on whether that bank is judged to be solvent . . . because extraordinary advances obviously cannot remedy the problems of an insolvent bank. Such liquidity support, while enabling a bank to pay its liabilities as they accrue, does not create new capital for an insolvent bank and thus cannot remedy the negative

net worth of a bank.' Although the Bank defines a bank as insolvent 'when the value of its assets is no longer sufficient to enable it to repay its deposits and other liabilities', it is clear from later discussion that their concern is with the long-term viability of the institution.

27 This assumes that the LLR's profits would ordinarily be handed over to the tax authorities.

28 It is questionable whether a central bank is the most appropriate institution to offer loans to insolvent firms. We have argued elsewhere (Guttentag and Herring 1983) that this responsibility is better lodged with a deposit insurance agency, but of course not all countries have a deposit insurance agency.

29 The Bank of Canada (1986, p. 23) acknowledges this potential problem, but asserts that it is empirically unimportant and that any potential cost is outweighed by the benefit of permitting 'the Bank of Canada to lend quickly and without hesitation, while at the same time affording appropriate protection of public funds.'

30 While none of these banks were liquidated, all of them required a capital infusion and underwent some type of reorganization.

31 When the LLR determines that the bank is insolvent, it may choose to let it go under or to facilitate a disposition. If the bank is so small that the LLR anticipates that an abrupt closure is unlikely to generate significant social costs, it may simply stop lending and let the bank fail. (The Fed took this option with regard to Penn Square National Bank.) If the LLR anticipates significant spillover costs from abrupt closure, it may attempt to shift responsibility to the deposit insurance agency if there is one. This might involve the LLR continuing to lend but with an indemnification from that agency. (The Fed took this option with regard to Franklin National Bank and Continental Illinois.) If no such agency exists, the LLR may arrange a disposition on its own. (The Bank of England took this option with respect to Johnson Matthey Bankers.)

32 Kane (1986, p. 227) argues that both deposit insurance and the LLR assistance should be regarded as guarantees. He presents an illuminating analysis of deposit insurance within this framework and suggest an application to LLR assistance.

33 See Kane (1985) for a discussion of implicit deposit insurance premiums.

34 Setting a uniform access fee that generated sufficient revenues to allow the LLR to break even would neutralize the first cost, but not the second.

35 In the absence of access to emergency liquidity assistance, illiquid assets constrain the bank's choice of risk since they function as a default penalty on shareholders. See Herring and Vankudre (1986) for a formal development of this argument.

36 Shafer (1982) notes that there is some ambiguity in this criterion since whether the bank is solvent may depend on the size of the penalty.

37 The report of Deutsche Bank's second quarter earnings in the *Financial Times* (Brown 1986, p. 19) is illustrative: 'Deutsche Bank, the largest West German commercial bank, appears headed for another record result this year after reporting a sharp jump in operating profits in the first half. As usual, the bank will not specify just how much operating profit it made. But it reveals that parent bank earnings "Grew by 54 per cent compared with half the previous year's result" – which (although also unavailable) is believed to be about DM 3 bn.'

38 See Eisenbeis and Gilbert (1985). For a more optimistic view of the effectiveness of holders of uninsured certificates of deposit in disciplining banks see Baer and Brewer (1986).

39 This is highly uncertain, however, because shareholders and supervisors might well have disciplined the bank's management even if depositors had not.

40 The tendency to infer implicit guarantees could be countered if the LLR committed itself to a random procedure such as the toss of coin to determine whether a particular institution would receive emergency liquidity assistance. But it seems unlikely that any LLR would adopt a capricious policy.

41 Joint Press Release by the Comptroller of the Currency, the Federal Deposit Insurance Corporation and the Federal Reserve Board, May 17, 1984.

42 For proposals to enhance the role of subordinated debtholders in disciplining large US banks see FDIC (1983) and Healey (1985).

43 Frankel (1975) emphasized this point in an early and insightful analysis of the problem.

44 While it is usually assumed that foreign interests will receive less weight than domestic interests, on several occasions the involvement of foreign bank depositors may have caused the central bank to do more than it would have preferred to do. In Chile, for example, the government bailed out insolvent banks because of pressure from foreign bank creditors (Harberger 1985, p. 246).

45 The ideal solution to these problems would be an LLR that represents the international community. We regard the development of such an institution, however, as no more likely than the universal adoption of Esperanto. Any practical solution must take into account existing national LLRs and their limitations.

46 As noted above, the value to a bank of access to emergency liquidity assistance is higher the greater the certainty that the LLR will act and the broader the range of circumstances in which it will act. A Group of Thirty (1982, p. 6) survey identified uncertainty over lender of last resort arrangements as one of the chief concerns of bankers regarding risks in international banking.

47 LLRs should, however, resist the temptation to exaggerate the number of banks that would not have access to emergency liquidity assistance. If important banks headquartered in the LLRs country are capriciously excluded, the list will lack credibility, and the market will rely on implicit guarantees.

48 At first glance it may seem more appropriate to follow the guidelines for supervision of liquidity. This would indeed seem appropriate for the provision of routine adjustment assistance. But the request for emergency liquidity assistance is most likely to arise when a bank's solvency is in doubt. Thus it is crucial that the LLR be able to make a judgment on the bank's solvency.

49 Spero (1980, pp. 148–9) notes that during the Franklin National Bank crisis, the Bank of England cooperated with the Federal Reserve Bank of New York, by holding assets in escrow to facilitate collateralized, discount window borrowings.

50 In some countries it is even clear which institution should agree to the allocation of responsibilities. In several countries the central bank is not the LLR, and in some the role has never been explicitly recognized. It is useful for the market to be aware of these institutional gaps.

REFERENCES

Aliber, Robert Z. (1985). 'External Shocks and U.S. Domestic Financial Stability', in *The Search for Financial Stability: The Past Fifty Years*, San Francisco, Federal Reserve Bank of San Francisco, pp. 87–111.

Baer, Herbert and Elijah Brewer (1986). 'Uninsured Deposits as a Source of Market Discipline: Some New Evidence', *Economic Perspectives*, Federal Reserve Bank of Chicago (September/October), pp. 23–31.

Bagehot, Walter (1873). *Lombard Street*. Reissued London, Kegan Paul, Trench, Trunber & Co., 1901.

Bank of Canada (1986). *The Submission of the Bank of Canada to the Commission of Inquiry on Certain Banking Operations*, Ottawa, Bank of Canada (May).

Bank for International Settlements (1983). *The International Interbank Market: A Descriptive Study*, BIS Economic Papers No. 8, Basle, Bank for International Settlements (July).

——— (1986). *Recent Innovations in International Banking*, Prepared by a Study Group established by the Central Banks of the Group of Ten Countries, Basle, Bank for International Settlements (April).

Benston, George, Robert A. Eisenbeis, Paul Horvitz, Edward Kane and George Kaufman (1986). *Perspectives on Safe and Sound Banking, Past, Present, and Future*, A Study Commissioned by the American Bankers Association, Cambridge, MIT Press.

Benston, George and George Kaufman (1986). 'Risks and Failures in Banking: Overview, History and Evaluation', Federal Reserve Bank of Chicago SM–86–1.

Bernanke, Ben S. (1983). 'Nonmonetary Effects of the Financial Crisis in the Propagation of the Great Depression', *American Economic Review* 73 (June), pp. 257–76.

Bernanke, Ben and Mark Gertler (1985). 'Banking in General Equilibrium', Working Paper No. 1647, National Bureau of Economic Research (June).

Blinder, Alan S. and Joseph E. Stiglitz (1983). 'Money, Credit Constraints, and Economic Activity', *American Economic Review* 73, (May), pp. 297–302.

Blunden, George (1977). 'International Cooperation in Banking Supervision', *Bank of England Quarterly Bulletin* 17 (September), pp. 325–9.

Brenner, Lynn (1986). '"Turning Assets Into Securities is Knotty Problem", Panel Says', *American Banker* (May 2), p. 2.

Brimmer, Andrew F. (1976). 'International Finance and the Management of Bank Failures, Herstatt vs. Franklin National', working paper (September 16).

Brown, David (1986). 'Deutsche Mark boosted by strong first half', *Financial Times*, Friday, August 1.

Clarke, Stephen V. O. (1984). *American Banks in the International Interbank Market*, Monograph Series in Finance and Economics No. 1983–4, New York University.

Committee on Banking, Finance and Urban Affairs, U.S. House of Representatives (1984). *Continental Illinois National Bank Failure and Its Potential Impact on Correspondent Banks*, Staff Report to the Subcommittee on Financial Institutions, Supervision, Regulation and Insurance, Washington, D.C. (October 4).

Corrigan, E. Gerald (1985). 'Statement of E. Gerald Corrigan, President, Federal Reserve Bank of New York before the Subcommittee on Domestic Monetary Policy of the Committee on Banking, Finance and Urban Affairs, U.S. House of Representatives' (December 1).

Diamond, Douglas (1984). 'Financial Intermediation and Delegated Monitoring', *Review of Economic Studies* **51**, pp. 393–414.

Diamond, Douglas W. and Philip H. Dybvig (1983). 'Bank Runs, Deposit Insurance, and Liquidity', *Journal of Political Economy*, Vol. **91** (June), pp. 401–19.

Dini, Lamberto (1982). 'Financial Problems of the World Economy', English translation of a lecture at the Instituto Centrale di Banche e Banchieri, Rome (November), pp. 1–21.

Eisenbeis, Robert A. and Gary Gilbert (1985). 'Market Discipline and the Prevention of Bank Problems and Failures', *Issues in Bank Regulation*, Vol. **8** (Winter), pp. 16–23.

FDIC (1983). *Deposit Insurance in a Changing Environment, A Study Submitted to Congress by the Federal Deposit Insurance Corporation*, Washington, D.C.

Flannery, Mark (1982). 'Retail Bank Deposits as Quasi-Fixed Factors of Production', *American Economic Review* (June), pp. 527–36.

Frankel, Allen (1975). 'The Lender of Last Resort in the Context of Multinational Banking', *Columbia Journal of World Business* (Winter), pp. 120–9.

Freedman, Charles (1986). 'Recent Developments in the Structure and Regulation of the Canadian Financial System' in *Shifting Frontiers in Financial Markets*, edited by D. Fair. Boston, Martinus Nijhoff Publishers, pp. 273–85.

Giddy, Ian (1981). 'Risk and Return in the Eurocurrency Interbank Market', *Greek Economic Review*, pp. 158–86.

Goodhart, Charles (1985). *The Evolution of Central Banks, a Natural Development?* London School of Economics and Political Science, STICERD (October).

—— (1986). 'Why do Banks need a Central Bank?', *Oxford Economic Papers* (November).

Gorton, Gary (1985). 'Clearinghouses and the Origin of Central Banking in the U.S.', *Journal of Economic History* (June).

Gorton, Gary and Joseph Haubrich (1986). 'Bank Deregulation, Credit Markets and the Control of Capital', Working Paper No. 8–86, Rodney L. White Center for Financial Research (February).

Group of Thirty (1982). *How Bankers See the World Financial Market*, New York, Group of Thirty.

Guttentag, Jack and Richard Herring (1982). 'The Insolvency of Financial Institutions: Assessment and Regulatory Disposition', in *Crisis in the Economic and Financial Structure*, edited by P. Wachtel. Lexington, Lexington Books, pp. 99–126.

—— (1983). *The Lender of Last Resort Function in an International Context*, Princeton University Essays in International Finance, No. 151 (May).

—— (1985). 'Funding Risk in the International Interbank Market', in *International Financial Markets and Capital Movements, a Symposium in Honor of Arthur I. Bloomfield*, edited by W. J. Ethier and R. C. Marston, Princeton University Essays in International Finance, No. 157 (September), pp. 19–32.

(1986a). 'Financial Innovations to Stabilize Credit Flows to Developing Countries', *Studies in Banking and Finance* **3**.

(1986b). *Disaster Myopia in International Banking*, Princeton University Essays in International Finance, No. 164 (September).

Harberger, Arnold C. (1985). 'Lessons for Debtor Country Managers and Policymakers, in *International Debt and the Developing Countries*, edited by G. Smith and J. Cuddington, Washington, The World Bank, pp. 236–57.

Hayek, F. A. (1978). *Denationalization of Money – The Argument Refined*, London, Institute of Economic Affairs.

Healey, Thomas J. (1985). *Recommendations for Change in the Federal Deposit Insurance System*, The Working Group of the Cabinet, Council on Economic Affairs, Washington, D.C.

Herring, Richard J. and Prashant Vankudre (1986). 'Growth Opportunities and Risk-Taking by Insured Intermediaries', Working Paper, Wharton Program in International Banking and Finance (February).

Horvitz, Paul (1983). 'The Case Against Risk-Related Deposit Insurance Premiums', *Housing Finance Review*, Vol. 2, No. 3 (July), pp.253–63.

Humphrey, D. B. (1986). 'Payments Finality and Risk of Settlement Failure', in *Technology and the Regulation of Financial Markets*, edited by A. Saunders and L. J. White, Lexington, D. C. Heath, pp. 97–120.

Humphrey, Thomas (1975). 'The Classical Concept of the Lender of Last Resort', *Federal Reserve Bank of Richmond Economic Review* (January/February), pp. 2–9.

Johnson, G. G. with Richard K. Abrams (1983). 'Aspects of the International Banking Safety Net', *Occasional Paper* 17, International Monetary Fund (March).

Kane, Edward J. (1985). *The Gathering Crisis in Deposit Insurance*, Cambridge, MIT Press.

(1986). 'Risk-Related Premiums', in Benston *et al.*, *Perspectives on Safe and Sound Banking, Past, Present and Future*, A Study Commissioned by the American Bankers Association, Cambridge, MIT Press, pp. 227–43.

Kane, Edward J. and George G. Kaufman (1986). 'The Lender of Last Resort', in Benston *et al.*, *Perspectives on Safe and Sound Banking, Past, Present and Future*, A Study Commissioned by the American Bankers Association, Cambridge, MIT Press, pp. 109–26.

Kaufman, George G. (1986). 'Consequences of Bank Failure', in Benston *et al.*, *Perspectives on Safe and Sound Banking, Past, Present and Future*, A Study Commissioned by the American Bankers Association, Cambridge, MIT Press, pp. 37–79.

Keeley, Michael C. and Frederick Furlong (1986). 'Bank Regulation and the Public Interest', *Economic Review*, Federal Reserve Bank of San Francisco (Spring), pp. 55–71.

Kindleberger, Charles P. (1978). *Manias, Panics and Crashes, a History of Financial Crises*. New York, Basic Books.

(1985). 'The Functioning of Financial Centers: Britain in the Nineteenth Century, the United States since 1945', in *International Financial Markets and Capital Movements, a Symposium in Honor of Arthur I. Bloomfield*, edited by W. J. Ethier and R. C. Marston, Essays in International Finance, No. 157, Princeton University (September), pp. 7–18.

Machlup, Fritz (1968). *Remaking the International Monetary System, the Rio Agreement and Beyond*. Baltimore, The Johns Hopkins Press.

Mayer, Thomas (1975). 'Preventing the Failures of Large Banks', in *Compendium of Major Issues in Bank Regulation*, Senate Committee on Banking, Housing and Urban Affairs, Washington, US Government Printing Office.

McMahon C. W. (1977). 'Central Banks as Regulators and Lenders of Last Resort in an International Context: a View from the United Kingdom', *Key Issues in International Banking*, Federal Reserve Bank of Boston Conference Series, No. 18 (October).

Moffett, Michael (1986). 'The International Interbank Market: a Behavioral Model of Credit Rationing and Bank Tiering', Brookings Discussion Papers in International Economics, No. 48 (May).

Mussa, Michael (1986). 'Safety and Soundness as Objectives of Regulation of Depository Institutions: Comment on Kareken', *Journal of Business* **59**, no. 1, pp. 97–117.

Olson, Wayne (1986). 'Securitization comes to Other Assets', *Savings Institutions* (May), pp. 81–85.

Pavel, Christine (1986). 'Securitization', *Economic Perspectives*, Federal Reserve Bank of Chicago (July-August), pp. 16–37.

Rolnick, Arthur and Warren Weber (1983). 'New Evidence on the Free Banking Era', *American Economic Review* (December), pp. 1080–91.

Saunders, Anthony (1986). 'The Interbank Market, Contagion Effects and International Financial Crises', in this volume.

Shafer, Jeffrey R. (1982). 'The Theory of a Lender of Last Resort in International Banking Markets', in *Recent Developments in the Economic Analysis of the Euromarkets*, Basle, Bank for International Settlements Monetary and Economic Department (September).

Spero, Joan (1980). *The Failure of the Franklin National Bank*, A Council on Foreign Relations Book, New York, Columbia University Press.

Thornton, Henry (1802). *An Enquiry into the Nature and Effects of the Paper Credit of Great Britain*, Reissued, London, George Allen and Unwin, 1939.

Wallich, Henry C. (1977). 'Central Banks as Regulators and Lenders of Last Resort in an International Context: A View from the United States', *Key Issues in International Banking*, Federal Reserve Bank of Boston Conference Series, No. 18 (October).

White, L. H. (1984). *Free Banking in Britain: Theory, Experience and Debate, 1800–1845*, New York, Cambridge University Press.

Discussion

MICHAEL BEENSTOCK

In common with other writers the authors spell out the need for LLR and regulation when 'the market lacks sufficient information to evaluate the soundness of banks'. It is well known that asymmetric information can give rise to contagious bank runs as risk-averse depositors who are unable to distinguish between idiosyncratic and systematic risk seek to be the first to withdraw their deposits, even from banks that in reality happen to be solvent. To safeguard the banking system from such confidence crises the central bank is required to undertake the LLR function.

Since LLR gives rise to problems of moral hazard, various types of bank regulation are necessary to limit the degree to which the banks assume extra risks that they would not undertake if there were no LLR. While Bagehot argued that LLR should not apply to insolvent banks, central bankers readily admit that they are often forced to save insolvent banks in order to avoid a run on the rest of the system.

The authors have served a useful purpose in reminding us that LLR and regulation would not be necessary if information were perfect. In such a world, 'the only losers would be bank regulators, who would find their employment prospects greatly diminished'. However, in common with other students of LLR, they take the asymmetry and imperfection in information as a datum and do not question whether this can be corrected. If it cannot, I accept their argument, but I think that these information constraints are at best artificial and at worst a regulators' conspiracy.

There are two types of information asymmetry. The first is inherently natural, where there is no feasible way in which the necessary information can be imparted. Perhaps Akerlof's 'market for lemons' covers such cases, but even here independent survey reports (e.g. of second-hand cars), guarantees and associated insurance policies limit the practical significance of information asymmetry. In any case reputation effects create strong incentives for suppliers to be as honest as possible.

The second type of asymmetry is inherently unnatural. In this case the information is withheld when in fact it is feasible to impart it. On the whole asymmetry in banking information falls into this category. This is demonstrated by the fact that the information is disclosed, but only to the bank regulators. My contention[1] is that provided there was proper public disclosure, not just to the regulators, there would be no need for LLR. Under such circumstances, market forces would do the regulating, as the authors note. The public would stand possessed of the information that would enable it to distinguish solvent banks from insolvent ones, and to distinguish idiosyncratic risk from systematic risk. In this way, contagion effects would be limited as far as possible.

Over the centuries, we have learnt that corporate disclosure is essential to the orderly operation of stock markets. The market must be provided with the information with which to form responsible judgements about corporate profits and insolvency. The vast body of evidence in favour of market efficiency suggests that on the whole the public uses this information in a sensible fashion. This is why we insist on high standards of disclosure for public companies.

Would matters be different in the case of the disclosure of bank information? Would the public use the information responsibly, or would it all be too confusing and even counter-productive? I do not think so. In any case, we would see the emergence of 'Which Bank' magazines which were marketed by bank analysts with the consumer in mind. These services already exist for sophisticated financial products such as pensions, so banks are unlikely to prove an exception.

This begs the question of why it is that banks do not disclose information except to the official regulators. It is very curious that banks are treated as a special case. My only explanation for this odd state of affairs is that by keeping this information to themselves the official regulators protect their monopoly position in the regulation market. It also gives them power over their regulatees. There must surely be nothing more thrilling in the life of a central banker than a fully-blown secondary banking crisis in which even solvent banks are forced to answer the becks, calls and threats of the supermen charged with saving the system from itself. The solvent banks acquiesce in the blackmail because the public at large is in no position to realize that they are not tarred by the same brush.

It is in the interests of sound banks to go for full disclosure. LLR might appear to be free insurance but it is not worth it. These arguments suggest that the underlying logic calls for less LLR, certainly less ILLR, and more disclosure. But bankers today seem to be as confused as they were 50 years ago as noted by a previous commentator.

> It is necessarily part of the business of a banker to maintain appearances and to profess a conventional respectability which is more than human. Lifelong practices of this kind make them the most romantic and least realistic of men. It is so much their stock-in-trade that their position should not be questioned, that they do not even question it themselves until it is too late. Like the honest citizens they are, they feel a proper indignation at the perils of the wicked world in which they live – when the perils mature; but they do not foresee them. A Bankers' Conspiracy! The idea is absurd! I only wish there were one! So, if they are saved it will be, I expect, in their own despite. (John Maynard Keynes)

NOTE

1 M. Beenstock, 'The Theory of Last Resort Lending' in Z. Res (ed.), *International Debt and Central Banking in the 1980s*, Macmillan, 1987.

Discussion

CHARLES FREEDMAN*

Guttentag and Herring (G–H) present a balanced account of the role of lender of last resort and the functions of last resort loans and I am in broad agreement with much of their discussion. Since about three-quarters of their paper focuses on the principles and considerations underlying such loans and only about one-quarter deals with the international aspects I will weight my comments in a similar fashion.

I would define last resort loans as the extraordinary advances which are provided to banks experiencing liquidity problems because of a loss of depositor confidence and unable to meet deposit withdrawals from their own resources or from additional deposits raised in the market at or near their usual rates of interest.[1] The policy of most central banks is to limit such loans to institutions that are believed to be solvent but which might fail without emergency liquidity assistance. The reason for such a policy is that last resort loans as such cannot remedy the problems of an insolvent bank; only a capital injection can deal with negative net worth and most central banks do not have the power to make such an investment.[2]

There are four aspects of last resort lending by central banks that I wish to touch on in these comments. First, its existence presupposes that there is some form of market failure such that even solvent banks can face liquidity runs. Second, there are believed to be substantial social costs to allowing a solvent bank to fail as a result of illiquidity problems. Third, a judgement can be made about whether a bank is solvent or not. Fourth, the existence of last resort lending may cause moral hazard problems.

(1) The need for a lender of last resort presupposes that there can be runs on solvent banks. As G–H point out, banks are peculiarly vulnerable because of the fact that their assets are imperfectly marketable and that they issue liabilities that mature on demand or at short notice. I would add the further condition that these liabilities are redeemable at a fixed or par value. It is therefore the case that any suspicion of insolvency, whether well-founded or not, leads not to an immediate fall in the price of the claims on the financial institution as in the case of a firm that issues variable price obligations (such as a mutual fund), but to withdrawals by nervous depositors. Thus, unlike most markets where bad 'news' results in a *pari passu* loss to all existing creditors, in the case of banks a creditor can avoid such a loss by withdrawing funds at virtually

no cost before other creditors act. Hence the rational corporate treasurer or creditor bank might well withdraw its funds on the least suspicion of insolvency because of the potential cost of not acting early should the suspicion prove to be well-founded. Thus the institutional structure can lead to very abrupt shifts of funds out of banks which cannot be offset by smooth adjustments in the interest rates paid on deposits by the bank that has come under suspicion.

(2)   A second element that underlies the traditional lender of last resort position is that the social costs of allowing the failure of a bank that is undergoing liquidity problems are substantial. The social costs of such failures are well discussed in the G–H paper in terms of their effects on depositors, borrowers, and the payments system. Furthermore, and of major concern to lenders of last resort, there is the possibility of 'contagion' effects which relate to the possibility that the failure of one bank as a result of a liquidity run may lead to similar runs on banks that are similarly placed in terms of their loans and deposits.

(3)   A third aspect of the proposition that lenders of last resort make liquidity loans to solvent institutions is the necessity for a judgement to be made on whether a bank is solvent or not. This requires either that the central bank itself house the supervisory authority or that a close relationship exist between the central bank and the supervisory authority.

The implication of the above remarks is that the lender of last resort (*qua* lender of last resort) is not in the business of providing injections of capital to insolvent banks. It may be the case that the authorities in other guises become involved in such activities for a variety of reasons. For example, given the magnitude of liquidation costs, it may be cheaper for a deposit insurer to inject capital into an insolvent institution and sell it as a viable institution rather than to liquidate it. Also, some authorities in the United States have explicitly stated that large banks will not be allowed to fail, presumably because of the impact on the economy of their failure. But, it seems to me, it is important to distinguish such actions and statements by deposit insurers and/or governments as investor of last resort from the role of the lender of last resort, *per se*. At points in the G–H paper I found some confusion arising from not disentangling the lender of last resort function from these other elements. For example, the authors treat the 'implicit guarantee' as resulting from the ambiguity regarding the lender of last resort's policy (pp. 45–6). But since lenders of last resort universally espouse making such loans only to solvent institutions it is hardly likely that the 'implicit guarantee' has resulted from the lender of last resort's statements or policies (even if in practice they have made loans to banks that have turned out to be insolvent). The notion of an 'implicit guarantee' is related to a belief that creditors of large banks will be covered either directly by the insurance authority or indirectly by government actions taken to save the banks.

(4)   A fourth aspect of last resort lending by central banks relates to the potential moral hazard implications of the availability of such loans and the effects of the terms and conditions on which the loans are made. The mere existence of a lender of last resort facility may lead banks to take risks in the direction of reducing their liquid asset holdings and relying more heavily on wholesale funding at very short terms. Thus central banks have tended to be rather imprecise about the conditions and terms under which banks might obtain last resort loans. However, as G–H correctly point out, there is a real difficulty in balancing the uncertainty generated by not establishing explicit terms and conditions against the moral hazard that arises from the existence of a lender of last resort which sets out explicit terms and conditions of access. No completely satisfactory solution has been found for this problem. The trade-off between explicitness and flexibility shows up clearly, for example, in the area of pricing last-resort loans. It is desirable to avoid a situation where such loans are used as a cheap source of funds at a time when alternative sources of funds are available. Because of the negative associations that are currently attached to borrowing from a lender of last resort, at least in Canada, it is not likely that any healthy institution would turn to the lender of last resort simply to reduce somewhat its cost of funds. However, for an institution that has already been forced into the lender of last resort for other reasons, there may be some incentive to increase its borrowing from the lender of last resort in order to fund its growing portfolio of assets more cheaply than it otherwise would be able to and the lender of last resort may wish to charge a higher rate on the loans that are used in this way. However, an explicit schedule of loan rates may result in higher rates being charged inappropriately in the case of a bank undergoing a liquidity crisis that is not abusing its access to a lender of last resort.

The application of the principles of last-resort lending to international banking is relatively straightforward even though the practical problems are more complex than in the domestic setting. It is worth noting in this connection that 'international banks' are largely foreign branches, agencies and subsidiaries of large domestic banks and only to a limited extent separate banks created for international purposes. Even the latter usually have connections to domestic banks (e.g. consortium banks).

As far as the question of the need for a lender of last resort is concerned, the argument is perhaps even stronger internationally than for a domestic system. Since most foreign depositors are not covered by deposit insurance (either because of the size of their deposits, their currency of denomination or their place of booking) there is relatively little in the way of 'core' deposits, which are less likely to be withdrawn quickly in response to rumours about the solvency of a bank. Furthermore, in a world with complex linkages among banks via the interbank market, the potential for contagion is extended across banking systems.

The social costs of a liquidity crisis appear to be just as important when arising from an international shock as from a domestic shock. As mentioned, the institutions engaged in international banking are largely the branches and subsidiaries of large national banks. In the case of such branches and in the case of subsidiaries whose parent bank has guaranteed its liabilities it is hard to envision a situation in which the branch or subsidiary comes under liquidity pressure without impacting on the parent bank, and causing the same problems vis-a-vis depositors, borrowers, payment system, and contagion as discussed in G–H.[3] Indeed, the contagion aspects are likely to be more severe in the international system than in the domestic because of the greater links among banks as a result of the greater relative importance of the interbank market internationally.

The third aspect of last resort lending, the need for a judgement about solvency, raises important practical questions about the links between lenders of last resort and supervisors. Clearly, a lender of last resort has much closer links with its own national supervisory authority than with foreign authorities although relationships with the latter have been strengthened over the last decade through the Cooke Committee. For those banking systems which prepare consolidated financial statements (including foreign subsidiaries) for the national supervisory authority, this problem is much less serious since the supervisor is able to make a judgement about the bank as a whole. This does not necessarily imply that the lender of last resort to the parent will take responsibility for a subsidiary abroad, only that it is capable of so doing if it chooses on the basis of information provided by its own supervisory authorities. Where consolidated data are not available, there is an added level of complexity for the parent lender of last resort.

The suggestion by G–H that the Concordat-type distribution of responsibilities be explicitly applied to lenders of last resort has a certain theoretical appeal but is unlikely to prove practical. As always in the case of the ambiguity issue there is a trade-off between the moral hazard problem and the uncertainty problem. The lenders of last resort have chosen to deal with potential international liquidity problems on a case-by-case basis, in part because of the overlapping responsibility of parent and host lenders of last resort in some cases. The close linkages between central banks should ensure that no major problems of liquidity contagion will develop without rapid and coordinated response. Nor would the G–H approach go very far towards clarifying responsibilities since it would only establish a primary responsibility *in principle* for the various institutions without clarifying the conditions under which the lender of last resort would act.

As banking systems become increasingly internationalized, more lenders of last resort will be faced with banks which have a substantial proportion of their consolidated balance sheet denominated in foreign currencies. If foreign creditors grew nervous about such banks and began withdrawing their deposits, the banks would likely turn to their domestic markets and, if necessary, to the domestic lender of last resort. As discussed by G–H in their earlier study of this subject[4] this could result in some circumstances in significant pressures on the exchange rate of the country.[5] In this connection it should be noted that standing behind the banks of the country is not simply the lender of last resort but the government itself. In some cases it is the government and not the lender of last resort which holds the foreign exchange reserves and it is the government that might have to issue foreign-currency loans to provide the foreign currencies to the banks with which to repay foreign depositors. In effect, in such a case the government would substitute its own credit abroad for that of the banks that have come under pressure.

One potentially important development that will have implications for the lender of last resort (and for the deposit insurer) is the growing trend for banks to engage in ancillary activities both at home and abroad. For example, many North American banks have established securities subsidiaries in London and eventually may have subsidiaries and affiliates in the securities markets at home. Can such subsidiaries be treated as completely separate from the parent banks or will problems in such subsidiaries infect the parent bank and hence require last resort lending? What will be the links between banking regulators and securities regulators? Such issues are under active consideration and, in a recent speech,[6] the Governor of the Bank of England raised the possibility of the need for banking and securities supervisors to cooperate internationally to deal with such problems.

NOTES

* Adviser, Bank of Canada. The views expressed in this note are those of the author and no responsibility for them should be attributed to the Bank of Canada.

1 See Bank of Canada (1986).
2 One might characterize the institutions with the power to make such capital injections as investors of last resort as opposed to lenders of last resort.
3 There is one case in which a subsidiary or branch is unable to pay depositors without the parent bank being affected and that is a situation in which the host country imposes exchange controls or other regulations on the branch or subsidiary which prevent it from meeting its liabilities as they come due.
4 See Guttentag and Herring (1983).
5 One possible way of responding to a temporary run on the foreign currency deposits of a banking system is for the central bank to enter the foreign exchange swap market and to buy spot foreign currency in exchange for forward delivery of the foreign currency. It could then do a reverse transaction with a domestic bank. In effect the central bank interposes itself between the market and the domestic commercial banks who no longer have access to this market.
6 See *Bank of England Quarterly Bulletin* (1986).

REFERENCES

Bank of Canada (1986). *The Submission of the Bank of Canada to the Commission of Inquiry on Certain Banking Operations*. Ottawa (May).
Bank of England Quarterly Bulletin (1986). 'Innovation in Central Banking' (June), pp. 225–29.
Guttentag, Jack and Richard Herring (1983). *The Lender of Last Resort Function in an International Context*, Princeton University Essays in International Finance, No. 151 (May).

Discussion

J. RICHARD ZECHER

The authors provide an excellent review of the history of thinking on the issue of the lender of last resort function. The ambiguity surrounding this function is no accident, as they point out, but is part of the 'game' of inciting more prudent behaviour through more market discipline of banks. Like some young ladies who say they may or may not do it, or would do it only under certain circumstances, lenders of last resort almost always end up doing it, and even if the circumstances are wrong (insolvency! but I wasn't sure, and who could have known at the time?)

Thus the lender of last resort issue continues to resist successfully the efforts of economists to lay down clear decision rules for when and precisely under what circumstances lending in a crisis situation will occur. Bagehot attempted to clarify this over 100 years ago by requiring last resort lending only (1) to solvent banks, and (2) at a penalty rate of interest. Lenders of last resort like the sound of these 'rules of the game'. They sound tough and businesslike. But history teaches us that they don't act according to these rules; that when a bank large enough to impact the working of the payments system is in trouble, they lend. And that this lending is coordinated, where a separate agency is involved, with the *investor* of last resort (in the USA, FDIC would be involved).

The authors, being realistic, know that this practice is unlikely to change. They make a very conservative recommendation that lenders of last resort identify those banks, or bank branches, that they will consider being a lender of last resort for. One problem with this notion is that it could provide a barrier to entry into a national market, and history also teaches us that it frequently would.

Now I speak from here on as a New York international banker, or a regulatee in the terminology of this conference. I would like to raise the issue that New York banks, in particular, are overregulated in several important ways, and that concern about crisis management – lender of last resort being an important part of this management – has contributed to the glacial pace at which this overregulation is being dismantled. It would appear that regulators and legislators use the possibility of a crisis in the payments system, for example, to continue archaic regulatory restrictions particularly on New York banks and particularly on our ability to expand into the domestic US banking market and our ability to move into new or non-traditional products.

What would be highly desirable from my perspective would be an unlinking of payments system regulation from all other regulation. The argument that banks are different (because of their role in the payments system) and therefore it is justified to regulate *all* of their activities heavily has been very harmful to New York banks. As was mentioned in our discussions, only one New York bank retains its AAA rating, and it is the least committed of all New York banks to traditional banking businesses. Also, New York banks generally have diminished in importance compared to European and Japanese banks. I believe these trends are directly related to the extraordinary regulatory restrictions on New York banks. A solution to this problem might be for regulators to focus their efforts much more on the payments system, somehow defined and perhaps organized differently than now, and to remove regulatory barriers to competition on all other activities.

6   The inter-bank market, contagion effects and international financial crises

ANTHONY SAUNDERS*

I   Introduction

The Eurocurrency inter-bank market encompasses over 1,000 banks from 50 different countries. As of September 1985, cross-border inter-bank claims stood at $1,378.7 billion or approximately 59% of a total market size of $2,346.6 billion.[1] Apart from transactions in US dollars, which usually account for more than 55% of total external assets of BIS reporting banks, there are flourishing inter-bank markets in German Marks, Swiss Francs, Yen, Sterling, French Francs and Dutch Guilders.[2]

Its size and importance in providing an efficient mechanism for reallocating funds from surplus countries to deficit countries (see below) raises important public policy and regulatory issues regarding the integrity and 'safety and soundness' of the Eurocurrency inter-bank market. Specifically, a major breakdown in the mechanism of inter-bank fund transfers may significantly distort the size and composition of international capital flows and lead to externalities that adversely impact the level of (world) social welfare. Indeed, the very nature of the market itself, characterized by a strong interdependence of banks in a market for uncollateralized claims, provides a very fragile structure. In such a market, shocks, either informational or real, may be quickly transmitted among banks; that is, Eurocurrency markets have a strong potential for contagion.

In this paper, the potential sources of contagion in the inter-bank market are analysed and empirical evidence regarding contagion effects on interest-rate spreads, loan/deposit flows and bank equity market values is discussed. Policy questions as to what types of (central bank) regulatory response should be forthcoming are also addressed.

In Section II the role the inter-bank market plays in facilitating international capital flows is described and the risks relating to this market identified. In Section III potential sources of contagion are analysed. It is argued that while a considerable potential for contagion results from asymmetric information among contracting parties (due to imperfect information collection and monitoring costs in markets for uncollateralized loans) the actual settlement process itself, through CHIPS, creates an 'institutional' contagion potential. In Section IV the theoretical effects of inter-bank market spreads, loan/deposit flows, and bank equity market valuations are more formally described. Section V presents some empirical evidence relating to contagion effects that have materialized following recent international debt repayment problems (e.g. Mexico and Brazil) and large bank failures (e.g. Continental Illinois). Finally, Section VI critically considers current public policy/ regulatory responses to mitigate the potential for contagion.

II. The inter-bank market

In recent years a number of papers have been written describing the functions of the Eurocurrency inter-bank market. At least four, inter-related, functions are apparent:

(i) *A Distribution Function*: efficiently allocating international funds from non-bank surplus units to non-bank deficit units (see Niehans and Hewson 1976).

(ii) *A Liquidity Function*: providing an efficient means of liquidity adjustment to cover temporary shortfalls of funds domestically or internationally (see Guttentag and Herring 1985).

(iii) *A Hedging Function*: providing an efficient market mechanism through which banks can optimally hedge their foreign interest-rate and foreign exchange exposures (see Grammatikos, Saunders and Swary 1986).

(iv) *A Regulatory Avoidance Function*: to minimize the costs of domestic regulation and taxes (see Aliber 1980).

However, of the four, the role of the inter-bank market in facilitating the international distribution of capital is the most important. It is this function that provides the very rationale for international financial intermediation being used as the main vehicle for international financial flows instead of international securitization – i.e. the direct transfer of funds (primary claims) between non-bank units. The more 'cost efficient' it is for trans-national non-bank borrowers and lenders to transact indirectly, through holding the (secondary) claims of financial interme-diaries, the more likely it is that international financial intermediation

SECURITIZATION

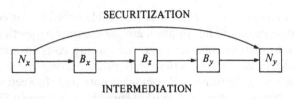

INTERMEDIATION

Figure 6.1   Securitization vs intermediation
N_x = surplus unit in country X
B_x = regional bank in country X
B_z = large correspondent bank in country Z (an international banking center, e.g.
London)
B_y = regional bank in country Y
N_y = deficit unit in country Y

will be the dominant mechanism through which international capital movements take place.

To see this, consider the stylized example in Figure 6.1 representing two alternative mechanisms for facilitating international financial flows between non-bank units in a funds surplus country (X) and non-bank units in a funds deficit country (Y).

Following Niehans and Hewson (1976), Niehans (1971) and others, financial intermediation will be chosen when the total costs relating to the intermediation process (T_{FI}) are less than those for direct security market transactions (T_S). These costs include search, administrative, taxation, inventory, regulatory and information costs. Notice that international financial intermediation geographically separates the deposit taking from loan making functions.[3]

Much of the recent theory of (domestic) financial intermediation has concentrated on the role of information collection and monitoring costs in describing why the costs, for non-bank agents directly transacting in primary (security) markets, may be inordinately high compared to indirectly transacting *via* financial intermediation (see, for example, Boyd and Prescott 1986, Diamond 1984, Ramkrishnan and Thakor 1984 and Millom and Thakor 1985). In the case of international security investment, information collection and monitoring costs regarding the quality (honesty) of the borrower and quality of collateral are compounded by increased geographical distances as well as sovereign risk considerations. Such costs will be reflected either in 'required yield spreads' or, if extremely high, in borrower exclusion from the securities market.

The financial intermediation process, in Figure 6.1, has three distinct stages. Stage 1 is where N_x deposits funds with B_x. Normally, if N_x and B_x have developed a close customer relationship over time the information (and search) costs will be relatively low. That is, through frequent transactions reputation capital has been built up between depositor and banker in country X in the form of 'implicit' contracts – these might be notably absent in the direct securitization case. In effect, N_x is choosing a liquid, 'almost surely' fixed payoff contract (a domestic deposit) over an illiquid uncertain payoff contract (an international security).

Stage 2 is the inter-bank market transaction between B_x and B_z. Perhaps because of a lack of profitable domestic investment opportunities, B_x on lends excess funds to a large bank operating in a major international banking centre (possibly a correspondent). In our stylized example, B_z will immediately resell these funds to bank Y, the latter operating in a net funds deficit area. In essence B_z, the large bank located in the banking centre, acts as a deposit broker by setting a bid-ask (offer) spread to optimize its Eurocurrency net deposit inventory(ies) in the face of non-synchronous deposit supplies and loan demands from surplus and deficit areas. This type of broker behaviour has been modelled elsewhere by Ho and Saunders (1981) assuming there is no credit risk (default uncertainty) i.e. the only uncertainty is over the arrival frequency of deposit supplies and loan demands. Assuming that banks B_x, B_z, and B_y have developed close customer relationships over time, so that considerable reputation capital exists among these banks, this assumption may not be far from the truth. In such a world, Ho–Saunders show that as bank risk aversion approaches zero and the inter-bank market becomes more competitive, the bid-ask (offer) spread will approach zero. However, as already noted in the introduction, there are over 1,000 banks transacting on the inter-bank market. If B_x and B_y are imperfectly known to the money centre bank B_z the *quality* of these borrowing/ lending banks may be important. Just such a system has been modelled by Allen and Saunders (1986) for the domestic US federal funds (inter-bank) market. It is shown that large money-centre banks (such as Z) will tend to sort smaller peripheral banks (such as Y and X) into imperfect default risk-classes based on 'observable' risk characteristics – which in the case of Eurocurrency inter-bank markets may include size, location, nationality and jurisdiction. Such default risk rankings will be reflected in either risk-premiums over the pure spread (so called tiering) or even in credit rationing.[4] Those banks who feel they have been sorted unfairly into too high a risk-class may seek to develop reputation capital for themselves (in lieu of actual collateral) by frequently trading on both sides of the market – thereby signalling that they are good credit risks and developing long-term implicit contracts with money-centre banks.

The third stage (described by Figure 6.1) is B_z, the regional bank in country Y lending funds to a local deficit unit, N_y. As in stage 1, it may be presumed that the bank and loan customer in country Y have developed a close customer relationship over time which serves to materially resolve any underlying information asymmetries among the contracting parties.

Hence, in summary, it has been argued that whether international intermediation takes place rather than securitization depends on the relative costs (both to borrowers and lenders) of engaging in each process. Concentrating largely on information costs, it was argued that even with a relatively heterogeneous pool of non-bank borrowers/ lenders, banks acting through their relative advantages in information collection and monitoring (and through the ability of the inter-bank market to separate geographically deposit and loan functions) should 'normally' provide the most efficient-least cost method of distributing international financial capital. However, if the costs of inter-bank information collection/monitoring rise the relative cost advantage of international intermediation over securitization will diminish and may even disappear.

III. Risks and contagion

(a) Risks

One important aspect of the current inter-bank market, already discussed in Section II above, is that both the number and diversity of players has increased. Currently there are over 1,000 participating banks compared to 200 in the mid-1970s (see Giddy 1981). This has increased considerably the information collection and monitoring burdens of banks currently participating, making them increasingly susceptible to credit (default) risk. However, in addition to credit risks banks face at least three other types of risk in the inter-bank market:[5]

   (i) sovereign risk
   (ii) liquidity or 'bank-run' risk
   (iii) settlement risk.

As is well known, in the absence of an international agency (legal authority) to enforce international debt contracts an additional risk dimension exists in international banking in the form of sovereign (or country) risk. Thus, even if bank Y wishes (and is potentially able) to repay bank Z, in the example above, government imposed foreign exchange restrictions, foreign exchange controls, moratoria on debt repayments or even wars may interfere with the repayment process. Thus a money-centre bank, such as Z, faces the risk of either costly re-negotiation/rescheduling of its inter-bank loan contracts or even repudiation. Consequently the nationality and jurisdictional location of bank

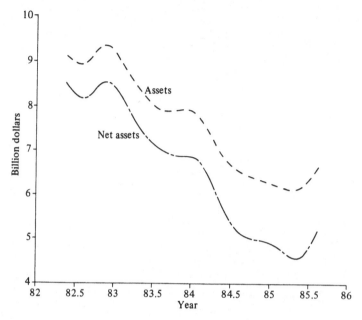

Figure 6.2   BIS banks' exposure to Polish banks, 1982–5

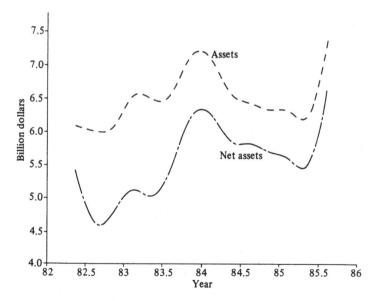

Figure 6.3   BIS banks' exposure to Argentinian banks, 1982–5

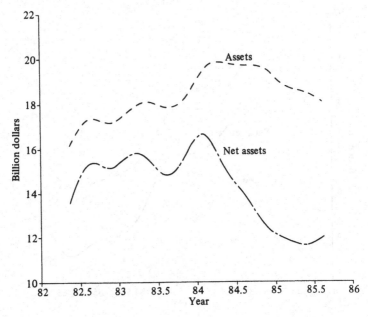

Figure 6.4   BIS banks' exposure to Brazilian banks, 1982–5

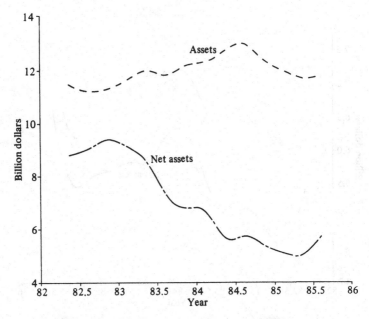

Figure 6.5   BIS banks' exposure to Mexican banks, 1982–5

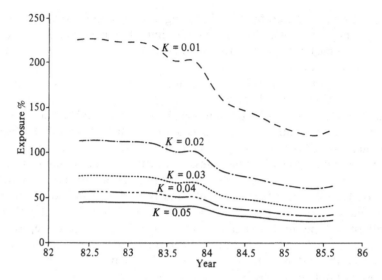

Figure 6.6 BIS banks' exposure to banks in four major debtor countries, 1982–5

borrowers and lenders becomes important in assessing inter-bank market risk (see Dufey and Giddy 1984 for a thorough discussion of these points).

In Figures 6.2–6.5 the gross and net claims of reporting BIS banks on *banks* located in four major debtor countries which have used reschedulings or moratoria to renegotiate (but not repudiate) international loan contracts are presented for the period 1982:Q1 to 1985:Q3.[6]

Although the net debtor positions of banks in three of the four countries, Brazil, Mexico and Poland, have apparently improved since the height of the debt crisis in 1982:Q3, the net amounts outstanding are still large: Argentina ($6.66 billion), Brazil ($11.97 billion), Mexico ($5.82 billion) and Poland ($5.23 billion).

Figure 6.6 uses the data represented in Figures 6.2–6.5 to show the (potential) BIS reporting banks' sovereign risk exposure by comparing the aggregate net claims outstanding on banks in these four debtor countries with different assumptions about reporting banks' capital adequacy. In the simulations in Figure 6.6 it is assumed that the 'average' bank capital – (*external*) asset ratios vary from a low of 1% to a high of 5%.[7] Thus, if on average, BIS participating banks held a 1% capital-external assets ratio in September 1985 a joint repudiation by banks in these 4 countries would more than exhaust capital held against international loans, forcing inroads to be made into these banks' domestic capital funds. Even a 5% capital-external asset ratio would see external capital funds reduced by 25% following a joint repudiation. While the above may be a worst case scenario the simulation nevertheless suggests that a significant degree of sovereign risk exposure currently exists in the international inter-bank market.

Banks in the international inter-bank market also face a liquidity (or depositor-run) risk. There has been a great deal of recent research interest in the theory of bank runs (see Ho–Saunders 1980, Waldo 1984, Chari and Jaganathan 1985 and Diamond and Dybvig 1983). These studies have shown that, in general, bank deposit contracts are efficient risk-sharing devices which have desirable attributes such as high liquidity and (almost certain) fixed face-value payoffs. However, unlike mutual funds deposit contracts are not continuously marked-to-market; so that if the market value of assets falls, the total face value of depositor claims will exceed the market value of bank assets. As a result all depositors have a rational incentive to be the first to run since 'place in line matters'. That is, those depositors who withdraw first may escape whole, while those last in line may be left with nothing.

Dean and Giddy (1981) have argued that this type of bank-run theory is more applicable to domestic than international banking. They suggest that this is because most international inter-bank deposits are time deposits and are not instantaneously 'callable' like domestic demand deposits. This argument ignores the fact that a considerable amount of transactions on the inter-bank market are *overnight* and therefore have similar liquidity attributes to demand deposits (see Ho and Saunders 1985 for a related discussion on overnight Fed funds).[8] Moreover, as has been noted by Furlong (1984), most time deposit contracts have interest penalty clauses for early withdrawal rather than absolute prohibitions on early withdrawal. Thus, even for small probabilities that a bank will be unable to repay its depositors in full, the incentive to run will be strong and likely to overwhelm any existing 'contractual' barriers inhibiting such a run.

Settlement risk relates to the institutional payment arrangement through which major banks settle borrowing/lending dollar transactions on the international inter-bank market. The primary mechanism of funds transfer is the Clearing House Inter-Bank Payments System (CHIPS), an electronically linked network of over 130 large banks. Unlike domestic US wire systems such as Fed wire, funds transferred on CHIPS *within* any day are provisional payments that *only* become final at the *end* of the day.[9] Thus if B_x, in our example, transfers funds to B_z at 11 a.m. the actual transfer of funds will not take place until the end of the day, normally through settling accounts at the Federal Reserve banks. Because this transfer of funds is not good or final until the end of the day, bank Z faces an *intra-day* settlement or '*daylight overdraft*' risk (see Humphrey 1986).[10] Specifically, bank Z may 'assume' the funds received at 11 a.m., from bank X, are good and then onlend them to a customer (Bank Y) at 11.15 a.m. However, if bank X does not deliver the promised funds at the end of the day, bank Z may be pushed into a serious net funds debitor position. Indeed, it is conceivable that this net debitor position may exceed its capital and reserves – rendering it 'technically' insolvent. In general such a disruption might only be expected to occur if a major fraud was discovered in bank X's books during the day and it was closed (the same day) by bank regulators. Alternatively, a bank might be transmitting funds (which it does not have) in the hope of keeping its 'name in the market' so as to be able to raise funds later in the day. It is conceivable that other banks may revise their credit limits for this bank during the day, making it unable to deliver all the funds promised.[11]

(b) Contagion

In Section III(a) the risks arising from inter-bank transactions for an *individual* bank were discussed. In this subsection the economic mechanisms for inter-bank contagion effects are considered. This is followed by a more formal discussion of contagion models in Section IV, and empirical evidence relating to contagion in Section V.

Mechanisms for contagion effects Contagion effects can be transmitted through either informational channels or real (institutional) channels. With respect to information effects these can be sub-divided into *pure* information contagion and noisy (or information signal extraction) contagion – see Aharony and Swary (1983). Pure contagion would result if bank Y failed, either through fraud or from losses on loans made for investment in a type of project that no other bank would consider (in other words failure was due to idiosyncratic reasons), but the announcement of this failure adversely affected depositor/investor confidence regarding the safety and soundness of other banks.

A noisy (signal information) contagion arises when depositors/ investors have some imperfect information regarding all banks. An announced loss by a bank on its foreign currency dealings or a cut in its dividends due to loan-loss write-offs, may be perceived to provide a noisy (but systematic) information signal regarding other banks. As a result, banks viewed as being similarly positioned to the troubled bank will face adverse responses from depositors/investors, i.e. will be placed in a similar risk-class as the troubled bank.

There are at least two real and/or institutional mechanisms through which individual bank risk can be transmitted to other banks. The first is the real transmission of bank runs to other banks, i.e. a run on an individual bank, in the inter-bank market, can be converted into a systematic bank run due to the close pyramiding of interbank transactions. For example, a run on bank Z will lead to a deposit outflow from this bank; however, while bank Z may be a net debtor in aggregate it may be a net creditor (supplier of funds) to a large sub-set of banks. Thus bank Z may call in its deposits from banks $1, \ldots, d$, in an attempt to cover its positions; such calls may lead to liquidity problems for these banks who in turn have to call in their deposits with banks $f, \ldots, k$, and so on. It might be argued that a systemwide collapse cannot occur because funds withdrawn from these banks are simply re-deposited elsewhere in the system. However, in reality the inter-bank market is not a constant sum game, deposits can be switched back into domestic banking or, in a true flight for quality, into treasury securities.[12] Thus in a contracting market, with each bank trying to meet a funds short-fall through calling in deposits with other banks, systematic run problems can occur.

The second institutional mechanism through which individual bank risk may be transmitted to other banks is through settlement risk. In the case discussed above, bank Z was left at the end of the day in a net debitor position because of 'undelivered' funds. If bank Z cannot meet its settlement commitments, CHIPS resolves this by completely unwinding bank Z's whole daily position (transactions) with all other banks. That is, the end of day net settlement matrix is recalculated for $n-1$ remaining banks, excluding all transactions with the nth (insolvent) bank. As a result those banks that were net senders (suppliers) of funds to the insolvent bank – i.e. they sent more than they received – will have their net settlement positions improved, while those banks who were net receivers of funds from the insolvent bank will have their positions worsened. Consequently, some banks that were originally in a net creditor position may be forced into a net debtor position, while others will have their net debtor position worsened, in the revised settlement matrix. If some of these banks are then unable to meet their revised settlement requirements, a further rebalancing will be necessary by excluding them from the settlement matrix, and so on until all banks left can meet their settlement obligations.

IV.   Modelling contagion effects

In Section III(b) contagion mechanisms were discussed on a relatively heuristic level. However, some authors have sought to model contagion effects more formally. These models tend to concentrate on analysing the effects of contagion on either: (i) interest rate spreads in the (international) deposit/loan markets, (ii) the quantity of deposits/loans supplied (credit-rationing models) or (iii) bank equity returns in the capital market. It might be noted that no author has integrated these three dimensions of contagion into a single model.

(i)   Spread (risk premium models)

Examples of interest rate spread models in an international context can be found in Angeloni and Short (1980), Edwards (1985), Feder and Just (1977), and Saunders (1986) among others. For simplicity assume that if a debtor declares default the creditor loses all principal and interest. Let k be the interest rate on the loan, R_F be the interest rate on a safe loan (the risk-free rate), ϕ be the risk-premium or spread on the loan and p be the lenders' subjective probability of repayment. Then a profit-maximizing risk-neutral lender[13] would charge a loan rate such that the expected return on a risky loan just equals the return on a safe or risk-free loan. That is,

$$0(1 - p) + p(1 + k) = 1 + R_F \tag{1}$$

Solving for k, the required rate on the risky loan:

$$k = ((1 + R_F)/p) - 1 \tag{2}$$

with a risk premium ϕ equal to:

$$\phi = ((1 + R_F)/p) - (1 + R_F) \tag{3}$$

From equations (1)–(3) it is clear that given R_F (the rate on risk-free loans), both k and ϕ are driven by lenders' perceived probability of loan repayment (p).

$$p = f(C_i) \tag{4}$$

where $f' > 0$, and C_i may be viewed as the bank-specific or unsystematic default risk characteristics of the ith borrower.

Following Guttentag and Herring (1984), Minsky (1977) and others a crisis state or period may be defined as one in which lenders perceive that the probability of systematic default or default contagion is nonzero. Further, in such a disaster state the probability of repayment is zero for all loans.[14] Thus while in *normal* periods lenders may base their subjective probabilities of repayment of a given loan on $f(C_i)$ as in (4) above, in crisis periods p is determined by equation (5) below:

$$p = (1 - \pi)f(C_i) + \pi(0) \tag{5}$$

where π is the lenders' perceived probability of the disaster state occurring. Implicitly, in normal periods $\pi = 0$ while in crisis periods $\pi > 0$.[15] Note that $\pi > 0$ may be due to adverse information (signals) regarding one bank which depositors/investors believe contains adverse information pertaining to all banks. Indeed, in a crisis state all adverse signals affecting individual banks may increase π.

Note that this perception of systematic risk or contagion can be based on either actual real and financial linkages (e.g., through trade, inflation, money supply etc.) or it can be purely informational, i.e., the debt repayment problem of one sovereign borrower sends *adverse* signals to lenders regarding the repayment probabilities of all countries, thereby changing lenders' prior expectations as to π.

In the context of equations (1)–(5) an increase in the systematic or contagion probability (π) will reduce p, the perceived probability of repayment, *even if bank-specific risk, $f(C_i)$, remains unchanged.* Moreover, the larger is π, the more the systematic or contagion risk component will dominate the bank-specific risk component, so that perceived repayment probabilities for different countries will tend to become increasingly isomorphic. Thus the presence of a perceived contagion risk should not only result in increasing risk premiums or spreads on international loans, or π in equation (3), but also in a greater correlation or co-movement in the spreads charged to different borrowing groups (countries).[16]

(ii)   Credit rationing models

Contagion may not only have well defined effects on interest rates (k) and spreads (ϕ), but also affect the quantity and type of loan that a lender is willing to make. The optimality of credit-rationing risky borrowers instead of simply increasing risk-premiums or spreads has received extensive coverage in the banking literature (see, for example, Sachs and Cohen 1982, Eaton and Gersovitz 1981, Stiglitz and Weiss 1981 and Guttentag and Herring 1984). This also fits into the stylized facts we know about the international inter-bank market, namely that banks set (variable) credit ceilings or limits, for other banks, beyond which they will not lend *at any price* (see Giddy 1981).

The logic behind binding credit ceilings is that, beyond some point, raising interest rates (spreads) to risky borrowers becomes counterproductive. That is high interest rates provide both adverse selection (moral hazard) and incentive effects for borrowers that may actually reduce the lender's expected return, $E(r)$, on a loan.[17]

Similar to Stiglitz and Weiss (1981), the relationship between the $E(r)$

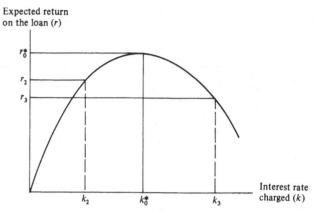

Figure 6.7 The relationship between the expected return and interest rate on a loan

on the loan and the contractual interest rate (k) can be shown in Figure 6.7. In this figure, as the interest rate charged to a borrower rises from zero, the lender's expected return may initially rise, since over the relatively low interest rate range $(k < k_0^*)$ the lender's expected return from higher interest rate charges will tend to offset any greater risk due to the borrower's increased risk-taking incentives after the loan is made. Eventually, however, the increased risk due to default incentives and adverse selection may come to outweigh the increased returns due to higher interest rate charges, so that at some point beyond (k_0^*) the lender's expected return on the loan will actually start to fall. Of course the logic of this argument is that extremely high interest rates, such as k_3 in Figure 6.7, will simply result in lower expected returns to the lender (r_3). Hence an important implication of Figure 6.7 is that at any moment in time there is an equilibrium rate on a risky loan which maximizes a lender's expected return, and this rate, or associated spread over the risk-free rate, is not necessarily large. In Figure 6.7 the optimal rate is k_0^*.

To see how credit rationing can occur, assume that there are two observationally distinguishable borrowing groups (in terms of bank-specific risk) A and B facing a lender. Group A might be thought of as other large banks operating in central market locations and Group B as banks on the periphery of the inter-bank market, i.e., here location and size may be thought of as the group risk sorting characteristics. Suppose the interest rate-expected return loci for these two groups take the forms characterized in Figure 6.8. Here, k_A is the optimal, expected return maximizing rate to be charged to Group A borrowers and k_B is the

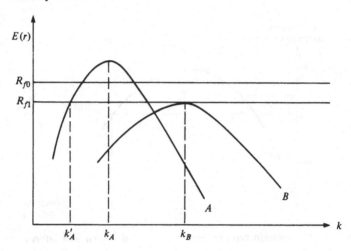

Figure 6.8   **Expected return – interest rate loci for groups A and B**

optimal rate to be charged to Group B borrowers such that $k_B > k_A$. Now suppose that the bank's cost of funds (assumed, for simplicity, to equal the (risk-free) bid rate is designated by R_{f0} in Figure 6.8. At this cost of funds, all borrowers in Group A, who are willing to pay k_A, will receive loans. However, because of the higher default risk of Group B borrowers, the whole expected return–interest rate locus for this group lies below R_{f0} and *no bank loans* to Group B borrowers are profitable *at any finite interest rate (or spread)*. Hence all type B borrowers will be rationed out of the international loan market. There are two ways that type B borrowers might regain access to the loan market. The first is if the cost of funds falls from R_{f0} to R_{f1} or below. The second is if lenders' subjective perceptions of Group B default risk is reduced, perhaps by some favourable shift in their credit-sovereign risk set (in Figure 6.8, the locus B would shift upwards).

A contagion effect on the supply of loans can also be analysed within this framework. Suppose Group B loans were initially credit-rationed because of some perceived adverse shift in these banks' future prospects. In the absence of contagion Group A and B borrowers are, by definition, mutually distinguishable and only B's locus would be affected. However, contagion implies that lenders, due to informational or real linkages, can no longer perfectly distinguish between borrowing groups simply by characteristics such as size and location. Hence an increase in the default risk of Group B's loans, due to a shift in its opportunity investment set for example, may also be viewed as increasing the default risk of all other groups: Group A, Group C, etc. As a result the lender's expected

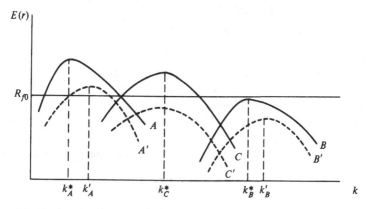

Figure 6.9   Contagion and credit rationing

return-interest rate loci will be revised downward for all borrowing groups even though the cost of funds remains the same for lenders at R_{f0}. This effect is shown in Figure 6.9 for the three borrowing groups A, B, C.

Initially all three groups have access to loans (with $k_B^* > k_C^* > k_A^* > R_{f0}$); although the bank lender prefers borrowers in Group A to those in Group C, and those in Group C to those in Group B. An increase in the default risk of Group B borrowers, when borrowers are mutually distinguishable, simply results in locus B shifting to B' and all borrowers in that group being rationed out of the market, while Group A and C retain access to the market at unchanged interest rates. When contagion is present a perceived shift in the default risk of Group B borrowers is also viewed as an increase in the risk of all other borrowers, so that borrowers become less distinguishable and the expected return interest rate loci of both Group A and C borrowers shift downwards as in Figure 6.9. The result is that now all Group C borrowers are rationed out as well as Group B, while Group A borrowers still have access only if they are willing to pay a higher interest rate (spread), i.e., $k_A' > k_A^*$.

The implication of the above analysis is that contagion should result in (increased) credit rationing, characterized by a falling quantity of loans for all borrowers.

(iii)   Capital market models

Capital market models have concentrated on analysing the effects of contagion risk on the required return on bank equity in the capital market (see, for example, Aharony and Swary 1983, Aharony, Saunders and Swary 1986 and Swary 1986 among others).

In capital market equilibrium:

$$E(\tilde{R}_i) = R_F + [E(\tilde{R}_m) - R_F] \beta_i \qquad (6)$$

where:

$E(\tilde{R}_i)$ = the expected return on bank i's stocks
R_F = the (constant) risk-free rate
$E(\tilde{R}_m)$ = the expected return on the market portfolio
β_i = Cov $(\tilde{R}_i, \tilde{R}_m)$/Var $(\tilde{R}_m)$ = the systematic risk on the ith bank's stock

Following Fama (1976) this may be rewritten in market model form

$$\tilde{R}_{it} = \alpha_i + \beta_i \tilde{R}_{mt} + \tilde{\varepsilon}_{it} \qquad (7)$$

where:

$\tilde{R}_{it}$ = return on bank i's stocks in period t
α_i = constant = $(1 - \beta_i)R_F$
$\tilde{\varepsilon}_{it}$ = residual or unsystematic risk on the ith bank stock.

Using (7) the total return risk (variance of returns) for the ith bank stock is:

$$\text{Var}(\tilde{R}_{it}) = \beta_i^2 \text{Var}(\tilde{R}_{mt}) + \text{Var}(\tilde{\varepsilon}_{it}) \qquad (8)$$

Thus, for any given variance of market returns (Var $\tilde{R}_{mt}$), total risk of bank i's stocks may increase because either systematic risk (β_i^2) has increased or unsystematic risk [Var $(\tilde{\varepsilon}_{it})$] has increased.

Note that as well as firm specific risk, $\tilde{\varepsilon}_{it}$ may reflect some 'bank industry' specific risk orthogonal to the market risk factor. Thus, for example, sovereign rescheduling may have some effect on the overall domestic economy (i.e., all firms) but their primary direct (non-contagious effect is likely to be on all those banks directly exposed.

In the market model framework, the 'announcement' effect, at time t, of adverse information pertaining to bank i will be reflected in its estimated abnormal return (AR_{it}) calculated as:

$$\hat{\varepsilon}_{it} = AR_{it} = R_{it} - (\hat{\alpha}_i + \hat{\beta} i R_{mt}) \qquad (9)$$

which is the difference between actual observed returns on bank i's stocks at the time of the announcement (t) and returns predicted by the market model ($\hat{\alpha}_i + \hat{\beta}_i R_{mt}$) – where $\hat{\alpha}_i$ and $\hat{\beta}_i$ are estimated over a 'stable' time period preceding the announcement. Thus if AR_{it} is significantly negative, the new information has served to depress equity values below their normal level.

Let AR_{jt} be the abnormal return on bank j's equity at the time of the adverse information reaching the market about bank i. Contagion occurs whenever Cov $(AR_{it}, AR_{jt}) > 0$ and is absent when Cov $(AR_{it}, AR_{jt}) = 0$.

In other words, contagion is present in the capital market whenever adverse information regarding bank i negatively affects the stock market values (prices) of banks j, k, l, m, n etc... Moreover, systematically declining equity values can have serious consequences on an industry that is either already capital constrained or is under pressure from regulators to increase capital-adequacy ratios.[18]

V. Empirical evidence on contagion

(i) Spreads

Evidence on spreads, the difference in spreads and the co-movement of spreads on inter-bank market transactions for individual banks is difficult to obtain. At best researchers have been able to observe bid/ask quotes on the Reuters screen. Unfortunately, however, these quotes may not be 'true' transaction prices. Giddy (1981) reports evidence on bid prices for 30 Eurobanks in London over *different* one-day periods in July and August 1981.[19] Estimating deviations from the mode on a 'typical' day, Giddy found the range of quotes across the 30 banks to be very small – at 5/16 of a percent or 30 basis points. Using bank size as a proxy for creditworthiness (along with earnings and capital adequacy ratios) as well as country of origin as a proxy for sovereign risk, he could find little correlation between any of these measures and the average size of the spread.[20] Giddy concluded that spreads tended to reflect relative daily demand pressures for funds at individual banks rather than different risks and that risk adjustments were more likely to be found in the quantity (loan size) dimension.

Giddy appears to be the only author to have looked at the distribution of spreads across banks at any moment in time. The vast majority of other studies have looked at the behaviour of *average* LIBOR across *all* borrowers from a given country either over time and/or across different countries at any moment in time. As a result, these studies have been primarily concerned with the degree of sovereign risk encompassing all borrowers (bank and non-bank) in a given country or jurisdiction.

In this context Saunders (1986) analysed *Euromoney* LIBOR spread indices for (i) the industrialized group of countries, (ii) the upper-middle income group of countries and (iii) the lower income (LDC) group.[21] Of particular interest was how correlations among these spreads performed around the time of significant adverse information regarding the LDC group (in this case the international debt crisis of Autumn 1982). Specifically was there an increase in the correlation among these indices around the time of the announcement (evidence consistent with

Table 6.1.   **Correlations among spreads, 1974:Q1–1983:Q4**

(a) *Non-Crisis period 1974:Q1–1978:Q4*

Variable	N	Mean (%)	Std dev (%)
Ind 1	20	1.17600000	0.31434811
Non-oil LDCs 1	20	1.56300000	0.28775172
Res 1	20	1.67900000	0.33486682

	Pearson Correlation Coefficients		
	Ind	Noil	Res
Ind	1.00000	0.87624	0.68260
Non-oil LDCs	0.87624	1.00000	0.92230
Res	0.68260	0.92230	1.00000

(b) *Crisis period 1979:Q1–1983:Q4*

Variable	N	Mean (%)	Std dev (%)
Ind 2	20	0.56700000	0.07987490
Non-oil LDCs 2	20	1.00650000	0.32627523
Res 2	20	1.61800000	0.55235953

	Pearson Correlation Coefficients		
	Ind	Noil	Res
Ind	1.00000	0.29604	0.01465
Non-oil LDCs	0.29604	1.00000	0.46462
Res	0.01465	0.46462	1.00000

Notes: 1 Raw data from Folkerts-Landau (1985), Table 4.
2 The Fisher test takes the form
$$Z_{12} = (Z_1 - Z_2)/\sqrt{1/N_1 - 3 + 1/N_2 - 3}$$
where
$$Z_1 = 1/2 \ln \left[(1+p_i)/(1-p_i) \right] \quad i = 1,2.$$

contagion), or were the spreads charged to the relatively safe industrialized group of countries uncorrelated with LDC spreads? Using a 17 month moving-window procedure to calculate monthly correlation matrices the correlation for the industrialized group and LDC group spreads was close to zero in 1981 before rising to +0.5 in the Autumn of 1982. However, by April 1983 this correlation had declined again to +0.25. This suggests a (temporary) contagion effect existed around the time of the crisis announcement, but also that it quickly dissipated soon after the shock.

It is also possible to gain insights from spread correlations for relatively tranquil and 'crisis' periods using quarterly LIBOR data reported in Folkerts-Landau (1985).[22] Raw data on average spreads are reported for the period 1974:Q1 to 1983:Q4 for (i) industrialized countries (Ind), (ii) non-oil LDC's and (iii) rescheduled countries (Res). This data set was split into two sub-periods; (1) 1974:Q1–1978:Q4 (a relatively tranquil period) and (2) 1979:Q1–1983:Q4 (a 'crisis' period). If contagion was present it might be hypothesized that the correlations among the different borrowing group spreads would be significantly larger in the 'crisis' sub-period.

Interestingly, there appears to be no evidence of contagion in the crisis period. Not only were the required spreads, in the crisis period, larger for the rescheduled group of countries relative to the 'safe' group of industrialized countries, the average spread between the re-scheduling countries and non-oil LDC's increased from 11 basis points to 61 basis points. More to the point, the correlations among the spreads were also significantly lower than in the non-crisis period. For example, the correlation among non-oil LDCs and rescheduled countries fell from 0.922 to 0.464 and for the industrialized countries and the rescheduled countries from 0.682 to 0.015. A simple bi-variate test, using the standard Fisher p to Z transformation[23] revealed Z-ratios of 2.37 and 2.90 respectively, i.e. the decline in both correlation coefficients was statistically significant at the 5% level. These results are consistent with clearer price-discrimination by lenders among borrowing groups in the post-1979 period and imply a low degree of contagion in this period.

Dooley and Isard (1980) have modelled sovereign risk as the *net* difference in rates on deposits in the same currency placed in different countries after adjusting for capital control effects. The case they look at is the spread between DM domestic interbank deposits and DM Euro-currency deposit in Zurich (of the same maturity) over the period 1970–4. The capital control adjusted sovereign risk spread was found to be small but time varying. With respect to contagion, the June 1974 Herstatt failure appeared to have no effect on this spread which reached a peak of 2% in mid-1973 and systematically declined to approximately zero by the end of 1974. More recently, Melvin and Schlagenhauf (1986) have applied the same methodology in deriving pure sovereign risk premia for Mexican Peso three month CD deposits at Mexican banks and French Franc three month deposits at French banks. Although the authors do not discuss the issue of contagion they present graphs showing the time-series evolution of both risk premia series that encompasses the August 1982 'announcement' of Mexico's debt repayment problems. From visual inspection of these graphs it is not possible to discern any adverse impact of the Mexican announcement on French risk premiums. Indeed, if anything, French risk premiums appear to be falling in the period immediately surrounding the August 1982 announcement.

Doukas (1985) has examined the informational efficiency of Euro-currency markets by analysing the adjustment of spreads to relevant 'news' about a borrower's economy. To do this he regresses monthly *changes* in spreads (for Mexico, Brazil and Argentina) on the *unexpected* monthly change in a country's export/international reserves ratio (a debt indicator variable). For the period 1978–83 he found a statistically significant impact of 'news' on individual country spreads. However, no contagion tests were conducted to see, for example, how 'news' for Brazil affects Mexican spreads etc. This would seem to be a fruitful area for further research.

There are also innumerable studies that seek to derive the determinants (*ex-post*) of sovereign risk premia using either regression (logit/probit) or discriminant analysis models. These have been extensively reviewed by McDonald (1982) and will not be discussed in great detail here. These studies seek to explain the cross-sectional variation in sovereign risk premiums (spreads) using some set of 'exogenous' economic and political risk proxies for each country in the sample. Presumably, if lenders can distinguish among sovereign risks there will be some well-defined vector of variables that accurately discriminates between high and low risk cases, not only in *ex-post* but also in *ex-ante* prediction tests (see Taffler and Abassi 1984). In a world of contagion, by contrast, the fit of such models should be poor and the number of Type I and Type II misclassification errors high. Moreover, the predictive ability of such models should be weak. With one major exception, Taffler and Abassi (1984), authors have largely concentrated on the *ex-post* explanatory power rather than predictive ability of such models. For example, a representative study is that by Edwards (1985) who found the most important discriminating economic variables to be the External Debt/GNP ratio, the Debt service ratio and the Gross Domestic Investment/GNP ratio. The only study of which the author is aware, to have found no systematically discriminating economic or dummy variables is that by Sargen (1976). As already noted Taffler and Abassi (1984) is a rare example of trying to test the predictive ability of this type of model out of sample. Using a discriminant function fitted for 1967–77, tests were conducted to evaluate how well the model explained 71 identified reschedulings over the 1979–83 period. On the whole the model appears to perform reasonably well, predicting 69% of these reschedulings, although there was a relatively high number of Type I and II errors in 1982 (the peak of the debt crisis).

On the whole, the existing body of evidence on spreads seems to suggest that, apart from the months immediately surrounding major crises such as the 1982 Mexican debt announcement, contagion effects reflected in spreads have not been very strong. This would be consistent with lenders compensating for risk by adjusting quantities (credit rationing) rather than prices (spreads). Evidence on this is considered next.

(ii)   Bank runs and credit rationing

(a) Bank runs   Although the theory of bank runs has received considerable attention in the recent banking literature, little empirical research
has been undertaken since the Friedman and Schwartz (1963) study on
historical banking panics in the US. Nevertheless, a run on bank deposits
in one country that leads to a major contraction in that country's money
supply, under a regime of fixed or quasi-fixed exchange rates, may be
transmitted *via* changes in international reserves to other countries'
money bases and therefore banking systems. In a recent paper Bordo
(1985) has matched common international business cycles (trough to
trough) for the US, Great Britain, Germany, France, Sweden and
Canada over the period 1870–1933. His objective was to determine
common international channels or linkages for historic recessions or
contractions (i.e. contagion effects). Specifically, were contractions
largely due to monetary factors such as systematic bank runs (increases in
currency-deposit ratios) or to other financial factors such as a stock
market collapse?[24] While bank panics appeared to be major determinants of 7 out of 12 contractions experienced in the US over this period,
such panics were noticeably absent in the contractionary phases for the
five other countries. Specifically, for Great Britain no banking crisis
occurred in any of the 12 contractions, for Germany 2 out of 12, France 3
out of 12 and Canada 2 out of 12. Bordo attributes the greater prevalence
of panics in the US to (i) the pyramiding of regional deposits with New
York banks (which bears a close analogy to the pyramiding in the current
international inter-bank market) compared to the more geographically
diversified bases developed by non-US banks and (ii) stronger and more
active Central banks in non-US countries. This historical evidence
provides some insights into the likelihood of systematic panics in the
current international inter-bank market. On the negative side is the
extensive pyramiding of deposits at a small number of central money
market banks (B_z in our previous example). However, mitigating against
panic effects are the greater fund diversification of today's international
banks,[25] more active market intervention by central banks (see later)
and the existence of relatively flexible exchange rates which weakens the
transmission effect of individual country shocks.

    In the more recent era the 'failure' of Continental Illinois in April 1984
provides a good case study for analysing any systematic bank run effects.
At the time of its failure Continental was the 8th largest bank in the US.
It had assets of $42 billion, 75% of which were financed by rate sensitive
liabilities. More importantly, due to restrictions on branching in Illinois,
Continental relied heavily on foreign inter-bank deposits (40% of total)

and domestic inter-bank deposits (16% of total), so that less than 10% of its deposits were liable to *ex ante* FDIC insurance guarantees.

Two important dates for analysing run and contagion effects were April 18th 1984, when Continental anounced an increase of $400 million in its problem loan portfolio, and May 10th 1984 when the Comptroller of the Currency publicly 'denied' rumours that Continental was in serious financial trouble. To analyse 'local' (US) contagion effects one can track the impact these announcements had on other large US banks deposits – specifically the large (over $1.4 billion weekly) reporting banks in the *Federal Reserve Bulletin*. The April 18th announcement had an imperceptible effect on large bank deposit flows, i.e. large banks' purchased funds increased by 1% that week. Nevertheless, the May 10th announcement appears, at first blush, to have had a more serious effect, with borrowed funds declining by 7% (or $13 billion) over the announcement week. However, this decline was largely offset by an 8% increase in demand deposits in the same week. Thus many depositors[26] appear to have reacted to the crisis by simply switching funds into safer banks and more 'secure' deposits rather than running *per se*, i.e., switching into currency or treasury securities.[27] Moreover, the very strong implicit guarantees provided by the Fed and FDIC as to the safety of all (domestic) deposits, large and small, effectively defused the incentive to run. However, while large depositors may have perceived that Fed guarantees applied to their deposits in the US it was not obvious that these guarantees extended to the *overseas/offshore* offices of US banks operating in the Eurocurrency markets. Further, Continental was heavily engaged in borrowing on the London inter-bank market. Table 6.2 reports the non-sterling overseas and CD deposits at American, Japanese and other foreign banks in London for the period January 1984 to October 1984. As can be seen, in neither April or May is there a net negative impact on deposit flows to American banks in London. Indeed in May overseas deposits (other than CDs) increased by 6.76%. It can also be seen that Japanese and other foreign banks weren't affected either. For example, between April and May all groups recorded total deposit inflows, i.e. American banks (+£2,074m). Japanese banks (+£3,841m) and other foreign banks (+£2,805m). These figures provide no evidence of a deposit flow contagion effect on the international inter-bank market at the time of the Continental failure.[28]

(b) Credit rationing   While bank panics or widespread runs do not seem to have characterized the recent international banking system, greater uncertainty about the creditworthiness of borrowers may have resulted in a systematic increase in credit rationing. Specifically, if loans

Table 6.2. **Non-sterling deposits at Eurobanks in London, February 1984–October 1984 (£m)**

1984	American Banks		Japanese Banks		Other Overseas	
	Overseas	CD's	Overseas	CD's	Overseas	CD's
J	52,880	28,312	65,850	20,756	86,539	11,221
F	51,281	29,502	66,423	20,830	87,068	11,396
M	51,891	30,768	70,763	21.374	88,674	11,349
A	52,019	30,792	69,594	22,740	90,083	12,014
M	55,538	29,347	72,109	24,066	91,897	13,005
J	56,933	27,915	76,273	24,062	94,107	12,843
J	57,453	28,159	82,934	26,367	96,742	14,426
A	58,338	27,520	83,435	25,440	97,694	14,286
S	59,296	28,456	94,188	27,211	101,596	16,483
O	58,499	27,555	94,074	26,732	105,102	16,167
% change						
A	0.2%	0.08%	−1.65%	6.39%	1.59%	5.86%
M	6.76%	−4.69%	3.61%	5.83%	2.01%	8.24%

Source: BEQB December 1984. Table 3.

are supply side determined and lenders are increasingly unable to accurately distinguish among borrowers[29] in terms of quality, there should be a strong positive correlation (contagion) in the flow of loans to borrowing groups over time; whereas a low degree of contagion (correlation) would imply that lenders are able accurately to distinguish among borrower groups.

It is well known that most banks place credit caps on the amount of funds they are willing to lend to other banks in the Eurocurrency markets. Unfortunately, other than anecdotal evidence (see Giddy 1981) there is little publicly available evidence on the size of individual bank caps or how they have varied over time. It is also conventional wisdom that banks apply caps on *aggregate* loan exposure to all borrowers (bank and non-bank) from a given country. On the supposition that there is a close link between perceived creditworthiness and the size of loan flows,[30] insights into credit-rationing and contagion may be gained by analysing loan flows to different country groups.

The Bank for International Settlements reports quarterly data on loan flows from BIS reporting banks to various areas. Table 6.3 summarizes

Table 6.3. **Loan flows from the BIS reporting banks to different borrowing groups, 1978–84 ($ billion)**

	1	2	3	4	5
		Reporting		Latin America + other LDC's +	
	Total	area	%	Eastern Europe	%
1978	208.8	122.8	58.8	34	16.28
1979	204.2	115.6	56.6	40.5	19.83
1980	208.6	116.1	55.6	41.5	19.91
1981	216.6	115.1	53.13	37.4	17.26
1982	134.4	74.3	55.3	9.7	7.21
1983	55.3	24.1	43.58	4.1	7.41
1984	57.3	58.9	102.79	1.4	2.44

Table 6.4. **Correlation matrix among loan flows from BIS reporting banks to various borrowing groups, 1978:Q1–1982:Q2**

		BIS	OFF	ODC	EE	OPEC	LA	OLDC
1.	BIS	1	0.653*	0.084	0.631*	0.630*	0.590*	0.441*
2.	OFF		1	0.037	0.446*	0.297	0.658*	0.327
3.	ODC			1	0.096	0.172	0.263	0.179
4.	EE				1	0.531*	0.422*	0.646*
5.	OPEC					1	0.456*	0.685*
6.	LA						1	0.682*
7.	OLDC							1

Note:
BIS   = BIS reporting countries
OFF   = Offshore banking centers
ODC   = Other developed countries
EE   = Eastern European countries
OPEC   = Opec countries
LA   = Latin American countries
OLDC   = Other less developed countries
* Significant at 10% level using t-test

(on an annual basis) loan flows from the BIS reporting banks to (i) all areas, (ii) the reporting area (industrialized) countries, and (iii) LDCs plus Eastern Europe for the period 1978–84.[31]

As can be seen the gross flows of external international bank leanding declined dramatically between 1978 and 1984, from $208.8 billion to $57.3 billion. Further, the decline for the 'high' sovereign risk group was

Table 6.5. **Correlation matrix among loan flows from BIS reporting banks to various borrowing groups, 1982:Q3–1985:Q3**

	BIS	OFF	ODC	EE	OPEC	LA	OLDC
1. BIS	1	−0.007	0.500*	0.507*	0.463	0.308	0.348
2. OFF		1	−0.025	−0.269	0.390	0.099	0.412
3. ODC			1	0.603*	0.531*	0.064	0.628*
4. EE				1	0.252	0.306	0.747*
5. OPEC					1	0.322	0.271
6. LA						1	−0.006
7. OLDC							1

even more dramatic, from \$34 billion (or 16.28% of gross loan flows) to \$1.4 billion (2.44%) in 1984. For the relatively safe group of industrialized (reporting) countries loan flows fell from \$122.8 billion in 1978 to \$58.9 billion in 1984. Tables 6.4 and 6.5 show the correlation matrices among loan flows for 7 borrowing country groups for two sub-periods (i) 1978:Q2–1982:Q2 and (ii) 1982:Q3–1985:Q3, with the latter period encompassing the Mexican–Brazilian debt crisis.

As can be seen in the first ('non-crisis') sub-period all correlations are positive with 11(13) out of 21 significantly positive at the 5%(10%) level. Further the loan flow correlations between the BIS group of countries and respectively Eastern Europe, OPEC, Latin America and other LDC's were all significantly positive. By contrast in the second (crisis) sub-period 5 out of 21 correlations are negative and only 4(6) out of 21 are significantly positive at the 5%(10%) level (none, at the 5% level, between the BIS group and the 'risky' group of borrowers). Rather than supporting contagion these correlation results imply that suppliers of loans were able to distinguish among different borrowing groups, i.e., there was selective rather than systematic (contagious) credit rationing. This is given further support by Tables 6.6 and 6.7 which show the results of principal components analyses for the two sub-periods.

To the extent that the first component reflects the common 'systematic' or 'worldwide' component underlying loan flows, this fell from explaining 54% of loan flow variance in the non-crisis period to 44% in the crisis period.[32]

However, these figures mask an important underlying trend in the international capital market. As was argued in Section II, international financial intermediation will only remain the preferred vehicle for international capital movements if the costs of using this mechanism are less than direct credit market transactions (securitization). As the costs

Table 6.6.   **Principal components analysis for loan flows from BIS reporting banks to various borrowing groups, 1978:Q1–1982:Q2**

EIGENVECTORS

	Prin 1	Prin 2	Prin 3	Prin 4	Prin 5	Prin 6	Prin 7
BIS	0.429516	−0.242357	0.096019	0.475512	−0.268810	−0.549659	0.383488
OFF	0.361643	−0.370220	0.564582	0.018066	0.057272	0.625875	0.134437
ODC	0.124311	0.855536	0.369094	0.312503	0.088665	0.067025	0.079761
EE	0.400908	−0.088043	−0.298674	0.320884	0.721436	−0.015602	−0.344435
OPEC	0.396400	0.139727	−0.440317	0.153978	−0.601476	0.371353	−0.325699
LA	0.421141	0.064786	0.357347	−0.531835	−0.085005	−0.398625	−0.491701
OLDC	0.417202	0.201956	−0.353575	−0.516119	0.164715	0.067930	0.601678

	EIGENVALUE	DIFFERENCE	PROPORTION	CUMULATIVE
PRIN 1	3.75178	2.71160	0.535969	0.53597
PRIN 2	1.04018	0.16068	0.148597	0.68457
PRIN 3	0.87949	0.30874	0.125642	0.81021
PRIN 4	0.57076	0.10549	0.081536	0.89174
PRIN 5	0.46527	0.25274	0.066467	0.95821
PRIN 6	0.21253	0.13254	0.030362	0.98857
PRIN 7	0.07999	—	0.011428	1.00000

Table 6.7.   **Principal components analysis for loan flows from BIS reporting banks to various borrowing groups, 1982:Q3–1985:Q3**

EIGENVECTORS

	Prin 1	Prin 2	Prin 3	Prin 4	Prin 5	Prin 6	Prin 7
BIS	0.415591	0.170905	0.130855	−0.858796	0.075436	0.124033	0.149491
OFF	−0.084610	0.667935	−0.300098	0.163229	0.587558	0.157209	0.245079
ODC	0.473695	0.010010	−0.371860	0.077026	0.021807	−0.789795	0.083956
EE	0.484207	−0.197575	0.185436	0.193250	0.532940	0.172073	−0.584073
OPEC	346777	0.488123	−0.233460	0.155922	−0.591204	−0.201493	0.255959
LA	0.196555	0.345683	0.800948	0.293502	−0.089969	−0.201493	0.255959
OLDC	0.449882	−0.357433	−0.155344	0.286518	−0.058415	0.429897	0.612699

	EIGENVALUE	DIFFERENCE	PROPORTION	CUMULATIVE
PRIN 1	3.07139	1.43730	0.438770	0.43877
PRIN 2	1.63409	0.67268	0.233441	0.67221
PRIN 3	0.96140	0.42461	0.137343	0.80955
PRIN 4	0.53679	0.15070	0.076685	0.88624
PRIN 5	0.38609	0.10808	0.055156	0.94139
PRIN 6	0.27801	0.14578	0.039716	0.98111
PRIN 7	0.13223	—	0.018889	1.00000

Table 6.8. **International bank lending and bond issues, 1981–4** [a] **($ billion)**

	1981	1982	1983	1984
Inter-bank lending	98.8	85.5	21.0	24.7
Bank lending to non-banks	165.0	95.0	85.0	95.0
Eurobond and foreign bond issues	32.0	58.5	58.0	83.0

Note: [a] Exchange-rate *adjusted.*
Source: BIS *Quarterly Report* 1985–II.

(particularly risks) of transacting in the international banking market have risen in recent years, low-risk high-quality borrowers and lenders have begun to withdraw (an adverse-selection effect) and turn to security market transactions instead. Many banks also prefer to act as either underwriters or guarantors in these markets compared to continuing as distributors of funds on the international loan market. This has not only resulted in a declining pool of lenders/borrowers on the international loan markets but also, more seriously, a decline in the average quality of the remaining borrowers.[33]

Table 6.8 shows inter-bank lending, bank lending to non-bank (end-users) and international bond financing (issues-redemptions-repurchases) for 1981–4.

Thus while inter-bank lending has declined from $98.8 billion to $24.7 billion and bank lending from $165 billion to $95 billion, Eurobond and foreign bond issues increased from $32 billion to $83 billion. Indeed, in 1985:Q1 alone total bond issues were $63 billion.

The implication of this trend is that, while credit-rationing *contagion* appears (so far) to have been absent, in the post-1982 crisis period, if the pool of low-risk borrowers continues to be depleted, as the relative cost (risk) of financial intermediation rises (relative to securitization) there appears to be a real possibility of future contagious effects.[34]

(iii) Contagion and bank equity values

Aharony and Swary (1983) have analysed the effect of the announcement of the three largest US bank failures, as of 1980, on the equity market values (abnormal returns) of three groups of US banks: money centres, medium-sized banks and small banks. The three failures analysed were the US National Bank of San Diego in 1973 (fraud), Franklin National Bank in 1974 (foreign exchange losses and fraud)[35] and the Hamilton

National Bank of Tennessee in 1976 (illegal inter-company real-estate loans). Since, to some extent, each of these events could be viewed as idiosyncratic (i.e. bank specific), as they involved financial irregularities of one type or another, contemporaneous negative abnormal impacts on the equity values of other banks would be consistent with the presence of 'pure' contagion effects. The results suggest that neither the USNB or HNB failures had any perceptible impact on other banks' equity values, which might be expected given their *relatively* small size on a US national scale. By comparison, at the time of failure, Franklin National was the 12th largest bank in the US and, because of its extensive international operations, was viewed as a major player in international inter-bank markets. The important event week for this bank was that encompassing May 10th–May 13th 1974 when Franklin suspended its second quarter dividend, announced sizeable foreign exchange losses and trading in its stock was suspended after sustaining abnormal losses/negative abnormal returns of 35% in the announcement week. This failure had a significant contagion effect on all three bank groups. Specifically, in the announcement week, average abnormal returns for the other (12) largest US money-centre banks was −9.51%, for the (31) medium sized banks −6.13% and (30) smallest banks −4.85%. In the same week the market index fell by only 0.16%. Interestingly, the period studied also encompassed the German Bankhaus Herstatt failure (seven weeks after Franklin National). In the week of the Herstatt bank failure abnormal returns for the US money centres was −4.91%, for the medium-sized banks −5.79% and smallest banks −3.15%, all significantly negative at the 5% level.

In a more recent study Swary (1986) has analysed the contagion effect of Continental Illinois' failure on other banks' equity values. Since this failure comes approximately 10 years after Franklin National, and both banks were of similar size and importance at the time, it allows one to compare the relative order of magnitude of contagion effects a decade apart. Indeed, it could be argued *a priori* that the Continental Illinois failure should have had a stronger contagion effect on other banks since its collapse was due to bad domestic and international loans rather than idiosyncratic 'irregularities'.[36] At best, the results show a very weak contagion effect on other US banks' returns (a portfolio of 67 other US banks). In the week of Continental's announcement of a substantial increase in problem loans (April 18th) the abnormal returns on Continental's stock were −8.88% compared to −0.64% for all other banks. In the next week in which Japanese and other investors withdrew a considerable amount of purchased funds, Continental's abnormal returns were −2.05% compared to −0.42% for all other banks. Even when the author segregated out 12 'questionable' liability managing banks their abnormal returns were still only −0.09% and −1.36% respectively. Hence these figures strongly suggest that the equity market contagion effects of the Continental Bank failure were considerably less than those experienced ten years before with Franklin National (and Herstatt).

There have also been studies of the announcement effect of the Mexican debt crisis (August 1982) on bank equity values. In this case since US banks did not fully disclose *ex ante* their sovereign loan risk (exposure) positions, questions arise as to whether the announcement had an adverse impact on the equity values of all US banks (contagion) regardless of exposure? Or, whether the US equity market was sufficiently 'strong-form' efficient that investors were able to accurately distinguish good (no-exposure) from bad (exposure) banks with abnormal return reactions directly linked to actual exposures (measured *ex post*)? In two recent studies, Smirlock and Kaufold (1987) and Lamy, Marr and Thompson (1986) similar conclusions were reached: namely that the US equity market was strong-form efficient. Specifically, in Smirlock and Kaufold the returns for 23 'unexposed' banks were statistically unaffected by the announcement, whereas for 23 exposed banks (measured by their total loans to Mexico divided by shareholder equity) abnormal returns were not only negative but also directly proportional to the size of their actual exposures. This implies that even without mandatory bank disclosure laws on sovereign exposure, US bank investors were able to distinguish accurately among different banks at the time of the Mexican crisis.[37] Consequently, the recent evidence seems to find no strong contagion effects in bank equity markets.

(iv) Settlement risk

Although a CHIPS settlement failure of the intra-day kind has yet to occur, Humphrey (1986) has simulated the contagion effect of a single large settlement failure on a random day in January 1983. The settling participant selected had a net credit position of $321 million for the day. (This failure was viewed as being a least worst situation since realistically only net debitors are likely to default). After deleting the transactions of this bank with all other banks and re-estimating the transaction creditor-debitor matrix he found that 24 banks had settlement obligations increased by more than the amount of their capital and ended up in a net debitor position. Of these, 8 had been in a net creditor position prior to the removal of transactions with the non-settling participant. It was then assumed that all banks whose net debitor positions deteriorated by an amount equal to or exceeding their capital were also unable to settle. Thus another revised transactions matrix had to be constructed. This process was continued until no participant failed following a transactions matrix revision. It was found that six such iterations were required and that the number of 'failed' banks was 50. These 50 banks accounted for 39% of the total dollar value of messages sent for that day.

VI. Contagion and public policy issues

The body of empirical evidence discussed above appears to suggest that except for major crises contagion effects measured either through spreads, deposit/loan flows or equity values have been relatively small. Indeed, if anything, the degree of contagion appears to have fallen since the early 1970s (the oil shock – Franklin National – Herstatt period). One possibility is that this has resulted from the more interventionist stance taken by bank regulators since 1974, as they become more aware of the social costs/externalities that could result from a major crisis in confidence in the international banking system. The massive financial support guarantees provided by the Fed and the FDIC to Continental Illinois, and the more clearly defined global responsibilities of central banks when overseas branches and subsidiaries of domestic parent banks are in trouble (following the Cooke Committee recommendations) have probably served to signal to the market that large bank failures will not be allowed to occur, or if they are they will not be allowed to adversely impact large depositors.[38][39] This, in turn, has raised questions regarding the 'price' of such guarantees (see, for example, Dean and Giddy 1981). For example, if banks transacting in the inter-bank market view such guarantees as a 'free good' then all manner of moral hazard and adverse selection problems could arise. Indeed, such problems have long been recognized in the context of US deposit insurance, where the FDIC charges fixed (explicit) premiums that are independent of bank risk (see Merrick and Saunders 1985 for a review of this literature). This has created incentives for banks to overexpose themselves in risky loans and to economise on 'costly' monitoring and information collection. As a result, while the financial system may be more stable in the short run, longer-term instability problems may be built in.

In actual practice banks currently operating in the international inter-bank market appear to be charged a heterogeneous set of *implicit* and *explicit* fees in return for Central bank guarantees. Specifically, virtually all international banks have had to face increased mandatory disclosure requirements since 1982. As disclosure (information production) is costly for the bank but, presumably, beneficial to outsiders, such as regulators, investors and depositors,[40] it can be viewed as a form of regulatory tax. Similarly, many large banks have had their required capital-assets ratios increased. Bank capital can be thought of as a costly form of co-insurance (with regulators) which acts as a cushion to protect depositors.[41] For example, US regulators are currently advocating a proposal to increase US money centre banks' capital ratios and to relate these capital ratios to both on- and off-balance-sheet risks.[42] A third aspect of this pricing system has been the move by the Fed towards the imposition of net intra-day depositor caps, both bilateral and aggregate, on bank daylight overdrafts on both public and private wire transfer systems.

Unfortunately, it is far from clear how this patchwork of fees controls risk on an individual bank level, especially as blanket Central bank guarantees are likely to modify, if not eliminate, risk premia being impounded by depositors and investors in deposit/loan rates and equity prices. Such a haphazard system of pricing and risk control may well be storing up problems for the future, especially if the trend towards securitization continues and international banking markets increasingly comprise a pool of relatively low quality/high risk borrowers and lenders.

NOTES

* The author would like to thank Messrs L. Price and A. Brillembourg for their comments.

1 BIS, *International Banking Developments*, January 31, 1986.
2 The relative size of each of these markets tends to vary with bankers' perceptions about foreign exchange movements and the need to hedge such exposure.
3 The model in Figure 6.1 is simplified. In actual practice banks not only play a brokerage function in the securitization process but also issue and hold a significant amount of Euro-bonds in their portfolios. In such cases the neat distinction between securitization and intermediation breaks down.
4 Giddy (1981) notes that in actual practice banks can and do refuse to supply funds in the inter-bank market at quoted (screen) rates if credit risk is perceived to have increased.
5 To this list may be added fraud and foreign interest rate/foreign exchange rate exposure risks.
6 It might be noted that these figures do not reflect the heavy borrowing of Mexican agencies in London and New York at the time of the debt crisis (since these offices are in the BIS reporting area). However, funds on-lent by these offices to their parent head offices are reflected in these figures. Such transactions may account for a significant proportion of 'inter-bank' business.
7 Since one of the rationales for international banking is to avoid domestically imposed capital-adequacy ratios (see Aliber 1980) it might be hypothesized

that actual capital/external asset ratios more closely approximate the lower (1%) bound than the upper (5%) bound.

8 For example, in recent years approximately 20% of interbank deposits on the London Eurocurrency markets have had maturities of less than 8 days.

9 CHIPS handles approximately 90% of all international inter-bank dollar transfers.

10 Note that prior to October 1981, when CHIPS moved to same day settlement, there was also an *inter-day* settlement risk. This inter-day settlement risk was partly to blame for the disruption in the inter-bank market after the Herstatt Bank failure in 1974.

11 It should be noted that bank Z has a number of other options to cushion the impact of a funds shortfall due to non-delivery by bank X. It can run down reserves, seek to call back the loan made to bank Y or borrow from the Central Bank.

12 This can be illustrated by the sharp fall in official reserves placed on the Eurocurrency markets by central banks in the 1980–83 period. Such a flight should also be reflected in asset-price adjustments.

13 This can easily be relaxed to allow for risk-aversion.

14 This could be made non-zero without adding any complications.

15 This idea of systematic and unsystematic risks of loans in the international market is also similar to that also found in portfolio theory (see Goodman 1981 and Walter 1981 for analyses along these lines).

16 See Carron (1982) for a similar argument.

17 Adverse selection results from the fact that low-risk borrowers may drop out of the market, leaving behind a pool of more risky borrowers, as rates rise. The incentive effect results when borrowers have a choice of project. The higher the interest rate on a loan, the greater their incentive to invest in more risky projects in order to be able to pay off the loan. This incentive is enhanced by limited stockholder liability on the downside and, possibly, sovereign immunity in the case of international loans.

18 Similar statements can be made if bank *groups i* and *j* are substituted for individual banks i and j.

19 This period occurred during recurring debt difficulties for East European countries (Poland, Hungary and Romania) and a move by the US economy into a recessionary phase.

20 Measured by the average (or standard) deviation from the mode.

21 As defined by *Euromoney*.

22 LIBOR is reported for all publicly guaranteed loans. Presumably, publicly guaranteed loans eliminate credit-risk exposure leaving only sovereign risk exposure.

23 See note at bottom of Table 6.1.

24 Bordo calls general financial panics, encompassing liquidity, interest rates and stock prices, the Kindleberger (1978), Minsky (1977) hypothesis.

25 The failure to diversify funds due to regulation, however, was one of the major reasons for the problems at Continental Illinois in 1984 (see discussion later in text).

26 Such as small regional banks and their agents the 'deposits brokers'.

27 This switching effect is apparent in the effect on the spread between 3 month CD rates and 3 month T-bill rates in the secondary market. Between January and March 1984 (prior to the Continental announcements) the

average monthy spread was 0.376%. This rose to 0.72% in April and 1.28% in May. In the three months following (June–August 1984) the average monthly spread was 1.30%.

28 However, spreads were affected (as in the domestic market). The average spread between 3 month Euro-dollar deposits and T-bills was 0.86% for January–March 1984. In April this rose to 1.14% and to 1.70% in May. In the 3 months, June–August 1984, the average spread was 1.68%.

29 For example, adverse information about one borrower is taken as a negative signal regarding all other borrowers.

30 Such a supposition underlies most of the credit rationing literature.

31 Including exchange rate changes – since they are part of a bank's risk exposure in making international loans. Note that columns 2 and 4 don't add up to column 1 since, for reasons of space, 'other items' are not included in the Table. Thus, for example, in 1984 *net* loans (change in the stock of loans) to areas other than the Reporting Area and the Latin American and other LDCs and Eastern Europe were *negative*.

32 This assumption is common in many multi-factor asset pricing models such as arbitrage pricing theory.

33 Many bank transactions are 'off-balance-sheet' and are therefore not subject to regulatory 'taxes' such as capital-adequacy requirements.

34 That is, all may be placed in high default risk classes – see Section IV.

35 Aharony and Swary (1983) attribute the Franklin National Bank failure to foreign exchange losses alone. This ingores the financial irregularities and fraud perpetrated by its chairman (M. Sindona) and others at the time of its failure.

36 In other words since many banks also had large domestic and international loan risk exposures the (negative) signal impact may be thought to have been important.

37 It might be noted that the 1983 US International Lending Supervision Act required more detailed sovereign loan disclosure by US banks. Interestingly, Cornell, Landsman and Shapiro (1986) could find little equity market impact from the passage of the Act. One possible interpretation of this result is that investors viewed the information disclosure requirements as redundant (i.e. the market was already strong-form efficient).

38 For example, in testimony before the House Banking Committee in September 1984, the Comptroller of the Currency stated that regulators would actually prevent the failure of the 11 largest banking organizations in the US.

39 However, the failure of Banco Ambrosiano identified a loophole in this global responsibility concept since the Luxembourg subsidiary of Banco Ambrosiano was classified as a non-bank holding company rather than a bank. As a result the Bank of Italy refused to take direct responsibility – see Guttentag and Herring (1985).

40 Although strong-form efficient market findings reviewed in Section V cast some serious doubt on this.

41 Higher capital ratios also dampen the growth prospects of the bank.

42 Capital ratios have recently been increased in Japan and the UK. Moreover, the UK banking authorities have announced their intention to impose the same (risk-related) capital ratios as are being proposed by their US counterparts.

REFERENCES

Aharony, J., A. Saunders and I. Swary (1986). 'The Effects of a Shift in Monetary Policy Regime on the Profitability and Risk of Commercial Banks', *Journal of Monetary Economics*, pp. 363–77.

Aharony, J. and I. Swary (1983). 'Contagion Effects of Bank Failures: Evidence from Capital Markets', *Journal of Business*, pp. 213–30.

Aliber, R. Z. (1980). 'The Integration of the Offshore and Domestic Banking System', *Journal of Monetary Economics*, pp. 509–26.

Allen, L. and A. Saunders (1986). 'The Large-Small Bank Dichotomy in the Federal Funds Market', *Journal of Banking and Finance*, pp. 219–30.

Angeloni, I. and B. K. Short (1980). 'The Impact of Country Risk Assessment on Euro-Currency Interest Rate Spreads: A Cross Section Analysis', *International Monetary Fund* DM/80/35.

Bordo, M. O (1985). 'Some Historical Evidence 1870–1933 on the Impact and International Transmission of Financial Crises', NBER W.P. No. 1606.

Boyd, J. and E. Prescott (1986). 'Financial Intermediary Coalitions', *Journal of Economic Theory*, pp. 211–32.

Carron, A. S. (1982). 'Financial Crises: Recent Experience in US and International Markets', *Brookings Papers on Economic Activity*, pp. 395–418.

Chari, V. V. and R. Jaganathan (1985). 'Banking Panics, Information and Rational Expectations Equilibrium', Northwestern University, BRC W.P. No. 112.

Cornell, B., W. Landsman and A. C. Shapiro (1987). 'The Impact on Bank Stock Prices of Regulatory Responses to the International Debt Crisis', *Journal of Banking and Finance, Studies in Banking and Finance, Supplement* 3, pp. 161–78.

Dean, J. W. and I. H. Giddy (1981). *Averting International Banking Crises*, Monograph Series in Finance and Economics, Salomon Bros. Center, N.Y.U.

Diamond, D. (1984). 'Delegated Monitoring and Financial Intermediation', *Review of Economic Studies*, pp. 393–415.

Diamond, D. and P. Dybvig (1983). 'Deposit Insurance, Liquidity and Bank Runs', *Journal of Political Economy*, pp. 401–19.

Dooley, M. P. and P. Isard (1980). 'Capital Controls, Political Risk, and Deviations from Interest Rate Parity', *Journal of Political Economy*, pp. 370–84.

Doukas, J. (1985). 'Syndicated Euro-Credit Sovereign Risk Assessments and Market Efficiency', Dept of Finance, Concordia University W.P. 1985.

Dufey, G. and I. H. Giddy (1984). 'Eurocurrency Deposit Risk', *Journal of Banking and Finance*, pp. 567–89.

Eaton, J. and M. Gersovitz (1981). 'Debt with Potential Repudiation: Theoretical and Empirical Analysis', *Review of Economic Studies*, pp. 289–309.

Edwards, S. (1985). 'The Pricing of Bonds and Bank Loans in International Markets: An Empirical Analysis of Developing Countries' Foreign Borrowing', NBER W.P. No. 1689.

Fama, E. (1976). *Foundations of Finance*, Basic Books: New York.

Feder, G. and R. E. Just (1977). 'An Analysis of Credit Terms in the Euro-dollar Market', *European Economic Review*, pp. 221–43.

Folkerts-Landau, D. (1985). 'The Changing Role of International Banking Lending in Development Finance', *IMF Staff Papers*, pp. 317–65.

Friedman, M. and A. Schwartz (1963). *A Monetary History of the United States 1867–1960*, Princeton, N.J.: Princeton University Press.

Furlong, F. T. (1984). 'A View on Deposit Insurance Coverage', Federal Reserve Bank of San Francisco *Economic Review*, pp. 31–7.

Giddy, I. H. (1981). 'Risk and Return in the Eurocurrency Interbank Market', *Greek Economic Review*, pp. 158–86.

Goodman, L. S. (1981). 'Bank lending to Non-Opec LDC's: Are Risks Diversifiable'?, Federal Reserve Bank of New York, *Quarterly Review*, pp. 10–20.

Grammatikos, T., A. Saunders and I. Swary (1986). 'Returns and Risks of U.S. Banks Foreign Currency Activities', *Journal of Finance*, pp. 671–82.

Guttentag, J. and R. Herring (1984) 'Credit Rationing and Financial Disorder', *Journal of Finance*, pp. 1359–82

(1985). 'Funding Risk in the International Interbank Market', Wharton School, University of Pennsylvania W.P.

Herring, R. (1985). 'The Interbank Market' in *Eurodollars and International Banking*, edited by P. Savona and G. Sutija, MacMillan: Basingstoke, U.K.

Ho, T. S. Y. and A. Saunders (1980). 'A Catastrophe Model of Bank Failure', *Journal of Finance*, pp. 1189–207.

(1981). 'The Determinants of Bank Interest Margins: Theory and Empirical Evidence', *Journal of Financial and Quantitative Analysis*, pp. 581–600.

(1985). 'A Micro-Model of the Federal Funds Market', *Journal of Finance*, pp. 977–88.

Humphrey, D. B. (1986). 'Payments Finality and Risk of Settlement Failure' in A. Saunders and L. J. White (eds.), *Technology and the Regulation of Financial Markets*, D. C. Heath: Lexington Mass., pp. 97–120.

Kindleberger, C. P. (1978). *Manias, Panics and Crashes: A History of Financial Crises*, Basic Books: New York.

Lamy, R. E., M. Wayne Marr and G. R. Thompson (1987). 'The Mexican Debt Crisis, the IMF and the Efficiency of Bank Share Prices', *Journal of Banking and Finance (Supplement)*, Studies in Banking and Finance, Supplement 3, pp. 203–18.

McDonald, D. (1982). 'Debt Capacity and Developing Country Borrowing: A Survey of the Literature', *IMF Staff Papers*, pp. 603–46.

Melvin, M. And D. Schlagenhauf (1986). 'Risk in International Lending: A Dynamic Factor Analysis Applied to France and Mexico', *Journal of International Money and Finance* (Supplement), pp. 31–48.

Merrick, J. J., Jr and A. Saunders (1985). 'Bank Regulation and Monetary Policy', *Journal of Money, Credit and Banking* (Part 2), pp. 691–717.

Miller, M. H. and A. V. Thakor (1985). 'Moral Hazard and Information Sharing: A Model of Financial Information Gathering Agencies', *Journal of Finance*, pp. 1403–22.

Minsky, H. P. (1977). 'A Theory of Systemic Fragility', in E. J. Altman and A. W. Sametz (eds.), *Financial Crises: Institutions and Markets in a Fragile Environment*, J. Wiley: New York, pp. 138–52.

Niehans, J. (1971). 'Money and Banking in General Equilibrium with Transaction Costs', *American Economic Review*, pp. 773–83.

Niehans, J. and J. Hewson (1976). 'The Eurodollar Market and Monetary Theory', *Journal of Money Credit and Banking*, pp. 1–27.

Ramakrishnan, R. and A. V. Thakor (1984). 'Information Reliability and a

Theory of Financial Intermediation', *Review of Economic Studies*, pp. 415–32.

Sachs, J. and D. Cohen (1982). 'LDC Borrowing with Default Risk', NBER Working Paper No. 925.

Sargen, N. P. (1976). 'Commercial Bank Lending to Developing Countries', Federal Reserve Bank of San Francisco *Economic Review*, pp. 20–31.

Saunders, A. (1986). 'The Determinants of Country Risk: A Selective Survey of the Literature', *Journal of Banking and Finance, Studies in Banking and Finance, Supplement* 3, pp. 1–38.

—— (1986). 'An Examination of the Contagion Effects in the International Loan Market', *Journal of Banking and Finance, Studies in Banking and Finance, Supplement* 3, pp. 219–48.

Smirlock, M. and H. Kaufold (1987). 'Bank Foreign Lending, Mandatory Disclosure Rules and the Mexican Debt Crisis', *Journal of Business* (forthcoming).

Stiglitz, J. E. and A. Weiss (1981). 'Credit Rationing in Markets with Imperfect Information', *American Economic Review*, pp. 313–409.

Swary, I. (1986). 'The Stock Market Reaction to Regulatory Action in the Continental Illinois Crisis', *Journal of Business*.

Taffler, R. J. and Abassi, B. (1984). 'Country Risk: A Model for Predicting Debt Servicing Problems in Developing Countries', *Journal of the Royal Statistical Society (Series A)*, pp. 541–68.

Waldo, D. G. (1984). 'Liquidity Services, Bank Runs, and an Insured Banking System', University of Florida *WP*.

Walter, I. (1981). 'Country Risk, Portfolio Decisions and Regulations in International Bank Lending', *Journal of Banking and Finance*, pp. 77–92.

Discussion

ARTURO BRILLEMBOURG

From Professor Saunders's stimulating and thorough paper, I have drawn three observations.

1. The banking system is facing growing competition from the ever expanding and less regulated securities market. This competition has left the banks with the riskier businesses of lending to less credit-worthy borrowers and clearing the settlement system, the failure of which the paper identifies as the event most likely to create a contagious financial crisis.

2. Empirical evidence shows that a contagious financial crisis is unlikely. Both markets and banks have effectively identified and

discriminated among the credit categories in a pool of borrowers. There is little evidence of contagion effects either on country credit allocation or on bank stock and bond prices.

3. Regulators have become aware that they belong to a service industry. Therefore they must be responsible for the quality of these services as well as for the costs they impose on the industry.

Before examining what response one could have to these observations, let me add a few of my own.

1. The financial system should above all strive to provide a clear transmission of information. After all, contagion effects may be only misplaced responses to a noisy, low-quality financial signal. What makes the system less noisy? Higher bandwidth and more discriminating components. In other words, greater competition among financial institutions and a greater variety of risk diversification instruments.

2. The financial system is and has always been a continuous spectrum of activities that range from a father's advancing a son's allowance to the issuing of junk bonds by Mike Milken. (By the way, I am told that some regulators may regard both activities as equally reprehensible.) Regulators cannot hope to cover the full spectrum but rather have to choose which sector they cover.

3. In my opinion, financial and technological innovations, though not without their problems, are helping the financial system to evolve into a more efficient and less noisy distributor of risk. Globalization is creating competition among previously isolated domestic institutions and is providing greater international sharing of risk. Securitization is creating new competition to both the banks and their regulators, thereby providing both borrowers and lenders greater choice. The increasingly comprehensive rating agency services are providing a private alternative to government regulatory services. For example, many US rating agencies are opening branches in London so that they can provide adequate coverage of the Euro market – something that the regulators have yet to do. Indeed, one can call the latter trend the 'privatization' of the regulatory system.

Now to get back to the main subject of Professor Saunders's paper – the containment of financial crisis in light of these world trends. It seems to me that governments can respond to these trends in one of two ways. They can either increase the scope of their regulatory services or increase their intensity. In other words, they can choose to do many things adequately or they can choose to do a few things well. As is their tradition, the French government has chosen to do the first. They have passed a new Banking Law which attempts to regulate most facets of financial intermediation.

My purpose here is to exhort governments to take the second route. In my opinion, the area in which the government has the greatest comparative advantage is the same area that has been identified as having the greatest systemic risk – the settlement system. The recent Bank of New York computer failure showed how fragile the system could be and how disastrous would have been the consequences were it not for the Fed's timely intervention.

Many of the papers presented, including Professor Saunders's, have commented how perilous it is for the central bank to take on the role of guaranteeing the payment system. In my opinion, these difficulties are inherent in the present system and no amount of additional regulation would eliminate them. Rather, I believe that more efforts should be made to explore alternative systems which eliminate these difficulties. In particular, greater efforts should be made in designing a financial system which would separate the payments system from the other banking functions. It seems to me that by closely regulating such a separate payment system and requiring adequate capital, one could assure that there is no solvency risk to the system and that only liquidity risk remains. As has been mentioned by other participants, central banks would not have any difficulties in guaranteeing the soundness of such a system.

In closing let me conclude that new financial trends have led to a diversification of risk and a privatization of many of the regulatory services. Let me exhort the government to concentrate their efforts on what they do best – maintain the solvency of the payments system and, while not neglecting the rest, let the market take the greater burden over regulating the rest of the financial system.

Discussion

LIONEL D. D. PRICE

Anthony Saunders's paper surveys a wide range of evidence of possible contagion effects in the international inter-bank market – a market which he asserts on the first page of his paper is a 'very fragile structure'. He is by no means the first person to point to the potential problems to which the market's structure could give rise, but the evidence produced in the paper is if anything comforting, as is the rather robust reaction of the inter-bank market to various shocks over the years.

Saunders offers us quite an extensive bibliography on the subject. As a central banker, I can only regret that he does not include the study of the inter-bank market made by an international central bank study group in 1982–3, and published by the BIS.[1] That study made use of structured discussions held with market participants in a variety of centres, about the functioning of the market, the purposes for which banks use it, and the contribution of the market to banks' management of their liquidity and maturity transformation. The evidence from these discussions and from statistical data did not provide support for many of the concerns often voiced about the market. The study group would, I think, have shared Saunders's view that the market provides 'an efficient mechanism for reallocating funds'. On questions relating to the market's liquidity in a crisis, they were more equivocal – not surprisingly because, as Saunders finds, there is a lack of evidence on these questions.

Perhaps the most serious worry of the study group related to banks' assessment of the credit risk attaching to lending to another bank. At that time, banks typically placed funds with a large number of other banks, including many for which they had only limited information. The degree of care shown by banks in assessing the credit-standing of their commercial customers was not usually applied to other banks. Lending on the basis of inadequate information must have been risky not only for the individual bank but also systemically, as it would increase the probability of contagion following the failure of a single bank. Partly in response to pressures from supervisors since the study group's report, and partly in response to events in the market, banks are now paying much more attention to the assessment of the creditworthiness of their counterparts, and such risks should now be reduced.

Turning to look at Saunders's paper in more detail, I must say that I found the model of intermediation vs. securitization deficient. Securitization is seen in the model only as the bringing together of non-bank investors and users of funds; yet of $125 billion of net international bond issues in 1985, the BIS estimate that as much as $55 billion comprised either issues of bonds by banks themselves or banks' purchases of bonds issued by non-banks. These figures show that securitization by no means always leaves no role for banks as intermediaries. That said, I do agree that information costs are a key factor in determining whether or not banks will intermediate flows, and I believe that technological changes are reducing banks' comparative advantage in this area.

In Section III of his paper, Saunders presents various figures and charts showing BIS-area banks' exposure to banks in Poland, Argentina, Mexico and Brazil. Certainly one of the most serious threats yet faced by the interbank market came in 1982 when Mexican banks seemed unlikely to be able to fund maturing inter-bank liabilities in the market. A crisis was averted by central banks intervening to persuade creditor banks to roll over their claims, and this experience was one of the events which increased the awareness of lending banks of the need for proper credit assessment in the inter-bank market. But the figures presented by Saunders do not directly capture that risk. The banks which would have been unable to meet their obligations were largely the Mexican banks' agencies in New York and London, which had borrowed heavily in the inter-bank market to fund lending back to Mexico. As the London and New York offices of the Mexican banks are *within* the BIS reporting-area, the figures used by Saunders do not show the size of their liabilities in the inter-bank market; instead, they indicate the extent to which these offices of Mexican and other nationalities of banks have been lending to their own head offices. More generally, it needs to be remembered when using BIS statistics on the inter-bank market that these figures include cross-border transactions between offices of the same bank. Such transactions account for some 40% of the total reported inter-bank claims, so that the scale of 'genuine' inter-bank business is significantly less than at first appears.

The problems of Mexico and several other countries do raise the question of the extent to which the apparent contagion of the decline in their ability to raise finance in international markets was unjustified, or whether it reflected the fact that they shared common problems. Saunders spends some time looking at evidence on this question, though I doubt that any conclusions reached on the presence or absence of unjustified contagion among borrowing countries tell one much about the likelihood of contagion among banks borrowing in the inter-bank market. But I should comment on his results showing a significant decline in the correlations between lending to different areas after 1982. It is evident that banks and other lenders have discriminated between these broad, continental groups of countries in reacting to debt problems. More investigation is needed, however, to determine whether they have discriminated realistically between countries within the same region. In any case, looking only at *ex post* flows begs the question of why they changed: was it because the banks decided to lend less or because the borrowers decided to borrow less? The falling correlation may reflect a growing disparity in the economic conditions in different parts of the world, rather than banks' changing preferences.

Saunders looks at contagion between borrowing countries because, as he explains, the lack of data on the distribution of spreads across *banks* makes it harder to investigate contagion in the inter-bank market itself. However he is able to draw some lessons from the experience of the failure of Continental Illinois in 1984. *Inter alia*, he notes that other US banks do not appear to have lost deposits by being associated, justifiably or otherwise, with Continental's difficulties. That does seem to have been the case. Nevertheless, there is some evidence of an *ex ante* run from bank deposits into Treasury paper. The gap between the rate paid by major US banks on three-month CDs and the US Treasury bill rate rose significantly as Continental's difficulties became known: from an average of under 50 basis points in the fifteen months to March 1984, the gap rose to 70 bp in april, 130 in May and 150 in June, before gradually falling back to more normal levels by the end of the year. This yield gap opened because – contrary to the suggestion of Saunders's paper – it was not possible *ex post* for depositors in aggregate to switch into Treasury securities. In the absence of additional sales of securities by the Treasury to meet the increased demand, asset prices had to adjust to equilibrate demand and supply. In addition, the maturities at which banks could raise funds shortened. In this instance, market mechanisms acted to stem any potential run from the banking system as a whole.

A sudden drain of funds from an individual bank is of course still possible and was experienced by Continental Illinois. The conventional wisdom seems to be that Continental's problems were aggravated by the bank's reliance on inter-bank deposits, but the evidence on this is far from clear. Certainly there have been a number of instances of runs by retail depositors, notably from savings and loans institutions, in recent years. I have no information on the behaviour of Continental's retail depositors in 1984: possibly deposit insurance helped to keep them in; if so, it should be remembered that the comprehensiveness of deposit insurance in the United States is not matched in most other countries. More is known about the behaviour of corporate depositors, the withdrawal of funds by some of whom was important in bringing Continental's problems to a head. Some bank depositors in contrast remained loyal throughout. In sum, inter-bank deposits were not obviously less stable than corporate deposits.

Overall, I agree with Saunders's conclusion that contagion effects in the inter-bank market are usually relatively small and if anything declining. He ascribes this in part to action by bank supervisors and central banks, with emphasis on what he sees as the guarantees of financial support for a large bank in trouble. (In this context he wrongly suggests that the Cooke Committee's agreement on *supervisory* responsibilities for overseas branches and subsidiaries embodies an allocation of support operations.) I would put more emphasis on the steps taken by supervisors to ensure that banks are adequately capitalized and also aware of the risks of the different aspects of their business, including inter-bank lending. Saunders sees these more as implicit fees to mitigate the moral hazard and adverse selection problems generated by deposit insurance or expectations of support. That is certainly part of the story, but we should not forget that in the event of a bank failure, even if depositors are safeguarded, shareholders and management are not. That does offer some significant protection against excessive risk-taking on the back of expectations of official support.

NOTE

1 'The International Interbank Market, a Descriptive Study', *BIS Economic Papers* No. 8, Basle 1983.

7 Public policy and international financial stability: a report of the conference discussion and panel

JOAN PEARCE

I General discussion

The basic quandary that faces public policy-makers in dealing with financial markets has changed very little since the development of deposit banking systems, as was clear from the paper by Eichengreen and Portes and the discussion that followed it. Some aspects of banks' activities affect the public interest in a way that differs from any other industry. In particular, banks are the focus of the transmission mechanism of monetary policy, are at the centre of the payments system, and are entrusted with other people's money. Policy-makers aim to strike a balance between intervening to prevent or mitigate damage that might be caused to the economy as a whole by problems in the banking sector and leaving banks to pursue their business in a competitive market free from distortions.

The context in which banks and regulators operate, however, has changed dramatically. Economies have become more interdependent, and national markets have become global. These related trends have been accelerated by rapid technological development. The macro-economic policies of the 1970s created a high-risk environment, which altered the attitudes of existing market participants and encouraged new ones to enter. Consumers have sought and financial institutions have supplied an array of innovative products. Regulators have responded by dismantling barriers between different segments of the financial markets and revising the rules by which they supervise banks. They have as yet done little to deal with the greatly increasing presence of non-bank institutions in financial markets.

The response of regulators to financial innovation was a recurring theme of the conference. Deposit insurance has been introduced in a number of countries in recent years and was extensively discussed, together with implicit guarantees by lenders of last resort. More generally, participants considered the growing complexity of the role of lenders of last resort and whether this could be alleviated. Disclosure of information is a long-standing issue that has been accentuated by technological advances. Attention was focused too on structural changes, particularly securitization, though some thought this would prove to be a temporary phenomenon. The last session concentrated in particular on issues that are likely to assume increasing importance in the years to come.

1   Regulation

Throughout the conference there were reminders of differences in regulation from one country to another. It is broadly recognized that, short of a crisis, the market can exert control and discipline banks' behaviour to only a limited extent, and there are wide variations in non-market intervention. Much bank regulation has originated from bankers themselves, who have seen a need for rules and standards of conduct to protect the system and people within it from the repercussions of any individual's careless actions. In some countries this responsibility has been assigned to government regulators and in others to private regulators. Government regulators are concerned with the interaction between the banking industry and the rest of the economy. They provide a measure of consumer protection and seek to ensure that activities in the banking sector do not threaten the stability of the economy as a whole. Often government regulators are also a source of revenue for the central government, though they may confer subsidies, for example, through free provision of implicit guarantees or underpriced deposit insurance.

Access to the facilities of government regulators is relatively easy. In contrast, private regulators aim to produce confidence and coordination services very efficiently, but they are apt to deteriorate into cartels which block evolution in the industry. A number of participants who viewed the regulator's role as that of an umpire challenged Ed Kane's depiction of regulators as an industry.

Regulatory differences complicate cross-country comparisons. One speaker pointed out, for example, that to compare capital adequacy requirements across countries, it is necessary to look at how off-balance-sheet items are treated in assessing liquidity ratios and gearing ratios. Another warned that though discussion often focused on the United States, that country is something of an anomaly. Partly this reflects the size and scope of the US industry, which comprises 15,000 banks and 40,000 depository institutions. Also, US public policy in ensuring financial stability has been developed through Congress and represents various interests. Regulation and supervision in the United States are more comprehensive than in many other countries.

Many speakers referred to the enormous changes that have taken place in the financial services sector and their implications for regulators. The increased volatility in interest rates and exchange rates that resulted from the macroeconomic events of the 1970s has prompted the market to develop large numbers of new instruments, such as futures, options and swaps, which would never have emerged in a low-risk environment. Thanks to these, and to the technological advances that facilitated them, almost any kind of liability can now be easily and cheaply transformed into almost any other kind, in terms of its maturity, currency, and whether it is fixed or floating. In this situation even the distinction between loans, bonds and equities begins to break down. Now that these enormous changes have occurred, there can be no going back to an earlier state. The changed environment means that the business of banks is greatly altered, and there is strong pressure on regulators to adapt.

But the financial revolution is not only a matter of new instruments: there are also many new players on the scene. The economic costs of entry into banking have declined steeply in recent years. With the emergence of well-developed international wholesale markets, it has become possible to enter large areas of banking, particularly corporate banking, without having to set up an extensive retail network. The continuing electronics revolution will probably lower the cost of entry further. At the same time the proportion of transactions that is handled by non-bank intermediaries has risen steadily. In many aspects of international capital markets the banking function is not central. Events in the bond market, the futures market and the foreign-exchange market, and the interplay among them sometimes affect national and international stability more than the relatively well-behaved and certainly better known and regulated banking systems.

In several cases changed circumstances have rendered existing rules irrelevant or unrealistic, making them difficult to enforce. Perhaps worse, in the new environment some old rules cause US banks at least to operate in a manner that is unsafe and unsound. All three banking agencies in the United States are advising Congress to liberalize rules that exclude banks from certain operations. Their argument is that the banks have lost other operations to more efficient competition, and restoring their financial health requires that they be allowed to enter areas from which they are at present barred.

Besides adapting rules in response to developments in the banking industry, bank supervisors are becoming more active in seeking to anticipate problems and suggesting precautionary steps to banks. A number of participants saw disturbances originating from high-risk activities in the unregulated sector as posing the greatest threat to the financial system. Many of these institutions have large credit lines with banks. Yet bank regulators appear to be totally unprepared, for example, for a situation where a major securities house suddenly shows substantial losses.

2   Deposit insurance, implicit guarantees and moral hazard

Protection in the form of deposit insurance was discussed in the session dealing with the Baltensperger and Dermine paper, and implicit guarantees by the lender of last resort in connection with the paper by Guttentag and Herring. In both contexts the problem of moral hazard was explored. In most countries deposit insurance is viewed as a measure of consumer protection, but the purpose is not consumer protection as such. There is no reason for governments to insure individuals against the private costs they would incur were a bank in which they had deposited money to fail. Depositors are protected to prevent them initiating a run on a bank, which might then spread through the banking system, that is, to avoid the social costs of a banking crisis.

Several participants remarked that in the United Kingdom and other European countries, depositors were largely oblivious of the existence of deposit insurance. Some thought that if depositors did not know about it, deposit insurance would not contribute to reassurance, and hence to stability. Public confidence in the financial system may derive less from deposit insurance than from confidence in the central bank as adviser to the banking sector and as lender of last resort. But do depositors need to be aware of the existence of deposit insurance, or is it sufficient if they know that in their country bank depositors do not lose their deposits? An additional advantage of deposit insurance schemes to the authorities is that they can reduce the cover that the central bank would in any case have to provide for banks. With an explicit scheme the central bank can charge for its services, and to some extent control the risks that banks take on, and it may even succeed in reducing its financial exposure.

One speaker questioned the view that deposit insurance raises problems of moral hazard, that is, creates an incentive for insured banks to take less care. In the event of a bank failure, deposit insurance protects depositors but not the bank's shareholders, directors and management. They will want to avoid failure in their own interest. Others described the rationale of moral hazard in the context of deposit insurance as being that a bank can get cheaper funding with deposit insurance than without, so the costs of taking on risky business are less. In this way deposit insurance indirectly promotes risk-taking. Without deposit insurance depositors would screen banks much more carefully and would require a larger return for a given degree of risk.

There is evidence to support the existence of moral hazard in deposit insurance. Experience of deposit insurance in West Germany has been too brief to draw conclusive lessons, but the private banking sector's approach to organizing its own scheme indicates that it foresees the possibility of moral hazard. For example, members are not allowed to mention their membership in advertisements, and they have established their own auditing system, whose instructions banks must obey or be excluded from the scheme. From the United States, where deposit insurance dates back much further, there is theoretical and empirical evidence that banks have substituted deposit insurance for capital. Bank capital is a very opaque statistic, and what it signals to depositors is unclear. Continental Illinois, for instance, failed despite having a published capital ratio larger than the average for the banking industry. Some participants thought that the problem of moral hazard could be solved by varying the fee charged for deposit insurance to reflect the riskiness of the insured bank, or by improving the publicly available information about banks.

The dilemma for the authorities is that they want to prevent depositors causing a banking crisis, but if a bank takes undue risks, they would like the shareholders to pay the bill. A comparable dilemma arises for central banks, in their role as lenders of last resort, from the cover that they provide for banks that experience liquidity problems. The market solution would entail no guarantees, and re-establishing market conditions (risk) in the banking industry might be a preferable course if the starting point was a sound situation. But total liberalization and deregulation at a time when there are many bad loans on banks' books and a number of banks are in trouble is very difficult, because it endangers the whole system. Probably there is no government at present that can credibly guarantee that it will not intervene.

Nonetheless, guarantees by the lender of last resort may have to be implicit rather than explicit. Several practitioners thought even the limited proposal for an explicit guarantee in the Guttentag and Herring paper to be unworkable. One reason is that each case is likely to be special and complex, and it would not be possible to insist on the kind of collateral that the central bank would want to stipulate in exchange for an explicit guarantee. There would also be problems associated with adding to or removing from the list. A procedure would be needed for determining which banks were eligible. If a new bank were set up, the authorities would want to wait before deciding whether to signal support for it by adding it to the list, but without that support the bank might not be able to function. In this way the list would be a barrier to entry. If, on the other hand, a bank already on the list got into trouble and the authorities removed it, this would be a signal to depositors to withdraw funds. The authorities would have contributed to a loss of confidence, with the opposite effect of what was desired. One regulator saw the only solution as to engage in neither implicit nor explicit guarantees, but to create a procedure for dealing with problem cases, whether relating to liquidity or to solvency. Since these situations are exceptional, there is no need for a precise rule. The sharing of responsibility and cost can be decided case by case. Another participant, however, considered ambiguity to be unhelpful. If it is believed that there are no guarantees, ambiguity will not help to prevent a bank run; if guarantees are believed to exist, there are problems of moral hazard.

3   Lenders of last resort

The role of the lender of last resort is being made more difficult as the large international banks and the instruments they deal in become more complex. Yet the lender of last resort is concerned with only one aspect of banks' activities, namely, the payments system. This prompted some participants to ask whether it would be possible to isolate within banks that part of their activities that would put society at risk if it were to fail. Such a move would simplify the task of the lender of last resort and permit further deregulation of banks' other activities.

Richard Herring was not persuaded, however, that this would solve the main problem. Much of what banks do is to provide credit to people who do not have access to the securities markets, and a large part of that credit is vital to the functioning of the payments system. If banks set up separate payments transfer subsidiaries that were strongly regulated, the inevitable result would be the emergence of near-banks, some of which would need deposit insurance and lender of last resort facilities, or something similar.

It was suggested that the Swiss system managed to minimize the role of lender of last resort. From the outset the central bank took the view that banks should be able to handle liquidity problems themselves, and they do so by having adequate cash reserves. This may make for inefficiency in that costs are imposed on banks because they hold cash reserves that they would not otherwise hold, but it does avoid continuous interference when there is a problem in the payments system. Furthermore, the payments system has been designed to ensure that such problems are unlikely to arise. Instead of a clearing system for settling inter-bank balances, Swiss banks use a system where each transaction is associated with a transfer of central bank money. An electronic system of inter-bank clearing is now being set up to effect these transactions. Problems do still arise in the payments system that can be solved only by giving assistance to an individual bank, but these are rare.

One speaker noted that much emphasis is placed on the distinction between liquidity and solvency as a basis for the operating procedure of a lender of last resort. In practice, however, it seems to be difficult to draw a line between the two concepts. In that case, the distinction is not useful to a lender of last resort in formulating policy, and it should either be refined or be discarded.

4 Disclosure

The question whether it would be desirable to disclose more infor-mation about banks cropped up repeatedly, particularly in relation to the lender of last resort and to contagion. Opponents of more disclosure argue that since it is impossible to have perfect information, increased information heightens the risk that the market will draw the wrong con-clusions and behave in a way that harms all concerned. Proponents believe that this argument serves the interests of regulators, enhancing their importance as sole custodians of much of the most useful infor-mation and protecting them from questions that might be asked about their activities if others had access to this information. Were it more widely available, the market would be quite capable of assessing it appropriately.

Discussion is complicated by the widely differing approaches of various countries. In the United States, for example, a great deal of information is disclosed about large banks, but for small community banks this is not required. One prohibition, however, is disclosure of the examiner's rating of a bank. This was cited as an instance of regulators restricting disclosure so as to avoid criticism of their performance. In other countries, such as France, West Germany and Switzerland, much less information is disclosed. This led one participant to ask whether there was evidence to show that the markets were better able to assess US banks than banks in these countries.

In the context of contagion, one speaker thought it important to dis-tinguish clearly between a situation where contagion occurs because, though only one bank is in trouble, there is incomplete information about the real economic prospects of other banks, and a situation where problems in one bank are providing information that there are similar problems in other banks. The first case is best addressed by improving the diffusion of information; the second necessitates tackling more fundamental problems in the real or financial economy.

Several people observed that contagion has been exacerbated by groups of depositors, notably institutional investors, who are quick to withdraw their funds at the least sign of trouble. One reason is that these institutions have to report all their holdings frequently. They are reluctant to be seen to have holdings in banks that are the subject of adverse press comment, even though they know them to be sound. In this way they contribute to the information problem.

Some participants viewed as misguided the idea that more disclosure would help to avoid contagion. One reason is that the quality of loans is very important but cannot be readily measured or communicated to the market. Furthermore, the information that is disclosed can often be deliberately falsified, especially in the case of troubled banks. Herstatt, Johnson Matthey and Franklin National all misreported their capacity to meet large foreign-exchange commitments. In addition, banks can change their risk position, particularly through new financial instruments, with dramatic speed. And information relating to new financial instruments cannot be adequately assessed as long as a proper accounting treatment of them has yet to be established and the legal framework remains untested.

A regulator saw information as a double-edged sword during periods of acute anxiety. Thanks to modern telecommunications, dealers all over the world see the same thing at the same time on their screens. Appropriate statements from authoritative sources can lower the level of anxiety immediately. But there is a proliferation of private supervisors and rating agencies, and they too can instantaneously transmit their views. Another regulator agreed that the constant stream of rumours, reports and comments made for a highly volatile situation.

Other people, however, felt that a high degree of disclosure was desirable. Market participants have proved to be quite skilled at recognizing the shortcomings of the data. Some bank analysts who pursued data on the exposure of banks in the Mexican debt crisis achieved quite accurate results, which were reflected in the market prices that emerged in a variety of areas. Clearly, they are willing to go to the cost of digging out this information, obtaining it through non-official sources. Rather than forcing them to do this, regulators should supply the information with a warning that it is known to have certain shortcomings and may have others unknown, and allow people to use it for their own purposes. Unless this approach can be shown to be positively harmful to the system, there is no argument against it.

A special plea was made for revision of accounting requirements in the United States. The present arrangements permit very important facts to be concealed. Banks can, for example, choose to report unrealized gains while keeping unrealized losses hidden. This is the main reason why it is not possible to distinguish a bank that is insolvent from one that has liquidity problems.

5 Securitization

Opinions about the significance of securitization were divided. Several participants pointed out that in the 1960s and early 1970s there were well-developed bond markets in the United States, Canada and the United Kingdom. Most very large first-class borrowers did not operate through banks but used the commercial paper markets and the bond markets for their borrowing purposes. Only in the 1970s, when very high and variable interest rates led long-term bond markets to dry up, did banks begin to make loans to these borrowers. This was partly because the banks were quicker to initiate term floating-rate lending than were the markets. From this sequence of events some concluded that what is happening now is a reversion to the traditional system, so perhaps the 1970s, and not the 1980s, should be seen as an anomaly. Others saw the resurgence of securities as part of a cyclical pattern. Hence it could be short-lived, particularly if interest rates began to rise significantly.

Some participants, however, believed that the rapid growth in securities activities and banks' exposure to them was a new phenomenon that merited further consideration. There is growing awareness that one problem of that exposure is the decline in the quality of business of banks in their traditional lending activities, but the most rapid growth in their business has been in their own securities activities. For some US and Japanese banks there is an added dimension. To avoid the regulatory framework, much of their expansion in these activities is taking place offshore. But it is precisely in these areas that the regulatory framework is most fragmented, because of the Glass-Steagall Act and similar legislation in Japan. It would be unwise to underestimate the risks to a bank, and hence to the interbank market, if it faced a very substantial capital loss either through subsidiaries in its onshore or local market, or on the part of a securities house to which it was exposed through its lending.

A regulator thought that the failure of a security company that was an independent company would not have unduly serious implications. If banks had well-diversified portfolios, some of them might suffer some losses but if their exposures were not large in relation to their capital the banking system would act as a cushion. The same should happen in the inter-bank market if one bank fails: there should not be knock-on effects unless banks are over-exposed to another individual bank. A greater problem would arise when a securities operation was a subsidiary of a major banking group, which, Glass-Steagall notwithstanding, could apply to US banks as well as to European banks. There could be very difficult problems, from which the banks, and the central banks potentially standing behind them, would not be immune. Regulators have begun to think about these problems, but there will be no easy answers.

II   Containing financial crises: Panel discussion

Sam Cross recalled the enormous transformations occurring in the basic structure of the financial system. Financial markets are becoming increasingly integrated and globalized; financial instruments are becoming highly innovative and securitized; and financial institutions are becoming functionally indistinct and homogenized. All these developments yield large and valuable benefits to users of financial services in terms of efficiency and cost-saving. There is now a wide choice of products tailored to meet the particular needs and preferences of investors and borrowers, and enormous opportunities to hedge and to arbitrage in a variety of markets. But this new and untested environment also poses problems, because it introduces into the financial system new areas of vulnerability and new potential for accidents. Change in itself is not a problem, and is indeed necessary to maintain a flexible and vigorous system. The difficulties are with the pace of change and with the ability of those involved to keep abreast of and to cope with the very rapid structural modifications that are taking place in the financial system.

There are three broad areas of concern. First come fears that the new financial system will be more accident-prone. Technology has greatly reduced the cost of financial transactions, while deregulation and innovation have enormously expanded the variety and sophistication of new financial products. As a result there has been a massive growth in the volume, value, spread and complexity of financial transactions, which are now at levels that only a few years ago would have been impossible. This expansion has increased the scope for disruptions or mechanical failures commensurately. Moreover, because markets are now more integrated and globalized, shocks are transmitted much more readily from institution to institution, market to market, and country to country.

Second, the disintermediation of lending by large banks indicates that what is thought of as the traditional role of the banking system is in secular decline. The view that securitization marks a return to the norms of an earlier period is in some respects valid. Nonetheless, developments in some markets may reduce the ability of the traditional lending-based banking system to provide the financial system with the sort of buffer that is needed to respond to liquidity problems and other shocks.

A third concern is uncertainty about the implications of the array of new financial products and instruments for the health and safety of the financial system. One worry is that severe competition, together with inexperience of new instruments, may lead to underpricing. Another is that understanding of where and how all the risks in the system are being redirected is incomplete, and that in some cases risks are being shifted to other economic agents that are less able than banks to carry these burdens. There is also a range of problems relating to liquidity, which is a motivating factor in many of the new instruments. It is widely assumed that there is great liquidity in the system, but in times of stress this assumption may prove to be mistaken.

Many questions arise, and it may be too soon to answer some, because our knowledge and experience are inadequate. This is why the pace of change presents difficulties. Innovators are, by definition, far ahead of other participants, but if the institutional infrastructure falls behind too much there will be problems, not only for regulators but for many others. Financial innovation has profound implications for accountants. The US professional body is studying these, but will probably take several years to reach firm conclusions, because the issues are very complex and the answers are not self-evident. Lawyers, too, are affected, since many of the new products have never been tested in court and may conflict with certain existing laws. The statistical services will also need time to determine what new information should be collected to provide a clearer picture of what is happening in the financial system, so that the regulators will be better able to cope with problems when they arise. Finally, the banks and investment houses themselves may not yet have fully mastered their new environment in terms of management and internal controls. In sum, if accidents are to be avoided a coherent view is required of the future structure of the financial system.

Christine Downton took up the subject of stresses within banks and other financial companies, and focused on three aspects. First, as markets have grown and become more globally integrated, companies have felt compelled to expand to meet these new challenges. This has entailed a large increase in staff, above all on the securities side of the business. Managing rapid staff growth is a major management task, particularly when it involves integration of different cultures, be they merchant banking, broking and market-making cultures, or British, American and Japanese cultures. Management has to contain the tensions arising from this growth and the associated changes, and to devote resources to training and building communications.

Another source of stress is the changing technological capabilities and innovation, which, together with entry into new markets and rising volumes, generate intense pressure on systems development and the whole range of back-office support. All the major companies involved in global financial markets are going through constant system changes and adaptations. This creates enormous stress on technology and administrative staff, in markets where there are limited supplies of these skills. The problem is particularly acute because if the systems are not available, the deal-makers leave a firm to work for a competitor. Many of the highly publicized walkouts of staff are over inadequate technology rather than inadequate remuneration. The process of managing the tension between the deal makers and the new systems they require and demand, and the ability of the back office to deliver them, is also a major management task. Until the back office can provide adequate support, management has to resist the temptation to give in and allow the deal-makers to do the business.

Furthermore, some of the new instruments involve combining the roles of sections of the business that were previously somewhat segregated. Swaps are a classic example. They brought together treasury departments and the departments that dealt with the capital markets and debt securities, each of which had been relatively self-contained. Banks and financial houses are now integrating these departments, but there were risks when the swaps business exploded, since internally there were still separate financial control systems dealing with the different aspects.

A third major stress is the rapidity with which the competition is changing. A few years ago most American banks and securities houses would have seen other American firms as their main competitors, and their most important market as their domestic dollar one. Much the same could be said of the Japanese and even the London houses. Although London has always been more internationally oriented, its domestic market has competed behind regulatory barriers with people who have known each other most of their working lives. We are now all competing across national borders to a much greater extent. This means management is having to come to grips with understanding different cultures and regulations.

The outstanding change in this respect is the rapid rise of Japanese financial entities to become the most powerful in the world in terms of financial muscle. A few examples illustrate this. Nomura now has a market capitalization of over US$13 billion, more than the capitalization of the four London clearing banks. Japanese banks are now in the majority of the top 10 banks world-wide on the basis of total assets. Backed by this financial strength, these houses are rapidly penetrating global markets. This is probably the most dramatic and fundamental change we are facing. It is a major challenge for the management of both the Japanese institutions and the US and European institutions meeting this competition.

The global markets where these various groupings are now meeting head-on lack the degree of understanding and shared ethics that have characterized domestic financial markets. The major global financial players are going to have to work very hard to build such understanding across the traditional national groupings. This could well be the critical ingredient in the smooth functioning of the emerging integrated global capital markets.

The focus of the earlier sessions of the conference was on rules – capital adequacy, etc. – to ensure that the financial community does not do things that it should not. But, though rules have a role, they cannot be the whole answer, given the rapidity of the changes that are occurring. More attention should be directed to the analysis of stress and how it is being managed.

The Comptroller of the Currency has drawn up a list of characteristics of Continental Illinois as it moved towards crisis, which provides some useful stress measures. The most important are:

- rapid growth in staff and high staff turnover
- going for market share and rapid balance sheet expansion
- rapid penetration of new markets and concentration of risk in those markets
- no time for paper work and lagging back office support
- reduction of quality of clients in search for new markets.

In the current environment of rapid change, many financial houses share at least some of these characteristics. Those who are managing them have the responsibility to be aware of and manage these risks, while the regulators will need to monitor these qualitative factors as much as quantitative ones.

Ernesto Feldman described the problems besetting the financial system in a number of Latin American countries. These problems have been closely associated with difficulties at the macroeconomic level, where inflation, fiscal imbalances and managed interest rates have caused significant distortions and malfunctioning in financial markets. In particular, the financing of public-sector deficits has crowded out the private sector and severely distorted the structure of interest rates. Abortive efforts were made to contain financial crisis by imposing a variety of prudential and protective supervisory measures on the banking system, including deposit insurance, capital-asset ratios and liquidity ratios. Central banks have acted not only as lenders of last resort, but as permanent lenders and notably in Argentina, as the largest lender in the market. Central bank discounts in Argentina account for two-thirds of total outstanding bank credit to the private sector. This is the outcome of rescue operations launched by the central bank when solvency problems affected not only particular banks but entire industrial sectors or economic regions.

Despite this difficult background, banks have expanded their branch networks in an attempt to preserve their share in a shrinking and demonetizing market. The result has been counter-productive, since intermediation costs have risen and efficiency has deteriorated. The main questions facing the authorities in the field of regulation are how to deregulate systems that have been over-regulated, to supervise banks properly without jeopardizing their efficiency, and to insulate domestic financial markets from external shocks.

More important to the prospects for averting financial crisis, however, is the health of the real economy. Several Latin American economies were weakened by the policies of the late 1970s, including overvalued exchange rates. These, in the absence of exchange controls, encouraged capital flight, which governments sought to prevent by raising domestic interest rates to very high levels, with severe adverse effects on bank solvency. Hence the financial system was in a fragile state even before the debt crisis. The dramatic macroeconomic adjustment that followed it created further strains, which threatened the soundness of the system, and would have done so however much the quality of bank supervision had been improved. More rational supervisory policies are necessary and are being introduced, but they are not sufficient. The prime requirement for a robust financial system is sustained growth.

Alexander Swoboda focused on long-run problems. In the past few years the spread of severe strains has been effectively contained or prevented. The debt problem, for example, is causing much less serious concern as a threat to the short-run stability of the international financial system than it did two years ago. Nonetheless, there is a risk that technically competent solutions prompted by a crisis will in the long run make the system less resilient and less efficient. They make a return in the future to a more market-oriented system of distributing risks difficult, because they tend to impose losses on society as a whole rather than leaving individuals to bear them. More specifically, deregulation combined with implicit guarantees and rescue operations will generate not only moral hazard problems but also bad-debt overhangs, which will impede a return to greater market discipline in regulation. The balance between preventive and corrective measures, between supervision and protection (through the lender of last resort, deposit insurance and implicit guarantees), is extraordinarily important. Three broad examples illustrate the problem.

If sovereign debt problems are solved not by the market but by cooperation among the IMF, creditor governments and commercial banks, though this may be admirable in the short run, implicit guarantees will be extended not just to the banks but also to the borrowers. This raises the risk of moral hazard, perhaps mainly for the debtors.

In some industrial countries and many newly industrializing countries high debt/equity ratios are giving cause for concern. They have partly resulted from guarantees, which by directly or indirectly subsidizing interest rates have made available cheap finance. High debt/equity ratios make the financial system less resilient and more sensitive to the next shock. If a shock to the economy causes asset values to fall substantially, the real economy will be in trouble, and rescue operations will have to be organized.

The third instance is the interaction among macroeconomic policy, the regulatory framework and the way the financial and economic system copes with risks and unexpected shocks, in particular losses in capital values. Essentially capital losses can be handled in two ways. Either they can be allowed to fall where the market would allocate them, or they can be socialized explicitly through taxation or implicitly through an inflation tax or some other form of engineered redistribution. Many of the problems of the late 1970s and early 1980s have arisen from the negative real interest rates and the inflation that prevailed in the 1960s and 1970s. The distortions in the system created during this period led to a reaction and to innovation. But also, the problems, including a bad-debt over-hang, left over from the later period make the system today much more sensitive to high real interest rates.

*　　*　　*

In the discussion that followed the presentations by the panel, the view of Sam Cross, that it was not change but the pace of change that created additional risk, was endorsed by several speakers. One estimated that on average one significant new product emerges each month, developed by banks, investment banks or even insurance companies. This means that there is always much that must be learned. Nor is it only a matter of new products, for existing products mature. Swaps, for example, began several years ago as an investment banking product. They were complicated, tailor-made, commanded large fees, and were relatively few in number. As the product matured, however, it became more standardized and more routine, the fees declined and the number of deals increased. Swaps moved from the investment banking division to the treasury, and are now sold differently, booked differently and priced differently. This was not an easy transition.

Participants also emphasized the change in the nature of banking. The essential function of banks used to be to receive deposits and to make loans. Nowadays banks originate assets, which they may then transform, and may subsequently sell. But though banks are designing new products, the demand for these is being generated elsewhere. The role of the house banker and the situation where a company had relationships with a group of banks have completely disappeared. Multinational companies and other buyers of financial services now seek them transaction by transaction. A bank that makes a very good job of a deal for a company cannot expect that it will get that company's business on a future occasion. Even if the company wants precisely the same deal a year later, it will ask ten banks to bid for it.

Attention was drawn to a new group of banks which are not recorded as such anywhere. These are the treasury divisions of multinational companies, which no longer invest the liquidity of their companies in a passive and risk-averse fashion. Their activities are now highly geared and profit-oriented, and they exert pressure in the markets, on banks and on brokers. Although they have significant influence and themselves deal in a variety of currencies and products, awareness of them is limited. They do not appear in banking statistics, and they are totally unregulated.

The management problems associated with rapid change were also taken up in the discussion. One participant characterized the new culture as being essentially a change in attitude towards risk. There have been cases of conflict between directors and management, and it appears that a change is required in what boards of directors will accept. Attempts to merge traditional bankers with the newer breed of bankers within an existing institution have often failed, causing difficulty for banks seeking to enter a new line of business. Banks that have brought people from outside into an alien culture have had more trouble than those that have taken time to develop and train people from the existing culture into new habits and ways of thinking.

The absorption of new technology and the need for technological capabilities to keep pace with innovative products being designed by deal-makers is a problem that a number of US banks experienced in the mid-1970s in the context of their foreign-exchange dealing. This has given them a lead over others in developing the technological infrastructure for more recent developments in financial markets. It also taught them that if they did not have the technology they should not do the deal. A bank which ignores that lesson is vulnerable. Since management does not know what is happening, there is no control; the books do not balance; profits are not being taken correctly; and the situation is open to fraud. From a regulator's perspective, these dangers are greater than that of a group of deal-makers being enticed away by another firm. The evidence indicates that such people can be replaced quite easily, and that walk-outs cause little disruption to the functioning of the system.

It was suggested that, at least in the United States, stress is probably greater within the regulatory agencies than anywhere else. This results from a combination of constant pressure and salary levels that are very much lower than in the banks themselves. And it is reflected in a steady stream of experienced middle-management people leaving the agencies. One group not mentioned by Sam Cross which is also uneasy about new developments in the financial system is the macroeconomic policy-makers. Their world has been severely shaken by the extent of new instruments and fluctuations in financial and exchange markets. Many are unhappy about their changed environment, but while regulators succeed in maintaining financial stability and there is no crisis they are unlikely to contest it. Should serious problems emerge, however, questions will be raised about the desirability of innovation, which might generate pressure to contain and reduce it.

One speaker took up, in a different light, the interaction between the macroeconomy and the financial system referred to by Alexander Swoboda. The sequence of a huge rise in inflation followed by falling inflation delivered severe shocks to the macroeconomy. Resources were concentrated in the financial system because that was one way of coping with these shocks, and indeed helping to restrain and cure the inflationary process. The global economy benefited greatly from the role played by the financial system during that period, but as it moves into a period of more stable prices, the resources devoted to the financial sector will decline. Furthermore, activity in the financial sector is increasingly becoming a zero-sum game among professionals. This means that the vast expansion in the financial system and in the volume of trading may be coming to an end, because overall profits generated in the financial services sector will be smaller. Another participant believed that finance was a growth industry, but it would be helpful, if possible, to distinguish how far this characteristic was attributable to long-term structural changes, notably rising per capita income, and how far to transitory factors, such as inflation or other misalignments and distortions. Such a distinction would be useful in setting regulatory policy.

Alexander Swoboda commented that if the financial activity that we have observed has, given increasing instability, been providing a better distribution of risks, then the system is better off with it, even though it may be costly in real resources. If, on the other hand, this activity has been spurred by distortions elsewhere in the microeconomy, then it may be sending the wrong signals. In any event, financial innovation should be judged by whether it is good or bad for the economy and society as a whole, not whether it is good or bad for policy-makers or for bankers. On the whole it is very good. Bankers and regulators have the important task of ensuring that it does not destabilize the financial system, either in the short or the long run.

8 Policy and financial innovation: will there be a switch from deregulation to reregulation?

MARKUS LUSSER

I The consequences of innovations and deregulation for monetary policy and bank supervision

Discussions in central bank and bank supervision circles have increasingly concentrated on innovations and liberalization in the financial markets. Two issues – matters of concern – are at the centre of discussions.

What are the consequences of these new developments for monetary policy?

Do they threaten the stability of the financial markets?

To me the predominant monetary problem is whether innovations and liberalization exert an influence on the demand for money. A monetary policy with explicit money supply targets – such as that pursued not only by my country, but by numerous other industrialized nations as well – depends on accurate forecasts of the demand for money. However, many innovations are aimed at a more efficient management of cash holdings. The economy's demand for money declines – relative to the volume of transactions – for as long as it takes an innovation to gain general acceptance. The trend of such shifts in demand is clear, though lack of historical experience makes it impossible to predict either their extent or their duration. Deregulation can lead to a massive redistribution of assets, which likewise impairs the accuracy of forecasts of money supply aggregates, a phenomenon that has been particularly in evidence in the United States.

In the light of this experience, the authorities in a number of countries have begun to modify their views regarding the significance of money supply aggregates for monetary policy. In Switzerland we have not become aware – at least not up to the present – of any major shifts in the demand for money. In my view this is due, among other things, to the fact that the traditionally liberal order of the Swiss financial markets and our stability-oriented economic policy have to date provided little cause for innovations and deregulation.

A second monetary policy problem is the question whether new financial market instruments – such as interest rate futures – inhibit the transmission mechanism and thus the effectiveness of monetary policy. The experts differ in their opinions on the subject. It is frequently asserted that the possibilities of hedging against interest rate fluctuations diminish the interest rate sensitivity of investment demand. Consequently interest rate changes need to be larger than in the past in order to achieve the desired effect on economic activity. I have my doubts about this. For the opportunity costs which are of decisive importance for the rational entrepreneur are subject to variations regardless of whether or not a company hedges against interest rate fluctuations.

Finally, the question of the effects of innovations on the stability of the financial markets is addressed first and foremost to the supervisory authorities. It is, however, also of interest to the central bank as 'lender of last resort'. The central banks are agreed that, for two reasons, special attention should be devoted to the risks involved in various innovations. For one thing, these risks are extremely difficult to assess due to the complexity of the new instruments and to lack of experience. For another, most innovations do not figure in bank balance sheets, thus easily escaping traditional supervision.

II   How long should we expect the pressure for innovation to continue?

Anyone dealing with the problems under discussion will first ask himself how long the hectic pace of innovations on the international financial markets can possibly continue. This question can hardly be answered satisfactorily. However, in my opinion, some of the causes for innovations will not become less pressing in the near future.

(a)   Technological progress

Technological progress is the first reason to be mentioned here. New technologies in the field of telecommunications have led to a massive cut in information costs. Technological progress will continue to be made. The ongoing process of innovation is thus in the nature of things. This holds true for the financial markets as well, even if the innovation pressure on these markets – e.g. in connection with a potential shift of technological development from electronic data processing to other areas – should ease in future.

(b) Circumvention of regulations

Regulations that invite transactions made for the purpose of evading the law are a further major cause of innovations. Every regulation that bites tends to become ineffective since sooner or later the market will try to circumvent it.

The creation of new instruments, however, is only one such means of evasion. Regulations are also liable to force transactions from regulated markets into less regulated, non-regulated or even newly emerging markets. We will probably never be able to do without a minimum of regulations on the financial markets. Evasion tactics – i.e. innovations – must therefore continue to be reckoned with.

(c) Innovations as a consequence of unsuccessful economic policies

A third major cause of innovations on the financial markets – and this is one I particularly wish to emphasize – is the series of abortive economic policies pursued in the seventies. The stop-and-go strategies of those years have neither led to the smoother course of business aimed at, nor brought us any closer to maximum economic growth targets accompanied by an acceptable inflation rate. On the contrary: excessive inflation rates, unsatisfactory growth levels and high unemployment were the result. Instability in the form of enormous interest and exchange rate fluctuations and correspondingly high risks on the financial markets was an immediate consequence of these unsuccessful economic policies. They gave rise to innovations in several areas:

High liquidity costs made economy measures imperative. More efficient forms of cash management and payment transactions – such as the NOW accounts in the United States – established themselves.

The perceptible increase in risks in connection with excessive interest and exchange rate fluctuations promoted the development of new forms of risk transfer and risk distribution. Futures and options are examples of such innovations.

In countries with direct price regulation – I am thinking in particular of maximum interest rate levels – market participants were on the lookout for profitable circumvention possibilities. They found them, among other things, in money market funds.

Under the pressure of large budget deficits, governments favoured innovations such as CATS and STRIPS, which facilitate the placement of debt issues.

My feeling that some of the new instruments would probably have gained acceptance less easily if the policies implemented in the seventies had not created unnecessary uncertainty and risks, and consequently a justified need for safeguards, is supported by the experience gained in Switzerland. On the Swiss capital market, for instance, bonds with flexible interest rates, after being initiated at the beginning of the eighties, proved no long-lasting innovation. As a result of our stability-oriented monetary policy the fluctuations in capital market rates were not wide enough.

III   Are innovations and liberalization desirable?

Experience with financial innovation in the 1970s and 1980s gives rise to the question whether innovations and liberalization on financial markets are actually desirable. It is frequently argued that many of the new instruments were and are having a destabilizing effect on the market. However, one of the main functions of numerous innovations in recent years is to make risks tradeable, i.e. to permit them to be redistributed in keeping with prevailing preferences, irrespective of any credit relations. In other words, innovations make economic sense by helping to coordinate better the supply of and demand for risks. No new risks arise in the process; they already exist, e.g. in the form of open positions of exporters. Accordingly, most empirical studies come to the conclusion that after the introduction of such innovations the financial markets are not less stable than before; at times they actually tend to be more stable.

The fear that the liberalization process may have been taken a step too far is not only expressed occasionally among the authorities, but increasingly so in the international press. The latter, accordingly, interprets the new regulative measures introduced in several countries as a turnaround on the part of the central banks and the supervisory authorities. To the two catchwords 'innovation' and 'deregulation' a new one has now been added, namely: 'reregulation'. In my opinion, this approach misjudges two facts.

Most cases of deregulation are – firstly – the result, rather than the cause, of the recent tide of innovations. Supervisory authorities and central banks came to realize that numerous regulatory measures did not achieve their aims as they were being circumvented; circumventions, in turn, gave rise to new difficulties. By resorting to deregulation, the authorities were drawing inferences from this experience.

Regulatory and deregulatory measures – secondly – have different focal points: liberalization measures concentrate chiefly on direct market interventions in terms of volume and price and on limitations to market access. The regulatory process, by contrast, takes place in the field of prudential supervision. It does not imply reregulation, but new regulatory measures. Their aim is to ensure that both the organization and provisions in terms of staff and capital of the financial intermediaries are in keeping with market risks.

IV Some conclusions for economic policy

In my view, there are two aspects to this development in the field of supervisory policy:

First, it constitutes a – desirable – reorientation: supervisory concepts are increasingly tailored to meet market requirements. The decision not to intervene directly on the market strengthens the efficiency of the financial market without supervision having to suffer as a consequence. For regulations with respect to the organization of financial intermediaries, the quality of their managements, as well as minimum capital and reserve requirements are, in my opinion, more suitable than direct intervention in the market process. Such measures should be amply sufficient for the supervision of the banks and the financial markets.

Secondly, this reorientation constitutes an adaptation of the supervisory concept to recent market developments; this is necessary anyway from time to time due to the inevitable attempts at circumvention. The globalization of the markets makes it imperative, in my opinion, also to globalize supervision in two respects. For one thing, traditional bank supervision must evolve into an encompassing supervision of the financial markets. This development is already far advanced in the United Kingdom. For another, the supervisory concepts need to be increasingly coordinated on an international level. Otherwise we are liable to lose risky business – following the path of least resistance – mainly to countries with inadequate supervision. The Basle Concordat of 1982 is an important step in this direction.

The efficiency of markets depends not least on market transparency. Through the reorientation of the supervisory concept the authorities contribute towards the improvement of this transparency; for the direct regulation of volumes and prices usually led to market distortions that were difficult to predict. This sparked off – due to circumventions – a more or less rapid succession of further market interventions. Among other things, market transparency consists of adequate information on the price and quality of the various financial investments, and consequently also on the risks involved. The enormous progress in the field of electronics has paved the way for radical improvements in this field.

I should like to conclude with an observation on monetary and fiscal policies. The uneasiness befalling many an economic policy-maker confronting the innovation pressure characterising today's financial markets takes him back to himself. For some of the most considerable risks to which the market has reacted with innovations in the past ten years were artificially created, or at least increased, by the economic and monetary policies of the seventies. The malaise should therefore lead us to think seriously about the connections between economic policy and innovations. And from these considerations we should then draw the necessary conclusions. The high level of money supply growth rates in a number of major industrialized countries – the renewed calls for activist economic policies – make me doubt that we have really learned the lesson that the debacle of the seventies should have taught us.

Appendix: Country studies

The role of public policy in ensuring financial stability in the United States

ROBERT F. GEMMILL
Federal Reserve Board

Overview

Responsibility for supervision and regulation of commercial banks, and for support arrangements for those banks, is divided by statute among three agencies at the national level: the Federal Reserve, Comptroller of the Currency (Comptroller) and the Federal Deposit Insurance Corporation (FDIC). In addition, laws and regulations of individual states apply to certain banking transactions. Supervisory actions by these federal agencies are coordinated, formally through the Federal Financial Institutions Examinations Council, and more broadly through informal working arrangements among the top officials.

With respect to supervision, the Comptroller has responsibility for all nationally chartered banks, the Federal Reserve responsibility for all bank holding companies and for state-chartered banks which are members of the Federal Reserve System, and the FDIC responsibility for state non-member banks.

With respect to support arrangements, the Federal Reserve provides liquidity support, while the FDIC is responsible for insuring deposits, and for providing any longer-term support, including recapitalization, that may be appropriate. In support operations, as in supervisory matters, actions of the agencies are closely coordinated.

A majority of thrift institutions (savings and loan associations, savings banks and credit unions) have separate supervisors, a separate deposit insurance scheme, and access to special industry lenders that are not available to commercial banks. Historically most of their liquidity support has been provided by these special lenders, although in principle since 1980 they have had access to the Federal Reserve discount window. These institutions are not covered here.

Deposit insurance

The deposit insurance system of the FDIC covers all national banks, all state member banks, and nearly all state-chartered non-member banks; branches of foreign banks are eligible for coverage, but relatively few have applied for it. With the exception of these branches, deposits of insured banks now account for virtually all deposits in commercial banking offices in the United States.

Deposit insurance covers only the first $100,000 of any deposit in a US banking office, although individuals may hold insured deposits in a number of different institutions. The deposit insurance system is financed through assessments on deposits in US offices. Deposits in foreign branches are not covered explicitly by US insurance and are not included in the base for assessment of deposit insurance premiums.

In practice, the FDIC normally arranges for take-overs of troubled banks by other banks, including in some cases by foreign-owned banks, instead of paying off depositors in insolvent institutions. Under such take-overs, all deposits of a troubled institution have been assumed by the acquiring bank, and hence all depositors have remained whole, including depositors in foreign branches. US and foreign banks find the opportunity to take over a troubled US bank attractive, because the acquiring bank may gain access to a new customer base within a state, or expand into a state in which it would otherwise be unable to operate because of state or federal statutes restricting interstate banking. Federal bank supervisors until recently had temporary statutory authority to arrange for interstate mergers and acquisitions of failed insured banks with assets of more than $500 million, and it is expected that authority will soon be reinstated; in the interim, mergers can still be concluded when permissible under state law, and some states have recently amended their laws to allow interstate acquisition.

Takeovers of troubled banks have frequently been facilitated also by financial assistance provided by the FDIC. Such takeovers have involved no financial disruption and have generally been achieved at lower cost to the FDIC than if the troubled bank had been closed and insured deposits paid off.

Lender of last resort and other support and rescue operations

The Federal Reserve has statutory authority to lend directly on acceptable collateral to US-domiciled commercial banks and other depository institutions and to US offices of foreign-chartered banks. Such lending is most often in the form of short-term adjustment credit, but under certain limited conditions it may include extended credit. Access to the discount window is a privilege, not a right. Credit is provided to financially viable institutions, which are expected to draw on other reasonably available sources of funds before turning to the discount window. In the case of US offices of foreign-chartered banks, alternative sources of funds would include funds from foreign bank parents and their affiliates. US offices of foreign banks cannot expect to use the discount window to fund the needs of their non-US affiliates or to reduce reliance on those affiliates in meeting regular funding needs in the US market. In fact, offices of foreign-chartered banks have used the discount window only infrequently and in modest amounts.

These general rules do not constitute the detailed blueprint for emergency assistance sometimes called for in the academic community. The Federal Reserve philosophy is set forth in Congressional testimony by Governor Wallich in 1974:

> There are dangers in trying to define and publicize specific rules for emergency assistance to troubled banks, notably the possibility of causing undue reliance on such facilities and possible relaxation of needed caution on the part of all market participants. Therefore, the Federal Reserve has always avoided comprehensive statements of conditions for its assistance to member banks. Emergency assistance is inherently a process of negotiation and judgment, with a range of possible actions varying with circumstances and need.

The Federal Reserve has extended liquidity assistance to a number of banks that subsequently have sustained losses and reductions in capital. When the deterioration in capital position has become severe, and the needs of the bank have gone beyond liquidity support, that support has continued in the process of seeking a long-term solution.

Much of what is often referred to as lender of last resort assistance is recapitalization of troubled banks, and in the United States when this cannot be accomplished solely through the private market, recapitalization can be provided under the aegis of the FDIC. In a few instances, the FDIC has supplied capital infusion as part of a rescue operation to enable the bank to continue to operate by itself; in those cases, there has been a complete change of bank management and the transfer to the FDIC of a financial interest in the rescued bank (usually in the form of rights to purchase equity) in an amount that reduced or eliminated the equity interest of the former stockholders. As part of rescue packages, the FDIC has assumed a large part or all of the troubled loans, and the value of the surviving equity interest of the original stockholders may be dependent on the degree to which the FDIC has been able to recover on the loans that it assumed.

Two examples of this type of rescue operation are the assistance given to First Pennsylvania in 1980 and to Continental Illinois in 1984. The excerpt from the press release on the latter case indicates the general form of the package.

> After analyzing alternative solutions to Continental Illinois's problems, the agencies concluded that the best approach is to provide sufficient permanent capital and other direct assistance to enable the bank to restore its position as a viable, self-financing entity. This decision was based on considerations of cost to the FDIC, competitive consequences and the banking needs of the public.
>
> Pending approval by shareholders and consummation of the permanent aid package, the interim $2.0 billion subordinated loan to the bank from the FDIC and a group of banks made on May 17, 1984, remains in place. Also, the assurance given by the FDIC on May 17, 1984, remains in place. Also, the assurance given by the FDIC on May 17 that "all depositors and other general creditors of the banks will be *fully protected* and service to the bank's customers *will not be interrupted*" remains in full force and effect.
>
> As part of the interim financial aid program, the Federal Reserve stated that it was prepared, in accordance with customary arrangements, to meet any extraordinary liquidity requirements of the bank pending more permanent arrangements. In light of the FDIC's commitment of capital resources to the bank, the Federal Reserve will continue its lending assurance. The $6.6 billion facility provided by a group of major US banks will remain in place.
>
> Upon consummation of the permanent aid transaction, the bank will be strongly capitalized and virtually free of nonperforming loans. If, for any reason, the permanent assistance package proves to be insufficient, the FDIC will commit additional capital or other forms of assistance as may be required.

Once an institution is found to be insolvent by its primary supervisory agency, the responsibility for liquidation falls on the receiver, which for insured banks is the FDIC. In administering this responsibility, the FDIC has sought to have another bank assume as much of the liabilities and assets of the insolvent banks as is feasible. In the cases of the US National Bank of San Diego and the Franklin National Bank, the FDIC assumed certain liabilities and also provided capital assistance to successful bidders for the remaining assets and liabilities. In the Franklin case, not all potential bidders were willing to have Franklin's foreign exchange book included as part of the assets and liabilities to be acquired; the Federal Reserve Bank of New York therefore purchased the foreign exchange book before Franklin was declared insolvent, so that international markets would not be threatened by failure of these contracts.

Liquidity assistance to nondepository financial institutions, as well as to nonfinancial institutions, has typically been provided by commercial banks, although the Federal Reserve has statutory authority to make loans directly to such institutions in extraordinary circumstances. Thus, at the time of the Penn Central crisis in 1970, the Federal Reserve took steps to ensure that adequate bank credit would be available, as the following testimony by Chairman Burns makes clear:

> Once it became apparent that some firms were having difficulty in refinancing their maturing obligations in the commercial paper market and might therefore need to increase their bank borrowings, the Board moved promptly and on June 23 suspended Regulation Q ceilings on large-denomination certificates of deposit with maturities of less than 90 days. This action has enabled banks to obtain funds that investors might be hesitant to place in other markets and to rechannel these funds to borrowers previously dependent on issuance of commercial paper. Also, it was made clear that the discount window would be available to assist banks in meeting the needs of businesses unable to roll over maturing commercial paper, and member bank borrowings for this purpose subsequently have risen. Increases in bank credit resulting solely from a rechanneling of funds represent a redistribution, and not an addition to the supply, of loanable funds.
>
> These conventional tools are buttressed with standby procedures to permit the Federal Reserve to make funds available to creditworthy borrowers facing unusual liquidity needs through "conduit loans" – that is, loans to a member bank to provide funds needed for lending to a qualified borrower. Administrative arrangements for making such loans to nonmember banks to nonbank thrift institutions were developed in 1966 and updated in 1969. Furthermore, the Federal Reserve could – under unusual and exigent circumstances – utilize the limited power granted by the Federal Reserve Act to make direct loans to business firms on the security of Government obligation or other eligible paper, provided the borrower is creditworthy but unable to secure credit from other sources.
>
> The powers of the central bank as the ultimate source of liquidity can, and obviously should, be reserved for extraordinary circumstances. Our financial institutions have demonstrated that they are sufficiently strong and flexible to handle with their own resources the needs of creditworthy borrowers – even when these needs are exceptionally large.

In the intervening 16 years, the Federal Reserve has on several occasions encouraged commercial bank lending to sound firms in troubled sectors of the domestic economy that were adjusting to changing market conditions. (The Federal Reserve has not made loans directly to such firms.) Correspondingly, in recent years, the banking community has been urged to provide new loans to major international debtor countries that are engaged in appropriate economic adjustment programs, when such loans and programs are judged to enhance the value of outstanding loans.

Prudential regulations

Prudential measures are applied to US banks on a worldwide consolidated basis. The principal supervisory tools used by federal supervisory agencies have been on-site examinations, which focus on five aspects of a bank's operations (adequacy of capital, quality of assets, competence of management, strength of earnings and sufficiency of liquidity) and off-site surveillance based mainly on analysis of reports submitted by banks.

In 1981, federal bank supervisors adopted formal guidelines for capital adequacy (a gearing ratio of capital to total assets); pursuant to the statutory authority in the International Lending Supervision Act (1983), the guideline was raised in 1985, and capital adequacy has been an important factor in Federal Reserve review of applications by banks to acquire other banks. The federal agencies recently published for comment a proposal to differentiate among certain types of assets for purposes of calculating capital ratios, a so-called risk-related capital ratio. Under this proposal, certain off-balance-sheet items would be included with balance sheet items in calculating the capital ratios.

US national banks are limited by statute in the amount of credit outstanding to a single debtor, and state-chartered banks are subject to similar limitations by state laws. US bank supervisors have not adopted specific ratio requirements for liquidity or for diversification of certain assets (e.g., for foreign exchange exposure); instead bank managements are expected to ensure through their own internal rules and control procedures that excessive exposures are avoided. These management practices are evaluated in the bank examination process, which stresses the need for adequate liquidity and diversification. (In fact, the proposed risk-related capital ratios have been constructed so as to encourage banks to hold money market liquid assets, by giving them a low weight relative to standard risk assets.)

Restrictions on the maximum interest payable on deposits at federally insured banking institutions, other than demand deposits, have been eliminated as part of the process of financial deregulation.

In regulatory decisions on acquisitions, an acquiring bank is expected to be a source of strength to the bank being acquired. Interstate acquisitions and entry are subject to state and federal laws; both foreign and domestic applicants are subject to broadly similar federal regulatory standards with respect to acquisitions and entry under the US policy of national treatment.

Banking supervision

The supervisory agencies are empowered to enforce their decisions to halt unsafe and unsound banking practices with legally binding cease and desist orders. Bank supervisors may require banks to write off assets of poor quality and to develop and implement plans for strengthening their capital positions.

Banks together with other financial and nonfinancial institutions file quarterly public statements. All banks are required to submit detailed periodic financial statements to their supervisors (call reports); national banks and state member banks are also required to publish their reports in local newspapers. In addition, banking organizations that offer public issues of securities in the United States are required to submit quarterly financial statements to the Securities and Exchange Commission (SEC); these reports provide a wide range of information on operating results and problems that the organizations may be encountering.

These rules for public disclosure afford more frequent and detailed information on the positions of US banks than is customary in many other countries. False or misleading information in reports to bank supervisors may give rise to penalties imposed by the supervisors, and in the case of reports to the SEC, may form the basis for legal suits by shareholders. Bank managements therefore seek to protect themselves by providing accurate and relatively full disclosure of the overall position of the bank. (For example, call reports to the SEC contain information on amounts of problem credits, e.g., loans to particular industries or countries that are not being serviced on schedule.) In order to avoid potential legal liability resulting from withholding of materially substantial information, banks and their accountants are likely at the present time to be making loan loss provisions to avoid understating risks. (Such provisions would be in addition to provisions or reserves that might be required by bank supervisors.) Other publicly owned financial institutions that have been participating in the spate of financial innovations of recent years are, by and large, also subject to the SEC reporting requirements.

Concluding observations

The US system to preserve banking safety and soundness involves a combination of governmental measures (including supervision, deposit insurance and financial assistance) and of market discipline; neither by itself is likely to yield a strong banking system.

Banks that have made major mistakes have taken losses. This is a general principle that is worth preserving, although there may in any single instance be a question whether the amount of loss has been appropriate. In the case of two major banks that were recapitalized with assistance by the FDIC (First Pennsylvania and Continental Illinois), bank managements were dismissed and the equity of existing stockholders was essentially wiped out.

Despite these and other instances in the United States and abroad where bank failure was a possibility, and in a few cases an actuality, there has been no financial contagion or panic. One element helping to avoid panic internationally has been the close contact among bank supervisors in various countries. In principle, each national supervisor has taken care of its own problem banks. That is also likely to be the practice in the future.

UK public policy on ensuring financial stability

L. D. D. PRICE
Bank of England

Responsibility for supervision of the banking system and other financial institutions

The Banking Act 1979 requires that institutions which accept deposits from the public be authorized for such purpose by the Bank of England.[1] At present, the Bank may grant either recognition as a bank or a licence to carry on a deposit-taking business. The legislation is likely to be revised in the coming year, however, and the present classification of recognized banks and licensed deposit-taking institutions[2] may be replaced by a single category of banks.

Other financial institutions, such as building societies, insurance, securities and other financial companies are subject to supervision by other regulatory authorities. Liberalization of the financial services sector has forced changes in the arrangements under which financial institutions are presently supervised. Institutions, especially banks, are seeking to broaden the range of their activities. As a result, the supervisory responsibility for a single financial group (or even single institution) is increasingly likely to be vested in more than one regulatory authority. Where a group includes a bank, responsibility may therefore be vested not only in the Bank of England but also in other bodies.

General approach to banking supervision

The Bank of England's general approach to the supervision of banks is based on the scrutiny of regular statistical returns accompanied by frequent interviews and discussions with senior personnel of the supervised institution, during which additional information is often requested. The Bank of England does not carry out inspections as a matter of routine procedure, although it may appoint people to investigate and report on banks where it appears desirable to do so in the interests of depositors. At present there are no particular auditing requirements imposed on banks apart from those applying to United Kingdom companies in general. Auditors have no duty to provide information to the Bank of England, which has no direct power over their appointment or removal. The Bank has recently published proposals, however, for a dialogue between itself and the auditors of banks. Some of these proposals are likely to appear in the new legislation. They develop the recommendations of the Committee set up by the Chancellor of the Exchequer to review the banking supervisory system in the United Kingdom following the rescue of Johnson Matthey Bankers.

In supervising banks, the Bank pays attention to a range of matters, including capital adequacy, liquidity and foreign exhchange exposure. Of these, the most important is normally considered to be capital adequacy.

Capital requirements

Under the Banking Act 1979, new institutions require minimum capital (net assets) of £250,000 to be granted a licence to carry on a deposit-taking business, £5mn to be granted recognition as a bank, or £250,000 for banks providing 'a highly specialized banking service'. These legal minima, even if raised by the new legislation, are less significant in the supervision of the banking system than the principle that each bank shall have an appropriate level of capital given the particular nature of the risks which it undertakes.

The Bank of England does not set general minimum capital ratios. Its assessment of the capital adequacy of banks incorporated in the United Kingdom employs two measures: a gearing ratio of capital resources to other liabilities and a risk asset ratio. The Bank emphasizes the latter ratio, which ascribes weightings to various classes of assets according to their susceptibility to the risk of loss. The capital base, less certain deductions, is measured against the total of weighted assets. A ratio is set for each bank having regard to its particular character and its degree of exposure to various categories of risk, including that arising from concentration of risk.

The Bank of England requires a bank to justify exposures to a single borrower or group of closely related borrowers in excess of 10% of the lending bank's capital base; it has also recently proposed a limit of 25% on such exposures. An exposure in excess of 25% will require prenotification and will be allowed only in the most exceptional circumstances.

These limits do not apply to exposures up to one year, inter-bank, country or sectoral exposures which are monitored separately.

The risk asset ratio takes account of on-balance-sheet and some off-balance-sheet risks. A review of off-balance-sheet risks is currently under way and is likely to bring a more comprehensive treatment of these risks.

For United Kingdom branches of overseas banks, the capital adequacy requirements are deemed to be fulfilled by confirmation from the overseas supervisor of the parent bank that it is satisfied with the overall financial soundness of the institution. Nevertheless, the Bank of England closely monitors any branch exposures that are large in relation to the branch's assets or deposit base.

Foreign currency exposure

The Bank of England does not impose formal limits on the foreign currency exposure of banks but agrees guidelines with each bank covering its net open dealing position in any one currency and the aggregate of its net short open positions. For United Kingdom incorporated banks these will not normally exceed 10% and 15% respectively of the bank's capital base. For United Kingdom branches of overseas banks, the Bank of England has regard to the foreign exchange guidelines imposed by their head offices.

Liquidity requirements

The Bank of England does not currently set any minimum liquidity requirements for banks. Rather it assesses each bank's liquidity individually using, as a first step, a cash flow approach which matches assets and liabilities on a cumulative basis in five maturity bands from sight to one year, taking into account future commitments and standby facilities as well as the marketability of assets. In the case of United Kingdom subsidiaries and branches of overseas banks, the Bank of England also takes account of their relationships with their parent banks.

The Bank is currently considering introducing a requirement for all banks to hold a proportion of their sterling business in the form of 'primary liquid assets' – short-term low-risk assets. The impetus behind this initiative derives largely from the removal, starting in September 1986, of money-market arrangements under which all institutions whose bills are eligible for rediscounting at the Bank of England undertook to maintain balances of secured money with members of the London Discount Market Association and with Stock Exchange money brokers and gilt-edged jobbers.

Other supervisory considerations

Consolidated supervision is applied by the Bank of England to all majority-owned subsidiaries of banks where there is a significant element of banking risk. Consolidation of minority interests may also be undertaken in certain circumstances. The Bank of England has published proposals for strengthening consolidated supervision, including complying with the requirements of the 1983 European Communities Consolidation Directive.

The size of provisions to be made by individual banks is decided by the bank's management. These provisons are reviewed by auditors when examining the accounts and may be discussed with the Bank in the course of the dialogue between bank and supervisor.

The Banking Act 1979 established a Deposit Protection Scheme funded by contributions from banks and providing a limited amount of protection for depositors with an insolvent institution. Broadly speaking, the Scheme protects three-quarters of a depositor's sterling funds with a bank up to a maximum of £7,500. Since it came into being in 1982, the Deposit Protection Fund has paid some £5 million to depositors with 11 licensed deposit-takers which failed. There is no policy to urge or incite banks to absorb failing banks.

The Bank of England provides lender of last resort facilities at its discretion. In a few instances where it has been evident that liquidity support for a bank would not be sufficient on its own and the Bank has been concerned for the systemic consequences of allowing the particular institution to fail, the Bank has itself acquired the failing institution. There have been occasions when other banks have joined with the Bank of England in providing liquidity support and in sharing potential losses on acquiring a failing bank.

NOTES

1 Various institutions – notably building societies – are specifically exempted from this requirement.
2 The term banks refers throughout to both recognized banks and licensed deposit-taking institutions.

The role of public policy in ensuring financial stability in Germany

PETER SCHMID

Deutsche Bundesbank

The Federal Republic of Germany is noted for a high degree of financial stability. Both the underlying macroeconomic conditions and the institutions of the German financial system have contributed to this. Fluctuations in inflation rates and interest rates have been less marked than in many other countries. Thus market participants have had less reason to secure themselves against economic risks by using new financing techniques. The German financial system is dominated by the banking sector. As 'universal banks', banks have always been free to offer their customers the whole range of financial services, and bank interest rates were decontrolled at the end of the sixties. So there have been no incentives for financial innovations, such as those which have resulted elsewhere from a high degree of fragmentation and regimentation in the financial markets. The monetary policy and bank supervisory authorities in Germany have not so far perceived insuperable difficulties caused by structural changes in the financial markets.

Insurance enterprises too are subject to (separate) supervision. The issuing of bonds also requires approval from the Finance Ministry. And finally, the individual Länder governments exercise control over the stock exchanges. The non-organized investment market is exempt from supervision.

Legal basis and organization of bank supervision

The legal basis for bank supervision is the Banking Act of 1961. The activity of banks is restricted only by general quantitative provisions and the obligation to open their books to the supervisory authorities; the supervisory authorities do not intervene directly in the banks' operation. The Banking Act defines the concept of 'bank' very broadly. Consequently, not only universal banks but also all specialized banks, building and loan associations and investment funds are subject to bank supervision.

The central supervisory organ for the banking industry is the Federal Banking Supervisory Office in Berlin. This office is subject to instructions from and reports to the Federal Ministry of Finance. It grants licences to carry out banking business and monitors compliance with the regulations of the Banking Act. Before issuing general regulations on banking policy, the Federal Banking Supervisory Office must reach agreement with the Bundesbank. Both institutions cooperate closely in obtaining and evaluating bank audit documents.

The banks have to submit monthly reports and annual accounts, render numerous special reports and have audits performed by certified auditors, banking associations or official auditors. The Banking Act grants the supervisory authorities almost unlimited rights with respect to information and audits in individual cases. In practice, the Supervisory Office relies heavily on the reports of external certified auditors, for which it lays down detailed guidelines.

If the Supervisory Office discovers problems at an *individual bank*, it can take many different courses of action. It can issue general warnings, warn the bank formally or insititute proceedings against it. In particular cases, where depositors' security seems endangered or where the orderly operation of the bank is at risk, the Federal Banking Supervisory Office can order that the bank be closed for public trading, can issue payment and sale prohibitions, can replace incompetent managers by specially appointed supervisory personnel or can revoke the licence to operate the bank.

The Banking Act includes special provisions for the rare case of a *general crisis of confidence* in the banking industry. In a bank crisis, the Federal Government can decree by Ordinance that a bank be granted a respite for meeting its liabilities (a 'moratorium'), that banks be closed for public trading and that bank and stock exchange activity be generally discontinued ('bank holidays').

Protective regulations

(a)   Permission to operate a bank

Any person who wishes to operate a bank requires a licence from the Federal Banking Supervisory Office. The licence may be refused only for specific reasons, e.g. if, the managers lack the requisite personal or professional qualifications, if the available funds are inadequate or if the bank does not have at least two full-time managers.

No check is made on the necessity to establish the bank. No particular legal form is prescribed, but since 1976 it has been impermissible to choose the legal form of a sole proprietorship. The setting up of branches of German banks does not require a licence; by contrast, the establishment of branches of foreign enterprises is subject to a licensing procedure. A licence may be refused for a bank from a non-EEC country if it is not considered to be justified on the grounds of general economic needs; however, this condition is insignificant in practice.

(b) Capital regulations

To guarantee that a bank always has an adequate capital base, the Act and the Principles derived from it provide as follows:

A bank's investments (land, participation rights) may not in the aggregate exceed its liable capital (section 12, Banking Act). Liable capital constitutes paid-up capital and published reserves and – since the beginning of 1985 – capital paid up against the issue of participation rights (to a limited extent).

The risk-bearing loans and participations of a bank should not exceed 18 times its liable capital (Principle I). Loans are weighted in accordance with risk groups. Loans to domestic public authorities are deemed to be risk-free and are not included. Since the middle of 1986, bank back-up facilities for third-party issuers such as the Revolving Underwriting Facility (RUF) and Note Issuance Facility (NIF) and other guarantees have to be included in credit components at 50% of their value.

The parent institutions of banking groups are required to ensure that Principle I is observed on a consolidated basis too. The consolidation is to include all domestic and foreign subsidiaries as well as leasing and factoring companies in which the parent bank has at least a 40% participation or over which it can exercise a controlling influence. The legislature assumed that the parent bank must normally accept liability for losses incurred by its subsidiaries in accordance with its shareholding. For this reason the 'pro rata consolidation method' was prescribed, i.e. the risk assets and the liable capital are to be consolidated in accordance with the share which the parent banks hold in the subsidiaries' capital.

At the close of business each day, the difference between a bank's asset items and liabilities items in foreign currency and in gold, silver or platinum metals (precious metals), irrespective of their maturities, should not exceed 30% of its liable capital; the difference between a bank's assets items and liabilities items in foreign currency maturing in any calendar month or in the first half or the second half of any calendar year should not exceed 40% of its liable capital (Principle Ia).

(c) Liquidity regulations

Pursuant to the Banking Act, a bank's funds should be invested in such a manner that it is solvent at any time. Traditionally, this has meant that the maturities of the assets held by the bank should not exceed the maturities of its liabilities ('golden banking rule'). Experience shows, however, that a certain 'deposit base' of sight deposits and shorter-term funds always remains at a bank for fairly long-term use. The Liquidity Principles drawn up by the Federal Banking Supervisory Office together with the Bundesbank take judicious account of this observation. They therefore permit banks to invest to a limited extent in long-term funds which are formally short-term ('maturity transformation'). Two different Principles are to be distinguished here:

Principle II stipulates that loans with a maturity of four years and over and participations, unlisted securities and fixed assets are to be financed in full by own funds and sufficiently long-term external funds;

Principle III specifies which resources can be drawn on to finance short- and medium-term loans and investments in listed shares. The Banking Act does not provide for the application of the Liquidity Principles on a consolidated basis.

(d) Limitation of credit risks

The Banking Act requires the banks to disperse their loans among as many borrowers as possible. So-called 'large loans' (i.e. loans which exceed 15% of a bank's liable capital), loans to bank employees and enterprises and persons closely associated with the bank may not be granted without special internal controls and are to be reported to the Supervisory Office; similarly, a single customer's bank debts of DM 1 million and over are to be reported to the Bundesbank every two months and where major loans are concerned (over DM 50,000), the credit rating of the debtor is to be inspected carefully. The individual large loan may not exceed 50% of the liable capital, and all large loans together may not exceed eight times the liable capital. These limits obtain for groups of banks too. However, there is only a consolidation requirement when the parent bank holds an interest in the subsidiary of at least 50%. There are no limits for credits to individual countries or groups of countries. The bank supervisory authorities do not carry out any 'country rating' but the banks must report their foreign credit volume classified by countries.

German accounting rules and practices encourage very prudent risk assessment by the banks themselves. In particular, if appropriate write-offs for dubious assets have been made for the corresponding banks, bank auditors are required by the Supervisory Office to draw attention to it via their reports.

Moreover, such precautionary write-offs are deductible from taxable profits. The above applies in principle also to the valuation of foreign claims. Accordingly, German banks usually provide for dubious claims as far as possible in periods of good profitability, both for prudential reasons and in the light of tax considerations. In addition, banks are allowed to undervalue specific assets. This undervaluation is allowed in so far as it is necessary, according to reasonable commercial judgement, as a safeguard against the particular risks of the banks' field of business. As a consequence of this undervaluation, most banks have substantial 'hidden' reserves in addition to their stated capital. These 'hidden' reserves, which are used primarily to even out fluctuations in earnings, are not accepted by the Federal Banking Supervisory Office in calculating the relevant prudential ratios.

Deposit guarantee schemes

Bank supervision based on free-market principles cannot completely prevent bank failures. Such supervision must therefore be complemented by deposit guarantee schemes to protect depositors from loss. In the Federal Republic of Germany there is no public deposit guarantee system. But virtually all banks which conduct deposit business belong to one of the deposit guarantee funds set up on a voluntary basis by the banking associations. The fund established for the commercial banks aims primarily at protecting depositors, while the schemes operated by the savings bank and credit cooperative sectors are designed to avert member banks' insolvency.

The Deposit Guarantee Fund set up for commercial banks at the Federal Association of German Banks safeguards, in cases of insolvency, non-securitized liabilities to non-bank creditors, per creditor up to the level of 30% of the liable capital at the time of the last published annual accounts of the bank concerned. Larger liabilities are protected up to this guarantee limit. Protection encompasses both deposits in Germany and those at branches abroad, irrespective of the currency in which they are denominated and of whether the creditors are residents or non-residents.

Although, in the case of public savings banks, responsibility for indemnifying depositors ultimately rests with the local authorities (e.g., town, district) which set up the savings bank, given the existence of what is known as 'guarantors' liability', the regional savings bank and giro associations have nevertheless set up guarantee funds. In addition, there is a reserve fund of the Land banks/regional giro institutions, which, notwithstanding the guarantors' liability, acts as an extra safeguard for the deposits of non-bank customers. The credit cooperatives' by-laws provide for a limited obligation of members to pay up further capital when called. Furthermore, the cooperative sector has created a guarantee fund.

A feature common to all the guarantee arrangements is that a fund is formed from the contributions of the member banks. Commercial banks, for instance, have to make an annual contribution of 0.03% of their total deposits from non-banks. If the available assets are inadequate for the purpose, the members are required to pay up further capital when called. Another common feature of the various guarantee systems is that neither the member banks nor the depositors affected have a legal right to assistance. In other words, they are not deposit *insurance* funds.

As the guarantee arrangements in the savings bank sector and the credit cooperative sector serve to protect banks, internal association policy is to come to the assistance of banks that have got into difficulties. For example, the guarantee scheme for credit cooperatives has so far prevented any insolvencies. In the area of the commercial banks, the SMH Bank was saved from collapse at the end of 1983 after joint action by the deposit guarantee fund and the bank's major creditors. This was the first time that resources from the deposit guarantee fund of the private banks were used to avert a bank crisis. If only for basic reasons of competition policy, however, one cannot derive from this action any general rules for future measures in the private banking sector which would go beyond guaranteeing customer deposits.

Lender of last resort facilities

The banks can acquire central bank funds on their own initiative by way of bills discounted and lombard loans. The Bundesbank's discount credit is limited by rediscount quotas. Basically, lombard loans should be used only to meet a temporary liquidity need. To date, the Bundesbank has not given particular banks special treatment, especially with respect to supporting insolvent institutions. After the collapse of the Herstatt Bank it did allow banks more generous access to its refinancing facilities to prevent a large-scale crisis of confidence.

In addition to regular central bank facilities, following the Herstatt episode the Bundesbank and the domestic banking industry joined forces to set up the Liquidity Consortium Bank (Liko Bank) to provide temporary assistance to banks with liquidity needs arising out of domestic and international payments problems. The Bundesbank holds 30% of the capital of the Liko bank and has granted it a special rediscount facility. Its relatively small capital base (DM 250 million paid up and DM 750 million callable) limits its assistance to smaller institutions.

Recent trends

The most spectacular bank failures in Germany originated in areas which were not subject to bank supervision or which were supervised only insufficiently, such as forward exchange trading at the Herstatt Bank and excessive lending to a single group at the SMH Bank. In the second case, moreover, there was at the time no credit surveillance or limitation on a consolidated basis. The legislature has responded to these problems by introducing Principle Ia, the consolidation regulations, more stringent risk norms and widened scope for the bank supervisory authorities to intervene. The legislature did not take up more far-reaching reform suggestions, which related particularly to banks' non-bank participations.

Apart from the supervisory system, the security of the banking system depends fundamentally on its capital provision. Here, the German authorities have adopted the course of not softening the concept of capital by permitting capital substitutes, and have thus prompted the banks to improve their capital base. This course has been successful. In view of the favourable trend in earnings in the German banking industry in the last five years, banks have been able to improve their capital from internal resources as well as by taking up external capital. Their own funds/assets ratio (i.e. the ratio of capital and published reserves to volume of business) in the middle of 1986 was 3.6% compared with an average of 3.4% over the last 15 years. At the same time, the good earnings position enabled banks to make risk provision for their national and international credit commitments on a large scale.

Certain problems have arisen for the German bank supervisory authorities from the increase in 'securitization' and the off-balance-sheet liabilities. German structural norms are geared to the risks inherent in book credit, while listed securities are subject to special treatment in that they are regarded as liquid funds. It is questionable whether this differentiation can be maintained in future. At present, it is also not apparent how the financial innovations which are associated with exchange rate and security price risks can be incorprated in the structural norms.

Maintaining a sound financial system in Japan

SHIJURO OGATA

Bank of Japan

This paper briefly describes the recent changes in public policy in Japan concerning the maintenance of a sound financial system. First the new business environment of financial institutions is reviewed, and then the recent changes in the framework to maintain a sound financial system are discussed.

The new business environment of financial institutions

The business environment of Japanese financial institutions is undergoing rapid change. Two features are noticeable: progress in deregulation and the globalization of financial markets.

(i) Deregulation

Regulations such as those on interest rates, business activities, and entry into markets were generally implemented to protect banks after the experience of financial crises during the 1930s. Japan was no exception. Moreover, in the case of Japan, those regulations, particularly those on interest rates, served to finance reconstruction of the war-torn economy cheaply after World War II.

Relaxation of regulations started in the mid-1970s to promote greater efficiency in providing financial services. The major factors for the change from 'regulated' markets to 'deregulated' markets are (i) slower economic growth, (ii) increased issues of government bonds, and (iii) further integration of international markets. The pace of deregulation has been picking up significantly during the last two years, and it will not be reversed. The transition to a new environment, including further relaxation of interest-rate regulations, will be accomplished in the near future.

Deregulation has taken place in the following areas: (i) deregulation of interest rates on deposits, which started out with larger denominations; (ii) introduction of new financial instruments whose yields are related to market rates, such as certificates of deposit, foreign currency deposits, and bankers' acceptances; (iii) relaxation of collateral requirements for inter-bank transactions and new bond issues; (iv) freer entry of foreign institutions (e.g., less restrictive licensing for trust banking and membership of the Tokyo Stock Exchange); (v) more flexibility in allowing the establishment of branches (including automated branches).

(2) Globalization of financial markets

The role of the Japanese economy in the world has grown rapidly, owing to the sizeable amount of external claims accumulated, which have contributed to increased international activities of Japanese financial institutions. In addition, the development of technology and the innovation in financial techniques such as currency swaps have blurred the borders between nations, and they can no longer protect players inside from competitors outside.

Changes in the framework to maintain a sound financial system in the new environment

The framework to maintain a sound financial system has been adjusted to respond to changes in the business environment. While respecting the autonomy of financial institutions and preserving effective competition among banks, prevention of the domino effect of bank failures has become the key issue.

The Advisory Committee on the Financial System submitted its report on Financial Liberalization and Sound Banking to the Minister of Finance on 6 June 1985. They discussed how to improve competitiveness and efficiency as well as how to stabilize the financial system. The report proposed (i) revising the Deposit Insurance Act, (ii) strengthening regulatory ratios such as capital ratio and liquidity ratio and (iii) strengthening supervisory functions.

(i) Revision of the Deposit Insurance Corporation

In accordance with the Committee's report, the Deposit Insurance Act was revised and became law on 1 July 1986. The main features of the revision are to strengthen the funding base of the Deposit Insurance Corporation and further extend its functions (details are described in Annex I).

(ii)　Strengthening of regulatory ratios

The Ministry of Finance announced new guidelines for prudent bank management on 23 May 1986 in accordance with the proposal by the aforementioned Advisory Committee. The main ideas of the new guidelines are to strengthen capital and liquidity bases of financial institutions and to tighten the monitoring of their performance. It then announced guidelines on overseas activities on 27 May which take new market techniques such as off-balance sheet activities into account in the regulatory ratios (details are described in Annex II).

(iii)　Strengthening of supervisory functions

The Bank of Japan and the Ministry of Finance, both of which are responsible for maintaining a sound banking system, have strengthened their supervisory functions through on-site examinations and frequent contacts with individual institutions to ensure that financial institutions do not resort to excessive risk-taking practices. For example, the Bank of Japan has increased the frequency of examination of bank branches abroad, and it has included on-site examination of securities houses in its examination programme from 1979.

Annex 1　Revision of the Deposit Insurance Act

The revised deposit Insurance act became effective on 1 July 1986. The main features of the revision are as follows:

(1)　Strengthening of the funding base of the Deposit Insurance Corporation (DIC).

(i)　The maximum amount insured rises from ￥3 million to ￥10 million.

(ii)　The premium rises by 50% from 0.008% to 0.012%.

(iii)　The maximum amount that the DIC can borrow from the Bank of Japan rises from ￥50 billion to ￥500 billion. Borrowing from the Bank of Japan should be substituted as soon as possible by borrowing from the private financial institutions.

(2)　Diversification of the functions of the DIC (financial support of mergers)

(i)　The DIC may provide financial assistance (loans, deposit placement and asset assumption) to a bank which assists a problem bank through merger, when both banks request such assistance from the DIC to the Minister of Finance.

(ii) The Minister of Finance will approve such a request, if the following conditions exist:

(a) the problem bank may not be able to repay deposits;
(b) financial assistance from the DIC is considered indispensable for the merger;
(c) cessation of banking operations by the problem bank would have a significant adverse influence on regional or sectoral financing.

The Minister of Finance may advise mergers without any request from banks, if the above-mentioned conditions exist.

(iii) The DIC may also provide financial assistance (loans and deposits) to the mutual assistance systems of each respective financial institutional grouping.

Annex II New guidelines on prudential bank management

The banking bureau of the Ministry of Finance announced new guidelines on prudential bank management in May 1986, and the International Finance Bureau announced separately its new guidelines on overseas activities by Japanese banks having branches abroad on 27 May 1986.

(1) *Capital ratio*

(i) Capital ratio (general standard):

$$\frac{\text{Capital account in a broad sense*}}{\substack{\text{Total assets (average outstanding)} \\ \text{(excluding acceptances and} \\ \text{guarantees with negligible risk)}}} \geqq \text{approximately } 4\%$$

In view of increased risk as a result of financial deregulation, a capital ratio showing the ability of each institution to assume losses has been revised. As a result, the denominator of the ratio has been changed from deposits to total assets. Capital components have also been revised. The target ratio has been set at approximately 4% and is expected to be attained by fiscal 1990. The previous target was 10%.

(ii) Additional standard ratio for financial institutions with overseas branches:

---

* 'Capital account in a broad sense' = total of stockholders' equity, reserve for possible loan losses, reserve for retirement allowances, special reserves for foreign loans and tax adjustment (tax paid on accumulated reserves).

$$\frac{\text{Capital in a broad sense} + \begin{array}{c}\text{70\% of the hidden} \\ \text{reserves resulting} \\ \text{from capital gains} \\ \text{on securities}\end{array}}{\begin{array}{c}\text{Total assets} \\ \text{(as defined in the general standard)}\end{array}} \geqq \text{approximately 6\%}$$

Since international business is more risky than domestic business, an additional standard ratio has been set for financial institutions with overseas branches. In this case, hidden reserves resulting from capital gains on securities will be included in the calculation of capital.

The target ratio has been set at approximately 6% and will be applied from fiscal 1987. The weight of the hidden reserves has been fixed at 70% taking into consideration fluctuations in stock market prices.

Table A.1. **Formula for calculating risk asset ratio covering claims of non-residents in foreign currencies and in Yen (including Euro-Yen)**

Item	Weight
Interbank money market transactions (deposits, call loans	0.2
Securities	
Publicly-offered bonds	0.3
Others	1.0
Overseas Loans and Advances	
Short-term	0.5
Medium-/Long-term	
to public sectors	0.5
to others	1.0
Export–import bills	0.2
Guarantees	
Guarantees with substantial risk	0.3
Others	0.1
Commitments*	
Short-term	0.1
Medium-/Long-term	0.3

* 'Commitments' means committed future lendings and committed future purchases of securities such as: Revolving Facilities, Stand by Credit Facilities, C/P back-up line Facilities, FRN back-up Facilities, Revolving Underwriting Facilities, Note Issuance Facilities, etc.

(2)   Risk asset ratio with regard to overseas activities

The risk asset ratio defined as follows must be no greater than 3.5.

$$\frac{\text{total weighted external assets}}{\text{Capital account in a broad sense} + \text{70\% of latent reserves resulting from estimated capital gains on securities}} \leqq 3.5$$

(3)   Liquidity ratio

Modification of the present liquidity ratio is being considered.

Table A.2. **Limit on loans to a single borrower**

		(Ratio to capital)	
	Present lending limit to any one borrower	Exposure limit to any one borrower	Including exposure to affiliated subsidiaries
Commercial banks	20%	approximately 30%	approximately 40%
Long-term credit banks and trust banks	30%	approximately 38%	approximately 45%
Specialized foreign exchange bank	40%	approximately 45%	approximately 50%

As a result of the progress of financial deregulation, the diversification of risk is becoming more important than ever. From this viewpoint, to complement the present regulation,
(i)   an exposure limit to any one borrower, including loans as well as acceptances and guarantees with substantial risk, and
(ii)   an additional exposure limit including exposure to specified affiliated subsidiaries
have been introduced as guidelines and will be applied from fiscal 1987.

The role of public policy in ensuring financial stability in Finland

JOHNNY AKERHOLM

The first article of the Central Bank Act of 1925 stipulates that 'the duty of the Bank of Finland is to maintain a stable and secure financial system and to promote and facilitate payments transactions' (author's translation). Looking back at history, in particular the turbulent 1930s, it does appear that this rule has very much guided the activities of the Central Bank in Finland.[1]

Many of the 'safety net' measures listed in the illuminating paper by Baltensperger and Dermine are in place in Finland. However, the motivation for their implementation has in many cases during the postwar period been something other than prudential. Most of the measures have in Finland, and in most other Scandinavian countries for that matter, been introduced primarily for reasons of monetary policy, even if ultimately many of them also serve prudential ends. Monetary policy has traditionally been pursued through strict control of the financial system, in particular the banks. Hence, the Central Bank has also had an indirect influence on and control over risk-taking in the banking system. Another indirect effect of these measures has been the protection of the domestic banking industry from external competition, with a consequent reduction of the risks of financial instability.

Throughout most of the postwar period, the central bank in Finland (as in Sweden and Norway) regulated bank lending rates with the intention of keeping them below the equilibrium rate implied by the market. Deposit rates, in turn, have been kept at a low level and bank margins secured by allowing the exemption of bank deposits, both principal and interest, from taxation. As official foreign exchange reserves have typically been low, the counterpart of the note and coin issue and of the government's traditionally positive net deposits with the Central Bank has been a net (and gross) liability position of the banking system at the Central Bank. This net liability position has been effected through the call money market. Monetary policy has aimed at regulating the lending capacity of banks, in practice by changing the marginal cost of bank borrowing from the central bank.

In these circumstances, the banks have faced an excess demand for loans at the prevailing lending rates and have therefore (in theory at least) been able to refuse to grant loans considered too risky. This has reduced the risk of defaults. At the same time, the regulation of interest rates has removed the incentive to compete in price terms; instead, banks have devised non-price forms of competition such as expanding branch networks and advertising. Though these forms of competition might have an influence on longer-term profitability, they are probably less likely to cause rapidly emerging instability than interest rate competition.

Besides protecting the banking industry from external competition, the tax rules are also highly conducive to the conclusion of cartel agreements among banks on the deposit side; tax exemption is granted only if at least two banking categories (the banking categories comprise the Post Office Bank, Postipankki, the commercial banks, the savings banks and the cooperative banks)[2] can agree to offer the same terms on deposits. This effectively precludes competition in the bulk of the deposit market and at the same time gives a strong cost advantage to the banks in comparison to other financial institutions and instruments.

In addition, the banks have almost always applied variable interest rate schemes on both the deposit and lending sides; all rates have been changed in parallel with the central bank discount (later base) rate. Consequently, the banks have not encountered any significant interest rate or maturity risks.

Last, but not least, the financial market in Finland, and in other Scandinavian countries, has until quite recently been effectively sheltered from the rest of the world. Finnish banks were not allowed to participate in international loan consortia in the 1970s, when the deterioration of international loan portfolios started. When the banks were eventually allowed to engage in this business in the 1980s, they could already see the risks involved. It is also only fairly recently that Finnish banks have gone international on a wider scale.

As mentioned above, owing to the financial system's structure, banks have been in a position of almost permanent indebtedness (at least on a gross basis) to the Central Bank. As a consequence, there have not been any special lender-of-last-resort facilities designed for emergency purposes; rather the Central Bank has kept its lender-of-last-resort window open every day. Though the arrangements have differed greatly over the years, credit has always been granted, but normally only at rising costs. Banks have not run any substantial risk of liquidity problems.[3] But, of course, if a bank has for some reason or other had to rely on an exceptionally large amount of central bank credit for a long time, profitability has suffered and thereby posed a threat to solvency.

This has happened on several occasions in the past. In these situations, the Central Bank has stepped in and in various ways effectively reduced the costs of Central Bank finance. Financial assistance has been extended, but the assisted bank has usually been required to take various corrective measures. Hence, there is no doubt that the Central Bank has been willing actively to protect the solvency of the system, even if there have been no formal rules in this respect. There seems to be a clear, if unspoken, understanding in the financial community that this can be expected to hold true irrespective of whether the source of the difficulty is of domestic or foreign origin.

But banks, and in particular depositors, are also protected in other ways. Banks are by law obliged to join a private insurance scheme; there are separate schemes for the commercial banks, the savings banks and the cooperative banks. The Post Office Bank is the only institution not subject to this requirement, but the Government has declared itself a guarantor of that institution. The insurance schemes require the participants to make annual contributions according to internal rules. These rules must, however, accord with minimum legal guidelines. The funds collected by the schemes are in practice small in relation to members' actual liabilities. However, if there were a bank failure and the funds turned out to be insufficient, the remaining banks within the scheme would have to make advance contributions so as to make up the shortfall.

As far as direct prudential regulations are concerned, there are mainly four rules in force: (1) the banks have to maintain a certain amount of liquid assets in relation to their short-term indebtedness (except for the Post Office Bank); (2) they are required to maintain a certain ratio of equity capital to (adjusted) liabilities (this varies between banking categories, and there are no requirements on the Post Office Bank); (3) there are limitations on the extent to which banks can grant loans to the same borrower; and (4) there are restrictions on the foreign exchange exposure of banks.

Of these regulations, the first three are stipulated in law, while the fourth has been instituted by the Central Bank. The reason for restricting the banks' opportunities to take open positions *vis-à-vis* the Markka has, however, had more to do with capital flows than prudential questions. In fact, banks are not subject to any formal restrictions on their open positions among foreign currencies. But, after unsuccessful speculation on a large scale by one bank in 1984, banks have been obliged to report their foreign currency positions to the Bank of Finland on a daily basis. It is quite obvious that this reduces the banks' willingness to take risks in this field.

It is also worth mentioning that banks are not required to make provisions for bad loans. However, the tax rules treat these provisions very favourably; since they have been equated to equity capital in the past, banks tend to make such provisions on a substantial scale.

With this kind of set-up in the financial markets, it has been natural to concentrate bank supervision in a separate institution; as in other Scandinavian countries, the Bank Inspectorate is subordinate to the Ministry of Finance. The Bank Inspectorate has, in these circumstances, largely concentrated on supervising the legal aspects of banking, including the fulfilment of the legally stipulated requirements. The Bank Inspectorate also supervises the activities of financial institutions other than banks and has quite extensive rights regarding the disclosure of information. If it is felt that an institution is not performing in accordance with the stipulated rules, the Inspectorate can as a last resort ask the Ministry of Finance to withdraw the institution's licence.

There are, however, a great many changes now taking place which will affect riskiness in the banking industry and hence also the public attitude towards prudential control.

First of all, the commercial banks have during the last few years expanded their foreign activities rapidly; business carried out in foreign currency accounts at the moment for almost a half of their balance sheets. This makes the banks subject to all the international risks also felt in other countries. Secondly, domestic regulation has been gradually relaxed and the domestic financial market is facing a new phase of development and competition; the only substantive protection of banks still in force is the tax exemption of deposits, which suppresses competition for the deposits of private persons. In other respects, the domestic market is free of restraints on competition, and banks and the financial system will no doubt enter a new competitive situation. The gradual development of short-term markets and the capital market will also introduce new risks related to maturity transformation. This represents a significant change in a system which will have to experience much larger variations in interest rates than was previously the case. Furthermore, there is an intense debate going on concerning the future of the tax system, and it is not impossible that the system will be changed at some point to foster more competition.

Third, as a result of the rapid growth in off-balance-sheet items, the regulatory authorities face the same kind of problems as supervisors in other countries.

These developments have implications both for the coverage of supervision and for the role of the Central Bank in prudential supervision. Changes are already under way.

In February 1986, a committee submitted proposals for changes in bank legislation. Most important from our point of view was the recommendation that different items both on- and off-balance-sheet should be classified according to assessed risks and that capital requirements should be increased in accordance with increases in risk. Furthermore, the Central Bank will have to involve itself more than hitherto in analysing risk exposures in private banking; as noted earlier, in the event of a major crisis in the financial market, the Central Bank would be most likely to emerge as the lender of last resort. The Bank of Finland has for some years now collected information and analysed banks' exposures in foreign operations and is now considering ways and means of adopting a similar approach to the monitoring of domestic activities.

In conclusion, one can say that the Finnish banking system has been well protected; risks have been small, there has been a safety net of prudential regulations and the Central Bank has, as a final resort, been ready to intervene. There is, however, no doubt that risks will increase substantially in the future as a result of the development of the market. This requires a reassessment of the tightness of prudential regulations, a task already under way. But the Central Bank will also have to scrutinize risk-taking more closely if it is to ensure that it does not become a lender of last resort on a major scale as a result of undue risk-taking.

NOTES

1 Note that, although the Central Bank Act does not explicitly mention the stability of the Markka as an objective, the first article has often been interpreted as also including price stability.
2 Despite the different historical backgrounds of these banking categories, their activities in the domestic field have started to assume many similar features. Thus the Post Office Bank is active in all market segments, and the savings and cooperative banks have a large number of (in particular small) corporate customers. Likewise, commercial banks include a large number of households among their customers. Note, however, that the savings and cooperative banks have to carry on their foreign currency business through and in the name of their respective 'central banks'.
3 The Bank of Finland has at times asked the banks to provide additional information, if their borrowing from the Central Bank has been large.

The Argentine financial sector

UBALDO AGUIRRE and
ERNESTO FELDMAN

I Overview

The Argentine financial sector is the reflection of the country's history of high inflation and administrative restraints. For most of the last thirty years, Argentine interest rates have been administered and kept negative in real terms. During this period, deposit rates were positive in real terms only in 1953, 1969, 1970, 1981 and 1985. As a consequence, a strong disintermediation process took place while the ratio of money, broadly defined, to GDP declined steadily, reaching a low of 9% in 1976 as compared with a 30–35% ratio during the fifties. The interest rate liberalization policies introduced in 1977 led to an increase in the ratio which reached a peak of 25% in 1980, but disintermediation resumed in 1981 and accelerated sharply after June 1982.

When the Austral Plan was launched in mid-1985, the economy was on the verge of hyperinflation, and the degree of monetization had fallen to around 10%. Under the plan, in the last six months of 1985, the stock of M1 grew 120 percent in nominal terms and 84 percent in real terms. This represents a large seigniorage gain that was made possible by the increase in money demands. During the first half of 1986, money aggregates continued to grow albeit at a slower pace, and the broad money to GDP ratio recovered to 20%.

The long trend of financial repression was accompanied by inadequate policies concerning the structural organization of the Argentine banking system. The number of financial institutions, of branches, and of bank employees grew significantly and without pause, while the demand for financial assets was shrinking in real terms. This pathological combination of financial repression with structural overexpansion gave rise to a dramatic increase in banking operating costs that resulted in extremely wide spreads between deposit and lending rates. Inflation, banking over-regulation and fiscal imbalances brought about market segmentation, deposit maturities concentrated in the very short term and a sizeable immobilization of banks' capital.

II   Description of the system

The banks

There are three main types of banks in Argentina: the official banks, the private national banks and the foreign banks. The official banks include 5 national banks and 30 provincial and municipal banks. As of mid-1986, there were 130 private national banks and 31 foreign banks.

The following table shows the evolution in the number of banks and in the number of branches:

Table A.3. **Number of banks and branches, 1978–85**

	Number of banks			
	1978	1981	1984	1985
Official banks	35	35	36	36
Private national banks	18	32	32	31
Foreign banks	104	139	142	130
Total	157	206	210	197
	Number of branches			
Official banks	1,771	1,876	1,914	1,943
Private national banks	1,250	1,705	2,305	2,224
Foreign banks	204	341	340	340
Total	3,225	3,922	4,559	4,507

As shown in Table A.3, in the last two years official banks kept on increasing the number of their branches while the number of private national banks and branches diminished. The number of foreign banks and branches remained basically constant. The Central Bank has also under its control around 100 non-bank financial institutions (which are not allowed to receive demand deposits). These intermediaries hold less than 2% of total deposits.

Market segmentation

Financial and fiscal policies have imposed a high degree of segmentation on the banking market. At present, financial resources flow through three broad segments: (1) regulated demand and time deposits,

Table A.4. **Financial system liabilities, 1983–6 (%)**

		Deposits			
	Currency	Current account	Regulated rate	Indexed	Free rate
December 1983	22.2	11.5	50.1	15.1	1.1
December 1984	21.7	8.5	43.1	12.3	14.4
June 1985	19.7	9.9	42.5	7.8	20.1
December 1985	25.8	12.7	30.2	0.6	30.7
June 1986	19.2	11.7	31.0	0.7	37.4

(2) non-regulated deposits and (3) rediscounts, largely financed through compulsory reserve requirements imposed on (1) and (2). When the Austral Plan was launched in June 1985, 52.4% of the liabilities of the financial system were in current account (9.9%) and regulated rate time (42.5%) deposits, subject to interest rate control and guaranteed by the government. Deposits at free rates and with no state guarantee amounted to 20.1% of total bank liabilities, guaranteed indexed deposits to 7.8%.

One year later, in June 1986, the share of current account and regulated rate deposits had dropped to 42.7% of total liabilities, while the share of free rate non-guaranteed deposits had increased to 37.4%. Index-linked deposits, on the other hand, practically disappeared, as inflationary expectations receded.

Each of the deposit segments has a different regime of non-remunerated reserve requirements and forced investments with the Central Bank. In the regulated segment, they amount to practically all deposits, and in the free segment they are approximately half of free-rate deposits. On average, reserve requirements and forced investments account for 75% of total deposits. There is also a wide dispersion of interest rates on deposits. The lowest rates are on regulated-rate deposits, reflecting the ceiling on these rates more than the government guarantee. Interest rates on rediscounts are about the same as rates on regulated-rate deposits, although the specific rate charged depends on the borrower.

The share of the three groups of banks in total deposits has evolved as shown in table A.3.

Deposits in official banks have grown continuously, especially last year, as a result of four factors. First, official banks, national, provincial and municipal, enjoy the explicit or at least the perceived guarantee of the state. Second, in 1985, the Central Bank intervened in a major

Table A.5. The distribution of deposits, 1978–85 (%)

	1978	1981	1984	1985
Official banks	44	46	47	55
Private national banks	44	38	37	31
Foreign banks	12	16	16	14

Table A.6. Deposit concentration, 1977–85 (%)

	1977	1979	1981	1985
Banco de la Nación Argentina	23	37	30	26
First 10 banks[a]	49	42	48	52
Second 20 banks	28	25	22	22
Total	100	100	100	100

[a] Includes Banco de la Nación Argentina

private national bank (Banco de Italia y Rio de la Plata). This intervention triggered a lasting flight from private national to official banks. Third, provincial banks paid very high deposit rates (in the free-rate segment) to finance regional fiscal and private sector needs. And fourth, Treasury deposits were transferred, at the inception of the Austral Plan, from the Central Bank to Banco de la Nación Argentina, the largest official bank in the country.

The deposit concentration of the financial system has not changed much over the last ten years.

II   Problems affecting the system

The public sector deficit and its financing (reserve requirements and rediscounts)

Argentina's banking system has traditionally been used as a main domestic source of public sector deficit financing, since there is no system for the direct placement of public domestic debt. Such financing takes the form of very high reserve requirements on demand deposits, on other bank deposits, and substantial forced investments in financial assets issued by the Central Bank to purchase Argentine domestic public debt. Latest available information indicates that total reserve requirements

Table A.7. **Anatomy of the Argentine banking system**

Liabilities and net worth		Assets	
Deposits	100	Reserve requirements	
Rediscounts[a]	50	and compulsory investments[a]	75
		Loans	82
Net worth	30	Fixed assets	23
	180		180

[a] Reserve requirements and compulsory investments net of rediscounts: 25% of deposits

and forced investments represent around 75% of total deposits. If Central Bank rediscounts are deducted, net reserve requirements are about 25% of deposits.

The fiscal deficit of the National Government is therefore a source of pressures on free lending rates. These pressures are exerted mainly through banks' intermediation spreads, because the Treasury's demands reduce the proportion of deposits that can be loaned by the banking system. Thus, besides 'crowding out' the private sector, the Treasury's demands require higher lending rates to cover banks' interest costs of deposits and their operating costs.

Since the implementation of the Austral Plan, the Central Bank has not provided additional direct credit to the Government, which has financed its deficits mostly from external sources. Nonetheless, the high reserves have continued to put upward pressure on spreads and interest rates. These reserves financed the existing stock of Government debt, the increase in the Central Bank's net foreign assets, and the increase in rediscounts.

Total rediscounts represent almost 50% of all existing deposits and 65% of bank credit to the private sector. Such a large volume of rediscounts is, to a large extent, a reflection of the economic difficulties experienced over recent years by various sectors of the economy, the regional economies and the financial system itself. These difficulties go back to the beginning of this decade, and the sudden cooling of inflation induced by the Austral Plan accentuated them perhaps more harshly. This is why there is presumably such a diversity of purposes, terms and interest structures in the current rediscounts. Each one has in fact been devised to take care of a particular critical situation that the market would have had problems handling spontaneously.

These critical situations had persisted over time and gave rise to a vast amount of intermediation activity on the part of the Central Bank and to what is known as the quasi-fiscal deficit. Many of these situations have now been surmounted, especially as regards their impact on the Central Bank's results. However, it has also proved necessary to provide financial assistance in new cases, thereby recreating once again the inefficient pattern of increasing rediscounts and, simultaneously, remunerated and non-remunerated compulsory reserves.

The Central Bank has run large losses in its intermediation role in the recent past. The average interest rate on forced investments has been higher than the interest rate charged on rediscounts. For instance, in December 1985, the average difference between these rates was about 1.5 percent (per month). The resulting loss was a major cause of the quasi-fiscal deficit, estimated at 1 percent of GDP in the last quarter of 1985 and 1.4 percent of GDP in the first quarter of 1986.

From a macroeconomic efficiency standpoint it is almost impossible to determine who is subsidizing whom through the forced investment–rediscount mechanism, and thus what are the efficiency and distributional benefits or losses from the system. Moreover, it must be recognized that depositors and borrowers are often the same people that operate in all market segments simultaneously. Although payers and recipients of the subsidies are not well-defined groups, it is clear that substantial rent-seeking activity is being generated by the opportunity to obtain subsidies and to divert funds from one market segment to another.

The net result of the present situation has been very high interest rates on banks' free-rate loans and low or negative returns on bank equity. The banks' lending capacity is reduced by the large amount of reserve requirements and forced investments, generating pressures on the spread between deposit and lending rates. Although the interest rates on reserves that the Central Bank pays do exceed the banks' average cost of funds, they are below the lending rates that would be charged in a free market. Thus, the spread between free-rate deposits and loans is increased and depositors, borrowers and bank equity holders are forced to transfer resources to recipients of rediscounted loans. Moreover, the large intermediary role of the Central Bank has propped up weak banks through the forced investment–rediscount mechanism, hurting the more efficient banks and delaying necessary adjustments in the sector.

The situation described has also led to the expansion of an intercompany unregulated market that competes unfairly with the financial market regulated by the Central Bank. This unregulated market, which of course has no reserve requirements, has large dimensions. This situation has adverse effects on the overall profitability of the financial system and hence on its stability. Furthermore, as this market functions free of controls or regulations, at a time of a credit crunch or failure to perform by a major participant, chain defaults may occur, which may ignite a major financial crisis for the whole economy.

The efficiency problem

Banks' operating costs are an important component of spreads in Argentina. Average operating costs of Argentine banks (as measured by the ratio of operating costs to total deposits) have increased substantially in recent years and are presently four to five times higher than the average for OECD countries. There are three main reasons why banks' average operating costs are so high: (1) the strong demonetization and disintermediation of funds experienced by Argentina's financial institutions, particularly after the reforms of July 1982; (2) the extremely reduced maturity of financial contracts; and (3) excessive investment in real resources (i.e., buildings and employees) in the sector. The demonetization and reduced maturity are related to macroeconomic factors, while overcapacity is related to structural factors.

Financial repression has been a constant feature of Argentine financial history. After the liberalization attempt of the late seventies, real deposit mobilization by the Argentine banking system began decreasing in late 1980, mainly as a consequence of the strong expectations of devaluation and the capital flight observed in this period. It declined further after 1982, mainly as a result of the policy of corporate debt liquidation through highly negative real interest rates. Real deposit mobilization decreased not only because asset holders switched to domestic real assets and foreign assets but also because an increasing volume of financial transactions went through the non-institutional financial system. Under the Austral Plan, deposit mobilization increased substantially. However, even if real deposit mobilization returned to the peak levels of 1980, average bank costs would still be significantly higher than international standards. This is so because the increase in average costs was not only due to a decreased volume of business, but also to increased real labour costs and other expenses.

One factor making for increased real costs has been the reduction in the maturity of deposits, caused by high and variable inflation and uncertainty. In Argentina this process has gone further than in most countries, as depositors and borrowers attempted to protect themselves against uncertainty. Bank deposits have an extremely reduced average maturity which is now estimated to be 19 days. The need to roll over deposits and loans on practically a two-weekly basis is an important element in the system's high costs and overstaffing.

The present physical dimension of the Argentine financial system is another important cause of high average operating costs. In the early 1970s, financial intermediaries exceeded 850, having more than 2,500 branches. The lack of a sound financial basis for many of the banks created during 1978–80, of which a significant number were finance companies and credit unions that were transformed into banks, became evident when economic activity faltered. The subsequent financial crisis led to the intervention in and liquidation of the largest and the second largest private commercial banks in 1980. By the end of 1985, the total number of banks had declined to 197, but the number of branches had increased to 4,507, with a corresponding rise in the number of employees.

Immobilization of banks' capital and solvency problems

As of December 1985, 75 percent of Argentine banks' capital was invested in fixed assets. Moreover, these fixed assets are overvalued in the banks' books since their equity was indexed while the market price of such assets increased much less. Since the immobilization of capital reduces the banks' lending capacity (in Argentina the share of banks' capital which is not immobilized can be lent at free rates) and may generate capital gains (or losses), it may also be a source of pressure on banks' lending rates. This pressure exists to the extent that the banks' managers do not realize capital losses and try to achieve positive returns on overvalued equity.

Argentine banks face significant portfolio problems. These problems have a long history; they were temporarily eased by the policy of corporate debt liquidation implemented in June 1982, albeit at the cost of a sharp demonetization of the economy. However, portfolio quality began to worsen again almost immediately, as the Argentine economy kept undergoing a dramatic adjustment to face the burden of its US $50 billion foreign debt.

III   New policies

Consolidation of the system

Consolidation of the Argentine financial system calls for a combination of monetary and fiscal decisions and more dynamic action on the part of the Central Bank Superintendency to deal prudently but firmly with existing problems. A new set of policies has been recently designed to get a firmer grip on monetary expansion. Central Bank authorities have taken a strong commitment to control growth of the monetary base. As fiscal accounts are kept under reasonable control, the Government will be able to stick to one of the cornerstones of the Austral Plan: it will refrain from borrowing from the Central Bank. This commitment implies the gradual elimination of rediscounts and compulsory reserve requirements.

The need to exercise a strict policy in regard to rediscounts is a fundamental one from various viewpoints:

it will enhance the credibility of the monetary policy in itself, since the Central Bank will exercise effective control over expansion of the monetary base:

it will make for greater transparency of the fiscal accounts and further elimination of subsidies, which are a source of the quasi-fiscal deficit; and

it will contribute to the goal of eliminating the excessive fragmentation of the system.

The Central Bank has decided to put an end to the self-destructive mechanism based on the granting of rediscounts, on the one hand, and on imposing compulsory sterilization mechanisms, on the other. Its elimination will contribute to lessening distortions in money markets and, particularly, the pressure that reserves remunerated at rates below the opportunity cost of the funds place on spreads. In the same way, its elimination will lessen the fragility of the system that gives rise to the unequal distribution of lending capacities among different kinds of banks. Rediscounts affect the institutions unequally since, although all of them maintain similar reserve requirements, the rediscounts are mostly concentrated in the official banks and in a small group of private banks which, due to the nature of their portfolios, have made extensive use of Central Bank credit support.

The simultaneous reduction of compulsory reserves and rediscounts will bring down the quasi-fiscal deficit through the elimination of implicit subsidies that often go to indeterminate beneficiaries. The adoption of an explicit rule for granting rediscounts will complement the commitment assumed when the Austral Plan was launched not to resort to money creation for financing the fiscal deficit.

The structural problems

The Central Bank is prepared to attack simultaneously the structural problems that affect financial system institutions: capital immobilization, insolvency of portfolios and high cost of intermediation.

There seems to be, however, a consensus in Argentina on the need to introduce gradual, non-traumatic changes in the operating structure of the system. Since the introduction of the Austral Plan, remonetization has done a great deal to reduce average costs. Average operating costs declined from over 2% *per month* in June 1985, to 1.5% in July 1986. This improvement, which is obviously insufficient by any international standard, will be maintained and enhanced by means of consistent monetary and fiscal policies, and by gradual restructuring of the system.

Finally, the Central Bank is committed to create appropriate mechanisms that will induce a steady reduction in intermediation costs and growing institutionalization of the financial markets. Legal and fiscal measures will clearly penalize the persistence of dealings in the marginal money markets. In this connection, the Superintendency of the Central Bank will be strengthened through strict application of a revised banking law.

Index